Sounding Off: Theorizing Disability in Music

Sounding Off: Theorizing Disability in Music

EDITED BY

NEIL LERNER
DAVIDSON COLLEGE

JOSEPH N. STRAUS
GRADUATE CENTER, CITY UNIVERSITY OF NEW YORK

Foreword by Rosemarie Garland-Thomson,
author of *Extraordinary Bodies: Figuring Physical Disability
in American Culture and Literature*

Routledge
Taylor & Francis Group
New York   London

Routledge is an imprint of the
Taylor & Francis Group, an informa business

Routledge
Taylor & Francis Group
270 Madison Avenue
New York, NY 10016

Routledge
Taylor & Francis Group
2 Park Square
Milton Park, Abingdon
Oxon OX14 4RN

© 2006 by Taylor & Francis Group, LLC
Routledge is an imprint of Taylor & Francis Group, an Informa business

Printed in the United States of America on acid-free paper
10 9 8 7 6 5 4 3 2 1

International Standard Book Number-10: 0-415-97907-2 (Softcover) 0-415-97906-4 (Hardcover)
International Standard Book Number-13: 978-0-415-97907-8 (Softcover) 978-0-415-97906-1 (Hardcover)

Library of Congress Cataloging-in-Publication Data

Sounding off : theorizing disability in music / edited by Neil Lerner and Joseph N. Straus.
p. cm.
Includes bibliographical references and index.
ISBN 0-415-97906-4 (hb) -- ISBN 0-415-97907-2 (pb)
1. Music--Philosophy and aesthetics. 2. Disabilities. 3. Quotation in music. 4. Music--Performance--Physiological aspects. I. Lerner, Neil William, 1966- II. Straus, Joseph Nathan. III. Title.

ML3920.S728 2006
780.87--dc22   2006007511

Visit the Taylor & Francis Web site at
http://www.taylorandfrancis.com

and the Routledge Web site at
http://www.routledge-ny.com

Table of Contents

Acknowledgments

We are deeply grateful to Rosemarie Garland-Thomson, who, in addition to contributing the foreword to this collection, served as our model of engaged, creative scholarship about disability. Simi Linton's early encouragement played a significant role in this project's coming to fruition. Ann Fox also was an important force behind our work, both individually and collectively. At Routledge, our editors (Richard Carlin, Constance Ditzel, and Devon Sherman, and Sylvia Wood at Taylor & Francis) supported the project from its inception and shepherded it through to publication with professionalism and meticulous care. We gratefully acknowledge the assistance of Patty Howland in copyediting the entire manuscript and in preparing the lengthy bibliography that accompanies it, and of Thomas Robinson in preparing the musical examples. Neil Lerner's work on disability issues has been supported in part by funding from the Davidson College Faculty Committee on Study and Research. Joseph Straus's thinking about these issues, and about everything else, has been guided by Sally Goldfarb and by Michael and Adam Straus-Goldfarb.

We gratefully acknowledge the following publishers for permission to reprint material under copyright:

Figure 3.1 STRING QUARTET NO. 15 IN E-FLAT MINOR, OP. 144. By Dmitri Shostakovich. Copyright © 1974 (Renewed) by G. Schirmer, Inc. (ASCAP). International Copyright Secured. All Rights Reserved. Reprinted by permission.

Figures 3.2-3. Henryk Górecki, SYMPHONY NO. 3. © Copyright 1977 by PWM Edition, Krakow, Poland. Transferred 1998 to Chester Music Limited. © Copyright 1998 by Chester Music Limited for the World Except Poland, Albania, Bulgaria, China, Croatia and the Rest of the Territory of the Former Yugoslavia, Cuba, North Korea, Vietnam, Romania, Hungary, the Territories of the Former Czechoslovakia and the Whole Territory of the Former USSR. Sub-Published for North America by Boosey & Hawkes Inc. Reprinted by permission.

Figures 4.2-3. Still images from Kieślowski, BLUE. Miramax. Reprinted by permission.

Figures 6.2 and 6.3. THE BEAST WITH FIVE FINGERS, by Max Steiner. © 1946 (Renewed) WB MUSIC CORP. This Arrangement © 2006 WB MUSIC CORP. All Rights Reserved including Public Performance. Reprinted with permission.

Figure 9.1. Caricature of Glenn Gould, 13 February 1970. Reprinted with permission from *The Globe and Mail.*

Figure 15.2. Webern, FOUR PIECES, OP. 7. Used with kind permission of European American Music Distributors LLC, U.S. and Canadian agent for Universal Edition.

Figures 15.3–6. Shulamit Ran, APPREHENSIONS, for voice, clarinet, and piano (1979). © 1980 by IMI Israel Music Institute, P. O. B. 3004, Tel-Aviv, Israel. Reprinted with permission.

All lines from "APPREHENSIONS" FROM WINTER TREES by SYLVIA PLATH. Copyright © 1971 by Ted Hughes. Reprinted by permission of Harper-Collins Publishers. Additional permission for world rights granted by Faber and Faber Ltd.

The image on the cover of this book is Braille notation of J. S. Bach's four-part chorale setting of "O Haupt voll Blut und Wunden" from the *St. Matthew Passion.* Source: *Lessons in Braille Music,* prepared by H. V. Spanner, edited to conform with American usage by Harry J. Ditzler (Louisville, KY: American Printing House for the Blind, 1961).

Contributing Authors

Paul Attinello lectures at the International Centre for Music Studies at the University of Newcastle upon Tyne, and has also taught at the University of Hong Kong and UCLA. He has published in the *Journal of Musicological Research, Musik-Konzepte, Musica/Realtá,* the revised *New Grove,* and several collections. Current projects include a monograph on music about AIDS, a co-edited book on Buffy the Vampire Slayer, and books on Meredith Monk and Gerhard Stäbler.

L. Poundie Burstein is an Associate Professor of Music Theory at Hunter College and the Graduate Center of the City University of New York. He also teaches music analysis at Mannes College of Music.

Maria Cizmic is Assistant Professor of Humanities at the University of South Florida. She completed her Ph.D. in Musicology in 2004 at the University of California, Los Angeles where she was a Jacob K. Javitz fellow. Dr. Cizmic currently teaches interdisciplinary courses that integrate musicology and the humanities, including Representing Trauma, and is working on a book project, *Performing Pain: Music and Trauma in 1970s and 80s Eastern Europe.*

Daniel Goldmark is Assistant Professor of Music at Case Western Reserve University in Cleveland, Ohio. He is the author of *Tunes for 'Toons: Music and the Hollywood Cartoon* (University of California Press, 2005), and is co-editor, with Yuval Taylor, of *The Cartoon Music Book* (A Cappella Books, 2001).

Kelly Gross is a recent graduate of the Critical and Comparative Studies in Music program at the University of Virginia. A private instructor for Charlottesville's Music Education Center, her current research interests focus on gender, embodiment, and vocality in music and film.

Dave Headlam is Professor of Music Theory at the Eastman School of Music. He has published on post-tonal music, rhythm, computers and music research, and popular music. His book, *The Music of Alban Berg,* was awarded an ASCAP Deems-Taylor award in 1997.

Jennifer Iverson is a Ph.D. candidate in Music Theory at the University of Texas at Austin. In addition to her work in disability studies, her research centers on analytical and aesthetic issues in twentieth-century music.

Stephanie Jensen-Moulton is a Ph.D. candidate in Musicology at the Graduate Center of the City University of New York, where she is also an active participant in the Women's Studies Certificate Program. Her research interests include the voice, feminist musicology, and popular music studies. Her dissertation focuses on women composers in New York City during the 1950s.

Marianne Kielian-Gilbert is Professor of Music in the Jacobs School of Music at Indiana University, where she teaches Music Theory. Her work centers on music experience and analysis and connections among music, feminist theory and cultural studies, and modes of perception (temporal, material, intersubjective). Her work in Disability Studies stems from personal experience and from music's expressive potential to listen and hear from alternate or inclusive positions and in different registers of the social/material.

Neil Lerner, Associate Professor of Music at Davidson College, teaches courses on music history, film, and the humanities. A specialist in U.S. film music, his most recent essays have studied various film scores by Aaron Copland, John Williams, and Dimitri Tiomkin. Trained as a pianist and bassoonist, he sometimes accompanies early films at the piano.

S. Timothy Maloney is the Head of the Music Library and an adjunct professor at the University of Minnesota, lecturing in music history, literature, and bibliography. Earlier, he was the Director of the Music Division at the National Library of Canada, where the archival papers of many Canadian musicians, including Glenn Gould, were under his care. In addition to speaking and publishing widely about Gould, he supervised the creation of the extensive "Glenn Gould Archive" Web site (http://www.collectionscanada.ca/glenngould/) and played First Clarinet in the chamber orchestra conducted by Gould for the Sony recording of Wagner's *Siegfried Idyll* (SMK 52 650).

Adam Ockelford is Director of Education at the Royal National Institute of the Blind in London, Senior Research Fellow at Roehampton University, and Visiting Research Fellow at the Institute of Education, University of London. He is secretary of SEMPRE, the Society for Education, Music and Psychology. Research. His research interests include interrogating exceptional musical development and abilities through a fusion of psychomusicological and music-theoretical techniques.

Andrew Oster is a Ph.D. candidate in Musicology at Princeton University, where he is writing a dissertation on postwar German music and radio. His other research interests include opera and the history of sound recording.

Stephen Rodgers is an Assistant Professor of Music Theory and Musicianship at the University of Oregon. He received his Ph.D. in music theory from Yale University in 2005, with a dissertation on form and program in Berlioz's instrumental music.

Laurie Stras is Senior Tutor in the School of Humanities, University of Southampton; she also co-directs the early music ensemble, Musica Secreta. Her research interests were once succinctly described as "girl groups from Ferrara to Motown." Current projects include an edited book on 1960s girl singers, a monograph on the Boswell Sisters, and the musical direction of a play set in the sixteenth-century convent of Corpus Domini in Ferrara.

Joseph N. Straus is Presidential Professor of Music at the Graduate Center of the City University of New York. He has published widely on topics in post-tonal music and music theory. He is a former president of the Society for Music Theory.

Foreword

I am thrilled that this book is entering the conversation that makes up the emerging field I call *cultural disability studies*. The compelling and wide-ranging group of essays collected here under the capable editorial direction of Neil Lerner and Joseph N. Straus affirms the central proposition of cultural disability studies: Disability is everywhere once you know how to look for it. The intellectual work of cultural disability studies is to show that the concept of disability saturates the cultural fabric. This new scholarly enterprise of tracing disability's threads can illuminate how we think about ourselves and one another and how we structure the world we share together. The exemplary academic analyses that make up *Sounding Off: Theorizing Disability in Music* demonstrate how what we are acculturated to think of as a medical condition or a personal misfortune is in fact one of the informing principles of musical artistic production. What is fresh here is the exploration of how the concept of disability shapes music and music shapes the concept of disability.

Cultural disability studies is one of the developing new areas that make up the larger field of inquiry sometimes called *identity studies*. Such recent research and scholarly enterprises as gender, race, ethnic, and gay and lesbian studies pose new research questions, develop new archives, and establish new knowledge about how identity operates in the social order, the political world, artistic and cultural representation, and individual identity. The kinds of questions that drive identity studies tended not to be asked in the academic world up until the political changes of the civil rights movement encouraged and demanded new ways of thinking about who we are and what social justice might be. Identity studies was born of the larger civil rights movement, which gave us a more integrated and just society. In addition to the black civil rights movement, the women's movement, and the gay and lesbian liberation movement was and is the disability rights movement. These movements' goals of producing a more equitable society and bringing attention to minority groups gave form to identity studies in the academic world. Cultural disability studies and other identity studies are distinct from the rights movements that inspired them because they are intellectual endeavors, not advocacy initiatives on the part of individual traditionally disenfranchised groups. Research, scholarship, and pedagogy drive identity studies, even though—like all academic work—they do have a political dimension.

What I have just defined as cultural disability studies understands and investigates disability as a cultural product, as a way of interpreting bodily variation and a social concept that widely influences our collective thinking and practices. It works against dominant traditional understandings of disability as medical pathology or individual inadequacy, which are the lenses through which disability has traditionally been viewed in the academic world. Cultural disability studies can be thought of, then, as an augmentation to the study of disability in the health and biosciences. Cultural analyses of disability in such traditional humanities disciplines as history, literary studies, philosophy, art, theater, and music are—like gender and race studies, for example—compensatory as well. That is, they build an archive of knowledge where none existed before. Disability as a category of analysis in artistic production is a new way of thinking in both research and critical explication. Just as gender was not imagined in the academic world as a relevant category of analysis thirty years ago, disability was also not imagined as a relevant category of analysis until ten years ago. Disability, gender, race, ethnicity, class, and sexuality are now recognized as ideological and social formations that affect all cultural products and material spaces in the social order. Before identity studies, such social systems and categories were generally thought to be incidental and privatized forms of individual difference that had little effect on the cultural order or material world.

At this point, I need to come clean. My own academic efforts have focused on developing cultural disability studies not only in my own scholarship and research but also as an institutionalized field of inquiry in the academic world. This means that I spend a good deal of time explaining to people, as I have in the previous paragraphs, what cultural disability studies is and does. In promoting an integrative model of pedagogy and scholarship, I am forever asserting that disability can be incorporated into any humanities discipline. I have done it myself, along with many colleagues, in literary studies. I have witnessed it, as well as edged there somewhat myself, in critical studies of art and performance. In spite of my ardent promotion of these research and teaching initiatives, I have always secretly doubted that disability could be represented in musical form. I understood that thematically music could carry the concept of disability or that disabled musicians such as Stevie Wonder, Itzhak Perlman, or The Blind Boys of Alabama might produce music that one could argue is informed by their personal experience of disability.

What I did not understand until I read the essays in this volume is that I and my colleagues are indeed correct: Disability is everywhere in culture once you know how to look for it. Reading these essays as a general humanist stretches my mind, enlivens my curiosity, and deepens my understanding of music.This exemplary work makes us think in ways and about things we have never considered before. These essays illuminate such fresh ideas as the role of stuttering in song, how musical scores can work against stereotyping, how one plays the piano single-handedly, what place music occupies in autistic culture, how the concept of normalcy might operate in musical form, and the role of damaged voices as vehicles of musical distinction.

In this sense, this remarkable collection of essays addresses the question: What is disability music? It poses several critical questions. First, how is disability a thematic element in music? Second, how is musical composition or performance structured by individual disabilities of the composer or performer? Third, how is disability signified in musical performance? Fourth, how do musical composition and performance narrativize disability? Fifth, how does disability as a concept structure musical form?

As such, *Sounding Off: Theorizing Disability in Music* sets an agenda for future scholarship, lays out the beginnings of a conversation, and poses innovative intellectual questions. This volume is a fine example of one of the most productive scholarly institutions: the inaugural collection of essays about a previously unaddressed topic. Like all path-breaking collections, it stretches the limits and challenges the assumptions that sink us into intellectual complacency. Disability, it shows us, is an inherent and enduring aspect of human variation that shapes human aesthetic and cultural productions, leaving its imprint for scholars like those whose work appears here to excavate and display in our collective archive of human knowledge.

Rosemarie Garland-Thomson

1

Introduction: Theorizing Disability in Music

NEIL LERNER AND JOSEPH N. STRAUS

Just as race, class, and gender have slowly entered the horizon within music scholarship, the lens of disability has now arrived. The lens metaphor brings some attention to the ways cultural constructions of disability—and language's complicity within those constructions—recur and inscribe understandings of the world. A lens, after all, can serve to focus light into patterns that are clearer and more easily perceived; eyeglasses are some of the simplest and most familiar technologies used to accommodate visual impairments. The verbal language musicians use also says much about their assumptions. For example, *sight singing* constitutes a basic element in music education. To perform music within the cultivated tradition, musicians are expected to read musical nota- tion, and so the study of sight singing cultivates the skill of translating printed musical notation into performed sound. Yet the implication behind the phrase *sight singing* assumes something more: that one must have sight to read music. Actually, one does not have to have sight to read music, as revealed through a number of sight-singing books that have been translated into braille—without any apparent irony over the paradox in the words.

The primary goal of blending music and disability studies is not, however, to set out new rules for policing language. Rather, attention to disability and impairment brings greater attention to music as a manifestation of our embodi- ment, whether that be as listeners, composers, or performers. The history of European and American music features a remarkably rich cast of characters whose bodies, both physically and musically, are marked by their impairments, whether they be medieval monks (e.g., *Hermannus contractus*—in English, Herman the Hunchback; Notker Balbulus, the "stammerer"), *trecento* organ- ists (e.g., Francesco Landini, blinded as a child by smallpox), baroque church musicians (e.g., J. S. Bach, who lost his sight late in life), or Viennese symphon- ists (e.g., Ludwig van Beethoven). Indeed, once one starts to think about music through the lens of disability, disability suddenly appears everywhere—in the bodies and minds of composers and performers, in the reception histories of musical works, and even in the works themselves, embedded there in the form of persistent narratives. As a paradigmatic example, Beethoven's deafness,

1

which has played such an important part in the reception of his music, has given rise to what disability scholars call the *overcoming narrative*: The central part of the mythology around Beethoven involves his decision to grab fate by the throat and—instead of killing himself over the loss of his hearing—to continue to compose. The person with a disability, in this case the increasingly deaf composer, overcomes the impairment, as perceived by people without disabilities, to relieve them of their own anxieties about experiencing similar fates.

Disability is generally understood in this volume, following what Rosemarie Garland-Thomson calls *cultural disability studies* (see Foreword), as a cultural and social phenomenon rather than a medical one. This intellectual project questions the familiar process by which bodies and minds are compared to a prevailing normative standard and by which deviant bodies or minds are defined as disabled. The essays in this book chart the cultural and social construction of disability in relation to many different kinds of nonnormative bodies and minds. Paul Attinello's subject is HIV/AIDS and the music that has emerged in response to it. Maria Cizmic discusses cancer as experienced by the protagonist in the drama *W;t*, particularly as that experience is inflected by the music accompanying the drama. Both Attinello and Cizmic consider the general question of the relationship between illness and disability.

Neil Lerner discusses dismemberment in the form of the one-handed pianism of his title. Blindness is the subject of Adam Ockelford's essay, a case study of a talented young girl's music making, and Jennifer Iverson's essay, which critiques the familiar conflation of physical and moral blindness in the film *Dancer in the Dark* (Lars Von Trier, 2000). Blindness is also one topic of Stephanie Jensen-Moulton's essay on the wildly popular nineteenth-century musician known as "Blind Tom," but her essay focuses more explicitly on her subject's cognitive impairments, which she identifies as characteristic of autism. Her interest in autism is shared by other essays: those of Timothy Maloney, who interprets the life and artistry of pianist Glenn Gould in relation to his asserted autism, and Dave Headlam, who argues for a distinctive way of making music autistically as a reflection of a characteristically autistic way of being in the world.

One of the distinguishing features of this collection of essays is its focus on mental, cognitive, and developmental disability, in contrast to the more typical focus within disability studies on physical impairments, particularly deafness, blindness, mobility impairments, and body dismorphisms. Not only are three of the essays about autism, but four more also treat other nonnormative mental conditions. Poundie Burstein reevaluates the music and career of the nineteenth-century French composer Charles-Valentin Alkan. Alkan's music is unusual in many respects, and there has been a strong tendency among critics to ascribe the eccentricity of the music to the alleged madness of the composer. Burstein suggests that this may have more to do with the persistence of the myth of the mad genius than with the lived reality of Alkan's life. Kelly

Gross's essay focuses on the mental trauma and dislocation experienced by the protagonist of the movie *Three Colors: Blue* (Krzysztof Kieślowski, 1993), with the film score as the principal bearer and expression of her interior mental life. Stephen Rodgers' essay on Hector Berlioz's *Symphonie Fantastique*, a work that has long been recognized as formally and harmonically deviant within the conventional world of the nineteenth-century symphony, explores the forms of madness experienced in the composer's life and expressed within the musical work, relating them to then-contemporary diagnostic categories such as melancholy and erotic monomania. As both Gross and Rodgers show, music has the capacity to reflect inner emotional and mental states perhaps better than art forms freighted with the baggage of language. This may account for the disproportionate interest in these essays on mental and emotional rather than physical disabilities.

Another group of essays in this collection deals with forms of vocal pathology or disfluency. As Laurie Stras observes in her essay on rough, hoarse voices in the performance of popular music, "The disrupted voice conveys meaning even before it conveys language; in Western cultures we hear disruption as pathology, in both the current and obsolete meanings of the word: It is indicative of passions, suffering, disease, malfunction, abnormality." Among these abnormalities of vocal production is one with particular resonance in the history of music: stuttering. Andrew Oster's essay describes a long tradition of stuttering characters in early opera, including particularly the character Demo in an opera by the seventeenth-century Italian composer Francesco Cavalli. These stuttering characters provide comic relief: "On the whole, the trope of stuttering remains a persistent vocal marker that distinguishes his and other stuttering characters' discourse from that of their fellow characters. Singing, represented on the opera stage as aria, fails to destigmatize this fundamental vocal difference." Within an entirely different musical tradition, Daniel Goldmark identifies a group of stuttering songs from Tin Pan Alley, including the famous "K-K-K-Katy." Goldmark observes that these songs reinscribe the most prevalent stereotypes about stuttering and thus may have more to reveal about contemporary anxieties about disability than about their ostensible subjects.

Just as the range of disabilities explored in these essays is large, with a perhaps understandable emphasis on mental and emotional impairments and vocal pathologies, the repertoire of music discussed is correspondingly large. Within the Western classical tradition, composers discussed in this collection of essays cover a wide range of historical periods and musical styles from seventeenth-century Italian opera (Cavalli, discussed by Oster) through eighteenth-century classicism (Joseph Haydn, discussed by Marianne Kielian-Gilbert), nineteenth-century romanticism (Alkan, Berlioz, and Johannes Brahms, discussed by Burstein, Rodgers, and Neil Lerner, respectively), early twentieth-century modernism (Arnold Schoenberg and Anton

Webern, discussed by Kielian-Gilbert and Joseph Straus), and a variety of more recent music in the classical tradition, including Henryk Górecki, Dmitri Shostakovich, and Arvo Pärt (Cizmic), as well as Shulamit Ran (Kielian-Gilbert). It is interesting to note that none of these composers is disabled in any evident way, but their music can nonetheless be understood to be about disability in some way, either by compositional design or by virtue of the dramatic context in which the music is heard.

Beyond the Western classical tradition, the essays in this collection deal with music in a variety of vernacular or popular traditions, including the songs of Tin Pan Alley (Goldmark), popular songs of a later generation (Stras), and the music of the popular singer Björk, as well as the musical *The Sound of Music* (Iverson). In addition, a number of the essays consider the role of music in film, video, or drama, including the music of one of the preeminent composers of film music, Max Steiner (Lerner).

A wide range of musical performers also comes under scrutiny in these essays, including a group of popular vocalists—Bing Crosby, Ethel Waters, Louis Armstrong, Connie Boswell, and Julie Andrews—discussed by Stras because of their particular means of vocal production, which are understood as deviant or unhealthy. Within the classical tradition, Maloney explicates the famous performance and lifestyle eccentricities of Glenn Gould in terms of his autism. Jensen-Moulton shows that the autism of Blind Tom can be seen in both his famous, popular, and widely documented performances and in his fascinating, but much less widely studied, compositions.

According to the authors of these essays, music has a variety of stories to tell about disability, many of which are familiar from the extensive literature on the history and culture of disability. In some cases, music can tell, or can be enlisted in telling, a familiar story of disability overcome—of the abnormal normalized. According to Gross, "the narrative trajectory of the film *Blue* can be read as a typical normalcy narrative … that seeks to rehabilitate and repair deviance or to obliterate difference through a cure." Part of the cure in this case involves the protagonist of the film asserting her own creative powers through musical composition. In the genre of the horror film, as discussed by Lerner, the narrative trajectory involves normalizing a monstrous deviance of some kind: "Finally the film reveals that the presumed monstrosity of the disembodied hand was nothing more than a hallucination, removing even the possibility of the one-handed pianist and his ostensibly horrific threat to the normal body, as well as the presumably horrific threat to the symbolic body of classical music and its implicit messages of perfect form and perfect execution."

In his analysis of Berlioz's *Symphonie Fantastique*, Rodgers describes a musical narrative of bodily difference with its own means of representation distinct from those of language. Rodgers pursues this primarily in the formal domain, in terms of formal deformations. He shows that Berlioz's deviations from standard forms can be understood as one means by which he expresses a notion of mental deviance or abnormality. A similar narrative, in similar musical terms, is the focus of Straus's discussion of short works by Schoenberg and Webern. A central musical issue in these pieces is that of inversional symmetry, a sense that notes may balance each other around some central axis: "In all of the literature on musical symmetry, there is an emphasis on balance, on the physical sense of symmetrical balance around a fulcrum, of a body in a physically balanced state. In this context, deviations from inversional symmetry are felt as physical disruptions that unbalance the musical body, that create the threat or the reality of a disability, with which the music must then deal in some way. Inversional symmetry and symmetrical balance thus create the possibility for musical narratives that depend on a contrast of normative and nonnormative bodily states."

A related narrative trajectory involves the marginalization and expulsion from the human community of a disabled character. This is the trajectory traced by Iverson in her discussion of the film *Dancer in the Dark*: "Expelling Selma [the film's blind protagonist] from rational, safe society is justified not only by the plot line, then, but also by her irreversible blindness. The plot thus reflects the sociohistorical formula that the physically disabled and emotionally disfigured must be removed from able-bodied society." Iverson goes on to argue that the film's soundtrack offers a counternarrative, one in which the protagonist's disability may be understood in a sympathetic light: "Cutting the other way, it is indeed the soundtrack that offers the opportunity to read a sympathetic representation of disability against the ableist ideology of the narrative."

In addition to narratives of overcoming, cure, normalization, or expulsion, music has other stories to tell. For example, as a temporal art often concerned with deploying a goal-oriented musical language toward some predetermined end, music is well suited to speaking of a passage toward death. Indeed, as Attinello shows, music may be better at depicting death than at conveying the daily routine of living with an illness: "Much music about AIDS avoids the realities of illness or incapacity ... I suggest that a larger teleology is guiding the musical rhetoric, pushing it to ignore the immediacy of daily illness in favor of what comes after. ... These songs seem almost eschatological, not experiential—they always seem to outline inevitable and terrible futures, the kinds of futures that a dreaded progressive disease apparently must, by definition, reach. ... Though it may be unsurprising, it is also exasperating that so much music about AIDS, even when it foregrounds a variety of experiences or emotions, then allows its temporal universe to collapse into a foreshortened waiting for death."

In tracing these narratives, the authors in this collection have drawn on the insights of disability studies. Four lessons in particular seem to have been well learned. The first lesson is that disability is better understood as a cultural and social construction than as a pathology of individual bodies. A critique of the dominant medical model of disability is at work, either explicitly or implicitly, in most of the essays in this collection. For example, in her analysis of the drama *W;t*, Cizmic observes that "by expressing and performing aspects of [the protagonist] Vivian's physical sensations of illness, the film's music functions as a critique of the medical master narrative and aids Vivian's narrating voice to shape the representation of her own body." By amplifying her voice, music thus assists the dramatic character in articulating a nonmedical counternarrative. Similarly, Headlam's essay argues that autism is understood better as a culture than as a curable pathology: "Autism may be regarded as an alternate form of consciousness and a distinct worldview." Headlam goes on to adduce a distinctive style of autistic music-making as evidence of that consciousness and worldview.

In their essays, both Jensen-Moulton and Maloney engage in the potentially problematic practice of posthumous diagnosis. In what may initially appear as an embrace of the medical model, Jensen-Moulton analyzes the stage behavior and musical compositions of Blind Tom as symptoms of his autism, and Maloney does the same for Gould's famous eccentricities of demeanor and performance, complete with citations of the relevant diagonistic criteria drawn from medical manuals. But in both essays, the medical approach to disability is only the starting point for an effort to come to terms with two poorly understood musicians in a humanistic and holistic way: In both cases, autism is not the end of the story; rather, it is the starting point for a sympathetic account in which the life and artistry of these two musicians are understood, for the first time, in a persuasively integrated way. This kind of sympathetic identification also underpins Ockelford's case study of a vocal improvisation by a sight-impaired young girl whose music-making is shaped in interesting ways by her disability.

The cultural construction of disability, rather than its more familiar medicalization, is also a theme in Burstein's essay on Alkan. Burstein shows that Alkan has been constructed as mad by critics and audiences in thrall to the cultural trope of the mad artistic genius. But what has been constructed can be deconstructed, and Burstein shows that "it might well be that Alkan did not put his life into his music but rather that the public has put his music into his life."

A second lesson that the authors of these essays have taken from disability studies is the insight that disability is contextual—defined by local society and culture rather than an immutable and inherent quality of individual minds or bodies. Stras's essay, for example, shows that a certain kind of damage to the vocal chords may be disqualifying in one domain (e.g., classical performance, daily speech) and enabling in another (e.g., certain popular singing traditions): "This essay begins an examination of why and how damage signifies in the singing voice, how it is valued or not, and how a marker of corporeal impairment, normally a site of cultural anxiety, might also act as a catalyst for anxiety's release. Singers engaged in popular music might suggest that vocal damage has acquired the status of a culturally inscribed desirable mutilation."

Similarly, Lerner explores the ways one-handedness is disabling in a particular context, namely with respect to playing the piano—"the constructed monstrosity of the solitary hand." In this context, the significant number of works written for the left hand alone function as a way of accommodating a disability. This kind of physical accommodation of disability is becoming more common in our daily lives, but remains a striking phenomenon in works of art.

Like one-handedness with respect to piano playing, stuttering is a disability that is problematic in life, and even more so with respect to musical performance. As Oster observes, "Perhaps the most debilitating of vocal disabilities is stuttering, the spasmodic repetition or prolongation of certain syllables of speech." Vocal damage, one-handedness, and stuttering are thus impairments that may become disabling in particular musical contexts, and permissible or even desirable in others.

A third lesson the authors of this collection have learned from disability studies is that disability is extraordinarily pervasive as a dramatic element in works of art, where it is often "prostheticized" by the artistic narrative, which seeks to disguise or obliterate it (Mitchell and Snyder 2000, 9). According to Cizmic, for example, music functions prosthetically for Vivian, the protagonist of *W;t*. It reinforces her antimedical counternarrative and helps her communicate when language fails. Music is thus a supplement or prosthesis to compensate for the failure of language. Similarly, Lerner argues that the musical score for *The Beast with Five Fingers* (Robert Florey, 1946) functions prosthetically with respect to the apparent deficiencies of a one-handed pianist. Steiner's elaborate music functions as a "musical prosthesis, audibly giving us much more sound than one hand alone could produce. ... [It] substitutes a greater pianistic sound than the pianist pictured on the screen could have actually produced by himself."

In Björk's music, as described by Iverson in her analysis of the film *Dancer in the Dark*, "electronica can be thought of as a prosthesis, a mechanical supplement that draws attention to the lack latent in the natural voice. The electronic appears prosthetic, threatening, less than natural: It is disembodied. In Björk's music, the electronic prosthesis reminds us not only that the unity of the voice is threatened but also that the natural voice contains a latent insufficiency, even pathology, which must be compensated."

A final lesson from disability studies is the extent to which disabled characters are narratively reduced to their disability. As Garland-Thomson observes, "Literary [and, by implication, musical] texts necessarily make disabled characters into freaks, stripped of normalizing context and engulfed by a single stigmatic trait" (Garland-Thomson 1997, 11). Through this process of "enfreakment," the disabled character appears not for the purpose of sympathetic identification but rather to reaffirm the normality of the presumptively normal spectator. Certainly this is the case for stuttering characters in opera, as Oster describes: "Consistent with many of today's cinematic portrayals of stuttering characters, Demo's condition is better suited to elicit laughs than to raise awareness of the difficulties of stuttering. This is often also the case for deaf and blind cinematic characters, whose impairments are commonly cast in a comedic, not empathetic, light." The stuttering singers described by Goldmark are similarly depicted as humorous, as a way of creating a reassuring distance between disabled singer and normally abled spectator: "The almost transparent personalities given to those who stutter in these songs suggests that their disfluency is the only thing about these people that is interesting or noteworthy. ... In this way all sheet music of difference has a similar end product: conflating, flattening, and generalizing notions of other." The critical reception of Alkan (Burstein), Gould (Maloney), and Blind Tom (Jensen-Moulton) all betray a similar process of enfreakment—in each case the artist, like a character in a disability narrative, has been engulfed by the stigmatic trait of his disability. To restore to these important musicians a fairer, more balanced, more fully human understanding, the authors in this collection have attempted to resist the process of enfreakment by shifting attention to their music rather than to their obvious eccentricities.

The introduction has dwelled thus far on the lessons the musician-authors of these essays have learned from disability studies. But we hope it is also possible for our musical inquiries to enrich the field of disability studies. First, many of these essays demonstrate the advantages of working with a nonverbal medium. Music can represent mental states directly, including those classified as illnesses or disabilities, without the mediation of language. That expressive capacity may explain in part the unusual emphasis in this volume on cognitive impairments and mental illness compared to most work on disability. Gross, for example, observes that in *Blue*, "music becomes the privileged component of memory and acts as a signifier of and vessel through which [the protagonist] Julie's memories are mediated cinematically." Similarly, Lerner points out that in *The Beast with Five Fingers*, Steiner's score gives its audience important information about the characters, including their impairments and specifically including the mental instability of one of the film's central characters. More generally, many of these essays reveal the power of music to represent disordered, deviant, abnormal mental states and to suggest ways of constructing these states as disabilities. If the field of disability studies is interested in dealing more extensively with the cultural construction of cognitive, mental, and emotional impairments, it might well wish to look to music as a promising area of study.

Second, as a performing art, music can usefully call attention to the performative aspect of disability. As Goldmark points out in his essay on stuttering songs, "Since speech disfluencies, such as stuttering and lisping, are largely contingent on the person speaking, songs about such disabilities feature these people in the midst of their impairment, showing how it affects them." In other words, a disability may remain invisible until it is performed and, depending on the disability, may emerge precisely through the act of musical performance. In a slightly different sense, we might say—following Burstein and Maloney—that the composer Alkan and the pianist Gould perform as mad geniuses: their behaviors permit them to fill that particular disabled role.

Third, these essays suggest ways disability and cultural anxiety about disability may affect not only individual works of art but also entire repertoires. Attinello suggests that musical minimalism may have emerged in part as a response to the terror of death in the face of an epidemic of HIV/AIDS:

> However, the frequent incidence of cyclical forms—or, one might call it, the recurrence of recurrence—suggests an emotional or cultural demand as much as it does any trend or innovation; plausibly the structures of new age music, and also the increasing popularity and development of minimalism and process musics, fulfilled a rather desperate cultural need. If, in our teleologically oriented, progress-maddened culture, we find it difficult to keep our awareness in the present and are inevitably dragged ahead of ourselves by our expectations of the future—and also if, in our death-avoidant culture, we are alternately left numb or terrified by the inevitable end of that future—then it may seem plausible that the pleasures of minimalism are not only derived from a longing for a return to the womb (*pace* Schwarz 1997). They may also, in some cases, be calculated retreats from the terrors of death; all those images of the golden circles of heaven, of the timeless ecstasies of a safe and deathless existence, are constructed according to the same self-deluding blueprint. In fact, perhaps the causality is reversed: Could the popularity of 1980s minimalism at least partly be a cultural response to the threat of AIDS?

Cizmic makes a similar point in her discussion of the minimalist compositions of Arvo Pärt: "Although Vivian's pain is far more extreme than the dissonances of this piece, this music offers a truth about Vivian's physical experience of time and endurance for which her doctors' 'single-minded *telos* of cure' (Frank 1995, 83) cannot account." For Attinello and Cizmic, then, a process-oriented, nonteleological musical style may be a response to a widespread cultural awareness of and anxiety about disability and its destructive medicalization.

Straus makes a related argument about the emergence of twelve-tone serialism in the music of Schoenberg and Webern shortly after the Great War:

> The dramatic shift in the social and visual landscape of wartime and postwar Vienna may have been among the factors that gave rise to the twelve-tone idea, which, for Schoenberg and Webern, is fundamentally concerned with inversional balance and inversional symmetry. Typically in a twelve-tone piece by Schoenberg or Webern, the sense of inversional

balance is far more pervasive and far more stable than in their free atonal music. When people with physical disabilities were largely invisible to them, Schoenberg and Webern wrote music that explored extremes of asymmetry and imbalance. When people with physical disabilities become an everyday part of the visual landscape, with an attendant rise in social and cultural anxiety about disability, Schoenberg and Webern responded with a musical language that guaranteed stable balance—that virtually banished the possibility of lingering asymmetry. In this sense, in the twelve-tone idea can be seen an extreme avoidance reaction to the threat of deforming asymmetry and imbalance, now made shockingly real in everyday life.

In this sense, one of the cultural forces that led to twelve-tone serialism, like the forces that helped produce musical minimalism some sixty years later, was a pervasive anxiety about disability.

Finally, these essays suggest the special fluidity of music, unfettered by language or concrete referentiality. Kielian-Gilbert, for example, argues for the potentially transformative impact of music, particular its power to disrupt the seemingly hard and fast distinction between ability and disability: "Musical becoming, metamorphic transforming, is a particular way of expressing and materializing the movements between multiple conditions and identities, between abilities and disabilities."

In the first sentence of her foreword to this book, Garland-Thomson refers to "the conversation that makes up the emerging field I call *cultural disability studies*." Musicians and musical scholars have come late to this conversation. The initial entrance of disability studies into musical scholarship came about at the 2004 conference of the American Musicological Society and the Society for Music Theory in Seattle. A panel discussion there, titled "Disability Studies in Music," included presentations by several of the authors represented in this collection—Cizmic, Kielian-Gilbert, Lerner, and Straus—and provided the impetus for the present collection. This collection of essays, together with Straus (2006), represents the first published efforts to theorize disability in relationship to music, and vice versa. We may have come late to the conversation, but it is our hope that the energy, range, and intellectual vigor of these essays will help create a new dialogue between disability studies and musical scholarship, to the great benefit of both.

Part I
Narrating Disability Musically

2

Fever/Fragile/Fatigue:
Music, AIDS, Present, and …

PAUL ATTINELLO

Rising dizzily from that hazy dullness spiked with intermittent intensities which is the bed of illness, I focus my fragmented thoughts by sheer assertion, make a statement, throw down a gauntlet: the experiential is the source of the musical. Yes, well, I take your point: not always, and not the only source—but, for me, this is where the treasure is, the exciting aspect of studying all the arts: excavating the artistic product for its coded nugget of experience, whether it reflects the physical, the emotional or the rational. Such a nugget could even involve all three, as in the case of a disability or illness which affects the feelings (as they are experienced in the body), and also the feelings (as they appear in that body/mind response system we call the emotions—the double meaning of the word is a trick of English usage which can be useful and frustrating by turns), and also thoughts (under which we should remember to include received information, interpretations, predictions, causal constructs, and a host of other all-too-apposite terms). The experience of AIDS, for instance: it is a syndrome ("syndrome" is embedded in the acronym, and a good thing too—the term reminds us of the only really acceptable substantive that can be used in talking about it, unlike "disease," "condition," and other words which imply things which may or may not apply to individual cases) which is conceived as starting with an infection, which may itself affect the systems of the body but which more significantly can lead to other infections, and which tends, in the medical world, to create a condition that demands medication—medicines whose extensive side effects often induce yet more feelings (of both kinds) and thoughts, and frankly problems. Underneath all these, and forcing them into certain dark and culturally dangerous lines of development, is the complex cloud of feelings and thoughts that existed before, and which also grew up, amplified, around the historical construction of AIDS—in this case the dense cultural loci around sex, sexuality, guilt, repression, infection, good and evil, healthy and sick, straight and gay—and even a trichotomy so exhaustingly familiar as past, present, and future. Many of those lines have knotted, tangled strands in them; often the musical reflection of experience reproduces those knots—but some knots are more interesting than others; and if we pick at the largest and tightest knots, we cannot help but notice some unsettling things ...

This article is part of a larger project that has occupied me for some years, that of understanding the body of music that has been written in response to the AIDS crisis, along with the network of meanings on which it rests and to which it contributes. Unavoidably, that also involves understanding at least some of the broader aspects of the AIDS crisis itself, which has deformed and been deformed by so many powerful cultural forces; but, just as the music I have collected, although it crosses through many genres and styles, is chiefly produced in the urban West, so I must attempt to view the crisis from the standpoint of my experience as a witness and participant. This creates an interesting process that alternates deduction and induction: as the wide complex of ideas touched on in the first paragraph can develop and narrow down to a single knot, a single problem, so it may also be useful to acknowledge that the ensuing discussion of experiences and the metaphors created to invoke them fans out from a single point—the moment, brief or seemingly endless, but peculiarly singular in any case, of lying on the couch fatigued, or feverish, or only feeling fragile.

On my terms

In the midst of this barrage of constellated ideas and terms, with all the heavy baggage that they carry, some should be clarified in terms of this particular argument. AIDS, like many illnesses, has a problematic relation to disability; some legal and political systems define HIV/AIDS as itself a disability—due to all the considerations resulting from that definition—and some do not. Some significant political and financial changes over the past twenty-five years have in fact hinged on whether AIDS is a disability and, especially in America, whether various chronic and/or progressive illnesses can be classified as disabilities, and under what circumstances (Crimp 1988; Treichler 1999; Stine 2000). The legal definitions used by, among others, the Centers for Disease Control and Prevention and the National Health Services in the United Kingdom are produced through pragmatic medical fictions covertly understood among doctors, patients, and social workers, most of which were created in an attempt to sidestep the vast resistance put up by financial and bureaucratic systems to supporting the PWA, or person with AIDS. This has been necessary because such resistance often used to mean that by the time government institutions were forced to acknowledge that a patient was incapacitated in any way that suggested a need for financial support, the patient was no longer a matter of concern, being dead.

If disability is defined as a condition of not being able to function in certain ways, a person with HIV/AIDS may or may not have that condition: although it is not difficult to determine a PWA's relation to HIV and/or AIDS (using data both quantitative and anecdotal, including how many immune cells appear in a tested sample, how high an amount of virus is found in a sample, and how many significant opportunistic infections have been diagnosed), actual daily experience can vary considerably among PWAs and over time. In the terrible old days before we had even partially effective medications, people frequently went blind; developed difficulties in walking, eating, or breathing; and struggled with embarrassingly frequent diarrhea. These problems are familiar and openly presented in many memoirs, novels, plays, and narrative poems; a subtle but deeply felt example appears in Ron Schreiber's poem "your life," included in the famous anthology (Klein 1989) that was a source for many of the texts set to music in the *AIDS Quilt Songbook* (1993, 1994):

> first there's your health: I
> want you to have it, you were
>
> exhausted and sun-dazed when I
> brought you back from the hospital
>
> —after stopping to get your drugs—
> & you were sleeping when I called
>
> downstairs just now. I am tired
> beyond anything my body tells me
>
> is fatigue. & when you're sick,
> when I look into your tired, lovely
>
> eyes, I want you well

Since the introduction of vastly more effective antiviral medications in 1996, the dominant experience of HIV/AIDS in Western urban centers has moved toward that of a chronic illness that is—up to a point—manageable. Although any given group of PWAs will experience serious illnesses and deaths over an extended period, many patients are now familiar with something less eschatological in nature: occasional fatigue, minor opportunistic illnesses, and side effects. It is thus not surprising that musical, and in fact much artistic, production has decreased in the West since the mid-1990s, and that the music which is now produced tends to be politically assertive and somewhat abstract rather than immediately or dramatically personal. What remains appropriate to the discussion of disability is the experience of being unable to maintain normal or expected activities, as a result of the hazy, changeable experience of being "fragile": passing fevers, with their injection of a distracting dizziness into daily life, and physical fatigue, which can have its source in the virus, in other infections or their ensuing physical damage, or of course in the medications used to fight off everything else.

Tired music

As it happens, not many musical works include strong metaphorical or textual images of such fragility; much of the music written about AIDS focuses considerably more on fear, mourning, or existential crises around the idea of death. However, the *AIDS Quilt Songbook* (1993, 1994) did include at least two strong evocations of disabling illness, both settings of poems built around concrete everyday images. "Heartbeats," a poem by Melvin Dixon set by John Musto, refers both obliquely and directly to incapacity and various resultant feelings in a long chain of scatter-fire disyllables:

> Test blood. Count cells.
> Reds thin. Whites low.
>
> Dress warm. Eat well.
> Short breath. Fatigue.
>
> Night sweats. Dry cough.
> Loose stools. Weight loss.

Musto's setting, although splintered into sections that use different textures, maintains a relentless misery in the pounding "heartbeats" of its irregular meters (see also Ward 1999). This surface reference to the physicality of illness as experienced from the "inside" is emphasized by a partially hidden underlay—brief piano interludes that give the voice a rest quote the melody of the Stabat Mater, suggesting not only a grief-stricken witness but also, as the composer's note clarifies, the stations of the cross as symbols for various stages and experiences of misery. Of course, the stations of the cross led inevitably to Golgotha, and the entire structure of the poem and setting are in fact insistently teleological—the text skips through months or years of progressively worsening illness, ruthlessly hammering out an apparently unavoidable journey toward death. In fact, I suggest that the aural image of this beating, anxious heart is about passing time and the fear of death much more than it is about the febrility of illness. The second commercially recorded performance of the song, included in *Heartbeats* (1994), the second volume of the *Songbook*, exposed the blunt realities underlying these images and metaphors; William Parker, the baritone whose personal efforts originally created the cycle, was at that point audibly weakened, and his performance on World AIDS Day, December 1, 1992, was colored by a shaky vibrato and cracking climactic notes. The liner notes explain that "William Parker's voice, frayed from the ravages of AIDS, faltered; but the notes held pure. Those were the last notes he ever sang in public: he died on March 29, 1993." I am faintly suspicious of the claim that "the notes held pure," especially as the actual recording suggests this is an exaggeration: is this kindly reassurance intended to sidestep the reality of his singing on that day, reinterpreting the cracks as dramatic signifiers of an impending death? Such a directed understanding of the situation admittedly made medical sense at the time, and of course the brief flash of an imposed teleological drive is familiar in the way we tell stories about the events previous to anyone's death from any means; however, the lack of alternative interpretations worries me.

Another song from the first book of the *AIDS Quilt Songbook* explores similar miseries, tied to disintegrating bodily functions and overwhelming medications—but as seen from "outside" and over the briefer time span of a single night. "A Certain Light," a startlingly observant poem by Marie Howe in a setting by Elizabeth Brown, is a portrait of Howe's brother during a period of extreme illness: John vomits up his medications, sleeps for hours, and is "breathing maybe twice a minute." However, the central turning point of the poem, highlighted in the title, reveals that the poem is a deathbed scene: John wakens, and "the room filled with a certain light we thought we'd never see again." That finality, supported by the mournful, quasi-expressionistic cross-relations of the piano accompaniment, pushes any dramatic interpretation of the song out toward its apparently inevitable end; this is especially true as Howe's brother died in 1989—although John does not die in the space of the poem, it is clearly suggested that death is days, if not hours, away.

Naturally, most of the narrative works that include music, such as the musicals *Rent* (Larson 1996) and *Falsettoland* (Finn 1990), include scenes about being ill or incapacitated—that is also the norm for nonmusical dramatic works. However, these scenes are rarely set to music; real illness in these works happens in spoken dialogue or more often—and in a way that faintly recalls Medea's children—offstage. Other songs—many of them, in fact—are accompanied by dragging, incapacitated musical sounds; a famous example is Bruce Springsteen's "Streets of Philadelphia" (Springsteen 1993): when the song is sung over the scenes of rich and poor that begin the film *Philadelphia* (1993) and also fill the separate music video, its darkness suggests the distance that the lawyer–protagonist will fall in the course of the film. However, most other such songs seem more concerned with the fear of death than with the immediacy of illness; moments of incapacity do not really represent disability, at least as it is generally understood, but are both reduced and redirected to become symbols of loss that foreshadow the final loss. Lee's (1996) music therapy case study of a PWA shows that the client/pianist clearly experienced, and musically commented on, his own changing illness and weakness; yet much of the musical improvisation they shared, and much of Lee's commentary on the case, focuses insistently on the threat of nonbeing.

Tropes of incapacity remain rare in most music about AIDS, although they are common in other media. I have suggested elsewhere (Attinello 2000, 2003) that some of the various marked differences between music and other media might result from a tendency for music to sidestep concrete experience and terminology in favor of the expression of personal and private emotions. However, that seems inadequate in explaining this situation; I suggest that a larger teleology is guiding the musical rhetoric, pushing it to ignore the immediacy of daily illness in favor of what comes after.

The teleological versus the static: other illnesses, and other ways out

These songs seem almost eschatological, not experiential—they always seem to outline inevitable and terrible futures, the kinds of futures that a dreaded "progressive" disease apparently must, by definition, reach. This seems to be the great difference between two modes of responding to disability: some medical conditions may be treated as static, or at least partially static, existing in time that can be experienced and lived through, but others are constructed as inevitably dashing toward their dreadful endings. This suggests yet another reason for the rhetorical conflict between "dying of AIDS" and the deliberately constructed phrase, frequently used since the late 1980s, "living with AIDS": why do we have so much difficulty compassing the experience of the second, the patience and awareness it implies, the possibility of living in a real and thriving temporal present, despite the knowledge of our mortality? Of course, most of these songs gain their emotional power from the fear of death—it is not the present, with its limitations and discomforts, that makes good drama, but the point where that present begins to slide to its end. These pieces are predictive rather than descriptive; and the predictions seem to me to be, at times at least, pernicious.

Such a problem is not restricted to AIDS, though its status as a "dreaded illness" (Sontag 1989) may make the problem harder to avoid. Rorem's (1999) lengthy song cycle *Evidence of Things Not Seen* includes a setting of a remarkable poem by Jane Kenyon, "The Sick Wife." The poem bridges an experience within the body—"Not yet fifty, / she had learned what it's like / not to be able to button a button"—with broader metaphors for ability: "The cars on either side of her / pulled away so briskly / that it made her sick at heart." Although the poem is linked to Kenyon's death from cancer rather than from AIDS, it clearly foreshadows the songs about AIDS that appear in the final section ("Endings") of the same song cycle. These two songs, written on texts by Mark Doty ("Faith") and Paul Monette ("Even now …"), are about the threat of death more than illness; plausibly the Kenyon is used to stand for the daily experience of illness, something very familiar to Rorem after his own lover's death (Rorem 2000). Certainly, there are diseases that share some of the same problems: Sontag's *AIDS and Its Metaphors* (1989) is virtually a second volume of *Illness as Metaphor* (1978), which investigated cancer through the invisible filter of her own experience of it; in the sequel she makes new points about AIDS—especially about sexuality, guilt, and military metaphors—but many of the same ideas are applied. A less famous but highly interesting memoir, *Take It and Leave It: Aspects of Being Ill,* is Dutch journalist Renate Rubinstein's (1985) aggressively opinionated examination of her experience of muscular sclerosis. Some years ago I wrote a review of *Take It and Leave It* for an AIDS community newsletter (Attinello 1992), pointing out that Rubinstein shared at least some problems with PWAs, including anger, resentment, dealing with other people's problematic responses, and learning how to get on with things despite new limitations. Despite the vast differences between the diseases involved—there is no sexual guilt in cancer or multiple sclerosis, nor are they associated with specifically despised groups, international politics, or pharmaceutical economics—these writers point up some of the same personal problems: how can we continue to live with a progressive illness when so many cultural forces and ideologies work so hard to prevent us from seeing anything but our impending deaths?

Although much music about AIDS avoids the realities of illness or incapacity, some songs sidestep the problem of death in a different way. I wrote elsewhere (Attinello 2006) about works that refer to some kind of heaven, usually a broadly ecumenical, nonspecific, aestheticized sort of place; as it happens, many of those works use musical tropes that circle round and round through pleasurable, sensually textured harmonic patterns while avoiding final cadences. There are, of course, good musical and historical reasons for this: AIDS entered the public consciousness during the same period of time that minimalism, process music, and new age music became popular and accepted compositional styles. Certainly, the soft, meditative surface of new age music was not only related to pleasure and leisure but was also associated with the increased popularity of healing musics, which were largely publicized by figures such as Louise Hay and were fairly directly linked to the growing PWA community of the late 1980s. However, the frequent incidence of cyclical forms—or, one might call it, the recurrence of recurrence—suggests an emotional and/or cultural demand as much as it does any trend or innovation; plausibly the structures of new age music, and also the increasing popularity and development of minimalism and process musics, fulfilled a rather desperate cultural need. If, in our teleologically oriented, progress-maddened culture, we find it difficult to keep our awareness in the present and are inevitably dragged ahead of ourselves by our expectations of the future—and also if, in our death-avoidant culture, we are alternately left numb or terrified by the inevitable end of that future—then it may seem plausible that the pleasures of minimalism are not only derived from a longing for a return to the womb (*pace* Schwarz 1997); they may also, in some cases, be calculated retreats from the terrors of death—all those images of the golden circles of heaven, of the timeless ecstasies of a safe and deathless existence, are constructed according to the same self-deluding blueprint. In fact, perhaps we have the causality reversed: could the popularity of 1980s minimalism at least partly be a cultural response to the threat of AIDS?

A counter-example

Although many popular songs are unafraid of the more uncomfortable emotions and ideas that arise around AIDS—fear, rage, and even in some cases a vicious comic malice—few of them spend much time on physical incapacity or illness. Even ballads by such melancholy songwriters as Leonard Cohen (1988) and Lou Reed (1989) focus on death rather than on an uncomfortable but, perhaps exasperatingly, undramatic continuation of existence. Possibly my favorite song among all those I have collected is the bizarrely sexy jazz/pop/club *tour de force* "Fear No Love" (Ostertag 1994), which briefly but confidently opens the door to explore the realities of physical illness and fragility. The song is by Bob Ostertag, one of San Francisco's most unpredictable queer experimentalists, and is unusual among his works. It was written when John Zorn asked Ostertag for something "completely different"; according to Ostertag's website (Ostertag, n.d.), the queer press loved the result, but Zorn hated it. The song gives one side—the top side, one might say—of a confrontation between an aggressive, disturbingly seductive man and his uptight prey, in what is perhaps the most obnoxious "pass" ever recorded. The darkly hilarious musical setting emphasizes jazzy backbeats and bouncy background singers, pulling in edgy buzz-saw samples just for the fun of it. In a long, tangled mega-coda (after the climactic chorus that appears at 3:55—less than halfway through the song—and starting from around 4:35), where the strophic structure disintegrates into an extended stop-verse constructed out of astoundingly invasive questions, some blunt realities start to surface between the two men:

> What if you and I were only bones and skin [and]
> What if you and I had only seconds left to make it in
> What if the world was ending and not a single person cared
> Who was kissing who—would you still be so fucking scared?
> Would you be scared of love? …
>
> What if we wake up one morning and the sheets
>   are soaked with our sweat?
> [Has that ever happened to you? I'm
> speaking hypothetically …
> Am I being too vulnerable? Is it pushing you away?
> Come back over here, sit the fuck down,
> I'm not finished talking to you …
> Well] what if you wanted to touch me but
>   [like] my lesions [kinda] scared you?
> [Be a man about it. Come over here.]

What if you were too weak [someday]
to get out of the bathtub?
[What would you want me to do then?
I think you'd want me to bend down
and put my arms around you,
I think that's what you'd want.]

My transcription of the lyrics includes, in brackets, singer Christian Huygen's slightly demented, growling, whisky-and-cigarettes expansions of the text; his insistent but romantic demands give the song a late-night, kind-of-guy-your-mother-warned-you-about quality. This may be one of the reasons I love this song so much: it launches, honest and unafraid, into a future that may be dangerous, that might involve terrible hardship, but that will nevertheless have real joys, real hours and days of living in it. The same point is made more poignantly by another song on the same album: in the heterosexual duet "Positive," a woman fearfully tells her lover she is—well, positive—with punning meanings tossed back and forth among the lines and voices. An extended coda with pitched percussion and electric bass supports the voices winding erotically around each other as the woman chants, over and over, in an ambiguous kind of happiness: "Boy, you make me want to live: absolutely positive." Ostertag offers a sex-positive, and in fact a life-positive, view that manages not to collapse into the institutionalized optimism of the social worker: he refuses to be drawn into an abstractly teleological future where death is the focus of all imagination, the chilly drain that pulls all our thoughts down into it.

Terminal reflections

Though it may be unsurprising, it is also exasperating that so much music about AIDS, even when it foregrounds a variety of experiences or emotions, allows its temporal universe to collapse into a foreshortened waiting for death. This is, of course, a particular problem for music, as music is so often concerned with temporal metaphors, with constructing models for different ways of experiencing time. Too many of these songs dissolve the past and present into a future that has not yet arrived, thus causing time itself—our time, the time in and through which we live—to vanish. The frequency of tropes of mourning and fear, even in songs directed at or modeled on the relatively healthy, and the temporal opposition of the teleological and a visionary eternity are, in this context, simply opposing but mirrored schemes in the dangerous redefinition of the PWA as a death just waiting to happen.

… What then can we say, or do, to undo some of the dangerous patterns we have learned? What space is opened up, what conflict is unearthed, by speaking of those difficult moments where the body itself seems to threaten us, where our survival seems to be compromised—even when we actually

know we are fairly safe, that we are not in grave danger as so many people once were—and as so many people in other countries still are, but then that hardly bears thinking about—when we know we are to all extents and purposes certain that our deaths will not be as helpless, as disastrously incomprehensible and even apparently cursed, as were the deaths experienced by so many who are now gone? After all, whatever stories have been told, whatever constructions have been built, one thing remains to hold onto: I'm still alive ...

3

Of Bodies and Narratives: Musical Representations of Pain and Illness in HBO's *W;t*

MARIA CIZMIC

Beyond the Medical Master Narrative

In Margaret Edson's play *W;t* (1999), audiences encounter the fictional Dr. Vivian Bearing, a literary scholar specializing in the Holy Sonnets of John Donne—poems that wrestle with the difficulties of faith in the face of mortality.[1] Now from within her experience of illness, Vivian faces her own mortality and addresses her audience through frequent monologues, narrating her diagnosis of stage-four metastatic ovarian cancer, her memories, her treatment, her hospital experiences, and her physical pain. This story grew from Edson's experiences working as a clerk in the oncology/AIDS unit of a Washington, D.C., research hospital during the mid-1980s. *W;t* was first performed in 1995 and underwent a series of revisions and small productions until its staging at New York City's Union Square Theater in 1999. This version of the play garnered Edson the Pulitzer Prize. In 2001, HBO produced an adaptation of Edson's play directed by Mike Nichols and starring Emma Thompson as Vivian Bearing; the film also incorporates music into the fabric of *W;t*.[2] The central modes of representation integrated into the play and film center on Vivian's suffering body: Language, images, acting, and—of central concern in this essay—music all work to convey aspects of Vivian's physical and emotional experiences of illness.

Vivian narrates her self to the audience, making *W;t* simultaneously confessional and fictional. She describes her childhood fascination with language, her pride in being an uncompromising professor, and her experiences of illness. In *The Limits of Autobiography*, Gilmore (2001, 36) points out that the act of self-narration implies multiplicity: There is the self who experiences events and the self who can step outside those events and create a story. Scenes depicting Vivian's hospital life alternate with her self-reflective monologues, thereby exemplifying Gilmore's distinction. This multiplicity inherent in the central narrative voice becomes richer with the film's inclusion of music, particularly vocal music, which complements and expands on Vivian's perspective. Though Vivian is both subject and narrator of *W;t*, Edson also weaves in two different medical perspectives regarding Vivian. Her male doctors cannot cure her and instead subject her to the most experimental and difficult of treatments, viewing her body as a means for research and knowledge—an attitude with which Vivian identifies as a scholar. Her nurse, Susie, on the other hand, offers compassionate attention and care to Vivian's increasingly ailing body.

These interwoven stories within *W;t* raise a concern central to humanistic discourse regarding disability, illness, and trauma: the relationship between bodies and narratives. In *Enforcing Normalcy*, Lennard Davis (1995, 9) draws attention to two prominent narrative tropes that involve disability: (1) stories in which an individual's success erases his or her disability, as with Itzhak Perlman; and (2) stories in which an individual overcomes a disability to attain success, as with Ludwig van Beethoven. Davis finds such traditional stories of erasure and overcoming about disabled people equally repugnant. Dominant cultural master narratives shape and distort public perceptions, articulating the difference between healthy and ill, abled and disabled. It then becomes the task of writers within illness and disability studies, including the present essay, to draw attention to and to dismantle these dominant ideologies.

Although Davis (1995, 2) focuses on cultural narratives, he briefly mentions the "heavily medicalized orientation towards care and treatment" that has often regarded the disabled as "objects of study." Both Frank (1995) and Couser (1997) critique the medical establishment and describe a medical master narrative that privileges doctors' authority, medical jargon, technology, and the unrelenting search for a cure. Couser (1997, 19) articulates the resulting power imbalance between doctors and patients:

> Although physicians usually rely to some extent on information provided by patients, they assume total responsibility for diagnosis..., prognosis ..., and therapy. ... After a patient presents his or her case to the physician, the role of the patient in conventional medical discourse is to attend to, and to comply with, "doctor's orders." The politics of medical discourse thus favors the professional; doctors exercise their medical authority through their privileged place in a specialized discourse.

Although modern medicine can heal patients, it can also devalue patients' voices and alienate them from their medical treatment and bodies. Most pertinent to *W;t* is medicine's focus on curing illness. Frank (1995) writes about a woman with terminal cancer. As she dies, specialists subject her to continued invasive treatments that strive for an impossible cure: "Obsessed with cure, medicine cannot place the woman's story in any other narrative" (p. 83). The medical master narrative of cure can eclipse the need to care for people humanely—to help people like Vivian Bearing endure their illness.

W;t performs a critique of the medical establishment that is very similar to the critique posed by these writers and offers parallel solutions. Frank (1995, 10–11) sees the increase in published personal illness stories in recent decades as a way for individuals to reclaim their physical experiences in their own voices. Couser (1997, 291) writes along similar lines: "In the case of illness and disability often the foremost motive in life writing is to recover variously dysfunctional bodies from domination by others' authority and discourse, to convert the passive object into an active subject." The ameliorative response to the medical establishment's master narrative is an attention to patients' voices and bodies. Both Couser (1997, 5) and Hawkins (1999, 1) define *autopathography* as the act of telling or writing the story of one's own illness or disability.[3] Frank (1995, 3) emphasizes that such stories, though told by an individual's voice, "are told not just about the body but through it." As a genre, autopathography supplies a means toward the reclamation of people's voices about their own bodies. Edson's play speaks to the concerns raised by Frank and others by mounting a critique of the medical establishment through fictional autopathography.[4]

Trauma theory also addresses voice, body, and narrative. But because the psychological community understands post-traumatic stress disorder as a problem of memory—often involving violence and bodily suffering—their attention to narrative focuses on assembling memories as a path toward healing. Often, people do not consciously remember traumatic events, but they may unconsciously and even physically retain such memories, resulting in nightmares and flashbacks. The conscious construction of a narrative about a traumatic event may offer a path toward healing the self.[5] Scholars such as Gilmore (2001), Caruth (1996), and Felman and Laub (1992), among many others, translate trauma from the psychological to the literary to consider how cultural texts perform the difficulties of representing trauma and participate in a redemptive healing. Although the terms of trauma theory are quite different from disability and illness studies, Frank's (1995, 1) description of illness experience as "the loss of the 'destination and map' that had previously guided the ill person's life" implies that bodily disease, like trauma, can result in a radical disorientation of the self. Narrative and autopathography supply a possible venue for a reorientation and healing of the self.

These scholarly conversations regarding disability, illness, and trauma orient narrative in terms of an individual's voice and body. Edson's play represents two versions of Vivian's body: (1) her body as medical object of study; and (2) her shivering, crying, puking, hairless body that undergoes cancer and chemotherapy. De Certeau speaks to this plurality by distinguishing between the *flesh* and the *body*. The flesh references one's particular physical sensations before they are presented to or are represented for others; the body operates on the level of social discourse, and food, clothing, mannerisms, and medicine, among many other factors, shape how bodies interact with others, either directly or through a mode of representation. Klaver (2004, 662) discusses *W;t* in de Certeau's terms, articulating the difference between Vivian's experience of her ill flesh and her doctor's diagnosis of her diseased body: "The flesh may be ill, but the body has disease."

I wish to take Klaver's argument one step further. *W;t* does not simply perform a distinction between flesh and body; it mounts an intervention at the moment that the flesh becomes diagnosed as a body. Because Vivian is both subject and narrator of her story, she is able to determine the representation of her own body by telling her audience directly how she feels, both physically and emotionally. Vivian constructs the representation of her own body and shapes its nature within social discourse, recovering her flesh from the medical establishment.

The reclamation of one's voice, flesh, and body has specifically feminist overtones, as well as postcolonial associations.[6] In Edson's drama, the male medical establishment analyzes diseased bodies and aims at a cure. Since at least the mid-1970s, women with cancer have called for a reclamation of particularly women's voices, bodies, and stories from medical treatment.[7] *W;t*'s central achievement is the presentation of a woman who owns and creates the story of her own flesh and, in so doing, defines her body in counterpoint to the dominant medical narrative about her.

In HBO's film, music operates at the level of Vivian's narrative voice. Her autopathography emphasizes her physical experience of illness; because the film's music often represents Vivian's point of view, it reinforces her central, embodied position in her own story. After a brief consideration of the stage play's opening, the present essay focuses on the film's use of music as an extension of Vivian's voice, as a critique of the medical establishment, and as a representation of Vivian's ill flesh. Dmitri Shostakovich's String Quartet No. 15 (1974), used in the opening scene, immediately pulls viewers into Vivian's disorientation at the moment of diagnosis. In later scenes, this music draws attention to Vivian's physical experience of pain. Arvo Pärt's *Spiegel im Spiegel* (1978) offers a musical space of stasis and unresolving dissonances that express Vivian's need to endure rather than to cure her cancer. Henryk Górecki's Symphony No. 3 (1976) offers a musical extension of Vivian's voice and her cry of pain, fear, sorrow.[8] *W;t*'s soundtrack mediates between Vivian's flesh and her body. By expressing and performing aspects of Vivian's physical sensations of illness, the film's music functions as a critique of the medical master narrative and aids Vivian's narrating voice to shape the representation of her own body.

Two Beginnings (Shostakovich, String Quartet No. 15)

In the theater, *W;t* opens with Vivian walking onstage dressed in hospital garb, pushing her own intravenous (IV) pole. Vivian faces her audience "in false familiarity, waving and nodding" and poses to them what she

will later explain is the hospital's standard greeting: "Hi. How are you feeling today?" (Edson 1999, 5).[9] This common phrase bears the brunt of the
play's central epistemological and phenomenological concerns: How do
we know and experience pain, either of our own bodies or of someone
else's? How do we address someone in pain or, conversely, communicate
from a position of illness? The difficulty of communication about pain,
particularly within a hospital setting, forms the center of Vivian's opening
monologue (p. 5):

> I have been asked "How are you feeling today?" while
> I was throwing up into a plastic washbasin. I have been
> asked as I was emerging from a four-hour operation with
> a tube in every orifice, "How are you feeling today?"
>   I am waiting for the moment when someone
> asks me this question and I am dead.
>   I'm a little sorry I'll miss that.

Vivian's reflections point to the overlapping social situations that incorporate
the generic question: How are you feeling? In daily conversational practice
this question often functions as a convention of address rather than as an
actual line of inquiry. In the context of illness and hospitalization, the question's casualness can become an ironic "feigned solicitude," as Vivian will
later claim (p. 6). At the same time, though, this question can open a crucial
door to address how someone feels; in fact, the question will prove to
work successfully in conversations Vivian has with her nurse, Susie, later in
the play. Positioned in this opening monologue, "How are you feeling today?"
highlights the absurdly large epistemological gap between those who feel pain
and those who do not. Even doctors and nurses, the very people who study
and treat diseased bodies and who know on a certain level even more than
Vivian what is going on in her own body, have severely limited access to the
actual physical sensations of her flesh.

W;t points toward an incommensurability among language, representation,
and pain. Scarry (1985, 5), in *The Body in Pain*, argued that language breaks
down in the face of pain because it is so totally circumscribed by an individual's
flesh. To this point, Woolf (1925, 194) once wrote, "The merest schoolgirl
when she falls in love has Shakespeare or Keats to speak her mind for her, but
let a sufferer try to describe a pain in his head to a doctor and language at once
runs dry." Scarry articulated the difficulties inherent in moving from an experience of pain to representing that pain—from flesh to body, in de Certeau's
(1988) terms. With so much of the play and film presented as a monologue,
Vivian uses words, something over which she has authoritative ownership as a
literary scholar, to convey her physical and emotional sensations. Vivian tries
to communicate her pain to her doctors, to her nurses, to her former professor,
and to her audience with varying success. Even with her mastery of language,

Vivian's ability to take the experiences of her flesh and verbally represent her own body deteriorates due to her continuing treatment and suffering.

Although the path toward representation is fraught, Scarry (1985) also argues that a path toward social justice and change lies in successful linguistic representation. Scarry is preoccupied with the ways suffering bodies can be co-opted by political ideologies—particularly during times of war—that represent bodies in such a way as to divert attention away from the fact of physical suffering. To move beyond such challenges, representation has to hold the body in pain as a direct referent: "If the felt-attributes of pain are (through one means of verbal objectification or another) lifted into the visible world, *and if the referent for these now objectified attributes is understood to be the human body*, then the sentient fact of the person's suffering will become knowable to a second person" (Scarry 1985, 13, italics original). *W;t* consistently references the specific, if fictional, body of Vivian Bearing. When Vivian's narrating voice fails, *W;t* supplies her body—audiences see the consequences of her cancer on her shivering, crying flesh.[10] At times, when Vivian cannot put her pain into words, the film strategically introduces music in a way that helps Vivian express her voice and represent her body. By maintaining Vivian's body as her story's focal point, *W;t* manages to communicate aspects of her suffering.[11]

In a manner quite different from the stage play, the film opens with a black screen that fades into a motley, pastel background. This image looks like an out-of-focus photographic still of buildings, but because the film's opening offers no immediate context the image's subject is not readily apparent. The brief opening credits run over these blurry pink, beige, and blue colors as the beginning of the second movement of Dmitri Shostakovich's String Quartet No. 15 (the last of his string quartets; see Figure 3.1), plays.

Shostakovich composed this piece at a time when illness had burdened him for some years.[12] As with other late Shostakovich works, this quartet is generally understood as expressive of sickness and death. The quartet's movements, all in E-flat minor, are played *attacca*. The first violin sustains a B-flat from the end of the first movement into the second, playing one whole note for the entire first measure on a single up-bow. Beginning softly, this note dramatically crescendos and culminates with a sharp *sffff*, spilling over into the next measure with a tied eighth note. Just as the first violinist reaches the gesture's peak, the second violin enters on the second measure's downbeat and creates the same sonic effect on the note A. All members of the quartet except the cellist follow one another in this manner, performing the piercing gesture through all twelve chromatic pitches. Shostakovich's whole notes create an intrusive effect due to their sudden and repeated dynamic surge. Because the quartet plays the twelve chromatic pitches in no predictable order, this movement opens in a sonic disorientation that the director and music consultant of *W;t* synesthetically reinforce through the out-of-focus shapes on screen.

Figure 3.1 Dmitri Shostakovich, String Quartet No. 15, II, mm. 1–13.

These long, smooth whole notes abruptly shift to a series of quick *pizzicato* chords played by the second violin and viola. At this moment, actor Christopher Lloyd's face enters the frame, simultaneously blocking out the pastel scene and contextualizing it as the distant view from an office window. As Dr. Kelekian, Lloyd's face suddenly occupies almost the entire frame in an extreme close-up shot that cuts off the top of his head. He says, "You have cancer" (p. 7). The sonic, visual, and verbal juxtapositions of *W;t*'s opening hinge on disorientation and disruption: Vivian's cancer diagnosis is the disturbing event that fundamentally redefines her life. The brittle *pizzicato* chords infringe sonically just as Lloyd's face intrudes visually and as the diagnosis invades Vivian's life. Shostakovich's music supplies information about Vivian's experience that Dr. Kelekian's technical diagnosis cannot encompass. The film rearranges the order of the play's opening scenes; as a consequence, Vivian does not immediately narrate the film as she does in the play. The music supplies a framing device that expresses Vivian's point of view and initiates her counternarrative.

By including exclusively precomposed music for the film's soundtrack, *W;t* also interacts with existing musical narratives. Within the context of Shostakovich's string quartet, the chromatic whole notes emerge from the last note of the first movement in an unexpected deviation. This fissure is also deeply physical: The players shift away from ensemble playing to trade single, long, extended up-bows. But what seems discontinuous is really a framing device for an off-kilter chromatic waltz; once the waltz ends, the piercing gestures and pizzicato chords return to close the second movement. The film's opening scene has a strikingly similar structure. Once the music and credits end, Vivian receives her diagnosis, and Dr. Kelekian offers her an experimental treatment. Marked by the doctor's compassionless medical jargon and Vivian's almost blank response, this awkward conversation stands in the same structural space as the movement's disjointed waltz; as the scene ends, those surging whole notes return, just as they do in Shostakovich's composition.

When the pizzicato chords follow at the end of the diagnosis scene, the film abruptly jumps forward in time and cuts to Vivian's hospital room. She sits on her bed, her back turned slightly toward the camera, her head bald under a baseball cap. At the moment of diagnosis, Shostakovich's music performed Vivian's disorientation; here, in its return, the whole notes and pizzicato chords indicate the physical suffering from illness and treatment that repeatedly disrupted her life after diagnosis. As Frank (1995, 56) writes, "Disease interrupts a life, and illness then means living with perpetual interruption."

Later in the film, when Vivian takes herself to the hospital because her chemotherapy has made her incredibly sick, the String Quartet No. 15 recurs for the final time. Vivian sits on a chair in a hospital corridor, flushed with fever and shivering with pain. She is so ill that she will be admitted to the hospital for the last time—a crucial turning point in the film. Here, the knife-like whole-note gestures suggest an aural metaphor for the sharp pains that cause Vivian's body to shake so violently. By giving Vivian the experimental treatment, Dr. Kelekian perceives Vivian's suffering body as part of his research—in an almost exaggeratedly callous way. Through aural and visual juxtapositions, Shostakovich's quartet conveys aspects of Vivian's embodied experience that Dr. Kelekian's medical language cannot come close to describing: the disturbing nature of the diagnosis and the even more intrusive experience of physical pain. The music's focus on Vivian's body lifts her physical experience into representation and works as a counterpoint to the doctor's narrative about her cancer. In scenes when Vivian does not explicitly narrate her story, the music performs aspects of her ill flesh and shapes the representation of Vivian's body from her perspective.

To Endure (Pärt, *Spiegel im Spiegel*)

In contrast to the knife-like intrusions of Shostakovich's String Quartet No. 15, Pärt's *Spiegel im Spiegel* for violin and piano passes through many of the hospital scenes like a kind of melancholy wash over the film. *Spiegel im Spiegel* is schematic, repetitive, cyclical, and dependent on a process of addition. Using A as its focal pitch, the violin gradually adds pairs of notes, one above and below, until it spans two octaves. The piano supplies a triadic accompaniment that mirrors the violin's process. Slow and quiet, *Spiegel im Spiegel* is continuous in dynamics, range, and timbre; its constant nature focuses listeners' attention on the minute change from one note to the next. Although each cycle introduces new pitches, change is so systematic and consistent that *Spiegel im Spiegel* creates a space of continuity and stasis.

In one particular scene, *Spiegel im Spiegel* accompanies Vivian's monologue (pp. 34–5):

> In this dramatic structure you will see the most interesting
> aspects of my tenure as an in-patient receiving experimental
> chemotherapy for advanced metastatic ovarian cancer.
> But as I am a *scholar* ..., I feel obliged to document what it
> is like here most of the time, between the dramatic climaxes.
> In truth, it is like this:
> (*She ceremoniously lies back and stares at the ceiling.*)
> You cannot imagine how time ... can be ... so still.
> It hangs. It weighs. And yet there is so little of it.
> It goes so slowly, and yet it is so scarce.
> If I were writing this scene, it would last a full fifteen
> minutes. I would lie here, and you would sit there.
> (*She looks at the audience, daring them.*)
> [*Spiegel in Spiegel* fades out here]
> Not to worry. Brevity is the soul of wit.

Vivian knows that her narration does not capture precisely all her experiences as she lives them. Although *W;t* is a fiction, this moment draws attention to the disparity between real life and any representation of life.[13] Writers about trauma also consider the disparity between reality and representation due to the compromised nature of memory and the idea that any narrative is a falsification of events to some degree.[14] Vivian tries to compensate for what her story leaves out by describing the stillness and slowness of hospital life; this theme leads her to acknowledge her own mortality and the scarcity of time she has left.

The music expresses what the narration cannot encompass. *Spiegel im Spiegel* creates a temporal space that does not build to a dramatic climax; instead, it creates a static state of being, simply and slowly circling through the notes of F major. As Vivian describes her hospital life, the film provides a musical corollary for her temporal experience outside of the film's narrative scope.

As Vivian's illness and treatment progress, she is faced with the need to endure chronic pain; her diagnosis offers no real hope for a cure, and the experimental treatment only makes her sicker. *Spiegel im Spiegel* also acts as the film's expression of endurance. Pärt's compositional process supplies a structure that does not give in to the teleological nature of tonality—its cyclical repetition does not search for any goal. By remaining within the notes of F major and moving stepwise in the violin part and triadically in the piano part, *Spiegel im Spiegel* creates mild diatonic dissonances that do not search for resolution; instead there is a constant sense of tension that correlates to Vivian's experience of chronic pain. Mild dissonances caused by notes from within a single tonal area rub up against each other, never leading to resolution, never going away, never cured. Although Vivian's pain is far more extreme than the dissonances of this piece, this music offers a truth about Vivian's physical experience of time and endurance for which her doctors' "single-minded telos of cure" (Frank 1995, 83) cannot account. Kelekian continues to give her the full dose of treatment, inscribing Vivian into the medical master narrative of cure. Pärt's music, though, helps Vivian reclaim her own body and asserts a counternarrative that pays attention to her need to endure the cure for cancer.

W;t chronicles Vivian's last days in the hospital as she struggles with her memories and her pain, alone except for the company of her nurse, Susie. Vivian makes the crucial decision to endure her treatment no longer and signs a Do Not Resuscitate order. As she dies at the film's end, however, Vivian's intern, Jason, obliviously calls a team to resuscitate her, but Susie arrives just in time to stop them. The scene plays out an upsetting juxtaposition: A doctor's view of Vivian as an object of research conflicts with her need to die humanely. After the severe jostling about her body, the final scene depicts Vivian's deceased body exposed from the waist up on her hospital bed. Over this image, Vivian's voice recites John Donne's "Death Be Not Proud." Pärt's *Spiegel im Spiegel* returns in the underscore during the recitation, continuing after the poem's end and playing out over the closing credits. The film begins its storytelling with Shostakovich's intrusive music and ends with the most disruptive event we know, or can never fully know: death. Music of unrelenting smoothness and continuity accompanies Vivian's death.

As Vivian recites the last line of Donne's poem, she says, "And death shall be no more, comma, death, thou shalt die."[15] The spoken punctuation recalls a scene remembered earlier in the story, a scene in which Vivian as a young graduate student is taken to task by her advisor for a poor analysis of this very poem. Expounding on the metaphysical implications of punctuation, her professor says to her (pp. 14–5):

Nothing but a breath—a comma—separates life from life everlasting. It is very simple really. With the original punctuation restored, death is no longer something to act out on a stage, with exclamation points. It's a comma, a pause.

This way, the *uncompromising* way, one learns something from this poem, wouldn't you say? Life, death. Soul, God. Past, present. Not inseparable barriers, not semicolons, just a comma.

Spiegel im Spiegel performs no barriers, no abrupt changes, shifts, or pauses; this is music of continuity, a sonic experience that, here at the end of the film, highlights the idea that the boundaries between life and death, past and present are not as great as we may think them to be. As part of *W;t*'s counternarrative, *Spiegel im Spiegel* supplies a music of continuity in the face of pain, illness, and death. Pärt's process-driven composition conveys a kind of control that resonates with the function of narrative: Vivian cannot control her flesh, much less what others do to her flesh, but she can shape the story about her body.

Two Women, Two Voices (Górecki, Symphony No. 3)

For much of the film Vivian lies in her hospital bed, struggling with her body as it fails her and grappling with memories as they flood her. She recalls a particular moment when a student asked for an extension due to a death in his family. With little compassion, Vivian responded, "Do what you will, but the paper is due when it is due" (p. 63). The classroom scene ends with a stunned-looking student, and the opening strains of the second movement of Górecki's Third Symphony begin just as the film cuts back to Vivian's hospital room. In a close-up shot that excludes any of the IV poles and machines in her room, Vivian lies in bed, clothed in a pale blue hospital gown and shown from the shoulders up with her arms swung behind her bald head. Vivian reacts to her memories: "I don't know. I feel so much—what is the word? I look back, I see these scenes, and I ..." (p. 63). She tries but cannot find the right words to express regret about her own past behavior.

As Vivian speaks, the second movement of Górecki's symphony performs a shimmery and static A major, beginning on an open fifth on A that reaches immediately up to the leading tone (see Figure 3.2). A desire to hear the missing third coupled with the upward melodic leap to G-sharp creates an effect of longing and reaching. Arcing downward to a D–F-sharp third, the motive rests for a whole measure. The orchestra sustains all the notes played thus far; the D–F-sharp third arrives on the downbeat of the second measure and the next three beats resonate with a major seventh (A–G-sharp) filled in by a set of major seconds (D–E–F-sharp–G-sharp). This gesture repeats three times and is followed by a trailing string of alternating thirds (D–F-sharp and C-sharp–E) and one last iteration of the opening motive.

Górecki creates a sonic realm of diatonic dissonances that, not unlike Pärt's *Spiegel im Spiegel*, do not search for resolution. As Vivian struggles to articulate her emotional state, this musical expression of yearning resonates with her search for language. Shostakovich's string quartet worked in place of Vivian's narrative frame; Pärt's *Spiegel im Spiegel* expressed an aspect of time for which Vivian's narration could not account. Górecki's symphony layers over Vivian's narration and occasionally compensates for her faltering voice. The sustained diatonic dissonances almost seem to help Vivian

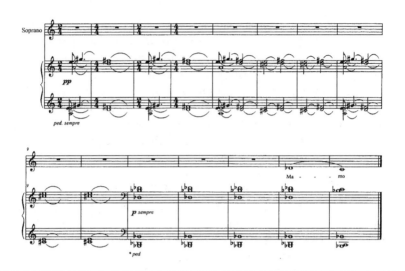

Figure 3.2 Henryk Górecki, Symphony No. 3, II, mm. 1–15 (piano reduction).

communicate what she cannot say—that she regrets her past behavior. When she stops speaking, the camera cuts away to show the only thing Vivian has in her room to look at: a blank television. Górecki's music enharmonically transforms at this moment from A major to B-flat minor by pivoting from C-sharp to D-flat (measure 11). The minor third on B-flat rearticulates Vivian's emotional landscape; overcome with loneliness, she pinches her IV tube and causes Susie to come to her side.

Subtitled "Symphony of Sorrowful Songs," Górecki's composition for orchestra and soprano is explicitly a work of mourning; the soprano's texts in all three movements invoke this overarching theme. For the second movement in particular, Górecki chose words inscribed on a prison cell wall in what was Gestapo headquarters in Zakopane, Poland, during the Second World War: "No Mother, do not weep. Most chaste Queen of Heaven, support me always."[16] An eighteen-year-old prisoner, Helena Wanda Błażusiak, inscribed and signed these phrases in 1944. Błażusiak's call of comfort as a child to her mother, the mother of God, seems to have been meaningful for Górecki on several levels, drawing on Polish historical and cultural memories, resonating with his personal recollections of war, and representing a form of address to his own mother who passed away early in Górecki's childhood.

Although much of this historical and musical detail may not be readily available to the average viewer of *W;t*, for the audience a different kind of cultural memory is at work. The film uses the 1992 Nonesuch recording of Górecki's Third Symphony, with Dawn Upshaw singing soprano; this is one of the best-selling classical recordings of all time. The second movement in particular helped earn the symphony its reputation in Britain and the United States as a World War II and Holocaust memorial piece. As Vivian mourns, Górecki's symphony supplies these associations of grief that arise from the symphony's historical content and reception.

After Vivian pinches her IV tube, Susie arrives to check in on her and even brings her a Popsicle, both as a form of comfort and a means of hydration. What ensues is a conversation of extraordinary difficulty. Dr. Kelekian views Vivian as a crucial part of his research: She is the first patient to take an entire series of the experimental treatment at the full dose, supplying him with important data. Because the doctor also sees Vivian as a colleague—as another scholar and professor—he never perceives her physical decline from her point of view. It is left to Susie to explain that, despite their best efforts and the most aggressive treatment, Vivian's cancer continues to spread. With the help of Susie's lucid explanations, Vivian makes a decision regarding life and death and decides to go on the charts as "Do Not Resuscitate." When Vivian's anguish regarding her own lack of warmth and kindness toward her students overwhelms her, the person she looks to for those very qualities is Susie.

This conversation about life and death is the heart of the story: It is Susie who calls Vivian "sweetheart," who listens to her voice, who pays attention to her body, and who cares for her successfully. Through this relationship, Vivian's reliance on intellect at the expense of kindness is transformed, even redeemed. After their conversation, Susie leaves Vivian alone in her hospital room; again the A major opening of the second movement of Górecki's symphony plays. With the camera aimed from the foot of her bed, Vivian sits and reflects on the preceding scene (p. 69); the music again shifts to the darker, B-flat minor passage.

That certainly was a *maudlin* display. Popsicles? "Sweetheart"? I can't believe my life has become so … *corny.*

But it can't be helped. I don't see any other way. We are discussing life and death, and not in the abstract, either; we are discussing *my* life and *my* death…and I can't conceive of any other … *tone.*

Now is not the time for verbal swordplay. And nothing would be worse than a detailed scholarly analysis. Erudition. Interpretation. Complication.

Now is a time for simplicity. Now is a time for, dare I say it, kindness.

As Vivian continues her monologue (p. 70), the soprano solo enters in the underscore with a sobbing, falling motive from D-flat to C on the word *mamo—mother* (see fig. 3.2, measures 14–15).

(*Searchingly*) I thought being extremely smart would take care of it. But I see that I have been found out. Ooohhh.

I'm scared. Oh, God. I want … I want … No. I want to hide. I just want to curl up in a little ball. (*She dives under the covers*)

At first, Upshaw sings rather low in her range and creates a full though covered sound. Upshaw almost moans the sob-like motive twice before trying to lift out of the D-flat–C descent. At measure 21 (not shown here), she sings, "Don't cry, Mother," rising from D-flat to E-flat before falling back down to D-flat and then to C. The orchestra continues its B-flat–D-flat pedal as the soprano attempts this upward gesture again at measure 25, singing the D-flat–E-flat motive twice before dropping again through D-flat to C.

At measure 32, Upshaw finally frees herself from the D-flat–C motive (see Figure 3.3). Beginning at D-flat, she sings through the B-flat natural minor scale, peaking at B-flat and arcing downward to G-flat. This is an important turning point in the soprano solo: The gravity of the sob-like motive has given way to a rising melodic arc that allows Upshaw to sing a kind of musical cry. As the soprano reaches up for the high B-flat, the orchestra releases the B-flat–D-flat pedal it has sustained for the preceding twenty-two measures and begins to alternate E-flat7 and D-flat7 chords. These musical changes correspond to a change in tone in Vivian's monologue: from reflection to fear. Vivian cries out to God and dives under the covers just as Upshaw reaches her high point and the music moves into the aural foreground. The harmonic rhythm increases to change every half note, the orchestral body rhythmically pulsing as Vivian's body throbs under the covers. Górecki voices these oscillating E-flat7 and D-flat7 harmonies as closely as possible, creating poignant diatonic dissonances as musical lines rub up against each other.

This music continues into the next scene as the camera slowly zooms out to show Vivian's entire figure under the covers. The scene fades out and into another shot of Vivian: She lies on her side with the camera focused in on her face from next to her bed. The only change that has been made to Górecki's composition occurs here: The recording has been edited to return to the soprano's initial entry in B-flat minor. This return to the minor third on B-flat occurs later in Górecki's score but briefly and without the soprano's voice. After peaking on B-flat, the music recedes into the underscore, and Vivian's cries and moans now enter the aural foreground. Vivian tries to find words to describe her extreme physical pain. As words fail her (p. 70), Upshaw moans the sobbing motive from D-flat to C.

Figure 3.3 Henryk Górecki, Symphony No. 3, II, mm. 32–34 (piano reduction).

(Trying extremely hard) I want to tell you how it feels. I want to explain it, to use *my* words. It's as if … I can't … There aren't … I am in terrible pain. Susie says that I need to begin aggressive pain management if I am going to stand it.

"It": such a little word. In this case, I think "it" signifies "being alive."

The music fades away after Vivian finishes this speech; no music plays at the end of the scene as Susie hears Vivian's agonized cries and runs to help her.

These scenes play out the struggle to depict emotional and physical suffering—to take Vivian's flesh and to represent it as a body. Vivian constructs her own story of cancer that draws attention to her ill flesh and suffering self. Górecki's music operates at the level of Vivian's narration and compensates for her fragmenting voice, at times expressing what she cannot. Upshaw's soaring B-flat cries out just as Vivian dives under the covers. At this moment, Vivian is too afraid to tell her story, and Upshaw supplies a musical cry of grief. Later, the falling D-flat–C motive performs a moan of pain as Vivian attempts to convey her discomfort in words; her voice falters as language becomes insufficient and her suffering too great. The music contributes to *W;t*'s fictional autopathography by vocalizing Vivian's pain and drawing attention to her embodied experience of illness.

The plurality of voices in these scenes emphasizes the need for listening because the voice—as Scarry (1985, 33) reminds us—is an extension of the body. De Certeau (1988, 145, 147) draws attention more specifically to "the cry," which for him is a direct vocalization of the flesh. He discusses the interaction between the flesh and the *tool*, a term including both writing that can represent the flesh and medicine that can diagnose the flesh. He sees two possible outcomes from the interaction between flesh and tools: either a fiction or a cry of pain. In Edson's drama, two fictions arise from the interaction between Vivian's flesh and the tools of medicine: (1) Dr. Kelekian's narrative of research and cure; and (2) Vivian's own story. Dr. Kelekian fails to attend to Vivian's pain because he inscribes Vivian into his narrative of research instead of paying attention to her body. Vivian's narrative frame maintains her body at the center of *W;t*, recalling Scarry's (1985, 13) argument that the body needs to be a stable point of reference to convey the felt-attributes of pain. Vivian's cries play a crucial role in expressing suffering; they are, as de Certeau (1988) wrote, emitted directly from her flesh. The film constantly focuses upon Vivian's body as it supplies her cries and further musical cries of pain. Audiences begin to learn something about Vivian's suffering through this repeated juxtaposition. Because Górecki's music functions as part of *W;t*'s narrative frame, the music ensures that Vivian's cries are central to the representation of her body.

Caruth (1996, 4) explains that "the story of a wound that cries out" represents and makes public events that exceed a normative frame of reference. The creation of such a story is a redemptive act (p. 83). Writing specifically about illness, Couser (1997, 289) echoes Caruth: "Although they [autopathographical narratives] may be unable to relieve the symptoms of the body, they may help to relieve the suffering of the self." Edson has notably, although ambiguously, commented that *W;t* is a story about redemption.[17] Vivian's redemption centers on her realization that she needs human connections and kindness. In her assessment of *W;t*, Jacqueline Vanhoutte (2002, 392–3) mounts a critique of redemption narratives about cancer: They can burden patients with the responsibility for the disease. The expectation that all cancer stories take the shape of a redemption narrative is distorting and often will not correspond to an individual's experience.

Neither Caruth (1996) nor Couser (1997) claim that all stories about disability, illness, and trauma have to take the shape of a redemption narrative. They assert that to represent disability, illness, and trauma is a redemptive act regardless of the particular narrative trajectory. Vivian's coherent representation of the physically disruptive events of her illness makes *W;t* a redemptive drama.

Bodies and Texts

In her primary physician, Dr. Kelekian, Vivian unfortunately and ironically finds a kindred spirit: a man as coldly intellectual as Vivian herself had been. As Donne was to Vivian, Vivian's body is now to Dr. Kelekian: an object to be studied, analyzed, and taught. It is this set of experiences, of being the object of research while in excruciating pain, that causes Vivian to reevaluate her own behavior. As a scholar of Donne's metaphysical poems, Vivian has taught texts and has treated life and death issues as texts. Once she physically enters into the palpable life-and-death situation that faces her as a cancer patient, she wrestles with her body's transformation into an object of her doctors' research and analysis. At the beginning of her treatment she says, "The attention was flattering. For the first five minutes. Now I know how poems feel" (p. 16). In another scene, Dr. Kelekian brings his group of students in to visit her, to analyze her, during "grand rounds." After a scene filled with students vying for the doctor's attention and approval, they leave Vivian to reflect on her situation: "In grand rounds they read me like a book. Once I did the teaching, now I am taught."[18]

In *The Object Stares Back*, James Elkins (1996) discusses the power relationships of seeing, claiming that often those who are clothed hold power over those who are not clothed. He draws examples from hospital settings and discusses the power relationships between patients and doctors (pp. 89–91). Edson dramatizes this point throughout the play. Vivian's body is an object to be read by her doctors, putting her in a distinctly disempowered position. Yet she is the central narrator of the story, creating and owning the story of her own body. To recall Couser's (1997, 291) point from the beginning of this essay, the goal of autopathography is the reclamation of "variously dysfunctional bodies from others' authority and discourse." *W;t* is a story that supplies a counternarrative to the dominant medical establishment and that focuses on Vivian's physical experiences. The compositions included in HBO's film reinforce *W;t* as counter-narrative by offering music that draws attention to Vivian's body—even helping her communicate when language fails.

Notes

1. The title of Edson's play has two common spellings: *Wit* and *W;t*. I use the latter in this essay because the 1999 edition of the play presents the *W;t* spelling. The insertion of a semicolon in place of the "i" references a conversation Vivian recalls with her professor, E. M. Ashford. As a graduate student, Vivian writes a paper based on an edition of John Donne's "Death Be Not Proud" that is falsely punctuated by inserting a semicolon rather than a comma in the poem's final line. Ashford asks her to rewrite the paper and to consider what the different punctuation expresses about the relationship between life and death (see Edson 1999, 14).

2. *W;t* contains no prohibition against music, yet stage productions of Edson's play do not conventionally use any music. From a personal e-mail correspondence with the film's music consultant David LaTulippe in August 2003, I learned that the musical choices for *W;t* were made by both LaTulippe and Mike Nichols. For more information regarding Edson and her play, see Martini (1999). For more information and a review regarding the HBO production, see Lyall (2001).

3. Hawkins defined *pathography* as an illness story, and Couser named the autobiographical illness story as *autopathography*.

4. Although these writers mount a credible reproach of modern medical practices, not everyone agrees with such criticism. Vanhoutte (2002, 407) countered *W;t*'s assessment of the medical establishment with her own touchingly humane story of cancer treatment.

5. See Herman (1992) for a clinical psychological account of the symptoms of and recovery from post-traumatic stress disorder.

6. Frank (1995, 10–11) explicitly borrowed the language of postcolonial theorist Gayatri Chakravorty Spivak in arguing that modern medicine has "colonized" patients' bodies.

7. See, for example, Lorde (1980). Although I believe that *W;t* has a potentially feminist slant in its attention to embodiment, Edson's drama unfortunately reinscribes some negative stereotypes. Vivian is an intellectual woman whose reproductive capacity is decimated; Vivian is also characterized as emotionally repressed, falling into what Sontag (1988, 39) defined as a stereotype of "the cancer-prone character: someone unemotional, inhibited, repressed. ..." For a detailed critique of the play along these lines, see Vanhoutte (2002).

8. *W;t* also includes an excerpt from Charles Ives's (1908) *Unanswered Question*. I do not discuss this work here because, unlike the other pieces of music in this film, *Unanswered Question* does not extend Vivian's voice in an autopathographical manner.

9. Subsequent *W;t* citations are by page number only.

10. See Klaver (2004) and Deshaze (2003). Both focus on the stage play's presentation of Vivian's body. In their respective arguments, they emphasize and explore the fact of embodiment as central to the play's philosophical and political meaning.

11. A sign of *W;t*'s success in communicating "the felt-attributes of pain" is the Educational Initiative Act, a program that tries to change the medical establishment by organizing performances of *W;t* at thirty of America's top medical schools (see Szegedy-Maszak 2001, 48).

12. For more on Shostakovich's illnesses and compositions during the early 1970s, see Wilson (1994).

13. Frank (1995, 21) reflected on the writing of his own autopathography, *At the Will of the Body*: The narrating and editing process led him to wonder whether he had "compromised too much and if the story was still 'mine.'"

14. See Felman and Laub (1992, 76–9). Psychoanalyst and Holocaust child survivor Dr. Dori Laub discussed his experiences with trauma and memory. He explored the unreliable nature of memory and the resistance many trauma survivors have to telling their stories.

15. The final recitation of this poem is not written into Edson's play and is a feature only of the HBO film.

16. The English translation of the Polish text is taken from the Boosey and Hawkes score (Górecki 1992). The Polish text is as follows: "O Mamo nie płacz nie / Niebios Przeczysta

Królowo / Ty zawsze wspieraj mnie. / Zdrowaś Mario." For more information about this source in Górecki's symphony, see Thomas (1997). Regarding this symphony's reputation as a Holocaust memorial work, see Howard (1998). Cizmic (2004) also discussed Górecki's symphony as a work of mourning wrapped up in its reception with Holocaust memory.

17. In an interview for *American Theater* with Adrienne Martini, Edson explicitly stated that *W;t* is about redemption and the experience of grace. She did not, though, specify what she meant by these statements, nor did she reference anything specific in her play (Martini 1999, 24–5). See also Eads (2002) for an attempt at interpreting *W;t*'s redemption in terms of Christianity.

18. This line does not exist in the original play but was added by Nichols and Thompson, who collaborated on the adapted screenplay for the HBO film.

4

Female Subjectivity, Disability, and Musical Authorship in Krzysztof Kieślowski's *Blue*

KELLY GROSS

Three Colors: Blue (Canada/U.S. title) is the first of acclaimed Polish filmmaker Krzysztof Kieślowski's French-language trilogy *Three Colors: Blue, White,* and *Red* (1993–94) and is ostensibly about music, the compositional process, and the haunting qualities of music that motivate character interactions. *Blue's* protagonist, Julie, possesses a unique relationship to music that is represented by her acts of composition and musical editing throughout the film. After losing her husband, Patrice de Courcy, a famed European composer, and young daughter Anna in a tragic car accident, Julie is haunted by fragments of her husband's last and unfinished work: the *Song for the Unification of Europe.* Shocked by the trauma of her loss, Julie severs all ties to her previous life and purposefully chooses a new life of isolation and emotional disconnection, hiding in anonymity in Paris. Throughout the film she is overwhelmed by the presence of musical fragments associated with her husband and daughter's joint funeral and the *Song.* Only through Julie's confrontation with this music, through the act of finishing the *Song* collaboratively with her husband's former secretary, Olivier, is Julie relieved of the disturbing musical fragments and able to begin the work of healing.

In addition to providing ample opportunities to explore the interplay of music and the cinematic depiction of Julie's subjective experiences, two particularly intriguing aspects of the film may also be situated within the context of disability. The first is the striking effect of Zbigniew Preisner's scoring for *Blue* during moments of visual obliteration where the screen fades to black. These highly stylized cinematic ellipses are suggestive of Julie's mental trauma; they arrest narrative flow and give way to music in a manner unique to Kieślowski's oeuvre. The second aspect is the film's narrative resolution, which involves Julie stepping into the role of author and composer, an act that relates to typical narrative strategies involving disability. How might Kieślowski's stylized narrative intrusions and often ambiguous handling of authorship provide new ways of thinking about the dialectical tension between female agency and the ways in which the character Julie is potentially disempowered?

41

The themes of female subjectivity, disability, and music are inextricably intertwined and act as vehicles for writer and director Kieślowski's deeply personal exploration of memory and trauma in *Blue*. Julie uses music as a powerful medium of expression to negotiate her identity as a composer and to achieve discursive power. Yet when seen through the lens of disability studies, Kieślowski's reliance on disability as a narrative catalyst and vehicle of textual disruption during the ellipses is also ultimately contained by Julie's cure. Before analyzing how these issues may function within *Blue* in a more detailed manner, this essay first looks more broadly at various critical responses to Kieślowski's depiction of women, music, and the metaphysical, or uncanny, connections between characters. These are powerful themes that repeatedly resurface in his late cinema.

Krzysztof Kieślowski died in 1996, leaving behind many critically acclaimed films including *Three Colors: Blue, White,* and *Red, The Double Life of Véronique* (1991), and the ten-hour *Decalogue* made for Polish television (1989). These films represent a striking contrast to the documentaries about quotidian Polish life Kieślowski made under the Communist regime in Poland from the late 1960s to the early 1980s. Notably, in the mid- to late 1970s Kieślowski gradually shifted from making documentaries to feature films. With *Camera Buff (Amator,* 1979), *Blind Chance (Przypadek,* 1981), *No End (Bez Końca,* 1984), and *Decalogue,* Kieślowski became increasingly comfortable in the arena of feature films as writer and director and later eschewed documentaries altogether.[1] This shift away from overt sociopolitical concerns coincided with Kieślowski's wider popularity in Europe. His later work is perhaps best known in France where, in the early 1990s, *The Double Life of Véronique* and *Three Colors: Blue, White,* and *Red* were coproduced. By the time of his death, Kieślowski had made his mark as one of Europe's most highly respected feature filmmakers, based almost exclusively on this later work.

This dramatic shift to feature films also reveals a remarkable change in Kieślowski's treatment of his female characters during the 1980s and early 1990s. Early films like *The Scar (Blizna,* 1976), *Camera Buff,* and *Blind Chance* revolve around the desires and conflicts of their male protagonists, whereas *Véronique* and the *Three Colors* trilogy of Kieślowski's late, French cinema concern the points of view of their respective female protagonists. The creation of female-centered filmic worlds also marks a fascinating change in Kieślowski's visual style. Alicja Helman (1999) made some of the first steps toward exploring this particular aspect of Kieślowski's films. In *Decalogue,* she argues, Kieślowski selected unattractive actresses or filmed beautiful Polish actresses in ways that accentuated their physical flaws, "suggesting a desire to destroy and devalue them in the viewer's eyes" (p. 120). Rather than acting as active subjects, female characters in *Decalogue* are tied to their biological roles and, when threatened, are depicted as hysterical, proving a danger to themselves and to male protagonists.

Helman (1999) also cites a radical change in the visual depiction, function, and agency of Kieślowski's female characters. She notes that the heroines of the *Three Colors* trilogy are not only "intrinsically beautiful" women but that they are "also treated as such by the director and his camera" (p. 120). Drawing on the work of Julia Kristeva (1982), Helman posits that women in these films access powerful feminine forms of feeling, emotional knowledge, and uncanny intuition. She argues that as a result, these heroines are no longer depicted as supplements to the masculine but as powerful alternatives to it. Though Helman did not feel that Kieślowski's later works are uncomplicatedly profeminist, she did little to problematize the concept of uncanny, extrarational feminine intuition usurping more rational and intellectual (i.e., masculine) forms of knowledge.

In *The Fright of Real Tears: Krzysztof Kieślowski between Theory and Post-theory* (2001), Slavoj Žižek broadly uses Kieślowski's films as a foil to critique modern-day methodological and ideological disputes within film studies and briefly touches on Kieślowski's treatment of sexual difference. In a direct challenge to Helman (1999), Žižek argues that praising woman's access to other forms of knowledge ironically reduces them to the prerational. Instead of transforming the earlier figures of excessive and dangerous women so prevalent in *Decalogue*, these heroines still pose no threat to the patriarchal order. Žižek argued that in celebrating these other knowledges, Helman relegates these female characters to a nondiscursive, powerless space.

As persuasive as Žižek's (2001) arguments are about the potentially limited role of women in Kieślowski's films, he does not critically address music—an issue that would complicate his arguments even further. Though her praise of Kieślowski's cinematic representations of woman's "difference" is problematic, Helman's (1999) exploration of music and its connection to his female protagonists' emotional knowledge creates an intriguing intersection. Helman draws on Kristeva (1982) in describing how music acts as a powerful medium of expression through which Kieślowski's heroines can express themselves "by means of a different 'speech'" (p. 126). It is no accident that for the female protagonists of *Véronique* and *Blue*, "[m]usic represents a certain value that is less aesthetic than existential" (p. 127). As well as bearing the burden of alternative female discourse, music also acts as a vehicle for Kieślowski's metaphysical explorations of characters connected by supernatural means.[2]

Music, female subjectivity, and metaphysics are aspects of these films that are inextricably intertwined, and the plot of *The Double Life of Véronique* demonstrates the difficulty of separating these themes from one another. In *Véronique*, aspiring Polish singer Weronika (Irène Jacob) wins a music competition and the opportunity to perform the music of composer Van den Budenmayer at a special public concert.[3] Not heeding the repercussions of a minor heart attack, Weronika chooses to sing in the concert and, in so doing, dies midperformance. Véronique (Weronika's double in France, likewise played by

Jacob) is also a singer suffering from a heart condition. The uncanny intuition about the fate of her Polish double influences Véronique to stop singing, and she continues her life in music as a teacher—teaching school children a work of Van den Budenmayer, no less. According to Helman's (1999) theoretical perspective, music in this context has a special status as that which exceeds and defies logic by playing an important role in linking Weronika with Véronique and is therefore heavily implicated in the metaphysical aspects of the film. However, Helman's view of music's special status seems limited, as seen in Žižek's (2001) critique of those Other(ing) elements of Kieślowski's films that relegate women—and by extension music—to a nondiscursive space.

Kieślowski's shift toward exploring metaphysical themes clearly marks a notable change in music's importance. Music in his late cinema is more foregrounded and "audible"—vitally connected to the narrative's trajectory. Already with *Véronique*, music can be seen to feature prominently for the first time as an essential plot element, inseparable from issues of female subjectivity and metaphysics. Kieślowski's shift toward depicting female-centered experiences parallels his shift in portraying music as an integral plot element, and both are heavily implicated in his examination of the metaphysical.

Disability and the trope of illness are also central thematic issues that permeate Kieślowski's musically centered later work. In *Véronique*, for example, the female protagonists are connected not only through music but also through the heart disease they share and that proves fatal to Weronika. Intrigued by the idea of music and disabling illness, Kieślowski twice featured storylines involving female singers with heart ailments who must make a literal choice between life and making music, or death. The minor character Ola (Jolanta Pietek-Gorecka) in *Decalogue IX* is a prototype for the two Veronicas. She is a young singer with a weak heart who, at the initial urging of her mother, elects to undergo a dangerous form of heart surgery to continue performing professionally. For Kieślowski, the physical limitations of Ola's illness catalyze her precarious choices (Stok 1993).

In *Blue*, Kieślowski explores the theme of psychological trauma. Julie, played by actress Juliette Binoche, survives the serious car accident that claims the lives of her husband and daughter. The rest of the film follows Julie as she recuperates from the physical damage of the accident and the tumultuous psychological repercussions of loss. Trauma and memory are powerful and important themes in the film that set the stage for highly stylized visual analogues of Julie's mental state, represented as ellipses and flashes of blue light. After the accident fragments of her husband's last unfinished composition, the *Song for the Unification of Europe*, as well as funereal music haunt Julie during these visually arresting moments.

The themes of physical and psychological illness pervade both *Véronique* and *Blue* and connect to the increased importance of music, the shifting emphasis toward the cinematic representation of female-centered worlds, and to the metaphysical in Kieślowski's later work. Disability thus offers a productive way to examine Kieślowski's reliance on Julie's mental instability as a means of textual disruption in *Blue*. How might the ellipses and Julie's musical authoring during the film's climactic conclusion play into the dialectical tension between powerful female agency and disempowerment? As part of a trifold axis of critical inquiry including women and music, disability is a crucial third perspective in my examination of the extent to which music emerges as a potentially powerful means of representing an alternative female subjectivity in *Blue*.

While recovering from her injuries at a hospital clinic, Julie is depicted sitting in a chair outside recuperating, dozing in the fresh air with her eyes closed and face still visibly bruised from the car accident. A diffuse blue light suddenly fills the screen and is shortly thereafter accompanied by elegiac music (see Figure 4.1)—music first heard at Anna and Patrice's joint funeral—which startles Julie into wakefulness (see Figure 4.2).[4] The camera focuses closely on Julie's face following this episode, when suddenly, an off-screen female voice says hello to her left. The same funereal music is heard, but this time, instead of being accompanied by blue light, the screen that depicts Julie resting in her chair fades to black—the visual marker of the first ellipsis (11:39).[5] Time stands still. When the diegetic world of the film comes back into view, Julie, seated in exactly the same manner, looks over to her left and answers hello in response, as though no time has passed. Then, from a point-of-view shot from behind her left shoulder the audience sees Julie looking at the woman who has just greeted her.

The ellipses are used to signify the temporary cessation of time for Julie. This cinematic effect halts the flow of the story and signals a synchrony between the funereal music and visual absence. Like the radiant blue light that preceded this first ellipsis, it radically interrupts the film's image track

Figure 4.1 Elegiac music from Anna and Patrice's funeral (author's transcription).

Figure 4.2 Blue light fills the screen, and Julie is startled into wakefulness.

and, in this case, dialogue. Ellipses occur three more times over the course of the film, returning as a function and mobilization of traumatic memory and accompanied by the same music (43:13, 1:02:17, 1:14:12). These unsettling moments of textual disruption and excess compete with the ongoing narrative by halting time and self-consciously focusing the attention of the spectator on the funereal music. The ellipses upset the conventionally subservient relationship of music to dialogue and image tracks commonly found in Kieślowski's oeuvre; however, music is allowed to come to the fore precisely because of the absence of image and dialogue.

The audience hears but cannot see. Music becomes the privileged component of memory and acts as a signifier of and vessel through which Julie's memories are mediated cinematically. Kieślowski's camera, which closely observes Julie's face just before and after each ellipsis in conjunction with the haunting musical fragments from the funeral, attempts to represent Julie's interiority—her subjective experience of trauma—visually and musically. Is Julie's mental state beyond the reach of the camera's gaze? Or does Kieślowski purposefully withhold spectators' visual access to Julie's mental images (Wilson 2000), which might more conventionally be represented by flashback imagery of some idyllic, sentimentalized past, or perhaps even horrific memories of the accident?

The powerful presence of music during the ellipses may stem from Julie's desire for her absent family. To draw on psychoanalytic theory, this desire is displaced on to musical fragments heard at their funeral. Julie tries to disassociate herself from her past life, but the emotional pain of the accident returns as music-laden ellipses that leave her psychic defenses disabled. The ellipses burst forth on the surface of *Blue*, signaling a return of repressed memory. These involuntary memories, whether experienced as blackouts—losses of consciousness—or as visually inaccessible mental images, create fissures and gaps on the surface of the film-as-text. The ellipses are not seamlessly embedded into the linearly unfolding narrative and seem to be beyond Julie's psychic control, shocking her into sensation (Wilson 2000, 2003). For Emma Wilson (2000), these moments function as symptoms of post-traumatic stress disorder, and because they refuse "temporal integration," the ellipses threaten to "undo the narrative teleology of the film" (pp. 48, 54). Wilson (2000) argues that Julie's denial of vision, her "loss of mental images," is a lack or absence she must ultimately confront (p. 42). However, it is precisely Julie's dissociation from past trauma that allows Kieślowski to "explore the denial of memory . . . in images and sound" (p. 45).

For Wilson (2000, 54), music, blue light, and fade-outs act as "cinematic analogue[s] for the flashback of psychic trauma" in Kieślowski's endeavor to depict Julie's subjective experiences. The portrayal of Julie's disabling psychological struggle is not pushed to the margins, nor is it suppressed; rather, it is narrativized and becomes one of the central themes of *Blue*. The heroine's mental "deviance" is embraced, not estranged or denied. *Blue*'s ellipses, a destabilizing technique unique within the context of Kieślowski's films, set up new expectations for the interaction of music and image tracks and work to collapse the distinction between spectator and object—Julie—drawing audiences into an intimate relationship with the protagonist's subjectivity, particularly through sound. These destabilizing techniques mark an important step toward creating a powerful and politically useful cinematic representation of mental disability. And in drawing on the kinds of potent representations of disability encouraged and sought by David Mitchell and Sharon Snyder (2000), *Blue* possesses the potential to offer audiences a nuanced glimpse of an alternative way of being.

Unfortunately, the radical potential of the ellipses to reconfigure audience perception is ultimately subsumed within *Blue*'s narrative framework. Though the ellipses continue to act as powerful emotional signifiers three more times over the course the film, once audiences develop an expectation for their reappearance much of the destabilizing potential of Kieślowski's technique loses its power. The ellipses may threaten but ultimately do not "undo the narrative teleology of the film" (Wilson 2000, 54); instead, they serve *Blue's* narrative.

Also, the film's insistent refusal to confront what must not be seen during the ellipses may be read as a form of disavowal (Lawrence 1991, 114).[6] Because audiences are denied spectatorial privilege during the ellipses, one is never quite certain whether (1) Julie confronts images from the past; (2) she is blacking out; or (3) like the audience, Julie is also denied visual representations of her past. Rather than celebrating the ellipses as a truly successful means of depicting an alternative female subjectivity, the ellipses remain shrouded in mystery, and Kieślowski thereby partakes of the "trope of the inexpressible" by leaving scenes of memory purposefully obscure and unarticulated (Rosen 2002, 101).[7] Ultimately, as Wilson (2000, 54) suggested, "[t]hese images, evoking the absence of the past and the disruption of the present, are not fully understood either by the protagonist or, it might be said, by the viewer."

On the one hand, the ineffable ellipses evade reductive categorization and are open to multiple interpretations. When analyzed in the light of disavowal, the ellipses act as a crucial mode of psychological defense for Julie. The fact that the ellipses—as signifiers or symptoms of Julie's trauma—defy explanation also sets them against traditional narratives, described by Mitchell and Snyder (2000, 53) as narratives that seek to "prostheticize" difference or to explain the "deviation's origins" as a necessary precondition for narrative closure.[8] However, Kieślowski's embrace of mystery, avoidance of looking and showing, and lack of explanation are likewise methods that stem from a similar discomfort with difference and ultimately fail to address that which we, as audience members, encounter. The ellipses also parallel performance theorist Barbara Kirshenblatt-Gimblett's (1998, 203, 214, 223) discussion of avant-garde cultural modes of encounter: *Blue's* emphasis on "making audiences experience, rather than interpret, what they see"—an aesthetic that revels in unexplained, "unmediated encounter"—is possibly informed by a European avant-garde sensibility.[9] In this way, mental trauma acts as a "crutch" on which Kieślowski relies, and disability in this context is exploited as a tool of avant-garde cinematic experimentation. Ultimately, like traditional, prostheticizing narratives, Kieślowski depends on Julie's mental instability as a disruptive narrative device (Mitchell and Snyder 2000, 49).

Though the ellipses may not be ultimately successful in cinematically depicting an alternative female subjectivity, Kieślowski clearly attempts to draw audiences into a sympathetic and empathetic relationship with Julie's mental instability through them; during these ellipses the heroine suffers not only from the psychic trauma associated with the loss of Patrice and Anna but also from a significant trauma that stretches back before the accident, involving Julie's inability to negotiate her own identity in relationship to her husband's. Early on just after the first ellipsis, a nosy reporter raises the questionable nature of musical authorship when she asks, "Julie? Is it true you wrote your husband's music?" Julie, upset and insulted, refuses to answer, but the reporter's question effectively implicates her as co-author, if not author, of music attributed posthumously to her husband, raising the issue of problematic authorship. Julie's reaction suggests that we are not only watching a woman going through the stages of grief after being instantly robbed of an identity informed by and molded through marriage and motherhood but that we are also encountering a breakdown of the protagonist's fundamental identity—one specifically connected to musical authorship. Composing is undeniably linked to Julie's psychic subjectivity and is the means by which she begins the work of healing.

Following his employer's death, Olivier—played by Benoît Régent—secretary to Julie's husband Patrice, tries to rouse her from her dissociative state to begin the process of mourning and presumably to rebuild a new life with him, as he has always secretly loved her. Not only does Olivier save a copy of Patrice's version of the *Song*, knowing that Julie has attempted to destroy the physical remnants of her past, but he also publicly announces that he will try to complete the work himself in a calculated effort to draw Julie out of her stupor. In the scene that follows Kieślowski cinematically depicts the creative process of musical composition and collaboration between the two.

Toward the end of the film, Julie visits Olivier in his apartment. As Julie looks over Olivier's *Song* revisions, her index finger touches the score, which is rendered in close detail (see Figure 4.3). Then suddenly the musical score is heard in fully realized orchestral sound, and the audience shares aural access to music that both Julie and Olivier seem to hear—violins and a single melodic piano line playing in unison (1:21:44). Then Olivier introduces a dramatic, percussion-driven section labeled *con tutta force*. A solo trumpet, violins, and a piano play in unison, dominating the upper registers. Heavy brass orchestration supports the unison line, and snare and bass drums provide its rhythmic drive (see Figure 4.4).

Moving away from the score, Kieślowski then presents a wide shot of Julie and Olivier working together. The shot slowly begins to lose focus, becoming so blurry that it obstructs the viewer's visual access to what transpires. Like the ellipses, this scene remains tantalizingly inaccessible to the viewer, and the increasingly diffuse image acts to focus attention on the music and dialogue. However, rather than signaling a moment of disjuncture like the ellipses, this effect creates an atmospheric dream-like quality as Julie begins to shape and edit the music, telling it what to do for her own pleasure. She says, "Lighter, without the percussion," and the music obeys her command, restarting at the *con tutta*

Figure 4.3 Julie's index finger touches the score of Olivier's version of the *Song for the Unification of Europe*.

Figure 4.4 Unison melody from Olivier's *Song* (author's transcription).

force section without the drums. Annette Insdorf (2003) suggests that these musical changes are "based on what is inside the characters' heads. When [Julie] suggests a lighter version . . . that's exactly what we hear. Music, we can say, is in the conditional tense. The: What if? The: Perhaps, if we do it this way, here's how it will sound, as opposed to a definitive version." The music's status with respect to the diegesis in this scene remains unclear. It seems to be diegetic—stemming from the story world depicted onscreen—but is simultaneously positioned as supremely nondiegetic. Whatever its status, as Insdorf suggested, music seems intimately linked to the characters' sonic subjectivities.

As the scene continues, Julie goes on to remove the trumpet as well as the piano, radically transforming the timbre of the music, and she does so utilizing technical musical language derived from classical training. Though Julie seems completely in charge of the alterations, clearly comfortable in her role as editor, the two do share a significant creative decision in scoring

Figure 4.5 Recorder solo from Julie and Olivier's musical collaboration.

for recorder (see Figure 4.5). By the end of this scene, however, gone are any traces of brass, trumpet, piano, or other percussion instruments from Olivier's *Song* revisions, making it increasingly unclear just whose music is being heard at this point.[10] Finally the image clears, and Julie is seen gazing straight ahead, listening to the final cadence of the recorder theme with a hint of a smile on her lips.

As Joseph Kickasola (2004, 278) notes, the visual abstraction of Julie and Olivier's collaborative effort cinematically depicts their "move into the realm of inspiration," and this "abstract loss of focus" can be said to signal a musical realm from which Julie begins her healing process. She no longer suffers from the intrusive ellipses, and by using her access to musical language, collaboratively composing in that language and continuing to work on finishing her own version of the *Song for the Unification of Europe* without Olivier, Julie is able to take part in her own cure. She is able to battle the symptoms of repressed, traumatic memory and to use her compositional ability as a tool with which she can now protect herself from the onslaught of music from the past. Julie's musical skill is complexly involved not only with curing the symptoms of trauma involved with the accident, but also with her negotiation of a specific kind of trauma that perhaps stemmed from her creative relationship with Patrice before the accident. However complex, her cure is implicated in traditional filmic narratives that ultimately contain female subjectivity in film. It is especially implicated in the narrative containment of subjectivities that are marked as somehow deviant or disabled.

Mary Ann Doane's (1987) work on women in classic Hollywood medical melodramas explores themes that resonate with my discussion of female subjectivity and repression. *Blue*'s disruptive ellipses that signal the "return of the repressed" mirror the "[b]reakdowns and instability in the representation of female subjectivity ... which are manifested as symptoms in the body of the [cinematic] text as a whole" (p. 44). Doane's focus on female protagonists who—as Freud would have it—"suffer mainly from reminiscences," illustrates how they must "tell their story," narrate, or be induced to narrate to stabilize a film and effect its narrative resolution (p. 52). Only in this way may a woman take part in her own cure. Through her act of musical authorship in the scene just described, Julie begins the work of healing and taking control of the ellipses, or involuntary reminiscences, through a nonverbal, musical version of the talking cure. The female subjects of the films Doane analyzes reach "self-knowledge" through "talking cures" often catalyzed by male figures such as doctors and analysts (Silverman 1988, 65). Similarly, in *Blue*, Olivier induces Julie to "narrate," or compose, by calculatedly luring her from her life of seclusion and emotional detachment.

Kaja Silverman (1988) argues that talking cure films blur and collapse the distinctions and boundaries between the female cinematic subjects' interiority and exteriority, as well as between their minds and bodies, in a manner related to the characters' hysteria and paranoia. As I argued previously, *Blue* operates in a manner similar to the medical melodramas discussed by both Doane (1987) and Silverman by working to collapse the distinction between spectator and object (Julie) and by drawing audiences into an intimate relationship with the protagonist's out-of-control subjectivity, interiority, and mind via images and sound. Through Kieślowski's representational strategies, audiences are called on to identify both with Julie's point of audition and her point of view during the ellipses and, in this way, to viscerally encounter her mental instability. However, at the same time, *Blue*'s narrative trajectory can be read as a typical normalcy narrative. According to Mitchell and Snyder (2000, 53) normalcy narratives seek to rehabilitate and repair "deviance," or obliterate difference through a cure. It follows that Julie begins to overcome her disabling mental instability and to take part of her own cure through collaboratively composing with Olivier.

Kieślowski's own rather provocative metaphysical philosophy of music's existence and what musical authorship entails also act to complicate the notion that Julie's composing lies solely within the context of female empowerment. For Kieślowski, *Blue* was an opportunity to explore how music can connect people. He believed that it was possible for two people, though separated by space and time, to perform or compose musical notes and fragments in the same order, thereby creating the same music. Rather than a mere coincidence or a matter of plagiarism, music is something essential, profound, and powerful that can connect human beings to one another (Kieślowski 2003).[11] Kieślowski's metaphysical philosophy acts to challenge the idea of a musical work as the sole property of one composer's original composition.

In *Blue*, for example, there are at least three composers of the *Song for the Unification of Europe*: Patrice, Olivier, and Julie. Julie's role as possible composer or editor of her husband's music during his lifetime and after the accident remains unaddressed. Kieślowski points to the purposefully ambiguous manner in which he handles issues of authorship in the film: "For some people Julie is the author of the music we hear. But it's not all that important whether [Julie is] the author or co-author, whether she corrects or creates. Even if she only does do the corrections she's still the author or co-author because what has been corrected is better than it was before" (Stok 1993, 224). Whether Julie and Olivier are merely finishing the "master's" work or if they had been co-collaborators all along during Patrice's lifetime remains one of the film's central enigmas. The fate of this music—whether it is ever publicly performed or if they make admissions about who has composed what—remains an intriguing mystery. Grounded in Kieślowski's metaphysical philosophy of music, the open and ambiguous manner in which *Blue* engages issues of authorship plays with the notion that the *Song* is a fixed musical work with one composer. Kieślowski and Preisner even go so far as to provide both Olivier and Julie's complete versions of the *Song* separately on the film's soundtrack.

One possible way to counteract the fact that Julie overcomes her mental instability through a normalcy narrative is to consider the ways Julie's cure through composing can be read within the context of empowerment. Due to the complex nature of authorship in the film, I do not believe that issues of empowerment can be solved simply by embracing Julie as Author. Instead, I attempt to tease out the complexities of the film to highlight the tension between the ways Julie is disempowered through *Blue*'s narrative drive to cure her "deviance," and the ways she gains power and uses her newfound agency through the film's conventional resolution. Therefore, I turn to a brief discussion of Julie's acts of composition toward the end of the film that highlight the complex ways she accesses power.

Through her musical collaboration with Olivier, Julie is able to step into a position that grants her mastery over sound, and she wields considerable discursive power over what audiences hear. She is no longer haunted by Van den Budenmayer's funereal music and *Song* fragments; rather, she controls music and shapes and edits it—she literally tells it what to do. Julie comes back to herself in the collaborative compositional scene with Olivier, and the music reflects "her"-ness, her voice, her agency—she is the maker of meaning.

Blue's dénouement—she a lengthy montage sequence—uses Julie's version of the *Song* to represent the interconnectedness of the film's major characters. At the end of the sequence, the final shot of the film is of Julie shedding tears for the first time. Over the course of the film, she makes a journey from withdrawal to open emotion through her creative involvement with music. In this sense, *Blue* ends with a personal sense of hopeful, redemptive *liberté* that links the film to the cathartic, bittersweet tears shed by male characters at the ends of *White* and *Red*. Though Julie's newfound agency seems to be at the expense of other possible narrative trajectories that do not cure her mental trauma, *Blue*'s narrative resolution may be read as ultimately empowering for her. At the end of the film, Julie is a female subject who enjoys active agency over music that previously dominated and tormented her, and she can now begin the work of mourning.

By critically examining the intersections of female subjectivity, music, and disability in Kieślowski's *Blue*, I have attempted to explore the complexities of these themes in a way that engages with the dialectical tension between Julie's potential empowerment and disempowerment. How might this trifold axis of inquiry provide insights into other potentially powerful cinematic representations of disability? I would ultimately like to open this study into a wider project that includes Jane Campion's *The Piano* (1993) and Lars von Trier's *Dancer in the Dark* (2000). Ada, the protagonist of *The Piano*, is an elective mute who communicates and expresses her desires through playing her own original compositions at the piano. In *Dancer in the Dark*, a factory worker who is becoming increasingly blind lives out her escapist fantasy life in the extravagant musicals she creates in her mind. Like Julie, these disabled female protagonists' subjectivities are intertwined with musical representation and the creation of distinctive musical worlds.

Notes

1. This shift in Kieślowski's career has been attributed to the dangerous negotiations he had to make while filming "reality" within the Communist system (Insdorf 1999).
2. Similarly, in her exploration of how music comes to bear the burden of utopic pasts in *Strains of Utopia: Gender, Nostalgia, and Hollywood Film Music*, Flinn (1992) emphasized how gendered subjectivity complicates the projection of desire onto lost moments of the past.
3. As well as bearing the "heavy" burden of metaphysical philosophy, Kieślowski and Preisner also enjoyed a playful relationship to music in the films they made together. As an inside joke, Preisner invented a personal alter ego that connects nearly every film he scored for Kieślowski. The "recently discovered" Dutch composer Van den Budenmayer is none other than Preisner himself.
4. This theme is attributed to Van den Budenmayer on *Blue*'s sound track (1993) and is first heard diegetically during Patrice and Anna's funeral, arranged for brass. (Film scholars use the term *diegesis* to refer to the fictional world of a film, so music emanating from a visible source in the film is described as diegetic, whereas music not coming from a readily apparent on-screen source is nondiegetic.) The funereal theme, with lush string orchestration, trumpet and low brass with oboe solos added, is subsequently heard nondiegetically during all four ellipses in a shortened form. All musical transcriptions are by the author with assistance of Daniel Pinkham.
5. All English translations of dialogue and DVD timings are taken from this subtitled version of *Blue: Krzysztof Kieślowski's Three Colors: Blue, White* and *Red*, the exclusive three-disc DVD collection, directed by Kieślowski (Hollywood, CA: Miramax Home Entertainment, 2003).
6. Freud's model of disavowal is gender specific—it focuses exclusively on disavowal as the male subject's "defense against castration anxiety" (Doane 1987, 140). Though important theoretical work by feminist psychoanalytic theorists like Kaja Silverman is predicated on Freud's models to illuminate the psychic differentiation between males and females, it is important to recognize more broadly here that castration, separation, and loss are forms of subject building that are relevant and applicable to both sexes.
7. In his analysis of *The Pawnbroker*, Alan Rosen (2002, 78, 101) examines the cinematic depiction of a Holocaust survivor's traumatic memories in relationship to the "trope of the inexpressible" and also briefly explored Alain Resnais's cinematic "response to trauma" in *Hiroshima, Mon Amour*.
8. In *Narrative Prosthesis: Disability and the Dependencies of Discourse*, Mitchell and Snyder (2000, 49) uses the concept of the prosthetic to illuminate the "discursive dependency" of literary narratives on disability as a narrative device: "Our phrase *narrative prosthesis* is meant to indicate that disability has been used throughout history as a crutch upon which . . . narratives lean for their representational power, disruptive potentiality, and analytical insight." They also used the verb form *to prostheticize* after David Wills (1995) to indicate a narrative's attempt to "resolve or correct ... a deviance marked as improper to a social context" (Mitchell and Snyder 2000, 53).

9. Though the 1990 Los Angeles Festival is Kirshenblatt-Gimblett's (1998) object of critique, the arguments she makes that compellingly link the festival experience with avant-garde modes of cultural encounter resonate with the kinds of experience Kieślowski's film engenders.

10. By "softening" Olivier's aggressive, percussion-driven version of the *Song*, it may be argued that Julie "feminizes" the music. The potential political ramifications of this act, which plays on stereotypes of "feminine" and "masculine"-type musical sounds in Western art music, are unfortunately beyond the scope of this essay.

11. Julie and Olivier even hear a homeless street musician—a recorder player—"coincidentally" performing music reminiscent of the *Song for the Unification of Europe*.

5

Dancing out of the Dark: How Music Refutes Disability Stereotypes in *Dancer in the Dark*

JENNIFER IVERSON

> Deformity of body symbolizes deformity of soul. Physical handicaps
> are made the emblems of evil.
>
> **Paul Longmore, "Screening Stereotypes: Images of Disabled People"**

The history of disabled characters in cinema is hardly a cheerful tale. Disabled characters are usually ostracized as *Others* and are isolated from the rest of society while we watch their impending and unavoidable downfall, if they are given much notice at all. As Longmore (2001, 4) said, Hollywood films play to the able-bodied myth that "disabled people resent the non-disabled and would, if they could, destroy them." The able-bodied characters' repressed lurking fear that they either will become disabled themselves or will be destroyed by the embittered disabled character precludes any unqualified social integration of the character with a disability.[1]

Martin Norden (1994) shows that disabled characters appear in films in a limited number of stereotypes. For example, the *sweet innocent* is an exceedingly demure young female, such as Louise in *Orphans of the Storm* (D. W. Griffith, 1921) and the flower girl in Charlie Chaplin's *City Lights* (1931).[2] The *tragic victim* is a pitiable character disabled due to an accident, war, or fate and suffering due to circumstances beyond his or her control—a famous example is Homer Parrish in *The Best Years of Our Lives* (1946).[3] Norden's stereotypes have a threatening side as well: The *freaks* are portrayed as practically inhuman aberrations of nature—examples are *Hunchback of Notre Dame* (1923) and Tod Browning's *Freaks* (1932); the *obsessive avenger* is the embittered and dangerously vengeful disabled male character—examples include Fritz in *Frankenstein* (1931) and Ygor in *Son of Frankenstein* (1939).[4]

Screening disabled characters according to stereotypes allows the audience to fetishize the disability while, at the same time, the film contains the threat of the disability in a formulaic and predictable narrative. Films typically depict disability as a pathology of individual bodies rather than a construct of social stigma and discrimination. As such, filmic narratives will offer to integrate disabled characters only if they can physically and emotionally come to terms with the disability and can muster up the strength to pass—to accede to the norm of able-bodied society. If the disabled character cannot pass or be miraculously cured, filmic narratives eradicate the character, thus implying that the external disability is a sign of internal deformations and that the character must be removed for the good of the society. In this way, the incurable disabled character is commodified, institutionalized, demonized, ignored, or murdered. In Longmore's (2001, 7) words, "Better dead than disabled."

In its portrayal of a blind immigrant woman, *Dancer in the Dark* (Lars von Trier 2000) conforms to prevailing practice. Selma (Björk), a Czechoslovakian immigrant living in Washington State in 1964, is quickly losing her eyesight due to a genetic disorder. Selma takes extreme measures to save her son, Gene (Vladica Kostic), from succumbing to her genetic blindness. Even after Selma becomes blind, she continues to work at her factory job because she wants to pay for an operation that will save Gene's already poor eyesight. After she breaks a machine at work, Selma's supervisor realizes that she is blind and fires her. Selma returns home that day to discover that her entire savings has been stolen. She knows immediately that Bill (David Morse), both a local police officer and her landlord, has stolen the money to support his wife's lavish spending habits. Selma kills Bill by bashing his safe deposit box over his head, reclaims her money, and prepays for Gene's operation. But she is subsequently arrested, tried, and sentenced to death. Her friends Kathy (Catherine Deneuve) and Jeff (Peter Stormare) try to persuade her to use the money for legal counsel, but Selma refuses all but one attempt to delay her execution and is hanged for Bill's murder.

This narrative puts blindness at the heart of the plot, especially since Selma is the film's protagonist. At first glance, it seems that Selma's disability reflects a predictable narrative formula: Selma dies for the good of society because her blindness—physical but also moral by association—is incurable. Yet there is already more to the story when the soundtrack is considered. The soundtrack, comprising ambient sounds and songs, reflects Selma's extraordinary ability to organize everyday sounds into rhythmic structures. The soundtrack conveys Selma's perspective on the filmic world and simultaneously adds complexity to Selma's character and the narrative. Because the soundtrack relies solely on Selma's perspective, the audience must identify with Selma in a real way. A film that foregrounds the theme of blindness cannot screen an entirely sympathetic visual representation of blindness, as it were, but the soundtrack offers the possibility of creating a sympathetic aural representation of blindness. Invoking the soundtrack, the film not only manages to portray Selma's plight from her perspective but also offers a biting critique of society's marginalization of disabled people.

The film premiered at the 2000 Cannes Film Festival and won many accolades including the Best Actress prize for Björk and the highest prize, the *Palme d'Or*. Björk, better known as an Icelandic pop star, made her debut acting performance in the film. She began her career in the late 1980s with the Icelandic band the Sugarcubes; her solo albums have since branched out to incorporate sophisticated electronic sampling techniques with her songwriting and have garnered a devoted international following (Ross 2004, 50, 53). Most critics agreed that Björk was excellent in the role of Selma, but critical reactions to the film overall were somewhat mixed. Some reviewers had high praise for *Dancer in the Dark*, saying it was a "thrilling, audacious work" (Guthmann 2001) that would "leave your mind and heart reverberating for days" (Covert 2000). Nearly every reviewer reacted passionately to *Dancer's* emotional tableau, but some reviewers believed the film was "crudely manipulative and implausible" (Wolf 2000) and objected to the way it played the audience's emotions off the archetypical fallen woman who dies for her sins and, in so doing, manages to restore her virtue. Stephanie Zacharek (2000) explains:

> A director isn't a misogynist simply because he shows us a suffering woman. But when that suffering becomes the axis of a picture (as in both *Dancer in the Dark* and *Breaking the Waves*), the force that generates all its momentum, with no redemption and no relief in sight, with no point beyond the suffering itself, you have to wonder if he's not just getting his jollies off it.

Zacharek's feminist critique focuses, and rightly so, on Selma's suffering. Blindness, however, is a pressing theme that, perhaps not surprisingly, few critics even mention.

Selma conforms in many ways to Norden's (1994) *sweet innocent* stereotype: She is female, blind, childlike with no sexual desires of her own, and dependent on the charity of men. Selma appears asexual when she repeatedly resists Jeff's romantic advances, and she has a childlike voice and overactive imagination. Furthermore, Selma benefits from Bill's charitable, paternalistic friendship, which surpasses the standard tenant–landlord relationship. Selma is portrayed as many *sweet innocents* are: victims of fate—genetic blindness, in her case.

However, Selma does not remain a harmless *sweet innocent* after she becomes blind; she succumbs to the blindness symbolically understood to possess her spirit. Selma displays her moral blindness when, instead of choosing a legal route to win her money back, she impulsively kills Bill. She resists telling the truth for the rest of the film, in court and even to her best friend, as if she cannot see how it might help. Furthermore, the onset of her blindness is associated with her fantasy daydreams. Beyond Selma's harmless childlike predilections, her willingness to indulge in fantasy daydreams suggests that as Selma loses her sight, she also loses contact with reality. For example, Selma fantasizes that Bill forgives her for the murder, but she refuses to come to terms with her crime in the private or the public sense; the only course of action that her blindness allows her to see is to surrender to the judgment of society. Society, therefore, seems somehow justified in expelling her as a dangerous *Other*. In refusing to fight her execution, Selma seems to have accepted and even to have embraced her downfall as a consequence of her blindness.

Though she never says as much, sticking instead with upbeat "It is not so bad" rhetoric, Selma's acceptance of her fate is revealed through her priorities. Selma named her son Gene, marking him with the disability she has passed on to him. In compensation, Selma invests her entire being in trying to prevent his eventual blindness. She judges her time at the factory, her earnings, and even her success as a mother only according to their effectiveness as tools to prevent Gene's blindness. If she were unsuccessful in preventing the onset of Gene's blindness, she would have nothing to offer Gene and no reason to live; she does not value her blind body or soul and cannot justify allowing her son to suffer the same fate. For that matter, once she succeeds in preventing Gene's blindness she has nothing else to offer him and no reason to live. Either way, her death is preordained on account of the disability.[5] Selma's dedication to preventing Gene's disability reveals the strength and depth of the ableist social myths that treat disabilities as tragedies. Expelling Selma from rational, safe society is justified not only by the plot line, then, but also by her irreversible blindness. The plot thus reflects the sociohistorical formula that the physically disabled and emotionally disfigured must be removed from able-bodied society.

Lurking just below this traditional treatment of disability, however, are undercurrents that cut against the ableist ideology apparent on the surface of the narrative. Zacharek's (2000) statement that there is "no point beyond the suffering itself" is not entirely convincing because *Dancer in the Dark* does not project a seamless diegetic world that would affirm the narrative without question. *Dancer in the Dark* instead projects a diegetic world littered with internal conflicts that invite us to read against the stereotypical portrayal of disability in the plot.[6] Indeed, the soundtrack offers the opportunity to read a sympathetic representation of disability against the ableist ideology of the narrative. In addition, rifts in the narrative open up a space for critical judgment of the narrative's apparent adherence to an ideology that demonizes and expels the incurable disabled character.

Even as it appears to condemn Selma, the film reminds us that she had no reasonable alternative to the course she chose. Could Selma have really gone to the law with the argument that one of the town's police officers—who was her seemingly helpful friend and generous landlord—stole her cash savings? Despite Selma's desire to keep working, what jobs would have been available to her as a blind immigrant woman? The narrative, and indeed the social climate of U.S. capitalistic society, dooms Selma from the start. Individual perseverance and hard work, the core values of the mythical American dream, are revealed here as figures of ableist ideology: Selma cannot remain a contributing member of society once she becomes blind.

In contrast to Selma's weakness and disability, Bill is clearly the signifier of lawfulness, hard work, and patriarchy. He serves as a police officer and as surrogate father to Gene and sometimes Selma; he is a seemingly charitable, generous landlord. Bill, as an able-bodied and hard-working patriarch, embodies values on which his country is based. But despite Bill's powerful able-bodied status, he is morally corrupt. His corruption allows him to be both police officer and thief, both guardian of Selma and the one who exploits her. It would be possible to argue convincingly that Bill should be held personally responsible for Selma's downfall. More importantly, the social power structure of the United States as idealized in Bill must be held responsible for Selma's fate. When Bill turns out to be morally corrupt, the values he is supposed to embody are revealed to be similarly polluted. The film discloses that Selma's downfall is due not to any evil inherent in her disability but rather to a bigoted and unaccommodating social structure.

> The evidence is building of a need for a theory of "difference" whose geometries, paradigms, and logics break out of binaries, dialectics, and nature/culture models of any kind.
>
> **Donna J. Haraway, "'Gender' for a Marxist Dictionary"**

As the film places Selma at the center of the narrative, the soundtrack asks us to identify with her. The aural realm is the space where we fully experience the world from Selma's perspective. Though we cannot see through her eyes, we nevertheless hear through her ears. The soundtrack defines, as it were, how Selma's blindness sounds. Ambient and environmental sounds, which comprise the majority of the sound-effects track, are mixed higher than usual throughout the film, giving the sense that Selma's acute hearing ability functions as a replacement for sight. Acute hearing as compensation for blindness is a stereotypical portrayal of the experience of blindness. However, it is important that the audience is deliberately drawn to Selma's point of view through soundtrack.[7] The soundtrack comments on what the world means to Selma. By hearing the world in the way Selma does, the audience occupies an empathetic position, set to judge the world as Selma does. Through the soundtrack, the audience learns how Selma copes as a blind woman in a society that is unwilling to accommodate her.

The soundtrack is indeed an essential element in sharpening the narrative themes in this or any film, though this soundtrack strays from Hollywood conventions. As Figure 5.1 shows, *Dancer in the Dark* contains few instances of nondiegetic music, or background underscoring, which is usually called on to convey some deeper emotional content than the narrative could otherwise communicate.

Though nondiegetic music typically packs an emotional punch, somewhat paradoxically it has a tendency to escape the viewers' direct consciousness;

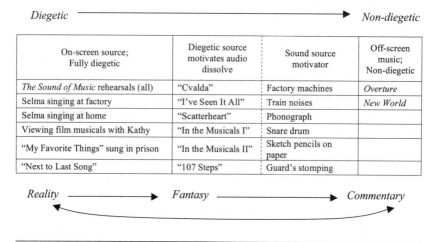

Figure 5.1 Origins of Selma's Songs and Other Music in *Dancer in the Dark*.

it simultaneously exposes deeper levels of meaning in the narrative without exposing itself as a filmic device.[8]

The absence of nondiegetic music in this film leaves many narrative functions to be filled by other devices: Diegetic music—music that is part of the filmic narrative and heard by the characters—along with dialogue and sound effects must articulate a range of emotions in this film. Diegetic music often occupies an obvious place within the narrative; as James Buhler (2001, 41) points out, "There is little need to devise theoretical explanations for the existence of diegetic music: its motivation is patently obvious." Although diegetic music may nuance and develop narrative themes, it does not stand outside the diegetic world offering commentary on the narrative as easily as nondiegetic music does. Hence, the diegetic music, sound effects, and dialogue carry an unusually large responsibility for adding depth to the narrative and articulating emotional states in this film.

As Figure 5.1 shows, the fully diegetic music in the film usually involves Selma singing in amateurish, realistic situations. These instances of diegetic singing function primarily to reinforce Selma's and the film's preoccupation with musicals; Selma sings at rehearsals for *The Sound of Music*, rehearses her songs at home and in the factory, and watches Hollywood film musicals with Kathy. In fact, Selma does not sing diegetically without the context of a musical.

As a genre, the Hollywood film musical depends on a progression from the reality of the narrative into an ideal realm signified by the song and dance digressions (Altman 1987; Feuer 1982). Selma's rehearsals, though preoccupied with musicals, are firmly anchored in the real: They do not involve lush background scoring or any dissolve to idealistic, choreographed dance numbers. Rather, Selma is accompanied by the out-of-tune piano used for the

Sound of Music rehearsals. The out-of tune piano suggests, in some small way, the pathology of the society in which Selma is immersed. In addition, the other *Sound of Music* actors question Selma's ability to play the part of Maria, complaining that her voice sounds funny, that she sings with poor intonation, that she cannot remember the choreography, and that she dances awkwardly. Despite Selma's confidence that musicals offer the perfect escape from reality, the poorly tuned piano, awkward dancing, and frustrated tone of the rehearsals suggest otherwise. The *Sound of Music* rehearsals never promise a smooth, idyllic escape for Selma.

The film moves from a preoccupation with musicals to an imitation of musicals when the audio dissolve is invoked (see the second column of Fig. 5.1). Nearly all of the musical numbers in the film—Selma's whimsical songs—occupy a grey area between diegetic and nondiegetic music. Diegetic noise always motivates the songs, but the audio dissolve that follows quickly takes us to a richly drawn fantasy world. As Altman (1987, 63) explains, this is a common tactic in musicals: "By breaking down the barrier separating the two tracks [diegetic and nondiegetic] the musical blurs the borders between the real and the ideal." Here, the diegetic sound source that motivates the dissolve anchors the ideal realm within the real, but the ideal quickly breaks off from the real to offer the audience a glimpse of Selma's fantasy dream world. In reality, and indeed in diegetic film worlds, sound obeys movement—an action produces a logically-motivated sound. Reversing this cause-and-effect logic lends a sense of enchantment to Selma's ideal fantasy:

> In leaving normal day-to-day causality behind, the music creates a utopian space in which all singers and dancers achieve a unity unimaginable in the now superseded world of temporal, psychological causality. The dominance of sound over image serves to unify groups by synchronizing their movements . . . (ibid., 69).

The logic behind the audio dissolves rests specifically on Selma's ability to hear everyday sounds such as factory machines and trains as musical, rhythmic structures. Significantly, Selma's daydreams, derived from her organized rhythmic structures, do not appear onscreen until the onset of her blindness. The musical numbers pull us away from the starkly rendered reality of the diegetic world and into Selma's fantasy dream world where she is the star of a musical. But the significance of Selma's fantasy dream space does more than merely offer a reprieve from the increasingly depressing narrative; this world of hers relies on her rhythmic hearing and talent for finding audio dissolves. The way Selma creates music from rhythms of the world represents her imagination, her perspective, and her space. Besides being drawn out of Selma's rhythmic hearing, some of the diegetic motivations for audio dissolves in this film also share a thematic logic. The rhythmic motivations for the first three songs involve sounds of technology (see again the second column of

Figure 5.1). The first number, "Cvalda," is motivated by the noise of the factory machines where Selma works; "I've Seen It All" is set on the train tracks that pass Selma's home and work; "Scatterheart" begins with a phonograph needle playing on an empty turntable. These technological sounds are retained as a layer of rhythm throughout the songs, and, as a result, the musical numbers themselves are preoccupied with technology.

Just as social preoccupations with technology belong in the film as part of the historical climate of 1960s America, music preoccupied with technology is also no surprise given Björk's considerable involvement in the soundtrack of the film.[9] Björk, who, in addition to playing Selma wrote the music and collaborated on the lyrics for Selma's songs, is an artist often characterized by her pervasive and deliberate juxtaposition of technology with voice. Electropop samples frequently collide and mingle with her remarkable voice, yet according to most critics, Björk synthesizes these strands of otherwise oppositional material seamlessly. For example, "by combining elements of herself and her Icelandic heritage with the technology of electronic music, Björk has created a unique space that blurs the line between nature/culture, feminine/masculine, body/mind, and self/other. She has, in one sense blurred the dichotomies and developed a new place in popular music" (Marsh and West 2003, 192–3). Grimley (2005, 38) argues that Björk's music likewise does not operate within a system of binary logic in the film: "Furthermore, by breaking down the barriers between sound object and visual image, Björk explores the way in which audiences (as listeners and viewers) construct their own sense of reality."

How has Björk created such an amorphous artistic space, articulated without relying on the binary logic that differentiates self from other? Binary logic relies on intuitive oppositional force to make distinctions between self and other and, as a result of its intuitive resonance, seems inescapable. Applied to Björk's music, binary logic would posit that on some level, Björk's electronica threatens her voice. The unquestionable naturalness and presumed unity of the voice is unbalanced by the artificiality of the intruding technology. Acoustic music also uses machines of course, but acoustic instruments are not fetishized as technological in the same way as electronic instruments. The so-called technology needed to produce the modern piano, for instance, is so outmoded by today's standards that it hardly seems like technology anymore. The time that has passed since the invention of acoustic instruments has naturalized them.

Acoustic music remains a natural extension of the voice in that the human body is needed to produce acoustic sound, whereas this does not hold true for electronic music. The human body is in control of the acoustic dimension, but the electronic dimension threatens to erase the need for human intervention. Haraway (1991a, 152) identifies the increasingly ambiguous relationship between humans and machines as a crucial boundary breakdown: "Late twentieth-century machines have made thoroughly ambiguous the difference between natural and artificial, mind and body, self-developing and externally designed, and many other distinctions that used to apply to organisms and machines. Our machines are disturbingly lively, and we ourselves frighteningly inert." Electronic music reveals our anxiety that the human will be superseded by the robotic, that the natural will be irrevocably fragmented by the artificial.

Disability studies scholars are beginning to analyze a similar binary logic that underlies cultural narratives of the prosthesis (see Crutchfield 2001; Mitchell and Snyder 2000; Wills 1995). The concept of the prosthesis is a useful lens through which we are able to reimagine the familiar cultural narrative of nature and technology just sketched here. According to Mitchell and Snyder (2000, 6), "In a literal sense a prosthesis seeks to accomplish an illusion. A body deemed lacking, unfunctional, or inappropriately functional needs compensation, and prosthesis helps to effect this end." In Björk's music, electronica can be thought of as a prosthesis, a mechanical supplement that draws attention to the lack latent in the natural voice. The electronic appears prosthetic, threatening, less than natural: It is disembodied. Yet more than threatening a hostile takeover of humankind by robots, prosthesis demonstrates that the wellness of the body is always in question. In Björk's music, the electronic prosthesis reminds us that not only is the unity of the voice threatened but also that the natural voice contains a latent insufficiency, even pathology, that must be compensated by electronica. On one hand, Björk's pervasive electronica suggests that the presumed wholeness and wellness of nature has failed—at least failed to satisfy us—yet as listeners and critics, we seem unthreatened by her electronic prosthesis. The question then becomes: Why is Björk's prosthesis not threatening?

If Björk's music succeeds in constructing an alternative space that does not insist that electronica and the prosthetic are locked into binary logic, forever opposed to the unity of the voice, it is because she can demonstrate that the presence of the prosthesis does not necessarily imply the perversion of the natural state. Ross (2004, 54) points out that the track "Modern Things" from Björk's 1995 release *Post* amounts to her thesis on this issue:

> "Machines," she sang over a gently burbling electronic stream, "have always existed, waiting in a mountain for the right moment, listening to the irritating noises of dinosaurs and people dabbling outside . . . It is their turn now." Digital technology, in other words, need not be a sleek, soulless force; it can embrace nature, teem with life.

Ross personifies Björk's electronica, naturalizing it in the process: It can have a soul; it can teem with life. Ross picks up the teleological progression that Björk's lyrics imply, and reads electronica as no less alive than the sounds of humans and animals. Yet it is questionable that naturalizing or personifying the electronica is enough to render the opposition moot.

As some scholars have suggested—and here is the real potential to deepen familiar binary cultural narratives—prosthesis offers an alternative to naturalizing difference. Prosthesis offers the opportunity to remember that the unity of nature is a construction, a farce. As disability studies scholars have pointed out, prostheses are everywhere: "The prostheticized body is the rule, not the exception" (Mitchell and Snyder 2000, 7; see also Davis 1995; Wills 1995). Furthermore, criticism is prosthetic to art but is no less necessary because it does not claim first-order natural status.[10] For Haraway (1991a, 178), "machines can be prosthetic devices, intimate components, friendly selves. We don't need organic holism to give impenetrable wholeness, the total woman and her feminist variants (mutants?)" Embracing the cyborg—part human, part machine—offers great potential in breaking down the presumed unity of nature and the binary opposition between self and other that is always contained therein. Björk's music, then, is cyborg music, and its influence on the character and music of Selma is not without consequence. When Björk's music suggests that the opposition between self (voice) and other (electronica) is a social construction, it is also suggested that the opposition between abled and disabled that is traced throughout this film might be similarly artificial. If we lose the concept of the whole self, the body is not denigrated by disability even if it is marked by prosthesis.

Two instances of nondiegetic music remain to be discussed: As the last column of Figure 5.1 shows, *Overture* and *New World* are the only instances of nondiegetic music; and not coincidentally they are drawn from the same musical material, as is "Next to Last Song." The *Overture* sets a serious tone for the film by calling up associations to sweeping symphonic and operatic overtures.[11] The *Overture* begins with an orchestral trope that signifies an epic quality—rising fourths and fifths played by the horns (see Figure 5.2A).

The melody then moves ahead with more anticipation but returns to the epic horn call motive, which is now played by the strings and reaches higher this time

A)

B)

Figure 5.2 Excerpts from the *Overture*: (A) Ascending horn call; (B) *Overture* melody plus horn call motive.

(see Figure 5.2B). The *Overture* melody is accompanied by a sequence of abstract watercolor images (see Figures 5.3 and 5.4) by Danish artist Per Kirkeby.

The perpetual fading among the superimposed abstract images is meant as an aesthetic imitation of the experience of losing one's sight (Kirkeby 2001).[12] From the *Overture* forward, the film intends to be taken seriously, perhaps even taken as an epic.

New World adds to the music of the *Overture* lyrics sung by Björk and also plays over the end credits. *New World*, when it incorporates the voice, suggests that there was a lack latent in the purely instrumental music of the *Overture*. The *Overture* thus appears to be ancillary to the main structure of the film, its instrumental music abstracted from the human dimension and the songs of the film proper. Yet *New World*, as it is sung over the end credits, reclaims the music of the *Overture* by suggesting that the framing music need not remain abstract and detached but instead can give voice to the issues at stake in the film.

At the emotional climax of the film, Selma sings this same melody *a cappella* in "Next to Last Song" moments before she is hanged. Selma sings alone, fully ostracized by society. She is denied instrumental support, just as she is denied the understanding of a compassionate society. Yet the reuse of the melody makes a tangible connection here between Selma's inner world and the outer world of the *Overture*, suggesting that Selma's story must be

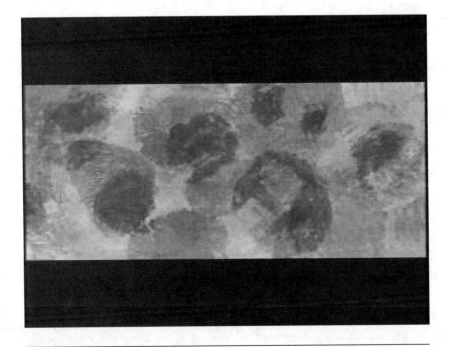

Figure 5.3 One of a sequence of abstract watercolor images used to accompany the *Overture* melody.

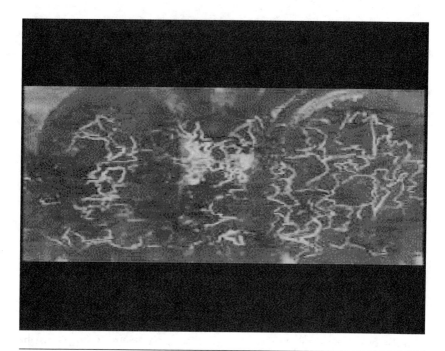

Figure 5.4 Another abstract watercolor image.

pulled from the diegetic world into our consciousness. In some sense, Selma is right when she sings, "This isn't the last song." When *New World* allows voice and instruments to occupy the same space again, it suggests that there is a possibility for reconciliation, if we are willing to create a society that makes distinctions between abled and disabled contingent rather than inherent. As Garland-Thomson (2004, 77) said, we must create a culture that realizes that "disability is a culturally fabricated narrative of the body, similar to what we understand as the fictions of race and gender."

> Dream involves fantasy and imagination, both directly opposed to reality, yet in some vague fashion, we sense that our dreams have the power to render reality more meaningful than it could ever be by itself.
> **Rick Altman, *The American Film Musical***

Any close reading of Selma's songs must acknowledge that the film is absolutely preoccupied with the genre of the musical. Stylized traits from musicals such as ballet and choreographed group dance scenes permeate Selma's fantasy dream world, and the fantasy sequences are visually marked by voluptuous colors not present in the bleak cinematographic palette of the rest of the film.[13] By invoking the fantastic enchantment of the musical, Selma dreams a host of potentially wonderful scenarios to replace her burdensome reality. The fantasy dream sequences grow in the gap, however large or small it may be, between reality and fantasy—a dichotomy that is played out on many levels in musicals—and grounds *Dancer in the Dark* within the musical genre.[14]

Selma's musical fantasy world allows her first and foremost to be an integral part of a community. When she is the star of the musical, she is the leader of her world. Selma yearns to be a part of a community that affirms her ability to lead and to be a star, if only in a musical. Being the star of a musical allows Selma to bring joy and contentment to her friends; Selma relishes the idea that she could give her friends the gifts of music and dance. In "Cvalda," the fantasy sequence in the factory, Selma coaxes the hidden dancer out of her friend Kathy—whom Selma has nicknamed Cvalda—which helps Kathy relax, laugh, and enjoy life. Imagining that she is in a musical allows Selma to believe that she is a vital part of her community of friends and that she has something powerful and beautiful to contribute to their lives.

In a society that disregards the contributions of people with disabilities, communal affirmation would be particularly significant to Selma. Selma's contributions to the community represent the potential for acceptance that she otherwise would not be granted. In another example of paired fantasy musical scenes, Selma asks herself, "Why do I love them [musicals] so much? / What kind of magic is this?" She comes in both scenes to the answer, "There's always someone to catch me . . . when I fall." [15] Selma longs not only to contribute to the community but also to reap the rewards—to know that she can depend on her community.

The emotional tone of Selma's fantasy scenes, however, is not happily idealistic; in fact, it is marked by melancholy, growing sadder through the course of the film. This melancholic character produces an emotional discord within Selma's fantasy world. To say it another way, if Selma can imagine any fantasy world, why does she choose a fantasy tinged with the imminent doom of reality? The lyrics from "I've Seen It All" try to remain upbeat but are trapped within a repetitive tune that cannot escape itself (see Figure 5.5A), just as Selma cannot escape her fate.[16]

The wordless vocalise that follows this melody seems to be an utterance that points to the inability of the lyrics to capture the enormity of blindness. When the repetitive motive finally breaks free of its bounds, it is firmly grounded within a minor key (see Figure 5.5B); hence, Selma's attempt at upbeat acceptance of her fate is tinged with the melancholy of her social exclusion.

Selma's melancholy fantasy sequences contrast sharply with the Hollywood musical Selma idolizes. The performative deflation of Selma's fantasy sequences is a source of considerable critical force, especially in its relationship to Hollywood musicals. As Feuer (1982, 92) explains,

> The Hollywood musical does not dare to take entertainment values out of musical performance . . . to dare not to be entertaining is the ultimate transgression, the ultimate form of reflexivity as critique. For

A)

B)

Figure 5.5 Passages from "I've Seen It All": (A) repetitive melody and lyrics from the verse; (B) melancholy minor melody from the chorus.

to be unentertaining means to think about the base upon which mass entertainment itself is constructed.

Selma's despondent fantasy leaves the audience wondering in what sense, if any, do these fantasy digressions transport Selma away from her dismal reality? It is upsetting to realize that Selma's dreams of social and self-acceptance are as unbelievable as her musical fantasy. Selma's fantasy digressions, the only parts of the film that allow her to reclaim the wholeness of the self, remain trapped within a society that would deny her life; she is denied even a figurative escape from a society that excludes her because of her difference. As the fantasy sequences devolve from melancholic to wretched, *Dancer in the Dark* levels a weighty critique against Hollywood-style entertainment—and by extension American culture.

Dancer in the Dark foregrounds its relationship to Hollywood in many respects; its normally drab color palette and jumpy, out-of-focus cinematography are aesthetically about as far as one can imagine from the seamless, highly polished production values normally associated with Hollywood filmmaking. Lars von Trier sparked controversy in the mid-1990s when he founded the *Dogma 95* movement with a minimalist manifesto stating that cameras must be hand-held, that all filming and sound recording must be done on location, and that adding optical filters, sound effects, or music after filming is strictly prohibited.[17] *Dogma* was intended to force directors to focus on telling a good story and to help them cleanse filmmaking of easy technological solutions and special effects that had served to mask poor storytelling. It was also intended to free filmmakers from the oppressive economic structure of filmmaking, providing them an opportunity to "try it un-plugged" (Stevenson 2002, 104). Von Trier's *Dogma* techniques have the effect of exposing the filmmaking apparatus by making the audience aware of camera movement and ambient sound and by calling attention to the absence of such common filmic devices as nondiegetic music and sound effects. Though *Dancer in the Dark* is not a *Dogma* film, von Trier's aesthetic in the film remains somewhat consistent with the *Dogma* aesthetic.

When *Dancer in the Dark*'s patently despondent fantasy sequences are coupled with von Trier's willingness to expose the cinematic apparatus, the effect pushes beyond mere technical avant-gardism into a critical engagement with the expectations of the musical genre. Von Trier uses the genre of the musical to make contact with sociocultural norms embodied by genre films. Yet as he positions his avant-garde aesthetics against the genre of the musical, von Trier seems ultimately to be embracing the role of cultural critic. According to Altman (1987, 330), "cultural criticism imposes itself on the genre critic, because the very constitution of a genre is in and of itself a cultural activity of multiple ramifications."

The genre at work in this film—the musical—is often described in terms of a dual-focus narrative logic that ultimately concerns itself with the coupling of a man and a woman, who are opposites in many respects. Musicals do not typically follow a single protagonist on a linear trajectory through the plot but instead are concerned entirely with the attainment of social harmony, exemplified through the socially sanctioned coupling of marriage. According to this logic, the dance numbers metaphorically encapsulate sexual fulfillment and the harmonious marriage of the couple (see Altman 1987, 16–58). By invoking the logic of the musical—a myth based on love, courtship, and sex—Selma becomes, at least in fantasy, a whole person again, living within society rather than outside it. Considering that films often represent disabled characters as asexual beings, the love, sex, and marriage symbolized in dance numbers of the musical are signs of what society denies to her.[18]

Dancer in the Dark is not structured as a romance, so the attainment of social harmony through marriage is present only as an absence or an impossibility. Selma is not clearly opposed to a male protagonist, but the role is filled symbolically by Bill as the representative of patriarchal social order in general. Already married, Bill is not an available suitor, again calling attention to the coupling denied to Selma. Yet even as an absent suitor Bill preserves the sociocultural norms that must subsume the challenge of the *Other* for coupling to occur in a musical. Despite the fact that the coupling never happens, the dichotomous relationship between sociocultural norms symbolized in Bill and a challenge to them—disability embodied by Selma—remains the essence of the plot.

The absence of marriage and narrative resolution in a genre film is crucial, according to Schatz (1981, 30): "The most significant feature of any generic narrative may be its resolution—that is, its efforts to solve, even if only temporarily, the conflicts that have disturbed the community welfare." Thus, the absence of marriage and narrative resolution in this film becomes crucial. Where there is no marriage to be had, the opposition between sociocultural norms and disability's challenge to them must remain unreconciled. The plot resolves by expunging the disabled character from society. As Zacharek's (2000) previously mentioned criticism of the film demonstrates, this violent and upsetting resolution draws attention to itself. For Zacharek it is pointless, but (*pace* Zacharek) its pointlessness speaks truth: It does not mask our culture's ableist ideology by claiming that conflicts can be resolved by marriage and true love. When the film strays from the traditional plot resolution of musicals, it unmasks the ideological core of the genre, its spurious image of social harmony. *Dancer in the Dark* refuses to endorse, as a happy, genre-appropriate ending would imply,[19] the idea that maintaining social order is more important than respecting the rights of each member of society.

> *They say it is the last song*
> *They don't know us you see*
> *It is only the last song*
> *If we let it be*

Intertitle after Selma's execution in *Dancer in the Dark*

The film reaches a crisis during Selma's rendition of "My Favorite Things" from her jail cell. While she waits to hear whether her stay of execution has been granted, Selma decides to sing to comfort herself. Selma listens to the ventilation system where she thinks she hears people singing but fails to find any rhythmic motivation for the song; she tries singing, but she cannot stop crying long enough to reach her fantasy world. The rich color tells the audience that this should be fantasy space, but the lack of dissolve shows that Selma's coping mechanism is no longer working. As Selma continues to sing she seems to convince herself a bit more, enough to finish singing the song without crying. Throughout, however, we continue to see Selma in her jail cell; there is no dissolve to Selma dancing on the set of a musical in her mind. Our perspective on the fantasy space has been radically shifted—or rather not shifted—from the confinement of the jail cell. Visually, we remain aligned with the voyeuristic position of the camera, watching Selma perform, barely convincing to her and painful for us. Aurally, instead of a rich, rhythmic sound world we hear Selma struggling to stop crying long enough to sing. Selma's fantasy world is exposed for what it is: a coping mechanism that is, at this point, rendered quite ineffective by oppressive, tragic reality. Indeed, instead of dissolving to her fantasy world, we witness the dissolution of that world.

As Selma's fantasy world dissolves on screen, the audience witnesses the stripping away of entertainment value in a film obsessed with singing, dancing, and Hollywood musicals. It is clear by the end of the film that Selma can no longer find refuge in the glossy Hollywood musicals she so idolizes. *Dancer in the Dark* turns back on its own subject matter, the Hollywood musical, and in so doing suggests that perhaps the audience can no longer find refuge in Hollywood-esque entertainment either. *Dancer in the Dark* is utterly depressing—the film turns on Selma's suffering and ends with Selma's violent, tragic execution. *Dancer in the Dark* implies then that the validity of film lies not in its ability to provide an entertaining escape but rather in its ability to signify within its cultural system and to comment critically on that culture.

At the heart of the film's powerful cultural critique is the binary logic that at once confines Selma to live within an uncompromising ableist society and sanctions her execution for defending herself against that society. It is easy to see Selma as a *tragic victim* of ableist ideology, dying at the hands of a society that has demonized her because of her disability. Yet the film goes further than to ask the audience merely to be sympathetic to the victimization of Selma; it suggests that the *tragic victim* trope must be done away with altogether.

The stereotypical *tragic victim* trope cracks when Selma's death is not celebrated as a social cleansing ritual that restores necessary balance and harmony to the society. There is never the sense that the world is a better, safer place now that Selma has been expunged. More importantly, the film does not allow the audience to leave the theater with the self-assuring thought that Selma did not die in vain. Selma seemingly dies for her son, but that sacrifice never seems necessary. In fact, Selma does die in vain. This film refuses to suggest that there is any point to Selma's suffering—that there is any reason for her death. *Dancer in the Dark* does not soften Selma's death by imbuing it with meaning; rather, the audience is left to grapple with Selma's fate—the consequence of blindness. The suffering of Selma is atrocious, and her death is wholly unnecessary. The pointlessness of Selma's suffering is the point: Within its utter meaninglessness lies the biting sociocultural critique.

The film forces us, as members of a society that victimizes and ostracizes disabled people, to bear the responsibility of her death. The intertitle that follows Selma's execution, cited at the beginning of this section, is a call to action. This song—unsung but seen by the able-bodied audience—asks us to remember that what society would inflict on the disabled, it would also inflict on everyone. Ultimately, we are all part of an unjust culture; if we ignore the social crisis that surrounds disability in this culture, we are all guilty of the injustices that prevail.

Acknowledgments

Thanks go to James Buhler and Jennifer Beavers for their careful readings of earlier drafts of this work as well as their many helpful suggestions.

Notes

1. In his 1919 essay "The Uncanny," Sigmund Freud argued that fear of becoming disabled symbolizes castration anxiety (see Norden 1994, 6).
2. For more on the *sweet innocent,* see Norden (1994, 33–42, 62–5, 131–6).
3. For more on the *tragic victim,* see Norden (1994, 26–8, 75–6, 168–70).
4. For more on the *freak* and *obsessive avenger,* see Norden (1994, 52, 84–105, 112–23, 138–43, 213–21).

5. Thanks go to James Buhler for this insight.
6. *Dancer in the Dark* is part of the avant-garde European art film tradition and as such represents a different set of production values than the highly polished Hollywood style. However, *Dancer in the Dark*'s play against Hollywood's seamless diegetic worlds is an important critical tool at work in the film. For a definition of diegetic and nondiegetic music, see Chapter 4, note 4.
7. For more on the significance of the audio world of this film with regard to recent film theory and criticism, see Grimley (2005, 39).
8. For more on the narrative functions of nondiegetic music, see Gorbman (1987).
9. For more on the historical climate of the 1950s and 1960s with regard to technology and music, see Taylor (2001).
10. The idea that criticism is a type of prosthesis is at the center of the arguments of Wills (1995) and Mitchell and Snyder (2000).
11. Grimley (2005, 40) went further, saying that "the timbral and intervallic characteristics of the brass writing in Björk's 'Overture' inevitably recall the openings of nineteenth-century Romantic works such as Wagner's *Das Rheingold*, gestures conventionally associated with the musical depiction of sunrise, birth, and the natural world."
12. "Audio Commentary by Artist Per Kirkeby," *Dancer in the Dark*, dir. Lars von Trier. New, Line Home Entertainment DVD.
13. This is a common cinematographic technique for visually marking fantasy space; see Feuer (1982, 67).
14. On the dichotomy between reality and fantasy in musicals, see Feuer (1982, 67–85).
15. This refers to Selma's fantasy song, "In the Musicals 1," during her last *Sound of Music* rehearsal before she gets arrested and its complementary scene, "In the Musicals 2," which occurs during her trial when Selma imagines dancing with Aldrich Novie (Joel Grey). The music and lyrics are quite similar in the two scenes, as are Selma's desperate and inescapable circumstances in each instance.
16. For more on the way accompaniments can support, amplify, or even contradict the meaning of the lyrics in pop music, see Moore (2005).
17. The ten-point manifesto can be found in its entirety in Stevenson (2002, 196, note 4).
18. For more on the way films portray the sexuality of disabled characters, see Norden (1994).
19. As Schatz (1981, 31) notes about genre films in general, "In their formulaic narrative process, genre films celebrate the most fundamental ideological precepts—they examine and affirm 'Americanism' with all its rampant conflicts, contradictions, and ambiguities . . . As social ritual, genre films function to stop time, to portray our culture in a stable and invariable ideological position."

6

The Horrors of One-Handed Pianism: Music and Disability in *The Beast with Five Fingers*

NEIL LERNER

Pianists must have two hands.

Does the severity of that claim unsettle or comfort us? The constructed normalcy, to borrow Lennard Davis's (1995) phrase, of the performing pianist within the European cultivated tradition expects two-handedness of keyboard performers.[1] To claim the title *pianist,* one must have two functioning hands. With only one functioning hand, someone who wishes to play the piano becomes not a pianist but a one-handed pianist. The default language for piano music assumes two hands; Maurice Ravel wrote a *Concerto pour piano en sol majeur* for both a left hand and a right hand, whereas the *Concerto pour la main gauche* marks itself as different in its declaration of single-handedness. Yet as Michael Davidson (2005, 616) notes, "most pianists at some point in their career temporarily lose the functioning of one or another hand."

As proof of the anxiety-provoking connotations attached to one-handed pianism, consider the horror film *The Beast with Five Fingers* (directed by Robert Florey, 1946), whose title draws attention to the constructed monstrosity of the solitary hand. The beastly hand in question belonged to a concert pianist whose right side was paralyzed because of a stroke, and the film presents scenes of left-handed pianism with the hand as attached to the pianist, as well as by itself, after the pianist's death. Following then with the cinematic tropes of the impaired body as freakish or monstrous, *The Beast with Five Fingers* explores the possibilities for one-handed pianists within the European cultivated tradition.

In *Piano Music for One Hand,* Theodore Edel (1994, 3–11) suggests four motivations for writing one-handed piano pieces: (1) technical development, with the goal being to improve the left hand to make for better two-handed playing; (2) injury of one hand; (3) compositional challenge; and (4) as a display of virtuosity. Edel notes that the vast majority of one-handed pieces are usually for the left hand, speculating that the larger cultural insistence of right-handedness through the nineteenth century caused most left hands to be weaker and therefore more in need of extra pedagogic attention. It may be significant to recall that through the nineteenth century in general, left-handedness was heavily discouraged; many examples throughout Western—and some non-Western—culture can be found where the left hand, the *manus sinistra,* symbolizes evil compared with the dexterity of the right hand.[2]

One-handed keyboard performances became increasingly popular through the nineteenth century—Edel (1994) discusses pianists Geza Zichy, Alexander Dreyschock, Adolfo Fumagalli, and twentieth-century pianist Paul Wittgenstein—and demand for one-handed piano music flourished, not by coincidence, after periods of war.[3] For instance, the number of one-handed piano works published in the United States rose in the 1870s and 1880s, just after so many Civil War soldiers left limbs on the battlefield or in the surgical theater.[4] And during the early 1940s, when production began at Warner Brothers on a horror film version of William Fryer Harvey's 1919 short story, "The Beast with Five Fingers," it did not require the gift of prophecy to foresee yet another wave of amputees. Indeed, Hollywood responded with both non-war-related maimings, as with Ronald Reagan's character in *Kings Row* (directed by Sam Wood, 1942), as well as soldiers who lost limbs in the war, as with the character of Homer in *The Best Years of Our Lives* (directed by William Wyler, 1946). *The Beast with Five Fingers,* which tells the story of a disembodied hand that seems to strangle people as well as to play Johannes Brahms' one-handed arrangement of J. S. Bach's Chaconne in D minor for solo violin, BWV 1004, contains characters with physical and mental impairments, although it treats these impairments with the familiar strategies of stigma, overcoming, and repression. In particular, Max Steiner's melodramatic score contributes a musical depiction of the social undesirability of the one-handed pianist by functioning as a kind of musical prosthesis, audibly providing much more sound than one hand alone could produce.

From Short Story to Hollywood Feature

Harvey's (1919) short story does feature an evil disembodied hand, but it was a *manus dextera,* not a left hand. Furthermore, Harvey's short story includes nothing about a stroke-paralyzed pianist, as the film version does. The short story opens with a narrator reflecting on his first meeting with a character named Adrian Borlsover; in both the literary and the cinematic versions, the perspective of who is telling the story contains significance. The audience discovers that Adrian was an eccentric naturalist, an expert on the fertilization of orchids—this detail, especially its relation to procreation, is important—and at the age of fifty Adrian suddenly went blind. A bachelor, his only relative was a nephew, Eustace. Eustace discovers something about his uncle Adrian: Adrian's right hand is capable of automatic writing. When Adrian sleeps, his right hand scribbles out long lines of seemingly nonsense prose, although it begins to write threatening messages to Eustace. Eustace is, like his uncle, a bachelor, and early on it is revealed that he "lived alone . . . with Saunders, his secretary, a man who bore a somewhat dubious reputation in the district" (p. 20).

Within the confines of early twentieth-century British culture, both Adrian and Eustace appear to be coded as homosexual, and one reading of the short story might be to see it as a reactionary, homophobic vengeance tale where the homosexuals are haunted by supernatural forces for their implied nonheterosexual behavior. After Adrian's death, Eustace and Saunders find themselves tormented by a disembodied right hand. The two men leave the hand-infested mansion but return as the servants begin to quit, complaining about odd occurrences. They flee to another town, but the hand follows them, stowing away in Eustace's gloves. They barricade themselves in a room but then realize the hand could sneak in through the chimney. They light a fire to destroy the hand, but in the process they accidentally set the room ablaze. Saunders escapes, and as he considers going back to save Eustace, he sees a black and charred thing crawling out of the flames. Eustace dies in the flames, and the story ends with the unidentified narrator explaining that he knew Saunders as his math teacher at his "second-rate suburban school" (p. 46).

In 1942, executives from Warner Brothers began exploring the possibility of making a film version of Harvey's (1919) short story, and after acquiring the literary rights from his wife for £200, a series of screenwriters were brought in to begin the process of adapting the story to the big screen, although only one writer—Curt Siodmak—ultimately received a screen credit.[5] When working on screenplays, Warner Brothers' writers could send questions about historical details to the studio's research department. Studio records document who asked questions as well as the question itself, the date it was asked, and when it was answered. In the case of *The Beast with Five Fingers*, the research record provides clues as to when, how, and even who was behind the story's change in the character of Adrian Borlsover, the blind naturalist, to Francis Ingram, a half-paralyzed concert pianist. Curt Siodmak's first question in the research log was for the "name of piece of music written for the left hand by M. Ravel. When written and performed?" (*Beast with Five Fingers* papers, 31 May 1945) to which he got the response, "For the Left Hand, Concerto for Piano, completed in 1931, first performed in Vienna, Nov. 27, 31, by Wittgenstein and conducted by Ravel. Info: LAPL [Los Angeles Public Library]." On August 14, 1945, Siodmak returned with another question, this time a request for an Italian translation of "Concerto for the Left Hand." Finally, on September 7, 1945, Siodmak sent a memo to producer William Jacobs suggesting "Concerto for the Left Hand" as an alternative title for the film. All of this archival evidence points to Siodmak as the likely culprit responsible for injecting not just music but specifically music for a one-handed pianist into the film version.[6] There were no copies of contracts with the composer, Max Steiner, and presumably he did not become involved with the film until relatively late in the process, as was typical with Hollywood films both then and now.

Other materials in the Warner Brothers archive also explain the shift from the Ravel concerto to the Bach–Brahms Chaconne. Executives from the music legal division of Warner Brothers exchanged urgent memos on November 2, 1945, seeking permission to clear the Ravel concerto for use in the film. A memo to Leo Forbstein, musical director of the film, responded that the concerto would have to be used in its entirety and thus was impractical. Forbstein responded three days later, on November 5, saying they should "forget about 'Concerto for Left Hand.' Will try and replace it with something else." (*Beast with Five Fingers* papers, 5 November 1945) None of the other records indicated who suggested the Bach Chaconne, but press releases for the film did contain a curious tidbit related to the Chaconne's appearance.

> Victor Aller, member of the Warners' music department, composed a Bach Choconne [sic] for [performance by] Victor Francen; this is a piece written for the left hand. Francen practised [sic] for some 200 hours in order to acquire the proper technique (*Beast with Five Fingers* papers, n.d.).

Victor Aller was related to Eleanor Aller, a cellist who recorded with the Hollywood studios and who, with her husband, Felix Slatkin, and Paul Shure and Paul Robyn, formed the Hollywood String Quartet. Aller was employed by Warner Brothers in the 1940s as the orchestra manager. He also gave piano lessons in Hollywood, sometimes to actors who needed to play piano onscreen, as in the case of Dirk Bogarde in the 1960 Liszt biopic *Song without End*. No documents surfaced clarifying who may have recorded the one-handed Bach performance captured on the *Beast* soundtrack, but Victor Aller seems at least as likely a performer as Victor Francen, despite his two hundred hours of practicing.

Among the musical parts preserved from the recording session is a three-page solo piano part titled "Chaconne (Study No. 5)," the subtitle making obvious the reliance on Johannes Brahms' "Studien für Klavier Nr. 5."[7] The unnamed reporter who attributed the arrangement of the Bach Chaconne to Victor Aller was probably mistaken, perhaps because he or she was told something about Aller and that piece—maybe that Aller performed it or that he was Francen's teacher for it?—but apart from a few minor differences, such as slight changes in slurring, Brahms' and Hollywood's arrangements are identical, perhaps most tellingly in their dynamic markings. As Brahms wrote to Clara Schumann in 1877, he wanted to have something of the experience of the violinist in playing the Chaconne and so arranged the piece for the pianist's left hand alone.[8] The decision to use the Brahms–Bach Chaconne instead of the Ravel concerto, though likely motivated first of all by financial considerations, still brought to the film a pianistic work already associated with questions of normative and adaptive keyboard writing.

The film version of *The Beast with Five Fingers* was an important project for Warner Brothers, commanding the healthy budget of $724,000—the total from the 6 November 1945 budget. It was directed by Robert Florey, a French emigré who had been involved with Grand Guignol plays as a teenager and who wrote the original script for Universal's film version of *Frankenstein*.[9] Strongly influenced by German Expressionist cinema like Robert Wiene's *Das Kabinett des Doktor Caligari* (1920) or Friedrich Murnau's *Nosferatu* (1922), Florey specialized in horror films, and his output included *Murders in the Rue Morgue* (1932), *The Florentine Dagger* (1935), and *The Face Behind the Mask* (1941). Peter Lorre was not the executives' first choice to play the role of Hilary Cummins, the odd secretary to pianist Ingram; producer William Jacobs had Sydney Greenstreet and Claude Rains higher on his list of casting possibilities dated September 11, 1945. Lorre's history with similar roles—including the psychotic child murderer in *M* (directed by Fritz Lang, 1931) as well as in his first Hollywood film, *Mad Love* (directed by Karl Freund, 1935), where Lorre played a doctor who replaces the damaged hands of a famous concert pianist with those of a criminal, leading to mayhem—made Lorre an inspired choice, even though some reviews criticized him for overacting in the role of Hilary.

Siodmak's script converted Adrian Borslover into a rich and eccentric concert pianist, Francis Ingram, who has suffered a stroke that paralyzed the right side of his body. Dependent on a nurse, Julie, and a wheelchair, Ingram continues concertizing because of an arrangement of the Bach Chaconne prepared for him by the composer and con man, Bruce Conrad, played by Robert Alda.[10] A frustrated composer, Bruce complains at one point in the film that he has been able to do nothing creatively since arranging the Bach Chaconne for Ingram, declaring that he has become "court jester to a cripple, dependent upon his charity, a dealer in modern antiques." When the audience first meets Bruce in the film, he is scamming U.S. tourists by selling them relatively worthless European cameos for inflated prices. Siodmak includes a subtle yet pointed criticism of one-handed pianism and performances by people with disabilities by linking Bruce's (or Victor Aller's or Steiner's or Brahms') arrangement of Bach, which allowed Ingram to continue performing, to the profitable sale of forgeries: Both are to be understood as fraudulent.

Yet even stranger characters inhabit Ingram's villa. Ingram's secretary, Hilary (Peter Lorre), appears to have little to do with his employer, insisting instead on spending his time with the massive library of ancient books housed at the villa. Ingram mysteriously dies, falling down the stairs during a stormy night, and his will leaves everything to Julie instead of to Hilary or to his relatives, including his nephew, Donald. Faced with the possibility of leaving his beloved books, Hilary begins to act oddly. Not long after Ingram's funeral, the local police *commissario* is shocked to find that Ingram's left hand is no longer attached to the rest of his corpse. Soon a number of stranglings plague the villa, and Hilary claims to see Ingram's disembodied hand crawling about and to see and hear the hand playing the Bach Chaconne at the piano. In one scene, Hilary confronts the hand at Ingram's desk, the hand waving around its middle finger in search of Ingram's ring, which Hilary lovingly slides onto the finger before shoving the hand into a drawer. Eventually the hand strangles Hilary to death, or so it seems—apparently Hilary has a heart attack from the fear of being attacked by this hallucination.

At times the tone of the film takes on a comic flavor, sometimes intentionally though sometimes perhaps not by design, as Lorre's exaggerated acting shifts the film toward a camp aesthetic.[11] When the stranglings begin to occur, Siodmak employs conventions of a mystery film, with each of the characters having motives and alibis. When the true murderer, Hilary, is revealed at the end—and the revelation gets overplayed to ridiculous proportions—the film lapses into sheer bathos as the *commissario* terrifies himself with his own hand, which threatens to strangle him. Siodmak did not approve of the comic relief, although his complaints to the producer failed to persuade him to make any changes.[12]

Audiences responded to the film with laughter, as several contemporary reviews in the studio's clippings file make clear. A February 6, 1947, review in the *Cleveland Plain Dealer* said that "the opening audience yesterday quite literally hooted it down," whereas the February 13 *Chicago Sun* reviewer, Henry T. Murdock, wrote that "as it progresses and Peter Lorre begins to chew big hunks out of the scenery the audience laughs instead of shivers." And Mae Tinée was repulsed that audiences would laugh at the supposedly gruesome scenes, as she wrote in the February 15 *Chicago Tribune*: "For some reason the audience at the Rialto found such scenes as that in which [Hilary] hammers the hand down with a nail and tosses it into a fire, only to have it crawl out, vastly amusing—a sentiment I could not share."[13]

The mobile disembodied hand has been a recurring motif within horror films, so much so that it has become a stock convention of the genre. Onscreen appearances of disembodied hands that do not move on their own go back further, including the presence of one in *Un Chien Andalou* (1928), by surrealist filmmakers Salvador Dali and Luis Buñuel. Buñuel returned to the image of the disembodied hand in *El Ángel Exterminador* (1962), and he is sometimes, probably incorrectly, attributed with having been involved with the production of *The Beast with Five Fingers*, perhaps because according to Taves, Buñuel claims in his autobiography to have written some of the scenes.[14] Skal (2001, 128) links the "bodiless pair of hands, clinging to a barbed-wire fence" in *All Quiet on the Western Front* to the hands of the creature in *Frankenstein* as he draws parallels between the bodily maimings of World War I and the Universal horror films of the 1930s. Other films involving disembodied hands include *The Crawling Hand* (Herbert L. Strock, 1963), *Dr. Terror's House of Horrors* (Freddie Francis, 1965), *And Now the Screaming Starts* (Roy Ward Baker, 1973), and *The Hand* (Oliver Stone, 1981). The trope of the disembodied hand was familiar enough for it to be parodied in the 1964 television series

The Addams Family, where the hand named "Thing" joins other stock horror characters like a Frankenstein monster and a vampire. Even an episode of *Buffy the Vampire Slayer* ("Life Serial," episode 0605 from season six) features an independently mobile disembodied hand, a mummy's hand roaming in the Magic Shop.

The Beast with Five Fingers builds up tension for the disembodied hand, which the audience does not see until relatively late into the picture. Although all of the circumstantial evidence causes it to appear that a bodiless hand has been crawling around and strangling people in the Ingram villa, Hilary is the only character who ends up seeing the hand. In one of the most radical departures from the short story, the film reveals its tricks and illusions by driving home, in a rather overblown manner, the information that Hilary, and no other character, sees the disembodied hand. After an increase in the level of the sound effects—the score calls for a wind machine here, but it sounds as though it may have been altered in some way—the solo piano version of the Chaconne returns with some impressive special effects photography showing the hand at the keyboard (see Figure 6.1).

As the camera pans between Hilary and Julie, both of them looking down at the piano, the level of the music rises and falls so that as viewers see Hilary,

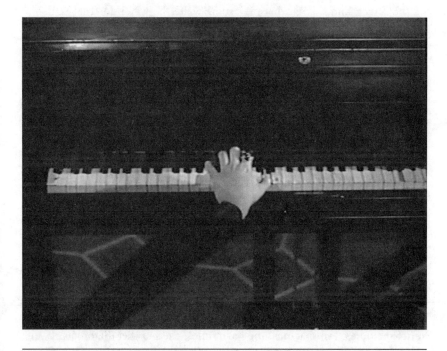

Figure 6.1 Ingram's disembodied left hand performs the Brahms-Bach Chaconne.

they hear the Chaconne; then with a pan to Julie, the music disappears.[15] This back and forth panning occurs three times; the overrepetition creates a comic effect and perhaps is some of the cause for the laughter reported by the reviewers, although normate anxieties over cinematic representations of disability might also have prompted some nervous snickers.

Max Steiner's Contributions

Most famous as a composer of epic, melodramatic film scores that employed the vocabulary of European post-romanticism, such as those for *Gone with the Wind* (Victor Fleming, 1939) or *Casablanca* (Michael Curtiz, 1942), Max Steiner rarely wrote for horror films, although his score for *King Kong* (Cooper & Schoedsack, 1933) revealed a penchant for dissonance in the service of images of fantasy.[16] Steiner prided himself on his ability to react musically to what he saw on screen:

> The way I approached writing music for films was to fit the music to what I thought the dramatic story should be and score according to the way a character impressed me, whoever he might be. He may be a bastard, she may be a wonderful woman, he may be a child. I write what I see. This is very difficult for anybody to understand. Especially for anybody with such bad eyesight as I have. But I see a character on the screen and that is what makes me write the way I do. That is also the reason that people enjoy what they hear because it happens to fit (Steiner 1970, 392).

Steiner's greatest gift as a musical dramatist was his skill at using music to encode an inner psychology for the characters on screen, using a musical language that was quickly recognizable to a film's mass audience. He had some experience representing bodies with disabilities: In the scores for *Of Human Bondage* (John Cromwell, 1934) and *The Informer* (John Ford, 1935), Steiner wrote rhythmically uneven melodies for characters whose leg impairments caused them to limp.[17] In *The Beast with Five Fingers*, Steiner's music gives us important information about the characters, some of whose impairments are more obvious at first than others.[18] In fact, Steiner's music says more about Hilary and his mental condition than it does about the more obviously impaired Ingram, whose one-handedness we learn visually.

In the scene first introducing Hilary, the secretary obsessed with Ingram's books (approximately ten minutes and thirty seconds into the film), Steiner presents a typically rich and informative underscore. The cue opens with shots of Hilary reading, as Steiner reacts with a Coplandesque style: The disjunct melodies, the spacings, the harmonies, the parallel diatonicisms, and the wind-dominated timbral palette all reflect the pastoralisms introduced into Hollywood scoring—at least partly—by Aaron Copland only a few years earlier in film scores like *Our Town* (1940) and in ballet scores like *Appalachian Spring* (1944) (see Figure 6.2).[19]

Figure 6.2 Steiner's musical evocation of Hilary's mental condition.

This music becomes a theme for Hilary that Steiner develops throughout the rest of the score, and as the audience first sees Hilary, the music suggests that he exists in a tranquil, pastoral space when left alone with his books. The drooping fourths, played first in the bassoon and then joined by the flute, suggest a certain obsessiveness through their repetitions and also through the triadic response in the lower strings. While the first four bars cadence on a D-flat major chord, the second four bars cadence on the much richer E-flat thirteenth harmony. After that point, the upper melody takes on a sighing, *Seufzen*-like character, against increasingly dissonant harmonies in the lower parts. As Julie tells Hilary that "what I need is a complete change" and as Hilary begins to realize his status at the Ingram villa may be in jeopardy, Steiner brings about a complete change stylistically, moving to much lusher harmonies and a more stable homophonic texture. Hilary becomes more agitated, saying "he's [Ingram] forgotten about me" and worrying about what will happen to his work.

From watching only the image without the sound, the audience would not get as direct an idea about Hilary's potential mental instability as they do when hearing the increasingly chromatic and dissonant underscoring. Diatonic clarity returns only when Hilary starts discussing his work on astrology, although the root position diatonic chords do not follow traditional voice-leading rules. As Hilary's explanation of his astrological work hits a climax (m.27), Steiner responds with a massive Straussian chord that spans from low octave B's to high octave F-sharps, including in the middle an F major seventh chord and a C-sharp major chord. As the scene quickly draws to a close and as Julie invites Hilary to dinner, the original Hilary theme returns, giving the cue an overall ternary form of ABA', as the descending perfect fourth melodies originally presented six times are now altered in the final measures of the cue to, first, a descending perfect fifth, then to a descending augmented fifth, and then to a descending fifth. The original stability of the descending fourth is replaced with a descending fifth that alternates with an augmented fifth. Together with Lorre's acting and Siodmak's dialogue, Steiner's music reveals Hilary's perceptual variability, giving the audience an early clue that Hilary's mood and mental state vacillate quickly and wildly.

It has become something of a commonplace in music history to note that characteristics of musical aesthetic modernism have been absorbed within Hollywood film music, but rarely are such assertions followed with specific examples. Genre plays an important role in determining what kinds of musical languages Hollywood adopts, and the genres of the horror film and science fiction—two genres that are sometimes overlapping and indistinguishable—have been particularly fruitful places for Hollywood composers to incorporate more avant-garde compositional techniques such as extended dissonances, atonality, aleatoricism, and timbral experimentation.

Steiner's score for *King Kong* remains an exemplary early example of a Hollywood score that employs extended dissonances, but in general Steiner is regarded as representing a more reactionary musical language.[20] Together with Alfred Newman, Erich Korngold, and Franz Waxman, Steiner was responsible for championing a musical vocabulary in Hollywood that relied heavily on the gestures of European post-romanticism, continuing the language of Richard Wagner and Richard Strauss. The most dissonant and nontraditional musical moments of *The Beast with Five Fingers* occur during the cue called "The Storm," which underscores the scenes of Ingram's death as he falls down a flight of stairs. The presence of dissonance here is not surprising, as these dissonant, unstable sounds present a direct analogue with the expressionist cinematic techniques. The nonlevel camera angles, the deep shadows, the unsettled camera movement, and the wavy shots of the double-exposed piano work together with the music to create an effect of confusion, fear, and suffering (See Figure 6.3).

As Ingram tries to focus on the piano, Steiner returns to the Chaconne theme introduced in the Main Title, played by both piano parts—only he writes them in close but different keys (E minor, F minor), creating a moment of bitonality that runs parallel to the double-exposure photography.[21] Here techniques of aesthetic modernism are put to the service of amplifying the horrific, the terrible—and in connection with the piano, the body with disability, for the piano serves metonymically as a reminder of Ingram's nonnormative body. Bitonality here serves as a reminder of Ingram's bifurcated body, split into active and passive sides by a stroke. One would not need two pianos, however, to create bitonality at the keyboard, and Steiner's—or Friedhofer's or Cutter's—decision to accompany Ingram's death with not one, not two, but four hands playing piano presents a moment of musical prosthesis, whereby the melodramatic underscore, the rich sound valued for the plentitude it brings to the image, substitutes a greater pianistic sound than the pianist pictured on the screen could have actually produced by himself. Just as Ravel constructed his piano concerto for Wittgenstein so that it would prosthetically create

Figure 6.3 Bitonal statement of Chaconne theme during Ingram's death (pianos 1 and 2 only from the full score).

the illusion of having been performed by a pianist with two hands, Steiner similarly generates a musical illusion of multihandedness, relying on the four invisible hands of the studio performers.[22]

Disability and Horror, Disability and Music

The Hollywood horror film provides an important site for investigating broader cultural anxieties about disability, and in specialized cases like *The Beast with Five Fingers* the focus narrows to music and musicians. Robin Wood's (1979, 14) formulation of the horror film—"normality is threatened by the Monster or the Monstrous"—raises the issue of normalcy, a concept of keen interest within disability studies. What is monstrous, and what is normal, after all?[23] As Wood points out, his formula causes potential overlap with other genres: Replace *monster* with *Indian* and suddenly it's a Western. Hollywood monsters during the period of the 1930s and 1940s were usually fairly well demarcated through acting, makeup, costume, lighting, and of course music. Monsters look different and threatening, and what they seem most to threaten is normality itself.

The entire horror genre repeats narrative patterns that see the continued repression and oppression of anything defined as nonnormative. Wood (1979) observes that sexuality often powers the monstrous element in these films—that libido threatens the bourgeois patriarchal system. From this Marxist and Freudian positioning, he reads films with a sharp eye toward the role of sexuality, particularly how sexuality gets repressed within the narrative structures of these films. Although the *Monster*, or *Monstrosity*, may have a sexual component to it, it may also be tied up with representations of bodies with impairments, or fragmented bodies, and it is at this juncture—the juncture between monstrosity and the nonnormative body—where disability studies has theories that can inform the readings of film and music.[24]

The Beast with Five Fingers uses conventions of the horror film to reinscribe the social undesirability of the one-handed pianist. Davis (1995) drew particular attention to a pervasive need within Western culture to hide the mutilated or fragmented body, an impulse articulated as *social erasure* by Mitchell and Snyder (2000). *The Beast with Five Fingers* provides multiple examples of these repressions and erasures. The film shows first a one-handed pianist playing Brahms' left-handed arrangement of Bach's Chaconne in D minor. Then, after the pianist's death, the disembodied left hand continues to play the same piece. Finally, the film reveals that the presumed monstrosity of the disembodied hand was nothing more than a hallucination, removing even the possibility of the one-handed pianist and his ostensibly horrific threat to the normal body, as well as the presumably horrific threat to the symbolic body of classical music and its implicit messages of perfect form and perfect execution. Hollywood did not simply make up this erasure of the one-handed pianist for a 1946 genre film; instead, Hollywood could turn to larger cultural institutions, including the traditions of European and U.S. music-making and musicology, for centuries of the invisible, yet performing, disabled body.

Acknowledgments

This chapter benefited from the advice and assistance of Ann Fox, Penka Kouneva, and Alice and Gertrude Lerner. I am also grateful to Jill Williams, for her patience during rehab, and Michael Lerner, for many lessons, including some about spinal cord injuries.

Notes

1. Davis (1995) devoted a chapter of *Enforcing Normalcy: Disability, Deafness, and the Body* to the topic of constructing normalcy.
2. Lubet (2004, 136) discussed left-handedness as both an impairment and a disability, observing that for orchestral string players, who must bow with their right hand and tune with their left hand, "WCM [Western classical music] may be unsurpassed in creating a major impairment from a common human variation that presents few if any limitations elsewhere: left-handedness." Lubet noted that "while adaptive options for lefties exist, some players like [Jimi] Hendrix simply invert right-handed instruments" (ibid.). No such options exist for string players in an orchestra.
3. Perhaps the most famous one-armed pianist of the twentieth century, Paul Wittgenstein (brother of Ludwig) commissioned works for the left hand from several famous composers, including Benjamin Britten, Erich Korngold, Sergei Prokofiev, Ravel, and Richard Strauss. Flindell (1971, 112) reported that one of Wittgenstein's teachers, Austrian composer Josef Labor, was blind, although he does not link that to Wittgenstein's later path; he does however resort to the familiar overcoming narrative when describing Wittgenstein's resolve after losing his arm, writing of his "heroic response to his personal catastrophe." Similarly, Arell (1950) compiled a set of musical overcoming narratives in "Defects into Dividends."
4. Several composers, including Arthur Foote (1853–1937), produced works for one hand. One popular compositional idiom at that time was the transcription of folk melodies; thus, many of the single-handed pieces were arrangements of such familiar tunes as "Home, Sweet Home." For example, see James M. Welhi's arrangement of "Home, Sweet Home" for the left hand, available electronically at the Library of Congress's *American Memory* website: http://hdl.loc.gov/loc.music/sm1870.03144.
5. This information, as well as the other production details noted in the following, comes from a study of the materials for *The Beast with Five Fingers* that I conducted in October 2003 at the Warner Brothers archive at the University of Southern California, Los Angeles. Siodmak worked the longest on the screenplay, and studio records reveal that some of the most interesting adaptations from short story to screenplay originated with him. Siodmak specialized in horror films, writing numerous scripts including *The Wolf Man* (1941) and *I Walked with a Zombie* (1943); his novel, *Donovan's Brain* (A. Knopf, 1943), another story about the fragmentation of the human body, has been made into several films.
6. In his liner notes for the Marco Polo CD of this score, Thomas (1996) wrote that Siodmak "suggested to Steiner that he utilize the left-hand version of Bach's D minor Chaconne played by the severed hand." Larson (1997) also declared Siodmak as the person responsible for suggesting the left-hand version of Bach's Chaconne to Steiner.
7. Brahms wrote to Schumann about his one-handed arrangement of the Bach Chaconne in June 1877 (Avins 1997, 515–6), comparing his achievement of transcribing the work for one hand to the story of the egg of Columbus.
8. "The similar difficulties, the type of technique, the arpeggios, they all combine—to make me feel like a violinist!" wrote Brahms (Avins 1997, 516).
9. In fact, Florey contributed the rather important story detail that the creature's behavior was malevolent because he had been made with a criminal's brain; a later writer developed that idea further, positing that the criminal brain was only stolen after the intended normal one was dropped. Universal somewhat unceremoniously yanked the

project from Florey, even though he had shot test scenes with Boris Karloff, but the film was given to James Whale (see Taves 1987a, 37; Curtis 1982, 72–3).

10. Alda had recently portrayed another composer, George Gershwin, in the film *Rhapsody in Blue* (Irving Rapper, 1945).

11. Warner Brothers released posters with taglines engineered to establish expectations for a horror film: "It lives but it's a corpse! It crawls like a spider! It kills like a cobra!" and "A sensation of screaming suspense! Sudden death striking from beyond the tomb! It's a terror-laden smash!" (*Beast with Five Fingers* papers, n.d.)

12. Siodmak to William Jacobs, producer: "About comedy relief in 'Beast with Five Fingers.' Not one of Edgar Allan Poe's stories, nor 'Dr. Jekyll and Mr. Hyde,' nor 'The Horla' by Maupassant—even 'Hamlet'—has any comedy relief. I think the classics are right." (*Beast with Five Fingers* papers, 21 September 1946)

13. All of these reviews are part of the clippings file at the Warner Brothers archives (*Beast with Five Fingers papers*, n. d.).

14. Taves (1987b) studied the archival records at Warner Brothers and concluded that Buñuel was not involved with *The Beast with Five Fingers*.

15. A document titled "Notes for *The Beast with Five Fingers*" (*Beast with Five Fingers* papers, n.d.) contained the suggestion that for this scene the camera should pan between the two characters, and the music should only be heard while Hilary is visible.

16. Steiner described his *King Kong* score as "modernistic" and "really screwy" (Steiner 1970, 393). Gorbman (1987) discussed Steiner's style as the template for the Hollywood sound of the 1930s, whereas Kalinak (1992) explicated his music for *The Informer*. See Marks (1996) for more on Steiner's scores for *Casablanca* and *The Maltese Falcon*.

17. A musical term for uneven rhythms in a melody is *alla zoppa* ("limping" or "halting" in Italian), and this rhythmic figure is part of the instrumental tradition of representing physical impairments. See Straus (2006, 148).

18. The main title sequence opens with the Warner Brothers fanfare before moving into a fully orchestrated version of Bach's Chaconne theme. The orchestra included two flutes, two oboes, three clarinets (one doubling on bass), two bassoons (sometimes on contrabassoon), four trumpets, four French horns, four trombones, one tuba, six violins, six violas, six celli, and four basses. Further, there were six percussionists, two harps, one Hammond organ, and two piano parts (each for two hands).

19. In Lerner (2001), I argue for Copland's role in establishing Hollywood's creation of a U.S. pastoral and nationalist musical language.

20. Besides examining over fifteen files of production papers, I also studied the musical materials preserved at the Warner Brothers archive at the University of Southern California, Los Angeles, which include copies of Steiner's short score (the original is housed at the Max Steiner archive at Brigham Young University), the full score in the hand of his orchestrator, and all of the orchestral parts. There are conductor's scores for all seven of the film's reels, but there are no full scores or parts for reels four and five, although there is music in those reels. One mystery I discovered when perusing the scores is that although Hugo Friedhofer receives screen credit for orchestrating this film, every full score cue in the archive contained the name and, likely, the handwriting of Murray Cutter. Friedhofer was Steiner's main orchestrator from the late 1930s until 1946, at which point Cutter became his principal orchestrator. I could locate no contracts or other records specifying musical personnel, although music department budgets from 1949—the only ones I was able to see—list Cutter as a staff orchestrator who earned a premium rate of $10 per page. Within the hierarchies of the studio system, it was standard practice for the established and bigger names to receive credit for work that may have in fact been carried out by several individuals. Such seems to have been the case with Friedhofer and Cutter on this score; it may be the case that at most Friedhofer orchestrated two of the seven reels.

21. In a similar way, Henry Mancini created tension in *Wait until Dark* (Terence Young, 1967)—a film that centers on the experience of a blind woman—by writing for two pianos pitched not a semitone but a quarter-tone apart (Marmorstein 1997, 334).

22. Russ (2000, 126) argued that "Ravel conceals the limitations of the pianist multifariously" in the concerto he wrote for Wittgenstein.

23. Tay Fizdale, who first introduced me to film studies at Transylvania University, once defined a *monster* as anything higher than you are on the food chain.
24. In the case of Fryer's short story, it should come as no surprise that the original homosexual components of the story get reduced to nearly nothing in the film; the relationship between Eustace and Saunders disappears, replaced with a new character, Julie the nurse, who finds herself in a love triangle involving Ingram and Bruce.

7

Stuttering in American Popular Song, 1890–1930

DANIEL GOLDMARK

At the height of its commercial popularity, the early twentieth-century music publishing industry in the United States, often referred to as Tin Pan Alley, manufactured thousands of songs yearly on every conceivable subject and for performing forces ranging from piano and voice to big band to saxophone and even mandolin orchestra. The historical importance of sheet music for this repertoire lies in part in the information about social issues reflected in the subjects chosen for songs and their lyrics. Songs about Prohibition, World War I, city life, and even new clothing fads were common fodder for songwriters and today provide humorous and often remarkably perceptive viewpoints about cultural trends.[1] A surprising number of songs from this period include disability—most notably stuttering—among their subject matter. With a thorough analysis of documentary evidence—all derived from sheet music—this chapter explores the formulaic narratives told by Tin Pan Alley to show how people who stutter were portrayed and to examine the stories being told about people with disabilities in general.[2]

Novel Disabilities

A songwriting guide from 1935 by Al Lewis, Tin Pan Alley songwriter and frequent collaborator with Rudy Vallee, offers precise descriptions of songs in "twenty-eight natural Classifications," including the novelty song, which Lewis wrote, "can be a ballad, a waltz, a march, a topical novelty, a philosophical or nature novelty, in fact almost any type or tempo. The chief requisite is that the idea shall be a little different, have some sort of an idea twist or play of words in it and shall be of a rather light and happy nature" (Lewis 1935, 9). Songs that qualify as novelties according to Lewis include "Who's Afraid of the Big Bad Wolf," "Shuffle Off to Buffalo," and "Piccolo Pete," among others (ibid., 17).[3]

The songs considered here are all novelties in Lewis's sense, with stuttering as the "idea twist" behind the song. Many of the songs about stuttering do not present the topic in any explicit way and do not even come to the simulated stutter until the chorus. Nevertheless, a person's disability, as Rosemarie

Garland-Thomson (1997, 12) described, "almost always dominates and skews the normate's process of sorting out perceptions and forming a reaction." Just as in literature, where people with disabilities "usually remain on the margins of fiction as uncomplicated figures or exotic aliens whose bodily configurations operate as spectacles" (ibid., 9), disabilities in general do not abound in Tin Pan Alley songs and generally occur as objects of fascination.

Songs about people who stutter were marked as such in several different ways. Some have repeated syllables as part of the title—"K-K-K-Katy," "Lil-Lil-Lillian," "M-M-Mazie"—whereas others self-identify with the word *stutter* or *stammer* in their titles, including "Stuttering Song," "I'm Always Stuttering," "Sammy Stammers," and "The Boy Who Stuttered and the Girl Who Lisped." Several songs leave nothing to chance and include descriptive copy or a subtitle that points to the song's topic, such as "A Comedy Stuttering Song" used to describe "Oh Helen!," "Possum Pie (or The Stuttering Coon)," and "Gussie (Guthie) A Stuttering & Lisping Song." Both "K-K-K-Katy" and "Lil-Lil-Lillian" also have text on their covers indicating that they are songs about stuttering, in case the titles did not make the point.[4]

In these songs, all of the people who stutter are male, perhaps reflecting the roughly four-to-one ratio of men to women who stutter.[5] Visually, these men are depicted in several different ways. Many of the songs feature photographs of famous performers (e.g., Walter Jones on "Stuttering Song"; Roscoe "Fatty" Arbuckle on "Oh Helen!"; Ray Benoit's Syncopators on "Lil-Lil-Lillian"), who either sang or popularized these songs, a common marketing tactic for attracting potential customers. The covers to several of these songs also have drawings or paintings of the title characters (e.g., "I'm Always Stuttering," "K-K-K-Katy," "You Tell Her I S-t-u-t-t-e-r," "Stuttering Jasper," "Gussie"). "I'm Always Stuttering" has no appreciable visual representation of stuttering, whereas the action on the cover of "You Tell Her I S-t-u-t-t-e-r" is ambiguous at best (see Figure 7.1).

The covers to "The Boy Who Stuttered and the Girl Who Lisped," "K-K-K-Katy," "Lil-Lil-Lillian," and "Gussie (Guthie)" all show men presumably in the midst of an interruption, with their mouths agape and their bodies tense or twisted, leaving no question as to the difficulty they are encountering. Because a stutter is typically apparent aurally, not visually, the cover artists who chose to draw consumers' attention to the disability emphasize and even exaggerate a stutter as unnatural, in effect caricaturing the very notion of speaking as an almost grotesque act.[6]

Lennard Davis (1995) argues that disability can become invisible in particular circumstances. Since speech disfluencies, such as stuttering and lisping, are largely contingent on the person speaking, songs about such disabilities feature these people in the midst of their impairment, showing how it affects them. Although songs like "Bandy Legs" and "Will I See Them: The Little Blind Girl's Pathetic Appeal" involve impairments that have visually

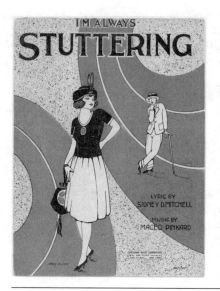

Figure 7.1 The covers of "I'm Always Stuttering" and "You Tell Her I S-t-u-t-t-e-r."

explicit cues on which an audience can concentrate, such a spectacle of disability does not apply to the speech disfluent, since audiences cannot stare unless the disabled person self-identifies. Songs about stuttering thus differ from other disability songs, not only because the impairment is not physically obvious but also because the impairment in other circumstances would be an impediment to performing, not its raison d'être.

The very notion of writing songs about people who cannot speak fluently to be sung by people who presumably have normal speech fluency is contradictory. An understood concept of normalcy applies not just to those people in the songs but also to those involved in the consumption of these songs—composers, performers, and especially consumers who either buy the sheet music or listen to its performance. Do all such songs assume that the listener is "normal," observing the damaged person who must live outside the norm? Is there some kind of voyeuristic pleasure to be gained by audiences from watching performances of these songs—or even by performers who take on such roles?[7] Though these questions must remain, for the moment, unanswered, they are posed here as a sampling of the complex issues surrounding the performance of cultural others in an entertainment setting, not unlike drag or blackface.[8]

The stuttering songs practically all situate stuttering in the context of romantic love, not surprising when considering that love was the main commodity trafficked by Tin Pan Alley. With all the songs about love, however, the character's disability will never be the true focus. Whether the man "stuttered very bad" in mixed company or only "gets tongue-tied when she's by his side," the underlying message remains: Stuttering complicates finding or pursuing a potential mate.[9] These songs do not portray or acknowledge stuttering as a disability beyond the pitching of woo; instead, it is often depicted as a personality trait, or possibly even a charming habit.

K-K-K-Katy

Geoffrey O'Hara's song "K-K-K-Katy" is exemplary not only because of its overwhelming popularity both in the United States and overseas with American soldiers fighting in World War I but also because it brings up so many of the presumptions about stuttering that appear in other pieces.[10] In the section of his guidebook *How to Write a Popular Song* on "Comic or Topical Songs," Charles K. Harris (1906, 43) reminds novice songwriters that "a little care and thought will often enable the composer to absolutely echo in his music the laugh of the line to which it is set." In "K-K-K-Katy," listeners can hear Harris's suggestion executed perfectly, as both the singer and piano create the effect of a stutter. The setting for the lines that include repeated letters (no words or syllables are blocked on in this song) is a simple musical figure (see Figure 7.2).

Each time the text calls on the singer to imitate a stutter, the melody and accompaniment both shift to a triplet figure before returning to the quarter-note beat that pervades the song. The triplet is not exclusive to the stutter, however. In two places—"beautiful" (from the line "beautiful Katy") and "Over the" (from the line "Over the cow-shed")—O'Hara repeats the triplet figure, not because the line features a repeated syllable but to maintain the parallel construction with the previous line. The performance of stuttering therefore becomes less essential to listeners' understanding of the song's construction; it is really only an incidental feature or selling point of an otherwise textbook example of a Tin Pan Alley novelty song.

The lyrics to "K-K-K-Katy," like the music, take little notice of Jimmy's stutter—the word is only mentioned once in the song, in the first verse:

Figure 7.2 The opening measure of "K-K-K-Katy."

Jimmy was a soldier brave and bold,
Katy was a maid with hair of gold,
Like an act of fate,
Kate was standing at the gate,
Watching all the boys on dress parade.

Jimmy with the girls was just a gawk,
Stuttered ev'ry time he tried to talk
Still that night at eight,
He was there at Katy's gate,
Stuttering to her this love sick cry.

(chorus)
"K-K-K-Katy, beautiful Katy,
You're the only g-g-g-girl that I adore
When the m-m-m-moon shines, Over the cowshed,
I'll be waiting at the k-k-k-kitchen door."

The noun *gawk*,[11] which refers to an awkward person or a simpleton, appears here as a stereotype of those who stutter; that is, Jimmy's stutter made him sound like an uneducated person—the presumption being that he was, in fact, intelligent. The cover image for the song shows Jimmy apparently in the midst of an interruption, with Katy looking somewhat uncomfortable, or impatient, as he pleads his case (see Figure 7.3).

Figure 7.3 Detail of the cover image of "K-K-K-Katy."

The lyrics for a number of other stuttering songs convey a similar concern: that the speaker not be mistaken for a fool despite his disability. The cover to "Lil-Lil-Lilian" makes this characterization quite explicit (see Figure 7.4). The illustration at the bottom of the cover shows a man stuttering, trying to say the name Lillian, with saliva coming out of his mouth while a woman—the object of his affection?—is shielding herself with an umbrella. The image also closely matches the lyrics of the song, in particular its first verse:

> Willie Brown, the village clown,
> Was known as the stuttering sheik,
> The girls and fellahs all raised their umbrellas,
> When Willie would start in to speak;
> The only one was Lillian who understood his stutter,
> And when he'd meet her on the street
> He'd start right in to splash and sputter …

In the image Willie is not just stuttering; his entire appearance is meant to look like he is less intelligent and less articulate than a normal person: he's hunched over, his arms hang by his side, and his hands are curled up. It may be that the image is meant to make him look not just awkward but even mentally disabled or to remind the spectator of a gorilla. Like the word *gawk* used to describe Jimmy in "K-K-K-Katy," Willie is referred to as both a *clown* and the *stuttering sheik*. This latter term is a play on the idea of the suave, mysterious

Figure 7.4 The cover of "Lil-Lil-Lilian."

character popularized by Rudolph Valentino in the 1921 film *The Sheik*; the song was published just two years later (Studlar 1996, 151). Both terms remind the listener that Willie's stutter trumps any possible efforts at being debonair and definitely distinguishes him as someone who is not normal. Moreover, the comparison to Valentino implies that like the movie star, Willie is, perhaps dangerously, effeminate, clearly tied to his inability to speak fluently. Thus, Willie's disability keeps him from getting anywhere with women; the second verse states, "He'd call on Josie and Posie and Rosie / But they all would give him the gate." Not all men who stutter would suffer such a fate, however. For almost all of the other hopeful lovers, their stutter becomes endearing, something that sets them apart from the others. Their stutter may prevent them from speaking fluently, but their beloveds always seem to get the message.[12]

Other songs vary in how clearly they address the disability itself—as opposed to its effects on others or the actual performance of the disfluency. The words *stutter* and *stammer* appear nowhere in "M-M-Mazie;" instead, the unnamed character's speech is described only once, as being "peculiar." The song's title and chorus with written-out interruptions clarifies this peculiarity. "I'm Always Stuttering" is equally vague, saying that Freddie Ray gets "tongue-tied" when he's near his "girlie"; once again the chorus confirms he has a stutter. The lyrics claim that it happens when he's near his girlfriend, as in "K-K-K-Katy," suggesting that his disability is conditional and therefore is not truly a disability. These themes misrepresent the causes of speech disfluency, implying that people who stutter from insecurity are not really disabled—which leads to the complicated notion of a stutter notated for the performer.

The artificiality of a singer affecting a block becomes most apparent in songs that, in an effort to keep the rhythmic pacing of the song regular and predictable, make sure the repeated syllables or words do not cross over strong beats or rhythmic phrases. In none of the songs surveyed did a phrase fail to end with either a complete word or at least the last iteration of a stutter. The chorus of "K-K-K-Katy" includes interruptions of four words: "Katy," "girl," "moon," and "kitchen." The point here is that O'Hara made a deliberate choice about which words would have the repeated syllables and, just like a high note in an aria or a melisma in a mass movement, the effect draws the listener's attention to those words and the meaning they might convey in that context.

In practically all these songs, the performed stutter does not happen until the chorus. A typical Tin Pan Alley songwriting device involved the story of the song being told by someone not directly involved: a friend of those described, someone who once heard the story, or an omniscient observer. The approach to the song's narrative ensures that the protagonist will speak, but usually in the chorus alone, providing an answer to some question set up in the verse. In "Possum Pie," a novelty "coon song" about a man who goes to school with the hope of getting a civil servant's job, the main character actually speaks in the verse just before the first chorus but does not block. He says, in defense of his stutter, "Now, teacher, don't guy me. I is not to blame." It is not until the chorus, where he is told to spell the words *possum pie,* that the stutter emerges. The artificiality of an enacted stutter is thus apparent not only when the stutter appears in the chorus but also when the performer can seemingly "turn it off" again to sing the second verse. This quick shift minimizes the complex nature of a speech disfluency, letting the audience easily dismiss and forget about it altogether, since it goes away with as much ease as it appeared.

There are several reasons to hold off from a song's novelty until the chorus. The chorus is, even in the early twentieth century, typically the most familiar part of a song (Harris 1906, 14). Placing the stutter in the chorus keeps the song's novelty from occurring too early. Audiences accustomed to the typical build-up of a Tin Pan Alley song would expect the musical and rhetorical pay-off—the catchy tune and verbal twist—in the chorus, often set as a punch line to the last line of the verse (ibid.). By confining the stutter to the chorus, all consumers of the music—not just the performers—temporarily enacted a speech disability in the process of singing along. Spectators in music halls or supper clubs were encouraged to sing on the refrain, especially because the audience had the first time around to learn it from the performer.[13] Although the performer might play the part of a man who stutters, the entire assembly joined in for the chorus, shifting the song's focus from one person enacting a disability to a roomful of people doing the same. Such a group performance would certainly have gone a long way to normalize the idea that a stutter is, as Lewis (1935, 9) calls it, something of a "rather light and happy nature."

The fact that Jimmy's stutter helped to drive the success of "K-K-K-Katy" can be seen in the ads for the song produced after it was first published. In 1918 Feist published a collection of songs (Anon. 1918) about war, patriotism, and home titled *Songs the Soldiers and Sailors Sing.* The ads for this compendium featured pages of sheet music with titles prominently displayed to let the consumer know some of the big hits inside, including "K-K-K-Katy," which is clearly subtitled "Stammering Song." This designation appears on neither the original sheet music nor on its smaller war-edition version. Another ad, from the *Saturday Evening Post,* includes a list of "Other Popular 'Feist' Songs," among them "'K-K-K-Katy,' stammering song."[14] In yet another such ad that features "K-K-K-Katy," the song is described as follows:

> Everybody sings it from California to France—
> and then some! It's the song of the doughboy—
> a real Yankee melody the Boys sing over and
> over again. You've got to stammer the chorus
> because Katy's beau was tongue-tied, but
> that's where the fun comes in. Composed
> by Geoffrey O'Hara, Army Song Leader.[15]

The line "but that's where the fun comes in" confirms the idea that the publisher was well aware that the saleable gimmick of "K-K-K-Katy" was the simulated stutter. Another ad from the back of another piece of Feist sheet music which includes the same marketing pitch also has a small illustration of Jimmy standing at a picket fence calling out "K-K-Katy!" while Katy sticks her head through the kitchen door (see Figure 7.5). So as not to miss the joke, another caption above Jimmy points to the full moon with the words "The m-m-moon".[16]

McCarron and Morgan's "Oh Helen!" from 1918 actually harnessed the resulting sound of the singer blocking for the purpose of a joke; that is, whereas other songs included blocks on single letters or indiscriminate syllables, the writers of "Oh Helen!" deliberately chose which syllables to have repeated for the comic effect, again, in the chorus:

(first chorus)
Oh H-H-Hel- Oh H-H-Hel- Oh Helen please be mine
Your f-f-feat- your f-f-feat- your features are divine
I s-s-swear I s-s-swear I swear I will be true,
Oh D-D-Dam- Oh D-D-Dam- Oh Damsel I love you.

(second chorus)
Oh H-H-Hel- Oh H-H-Hel- Oh Helen please be mine
You s-s-simp- you s-s-simp- you simply are divine,
You m-m-mud- you m-m-mud- you muddle me it's true.
Oh D-D-Dam- Oh D-D-Dam- Oh Damsel I love you.

When sung "correctly," the words *hell* and *damn* would be highlighted, as well as Willie being understood to say such ludicrous things as "Your feet, your feet," "I swear," "You simp," and "You mud," all of which are corrected as the block passes but which have the cumulative comic effect on the audience of mocking Willie not just for his stutter but also for something as seemingly benign as his choice of language.[17]

Figure 7.5 Advertisement for "K-K-K-Katy."

Performing Stuttering

There is a considerable difference between printed or published sheet music and its musical performance. Billy Murray, one of the most successful and well-known singers of popular music in the early twentieth century, recorded a version of "K-K-K-Katy" in 1918 for Victor.[18] His version of this song includes many stutters and even secondary symptoms not included in the original sheet music. He changes part of the first verse:

> Kate smiled with a twinkle in her eye
> Jim said, "M-m-m-meet you by-and-by,"
> That same night at eight, Jim was at the garden gate,
> Stuttering this song to K-K-K-K-K-K-Kate:

On the chorus he adds a stutter to create "c-c-c-cowshed." And lest we think he improvised the additional stutters on the spot, a male chorus joins him for a repeat of the refrain, with all voices stuttering together, including on the added stutter "c-c-c-cowshed." The deliberate artificiality of the disability is thus made evident: Having not just one but several singers stutter together shows anything but disfluent speech or lack of control—they are singing in harmony and in complete rhythmic unison.

After singing the second verse, Murray performs a brief skit where he and the chorus pretend to be soldiers in training, marching on dress parade (as the song's lyrics mention), who have stopped in front of Katy's house.

Katy.   Jimmy, come on over!
Jimmy.   I-I c-c-c-c-can't! I-It's against r-r-r-r-rules a-and r-r-r-reg-u-eg-u ...
Soldier 1. Aw, write it to her!
Soldier 2. They'll be soundin' Taps before he can tell it!
            [soldiers laughing]
Soldier 1. You'd better come over here, Katy.
Katy.   All right, I will.
Soldier 2. Say, wouldn't Jimmy make a fine officer? I bet it took him a long time to propose!
Soldier 3. He didn't propose.
Soldier 2. Who did?
Soldier 3. Why, Katy did!
            [soldiers laughing]
Katy.   Oh, Jimmy, Oh, say—can't you get a pass for tonight?
Jimmy.   I d-d-d-d- ... I d-d-d-d-d ... I d-d-d-d-d [clicks tongue and whistles] d-d-don't know. I'll t-t-t-t-try.
Soldier 1. Company, attention!

The recording ends as the soldiers, including Jimmy, walk off singing the chorus one last time, transforming the song from a love novelty into a militaristic-sounding anthem. This brief skit, which lasts less than a minute, provides much information about attitudes toward stuttering that would not otherwise have been transmitted through the sheet music. Jimmy's comrades tease him repeatedly, even in front of his fiancé, at one point calling into question his masculinity when they imply that the couple's sexual roles are reversed and that Katy had to propose to Jimmy. As seen earlier in "Lil-Lil-Lillian," men with a stutter are portrayed as effeminate and therefore weak and vulnerable. Murray also expands his portrayal of a stutterer beyond simply repeating syllables and interrupting words; he also mimics associated or secondary symptoms of having a block, in this case clicking his tongue and whistling—although as Bloodstein (1995, 19) points out, the secondary symptoms of stuttering are "many and extremely varied."[19]

Artificiality is still the issue here, and Murray's recording would indicate that consumers did not mind someone performing as a stutterer. Another example confirms this seeming willingness to let the abled enact the disabled. Jumping forward two decades, we meet the most famous stuttering performer of all time, one who was known to audiences by his voice alone—the essence of his disability. Joe Dougherty was the original voice of Porky Pig, a character who first appeared in 1935 in Friz Freleng's *I Haven't Got a Hat*, a Warner Bros. *Merrie Melodie*. As Freleng (1994, 90–1) indicated, the stutter was intended to be a comic foil—a novelty?—not a personality trait: "I made him stutter just to be different, 'cause back then everyone else was using falsetto voices—like Walt [Disney] was using a falsetto voice for Mickey Mouse. So I thought, 'Well, hell—I'll make him different.'"

Animation historian Michael Barrier points out that Porky Pig was not seen as the standout character of *I Haven't Got a Hat*: He appears early in the short, is on screen for a brief time, and does not have any significant personality development. It was not until the character had been altered considerably that he became a star. As Freleng also mentioned, however, Dougherty's "problem" was that he could not control his stutter, a condition that might have lent itself to comedy at first but that became problematic as the character grew more popular (Barrier 1999, 337–8). Eventually Dougherty was let go, and Mel Blanc—who had only recently been hired at the studio—was asked by producer Leon Schlesinger to voice the pig, including the now-defining speech disfluency (Blanc and Bashe 1988, 66–7).[20] What had made Dougherty invaluable to Warner Bros. in the beginning—his truly authentic stutter—became a terminal liability, since he could not turn it off on command. Blanc's ability to imitate the stutter meant that the writers could create gags incorporating the stutter, whereas Dougherty could only amuse with his inability to speak fluently. Because Porky was originally a young boy who eventually became an adult, his stutter was not as much emasculating as it was a sign that he was not yet a man. Thus, Porky never lost his stutter, although it did become much less a part of his personality as time passed.

This anecdote about Blanc and Dougherty, although cruelly ironic, demonstrates again that audiences were not overly concerned with the accuracy or authenticity of the person stuttering. The act is just that—an act, or rather, an enactment, in which Blanc took on the stereotypically explicit characteristics of one who stutters as a role. For someone like Billy Murray, it might be expected that singing a stuttering song like "K-K-K-Katy" was also like playing a role. The almost transparent personalities given to those who stutter in these songs suggest that their disfluency is the only interesting or noteworthy thing about them. And if these songs are considered in light of Lewis's (1935, 9) description of what makes a song novel, something that is "a little different, [has] some sort of an idea twist or play of words in it and [is] of a rather light and happy nature," then these songs are simply fetishizing the sound of the stutter, not even its source. In a competitive publishing market where literally thousands of songs were published every year, the ability to differentiate a single song and to make it stand out could have been just the thing to make it a hit.[21]

Murray's performance as Jimmy brings up another question: How do these songs characterize people who stutter? Are the people portrayed with disabilities multidimensional, or are their personalities entirely enveloped within their impairment? If the latter is true, then are they truly aware of their condition, and do they have an opinion of it? Gottschalk and Pemberton's "Stuttering Song," besides being the earliest song examined here, is the only song to be sung entirely in first person. The cover indicates the song as having been a vehicle for Walter Jones's well-known tramp act in E. E. Rice's production of *1492* (see Bordman 1992, 123–4; Gilbert 1940, 403). The character, Charley Tatters, acknowledges that he cannot sing or act like other performers but claims that his stutter is actually a positive attribute, not an impairment, as it is something he does better than anyone else.

> Oh I n-never could yodel
> And I n-never could t-trill
> But when it comes to stuttering
> I can s-s-stutter to k-kill
> I s-s-stutter and I m-m-mutter
> I s-s-stutter till I s-s-s stop
> I s-s-stutter when I m-m-mutter
> I s-s-stutter till I drop.

Of the other stuttering songs, the only character who seems at all troubled by his lack of fluency is Willie Meek in "Oh Helen!," who is "mortified" when he speaks. Bill McCloskey in "You Tell Her I S-t-u-t-t-e-r" does make use of a third party as a surrogate speaker, although it is not clear whether he does this out of shame or a desire to communicate his desire to marry his girl, Pearl. The other men who stutter carry on with their lives, and especially their lovemaking, despite their impairments. None of these men have much to distinguish them besides their speech. This brings up again the monothematic idea of the novelty that, combined with Garland-Thomson's (1997) discussion of an impairment engulfing any other characteristics a person might possess, means that these songs have little other focus.[22]

Naturally, Tin Pan Alley songs in general are not known for giving especially nuanced descriptions of people, apart from whatever wants and needs are the focus of the song. What these songs take for granted is that the men seem interested only in their verbal wooing and not in their disability. They do not deny having a disfluency—the songs simply do not acknowledge that other social effects of having a stutter exist. Neither of the soldiers portrayed in "K-K-K-Katy" or "Gussie" faces explicit ridicule at his compatriot's hands, yet Billy Murray's skit in the "K-K-K-Katy" recording indicates that such teasing might be a natural part of a stuttering man's life, especially in the military. Worse yet, the character who plays Katy does not seem phased by the other soldiers mocking her fiancé, endorsing the soldiers' contemptuous comments through her silence. The degree to which derision about stuttering centers on gender becomes very clear in this light, amounting to a disempowering or figurative emasculation of the men who have such an impairment. These songs, written at a time when the concept of masculinity was shifting radically, plainly reflect the confusion and paranoia about what was appropriately manly.[23]

Conclusion

It is no surprise that Tin Pan Alley enabled notions of ableist culture in America in the early twentieth century. It might also be too obvious to say that songs about stuttering engage with that impairment on only the most superficial level, like so many other forms of popular culture that engage with the idea of disability. Unfortunately, as Garland-Thomson (1997, 11) makes clear, such basic representations lead to reductionist notions of disabilities: "The more the literary portrayal conforms to the social stereotype, the more economical and intense is the effect; representation thus exaggerates an already highlighted physical difference." The stereotype becomes almost self-fulfilling as songs fetishize the few characteristics the normate knows about people who stutter—vocal blocks and interruptions combined with socially constructed stereotypes such as social ineptness or gawkiness, and secondary physical symptoms, such as spitting and whistling. The creation of a sense of stasis or normalcy by these songs—emotional and social equilibrium in the middle-class world of the early twentieth century—would make any stories about disability or deviation from the norm stand out considerably. Yet these songs barely rise to the surface among their thousands of competitors, as the disabilities described become gimmicks, novelties: They are routinized, ignored, and effectively made invisible.

The conceptual gap between the stories of men who stutter and realities about life for disabled people in early twentieth-century America establishes that these songs have little to do with disabilities per se and more about the same social anxieties Garland-Thomson (1997, 6) lists, including "vulnerability, control, and identity." Through the mocking scenarios set up in these songs, disabled people are subjected to the same sociocultural segregation that discourses of race, class, gender, sexuality, religion, and ethnicity—all the various discourses of otherness—face. Davis makes the point that all these categories have a totalizing effect, so that "disabled people are thought of primarily in terms of their disability" (Davis 1995, 10). In this way all sheet music of difference has a similar end product: conflating, flattening, and generalizing notions of other.

Notes

1. There is an extensive body of scholarship on Tin Pan Alley-era sheet music (see, for example, Tsou 1997; Garrett 2004; Elliker 1996, 1999; Graziano 1991; Levy 1967, 1971, 1975, 1976). Levy's vast collection is available online for researchers at http://levysheetmusic.mse.jhu.edu.
2. Songs for this study were found by surveying several online collections, including the Lester S. Levy Collection of Sheet Music from Johns Hopkins University, the UCLA Music Library Digital Archive of American Popular Music, the sheet music collections of the Lilly Library, Indiana University, the Maine Music Box, and American Memory at the Library of Congress. Thanks to Michael Barrier, Cyleste Collins, Marshall Fenig, Charles Garrett, Judy Kuster, Andrew Oster, and the editors for information shared and overall good counsel.
3. I was made aware of this text by an advertisement on the back cover of a piece of sheet music featuring Rudy Vallee, who wrote the introduction for the book.
4. Publication information for the stuttering songs discussed in this essay is as follows: "Stuttering Song," L.F. Gottschalk, L.B. Pemberton (Harry Pepper & Co., 1894); "M-M-Mazie," Wm R. Macaulay, Thos. S. Allen (George M. Krey Co., 1904); "Possum Pie, or The Stuttering Coon," Jos. C. Farrell, Hughie Cannon (F.A. Mills, 1904); "The Boy Who Stuttered and the Girl Who Lisped," Louis Weslyn (Witmark, 1907); "Oh Helen!," Chas R. McCarron, Carey Morgan, U.S.N. (Jos. W. Stern, 1918); "K-K-K-Katy," Geoffrey O'Hara (Leo. Feist, 1918); "Gussie (Guthie)," Royal Byron (Kendis Brockman Music Co., 1918); "You Tell Her I S-t-u-t-t-e-r," Cliff Friend, Billy Rose (Irving Berlin, 1922); "I'm Always Stuttering," Sidney D. Mitchell, Maceo Pinkard (Broadway Music Corp., 1922); "Lil-Lil-Lillian," Jack C. Smith (Orpheum Music Co., 1923).
5. This statistic holds true today as it had in the early twentieth century. "One of the strange features of stammering is that it occurs with far greater frequency in the male than in the female sex. There are four or five male stammerers to every female stammerer" (Bluemel 1913, 210). For recent statistics, see Wingate (2002, 78–9).
6. Another piece I found in the Levy Collection, "Stuttering Jasper" (by Robert Cohn, published in 1899 by F.A. Mills), is an instrumental march and cake-walk for piano yet has a drawing of an African-American man on the cover, clearly in the midst of saying something—or at least trying to.
7. This issue is discussed in Davis (1995, 14).
8. The concepts of drag and blackface have been discussed extensively elsewhere, whereas the performance of disability is not nearly as well theorized (see Lott 1993; Rogin 1996; Garber 1992).
9. These two lyrics are from "You Tell Her I S-t-u-t-t-e-r" and "I'm Always Stuttering."
10. The number of *answer* songs to "K-K-K-Katy"—songs written either in response to or spoofing it outright—gives us some indication as to how popular it was. Not surprisingly, these songs focus on the repeated syllable. The chorus of "Frenchy, Come to Yankee Land" from 1919 (Broadway Music Corporation) by Sam Ehrlich and Con Conrad—which is

actually the answer song to another hit from 1918, "Oh Frenchy" (Sam Ehrlich, Con Conrad; Broadway Music Corporation)—specifically refers to "K-K-K-Katy"; in this song Katy plays the other woman to the female narrator's love interest. In a recording of "Waitin' for Katy" by Fred Hall and His Sugar Babies (Okeh 41026; recorded April 14, 1928), Katy's name is sung with the trademark "K-K-K-Katy" stutter included. http://www.redhotjazz. com/sugarbabies.html.

11. *Oxford English Dictionary*, http://dictionary.oed.com.
12. Another instance of blocking caught in action appears on the cover of "The Boy Who Stuttered and the Girl Who Lisped." Though mostly decorative, it includes an inset photo of a well-known vaudeville team, William Rock and Maude Fulton, presumably enacting their roles from the song. The photo shows the "boy" attempting to speak while the "girl" is shielding her face from his verbal (and possibly expectoratory) onslaught (Slide 1994, 424–5).
13. Both Charles K. Harris (1926) and Edward B. Marks (1934) discussed, in their respective autobiographies, the importance of getting the audience singing on a song's chorus for a new song to be successful. Marks's anecdote about this is quoted in Crawford (2001, 473–4).
14. *Saturday Evening Post*, 23 March 1918, 105.
15. *Saturday Evening Post*, 21 September 1918, 74.
16. This ad is on the back cover of "I'm Sorry I Made You Cry" (War Edition) by N.J. Clesi, Leo Feist, New York, 1918. Author's private collection.
17. The implied profanity—not the stuttering—had adverse repercussions for "Oh Helen!" The song, performed by Arthur Fields, was pulled from an advertised record before it was released because of the language (Gracyk 2000, 130). Like so many other songs published at this time, "Oh Helen!" was made available as a piano roll, recorded in 1918 by Jack Clyde (Imperial 9773). Along with a reading that is quite faithful to the sheet music, the performer adds what might be called a third stutter chorus not in the original music, in which he imitates the sound of a person experiencing blocks by repeating certain chords of the chorus—and, in effect, stopping the rhythmic motion of the song—as the player tries to overcome the interruption. A midi recreation of this roll can be found at http://www.trachtman.org/rollscans/RollListing.php?showpage=3&sortby=catalog.
18. Victor 18455 (described in Gracyk 2000, 241).
19. Murray also recorded "You Tell Her I S-t-u-t-t-e-r" in 1923.
20. Even though people who stutter often can avoid blocking while singing, Porky cannot, as can be seen in his numerous performances in Warner Bros. cartoons. See *My Favorite Duck* (Chuck Jones, 1942) for one example, as Porky duets with Daffy on "On Moonlight Bay."
21. There is little evidence that any sales or marketing tactics besides actual performances of a song—either live or recorded—had any substantial effect on the popularity of a song. On this point, see Sanjek (1996), Jasen (1988), Harris (1926), and Marks (1934).
22. "Literary texts necessarily make disabled characters into freaks, stripped of normalizing contexts and engulfed by a single stigmatic trait" (Garland-Thomson 1997, 11).
23. For more on the concept of white masculinity at the turn of the twentieth century, see Studlar (1996).

Part II
Performing Disability Musically

8

Learning to Hear Autistically

DAVE HEADLAM

When listening to music, we often have the feeling that our consciousness is altered. Our sense of the passing of time becomes highly experiential, following the twists and turns of the tempi and rhythms. We shift between local details of motives and themes to larger groupings of formal sections, or we just revel in the sensory impressions from the colors of orchestration. We can engage in all sorts of behaviors (clapping, dancing, shaking, head-banging, etc.) that would be considered strange in the absence of music. It can be a shock when the "real" world impinges on our altered state; the musical world is a compelling place to be, and it serves many purposes. Musical experience seems to be a global human trait; virtually all societies have some role for music (Nettl 1983).

Although most people have some affinity for music, there is evidence that music has particular significance for those on the autism spectrum *(autistics)*.[1] If autism is viewed as a medical pathology, which is the prevalent view, it follows that music therapy plays a large role in its treatment. Indeed, music therapy is well established as an aid in learning, communicating, socializing, and controlling autistic behaviors. The basic elements of pitch, duration, timbre, and loudness are used along with the physical, social, and emotional efforts and effects of making music to promote "physical, mental, social, emotional and spiritual well-being."[2] In a more general sense it is clear, however, that music functions in therapeutic ways for many people; thus, even though music is perhaps particularly beneficial for autistics, it may have benefits for all.[3]

In another view, autism may be regarded as an alternate form of consciousness and a distinct worldview. Autism is then a defining trait of a group of people; as autistic Jim Sinclair (1993) writes, "Autism is a way of being. It is *pervasive*; it colors every experience, every sensation, perception, thought, emotion, and encounter, every aspect of existence."[4] These characteristics lead to an identification with a group and to the formation of an autistic culture to define the group. As with most cultures, autistics use music to define their place within their own immediate locales and within larger communities of autistics in the world. Not unexpectedly, autistics often experience music and express themselves musically in unique and interesting ways. Some autistic musicians draw upon the focus that an autistic disposition allows for in their musical endeavors and engage a rich talent for music. Others, perhaps less gifted, may to varying extents use music to communicate and to make sense of the world in day-to-day living.

This article explores the role of music in autism, drawing on the literature and personal experience with an autistic son.[5] I start from the premise that, although autism is typically seen as a defect, evidence from the writings and lives of autistic people suggests that, on the contrary, autism may be better understood as a culture. One defining attribute of this culture is the role of music. I show that autistics hear and conceive of music in distinctive ways that differ significantly from the ways in which music is heard and understood by people who are *neurologically typical* (NT). I suggest that trying to understand this distinctive approach to music—learning to "hear autistically"—may be an enriching experience for all of us and may be particularly revealing when applied to nontonal music of the last one hundred or so years. This music has many aspects related to autistic characteristics; I show that an appreciation of the autistic way of experiencing music can lead to insights into this musical expression.

The Medical Model of Autism and Its Limitations

In its medical definition, *autism* denotes a range of conditions defined in terms of abilities and behaviors.[6] Autistics are categorized over a range of symptoms and behaviors, variously as *high-functioning* persons with Asperger's syndrome, as persons evincing behaviors described somewhat vaguely as *pervasive developmental disorder not otherwise specified* (PDD-NOS), as *hyperlexic,* which includes early development of reading skills, and as *low-functioning* persons who need consistent care and may harm themselves unless controlled. Across this broad spectrum, three categories of behaviors and abilities are usually mentioned: (1) impaired social engagement; (2) delayed and limited communication skills; and (3) restricted, repetitive behaviors and responses to stimuli. More detailed characteristics are a lack of *simultaneous capacity,* or the ability to do two things at once; *face blindness,* or the inability to read and distinguish facial expressions; *mindblindness,* or the inability to appreciate differences in the minds of others; and two related to music, which are *central auditory processing disorder,* or the inability to stream multiple auditory sensations; and *lack of a chronological sense of time,* or the inability to estimate clock time.[7]

Autism can be diagnosed early in life, and often the symptoms become evident around two years of age. At that point many types of therapy, including music therapy, are applied. The topic of autism has been prominent in the scholarly and popular media in recent times, where it is generally treated as a growing epidemic in society—an overwhelming problem needing a solution—and this view is driving research. Although some anecdotal reports of alleged cures exist, it seems that autism is a permanent neurological state.[8]

This view toward a cure—that is, that a normal child may be developed from the autistic one, with all the treatments, attitudes, and research directions that it entails—has been questioned by the autistic community. As Sinclair (1993, 2005) describes, autistics are peculiar, abnormal, or disabled only when measured by the standard held up by NT persons. In his view, an NT society has its own problems of social dependence coupled with intolerance, among other characteristics, that tend to impose rigid standards on behavior and abilities. But autistic persons have their own distinctive ways of being, which include a culture and music. Even though some autistics suffer from depression or may harm themselves with physical actions, NT persons in similar states can be found. In sum, a wide range of cognitive abilities exists, which includes both NT and autistic consciousness. All along autistics have been living their lives and making contributions, many perhaps hitherto unrecognized, that stem from their characteristic sets of abilities.[9]

Autistic Culture

A culture emerges from shared values within a group, and in this view, autistics have their own culture. Describing this culture, writer and autistic Martijn Dekker (n. d.) begins with the role of individuals in the development of self-advocacy by autistics for their own forms of expression. Autistic writers such as Temple Grandin (Grandin 1986, 1995) and Donna Williams (Williams 1994) have described their experiences in terms that both other autistics and NT persons can understand. Grandin (1995) describes several modes of being, some of which apply to other autistics: she "thinks in pictures," translating concepts into visual images; her thought process is associational rather than logical; she finds abstract concepts difficult when they cannot easily be related to real world objects; and for her, transitions between locations and life situations are very stressful. Williams (1994) writes of discovering through friendship with other autistics the special characteristics of autistic social interactions, with the need for space, silence, and separation; she notes the shared lack of understanding of NT social conventions and therefore the appearance of being disengaged and unemotional and how this apparent problem is resolved within an autistic community.

From the important starting point of individual writings such as the ones from Grandin and Williams, Dekker asserts, an autistic sensibility has begun. The next stage, the rise of an autistic community, has been greatly aided by the Internet and the forms of communication it allows. As several autistic bloggers have noted, the Internet provides a safe conduit for self-expression and community among members of a group generally characterized by social disengagement.[10] Dekker notes that an e-list, the St. John's University Autism and Developmental Disabilities List (1991) used by parents of autistic children to bond and share information, actually prompted the emergence of an autistic Internet community. Autism advocacy developed in reaction to this list:

"Disappointed by the lack of acceptance of the autistic way of being on the AUTISM list, Jim Sinclair and Donna Williams founded Autism Network International (ANI) in 1992. ANI is a self-advocacy organization run by autistic people, for autistic people. It is the first of its kind" (Dekker n. d.). Here in an autistic space both the positives and negatives of autism are debated, with NT persons allowed but requested to avoid a pathological view of autism. This virtual space has a real world analog called *autreat*, a three-day conference and camping trip for autistics organized by Sinclair; in this place autistic ways of being are respected and indeed are the norm.

Dekker's comments on the rise of an autistic community on the Web are certainly supported by a number of Weblogs (blogs) that use the potential of the Internet both to inform and to promulgate different points of view. The political component is right on the surface here, as autistic advocacy develops in general conformance with other disability groups and with the principles of disability studies in general.[11] Many sites and blogs include personal experiences and expressions of autistics but also, of course, of all types of people; in this context autistics are no different than many people who find the anonymity of the Web liberating. From the musicians on such sites, the opportunity is there to distribute their compositions and to tell their stories. As with all such endeavors, there is good and bad music to be had, as well as sincerity alongside commerce. But the ability to connect with a community in a safe environment seems a boon to autistics as well as others.

Dekker compares the growing autistic advocacy groups with those of other disability communities. He asserts a link between the advocacy movement for autistics and that of the Deaf community in that a specialized form of communication is a shared feature. Sign language finds a parallel in the communication modes of autistics, which differ from those of NT persons. Dekker also compares autistic modes of expression with those of blind persons; what he describes as their heightened sense of hearing, which compensates for their lack of sight, may be understood as similar to autistic abilities: "Autistic people also often report a heightened ability to think in pictures, or to do logical reasoning, as a way of compensating for their lack of 'instinctive' understanding of the world" (Dekker n. d., para. 40). Whether or not these comparisons are accurate, Dekker clearly places autism in the context of disability studies. He notes similarities of the autistic advocacy groups to the disability pride movement and asserts that in representing a "neurological disorder," autism advocacy also has affinities with "psychiatric survivors," who have experienced some form of abuse during a treatment (Dekker n. d., para. 44).

Importantly, a sense of culture can arise from advocacy, and according to Dekker an autistic culture—including distinctive modes of communication—is being formulated. An aspect of autistic communication related to music is the rhythm of autistic discourse, where silence is not avoided. Though NTs find silence in conversation uncomfortable, autistic persons find it comforting.

A second aspect of autistic communication is the lack of body language or facial elements in the meaning, which relies wholly on the words themselves. The communication is direct and without hidden meanings or agendas. As discussed below, the enhanced use of silence and direct objective communication is characteristic of many forms of post-1900 music.

Dekker's views on characteristics of autistic society in comparison with NT society may also be related to musical structure. NT societies are often based on group structures and hierarchies, whereas autistic societies tend to be based on individuals, since autistics function less well in groups, and on networks where redundant connections among equals abound, which is more in line with an autistic worldview. Music has this duality as well: It is generally regarded as hierarchical in the common language of tonality; with the advent of new languages after 1900, a changed playing field in the form of flat networks of relationships becomes more common.[12] This chapter develops the comparison of hierarchical, tonal music with an NT sensibility and network-oriented non-tonal music with an autistic outlook in the next section.

Music and the Culture of Autism

Sarah Schuchardt (n. d.) provides a more formal definition of a musical context for autism culture. She defines *culture* as the human capacity for learning and transmitting knowledge about belief systems, social norms, and artifacts to succeeding generations. The term *social norms* is not necessarily as defined by NT societies but is generalized to include an autistic perspective, where social behavior is less group oriented. Also, behaviors in rituals are similarly more broadly defined to include self-stimulation to regulate sensory input, play rituals to provide order to experiences, communication rituals to include repetition, and scheduling rituals to provide security and predictability. All of these behaviors, in their autistic guises, are in this view evidence of a culture.

Schuchardt (n. d.) applies music to her discussion of autistic culture in several contexts. The first, a wider application, is related to the effects of music on the brain and nervous system of humans, which has been shown to have beneficial results for concentration and well-being. The second is related to music therapy and autism, to the effect that music can be used to moderate autistic behaviors and to provide a focus for concentration and learning. The third is related to rituals of behavior; although Schuchardt is not rigorous in her references to music in terms of these rituals, such rigor can easily be inferred.

In terms of rituals of behavior, it is clear that many people use music as a form of self-stimulation, and autistics are no different in this regard, although they may be more specific in their application. Music can shut out the world and can provide a focus for the senses, or it can be used to calm the senses after an overload. As a socially acceptable form of behavior, musical self-stimulation provides an effective conduit for autistics to relate to NT persons as well. A musical experience can be a communal one or a solitary one for all types of people.

According to Schuchardt (n. d.), the orderliness of play rituals is reflected in the types of musical expression favored by autistics. She draws some generalizations from a series of interviews with autistics; the sample group is small so her results must be considered speculative. Autistics, like NTs, have widely varying tastes in music, as indicated in the many autistic blogs and websites (see Ewing 2005). Additionally, many of the features of the preferred musical styles outlined below, such as a distinct beat and predictable, unchanging textures are common to most popular music styles that are preferred by many people. Nonetheless, the association of types of music and autistic characteristics is suggestive with regard to the role of music in developing an autistic culture.

Schuchardt's interviews suggest that autistics favor music with a strong pulse so that the music can be felt as well as heard; this division between the senses divides the input to avoid overload. Preference is given to music with repeating formal, melodic, and rhythmic or metric structures. The key to this preference, Schuchardt asserts, is that the predictability of the features is comforting, related to the difficulty autistics have with transitions. An overall homogenous structure with all parts smoothly operating within the whole, such as a clear and distinct melody line within a texture that does not obscure the lyrics, is preferred. Many of the interviewees responded that music provides comfort and that they prefer music with a "good feeling" that does not overwhelm. Schuchardt cites the music of Donna Williams, an autistic, for its simple, vocal-based textures. The music of autistic TrKelly's band The Raventones contains many of the features cited by Schuchardt; within songs the textures and vocal lines are predictable and clear, although Kelly does use vocal ornamentation that can overpower the lyric, but each song is in a quite different style (e.g., rockabilly, bluesy jazz, rock, etc.) so there is great variety between tracks on her CD. These changing styles are not homogenous on this larger level.

It is, of course, problematic to generalize across large, diverse populations; as mentioned, Schuchardt bases her assertions of musical preferences of autistics on a small sample. It is also not surprising that the types of music mentioned, with their characteristics of simplicity and predictability, are popular in the wider world as well and are elements of most popular music in any time period. Other points made by Schuchardt, such as that autistics prefer musical over verbal expression, are true of many performing musicians and listeners.

Clifton (2001) presents another view on music and autism concerning jazz music that often has none of the stable characteristics Schuchardt noted. He responded to spoken remarks by George Lewis, head of the Guelph Jazz Festival of 2001, in Ontario, Canada, in which the appropriation of jazz music from blacks by whites is given as evidence of an autism of culture (p. 2), an inability by whites to empathize with black jazz musicians. Citing Sontag (1977), Clifton called Lewis to task on this use of autism in the context of "illness as metaphor" (p. 2). Autistics do not have the type of insensitivity that whites ripping off blacks in the jazz world exhibit; Clifton cites Gillingham (1988) to show that they instead generally protect themselves from a state of too great a sensitivity and thus only appear to be insensitive. Therefore, the usage of autism in this context is false. Indeed, Clifton neatly turns the argument on its head by ending his article with an analogy between autistics and African Americans who produce jazz. He noted that both populations face discrimination and segregation and, continuing the musical analogy, that both live dissonant lives filled with recoils from "wrong note[s]" (p. 4).

Clifton (2001) goes on on to describe what he imagines as a specifically autistic approach to jazz. He speculates that many jazz musicians and recordings may have an autistic connection. This point relates to an earlier one in his article that some autistics can effectively hide in NT society, not risking letting their true natures come out for fear of losing opportunity. But in improvisation, one's nature will emerge, and the many stories of jazz musicians' strange behavior may be part of a hidden autistic component in improvised music.[13]

Autism and Musical Ability: Absolute Pitch

A particular trait of some musicians called absolute pitch (AP)—the ability to name a pitch with no reference point—has been associated with autism.[14] AP is of great interest to researchers, and its possible sources are debated. Two opposing models include: (1) early learning, where up to a critical age limit AP can be learned by musical exposure; and (2) gifted, a genetic endowment of AP in only some people, which may be activated by musical exposure. The prevalence of AP in autistics has suggested to some that the neurological characteristics of the two may be related (Brown et al. 2003).

Oliver Vitouch (2003) presents an overview of AP issues but advocates a nuanced developmental version of the early learning side, asserting that AP is a continuum—a fuzzy quality rather than crisp—which people can develop to varying degrees. As support, he indicates that latent forms of AP are widespread, that AP abilities seem parallel to early language acquisition, and that strong correlations between music training and AP exist. He notes several populations with AP as support for his advocacy of the developmental model: (1) the congenitally and early blind, who he notes, presumably rely more on their ears and thereby develop enhanced abilities like AP; (2) musicians in Japan, a country with a special tradition of early music training, particularly the Suzuki method, which favors ear training over score reading; and (3) people with different types of genetically based cognitive deficit syndromes, particularly autism and Williams syndrome.[15] Vitouch posits that the particular learning inclinations of these persons favor viewing AP as developmental rather than genetic. He directly addresses Brown et al.'s (2003) study, which suggests that a higher percentage of AP possessors are either autistic or have autism-like symptoms, by noting that autistic ways of learning—the autistic cognitive style—may facilitate AP development.

The many arguments about the nature of autism and AP and the possibility of a genetic or brain structural relationship present challenging problems for researchers. Parallels to the conditions are difficult to clarify and to test sufficiently, and a definitive answer may never appear. What is often left out of the discussions, however, is a musical view of the nature and value of AP. If autistics are more likely to have AP, what does that tell us from a musical point of view? A musician with AP has a great gift as well as an advantage in instantly being able to identify the names of notes. This ability can be related to performance considerations, such as tuning and memorization, and to long-range musical hearing, which depends on an ability to recognize the return of an original key. Another way of hearing, however, is called *relative pitch*, in which functional relationships between notes can be perceived without the need for absolute identification—for example, I may recognize that an interval distance is a perfect fifth, or seven semitones, without knowing that the boundary notes are C and G. This sense of the connectedness of notes is different from the separate labeling of notes in AP. An analogy may be drawn then between AP with autistic people and relative pitch with NT people if the generalization is made that autistics tend to prefer isolation and social separation whereas NT people prefer social connectedness. In this context, the tendency for autistics to have AP fits in with their social tendencies. Of course, not all people with AP are autistics, but the relation between this rare musical ability and autistic social interaction is suggestive.

In autistics, the ability to perceive AP may be accompanied by a general sensitivity to acoustic stimulus but also a dependence on acoustic self-stimulation. My son, Jerome, for instance, has AP and is sensitive to loud noises, but he often sings to himself continuously. He learns songs in a particular key and retains that key as part of the memory of the song; thus, recordings seem to be reassuring—he will listen to recordings of a song repeatedly. As I lack AP, when I sing a familiar song in the wrong key, he either ignores me or gets annoyed until I can correct my pitch. These characteristics suggest to me that this type of perceptual acuity may have relevance to the perception of structure in music. For tonal music, which is the music the general public prefers, having relative pitch is useful because the musical structure is hierarchical: The functional relationships among notes, chords, and keys is a distinguishing characteristic. But in non-tonal music since 1900, a type of music not widely accepted by the public, research to date has been unable to find similar types of hierarchies. Instead, the AP ability to label pitches instantly allows for an assessment of the nonhierarchical, network type of relationships that are prevalent. This line of argument is continued in the next section.

Music after 1900 and Autism

A perusal of the *Lexicon of Musical Invective* (Slonimsky 1984), a collection of music critics' responses to new compositions, illustrates that at least since Ludwig von Beethoven's time, new music has often been greeted with incomprehension and even outright hostility. But the tone grows notably harsher when nontonal music appears after 1900. A few examples from the *Lexicon* follow.

> [In Arnold Schoenberg's Three Piano Pieces, op. 11] one perceives a succession of tones and sounds which cannot be grasped in their continuity because they do not belong together. Schoenberg kills tonal perception; his sounds are no longer derived from one another (p. 149).[16]
>
> Arnold Schoenberg's latest work, *Variations for Orchestra*, is calculated and excogitated musical mathematics dictated by intellect alone to one obsessed with a single eccentric idea. I cannot take seriously someone or his work when his logic leads perforce to an absurdity because the premises of such a work are false (p. 161).[17]
>
> [Anton] Webern's *Five Pieces for Orchestra* required of the listener the utmost concentration of attention. Inevitably these faint rustlings, these tiny squeaks and titterings called to mind the activities of insects (p. 249).[18]
>
> It appears to me that the Bartók system of composition and performance is one of the most rigid-minded, rigid-muscled ever invented; that in shunning sentiment [Béla] Bartók has lost beauty, that in shunning rhetoric he has lost reason (p. 40).[19]
>
> [In Sergei Prokofiev's music] there are a few, but only a very few, passages that bear recognizable kinship to what has hitherto been recognized as music. No doubt there are what pass for themes, and there is ingenuity of some kind in manipulating them, but it seldom produces any effect but that of disagreeable noise (pp. 133–4).[20]

The focus in these and other similar reviews is on the seemingly incomprehensible behavior of composers who isolate themselves, who refuse to communicate sensibly with their listeners, and who apparently have no emotional empathy with them. In Schoenberg's music, sounds are isolated and disconnected, and the music characterized by obsessive ideas; in Webern's music, the listener is required to focus on minuscule motions; Bartók shuns sentiment and recognizable rhetoric; and Prokofiev displays ingenuity in producing noise.

What I want to suggest here is that the responses to the musical landscape of post-tonal music are remarkably like those of NTs to autistic culture: It is disconnected and uncommunicative. The music played in most concerts even today is music of the eighteenth and nineteenth centuries, with its NT-like qualities of a tonal hierarchy, a shared emotional experience, layers of meaning and symbols, and an arc-like life journey. Although this tonal form of expression continues to be written, most notably in film music, after 1900 many composers explore forms and expressions of isolation, solo journeys, static emotion with no satisfying arc, pattern for its own sake, and algorithmic compositional procedures stemming from logic rather than emotional intuition. The musical and aesthetic growth and effects of *total serialism* of the 1950s, in which each musical parameter is subjected to a serial or ordered set of transformations, is an example of a drive toward predictable, detailed patterning (Watkins 1988). The music and philosophy of John Cage, in which silence and detachment are celebrated, is another example of a musical tendency that is mystifying to most audiences but that has resonances with autistic culture.

Instead of viewing this music through an NT lens and finding it wanting, we can gain a greater understanding and appreciation for many of these compositions if we can learn to value the differences of an autistic worldview. An NT outlook and mode of expression that cherishes social interaction and hierarchical order is but one format. Other modes are possible and are explored in music after 1900. We can learn to hear this music on its own terms—that is, autistically—as an alternative and fruitful approach.

As an example, consider the piano etudes of György Ligeti.[21] Writers on this music point to a wealth of influences: the piano etudes by Frédéric Chopin and Claude Debussy, the keyboard style of Robert Schumann and Domenico Scarlatti, the pieces for player piano by Conlon Nancarrow, jazz piano from Bill Evans and Thelonious Monk, and music of Sub-Saharan Africa for its rhythmic polyphony. But listeners to the obsessive patterning will also recognize the ostinati of Igor Stravinsky, the motoric rhythms of Béla Bartók, the sonorities of Olivier Messiaen, and the slowly changing formations of minimalism. Above all, the impression is of a celebration of pattern for its own sake.

The Ligeti etudes are pure piano music, elemental in many senses: The concern is solely with pattern, amidst changes in register, density, texture, and dynamics wholly idiomatic to the piano. In the first two books, only no. 13 has a sort of ABA(B) form with a definite change in texture; in the remainder, only a vague formal outline is found—generally of expanding register to some climactic point followed by a retreat and then a return of the initial patterning. In the relentless flow of the patterns, usually one per etude with only slow changes if any at all, the listener may feel helpless and trapped in a musical world where logic arises only from the flow of patterns with no underlying harmonic progression to relieve or shape the machinations. The chromatic descending lines of no. 9 epitomize these forces: In unstoppable waves of descents, with growth in density and expansion in register and dynamics, in eleven pages of *prestissimo* tempo, the piece drives unswervingly to its end in the low register. To an NT listener, the obsession is bewildering: why these unbroken patterns above all? Listeners crave variety, change of mood, or some hierarchical undergirding or emotional arc. But, if we can learn to let go—to appreciate the patterning for its own musical qualities and to focus on it—we can gain an understanding of the art of Ligeti in these works.

I am reminded in these pieces of my son's obsession with patterns for their own sake, with his need for repeated ordering of patterns and for the pleasure elemental expressions of patterning give him. When I think of his worldview, the etudes make more sense, the flow of the patterns are their own logic, and their systematic exploration of the fundamentals of piano technique conveys a direct sense and meaning without an emotional conduit—or perhaps a fundamentally distinct one—that is quite different from that of earlier music.

If a similar approach is taken to other aspects of post-1900 music with their analogous obsessions—the exploration of extended silences, logical structures that do not call on familiar emotions, direct expression untempered by vibrato or other traditional tone devices, and different listening modes, other than a quiet concert hall, as alternate forms of musical consciousness derived from the characteristics of autistic communities—we will surely gain from the experience. The music of Anton Webern, with its quiet brevity and sparse textures, of Iannis Xenakis, with its formalized probabilities, of Milton Babbitt, with its serial complexities, of Morton Feldman, with its expansive durations, and of Barry Truax, with its timbral explorations, may come to seem more appealing and approachable if we allow different visions of expression into our ears and minds.

Again from my own experience, I can say that new musical understanding and my relationship with my son, who demands that I consider his worldview along with my own, have developed hand in hand. Whatever the sources of the changes in expression found in much music written after 1900, we can profit if we learn to hear austistically: to recognize alternate forms of beauty and expression in different modes of communication.

Notes

1. See Bonnell et al. (2000), Heaton, Hermelin, and Pring (1999), Heaton, Pring, and Hermelin (2001), and Thaut (1988) for information about musical processing and autism. Musical sensitivity exists even though autistics often suffer from auditory processing problems; see Society for Auditory Processing Techniques, "Auditory Processing Problems in Autism," http://64.202.182.52/saitwebsite/processing.html. The term *autistics* for persons with autism is used by Sinclair (2005), and this essay follows his usage.
2. Bunt (n. d.). The music therapy literature concerning autism is voluminous; see the journals *Music Therapy, Journal of Music Therapy,* and *Music Therapy Perspectives.* See also American Music Therapy Association, and Autism Society Canada; Alvin (1975); Baker (1982); Euper (1968); Shore (n. d.); Staum (n. d.); and Thaut (1984).
3. In addition to the emotional and spiritual components, music has been asserted to have physiological effects; see Schlaug et al. (1995) for a reported increase in connections between brain hemispheres as a result of musical training.
4. Sinclair (1993). Similarly, see Williams (1994) and Grandin (1995) for discussions of their autistic worldviews.
5. The scholarly literature on music and autism is almost completely from the field of music therapy; music theory and musicology have not dealt with the issues presented by autism and music. For instance, a search of the New Grove Online turns up only one mention of autism in the music therapy article. See Bunt (n. d.).
6. The *Diagnostic and Statistical Manual of Mental Disorders* (DSM) gives detailed diagnostic criteria for autism. See American Psychiatric Association (APA) 1994. The literature on autism is voluminous; see references listed in Volkmar (1998) for an overview.
7. This list is compiled from the Autism Society of America and Autism Society Canada websites.

8. Autism Network International (ANI), "What Is Autism?" http://www.ani.autistics.org/definitions.html

9. The best-known autistic is probably Temple Grandin (see Grandin 1995), who developed a new paradigm for treating livestock and has written several books on her life as an autistic. For discussion of autism not as disability but as difference, see Baron-Cohen (2000). The term *alter-abled* is used by autistic musician TrKelly (n. d.), who asserts, with a musical reference: "*Variation!* i won't accept the notion of 'DIS-abled' no matter what the paperwork has to say..., because i am more truthfully, ALTER-abled. This means that *i can do things that you can't*, as well as the more commonly noticed 'i can't do what you take for granted and expect as normal.'"

10. The many blogs and websites by autistics indicates the wide use of the Internet for expression and communication. Autistic culture even has a Wikipedia entry: http://en.wikipedia.org/wiki/Autistic_culture.

11. For a list of Weblogs on disability studies see Dorn et al. (2005).

12. The field of music theory has adopted both of these modes in analytical models in an attempt to explain differences in expression. The contrast is clearest in the theories of Schenker (1935), generally applied to music that appeared from the time of J. S. Bach to Johannes Brahms, and the theories of Lewin (1987), generally applied to music written after 1900.

13. Improvisation is presented as an important milestone in musical development in the music therapy literature. My son, Jerome, often improvises on the piano, seemingly enjoying sound for sound's sake but also singing along in a kind of free melismatic style. See Barton (n. d.) for the view that autistics cannot engage in complex rhythms and that this factor would limit improvisation.

14. AP is also called *perfect pitch* in the literature; see Brown et al. (2003), Heaton (2003), Heaton, Pring, and Hermelin (2001), and Bamberger (1986). In addition to perfect pitch, some autistics have extraordinary musical abilities and are described as *savants*. See the essay on "Blind Tom" in this volume for more on this topic.

15. Williams syndrome is a rare, congenital disorder characterized by physical and developmental problems including an impulsive and outgoing—excessively social—personality, limited spatial skills and motor control, and intellectual disability (i.e., developmental delay, learning disabilities, mental retardation, or attention deficit disorder). See National Institute of Neurological Disorders and Stroke, "NINDS Williams Syndrome Information Page," 2005, http://www.ninds.nih.gov/disorders/williams/williams.htm.

16. From *Signale*, Berlin, February 9, 1910.

17. From Fritz Ohrmann, *Signale*, Berlin, December 12, 1928.

18. From Warren Storey Smith, *Boston Post*, November 20, 1926.

19. From Percy A. Scholes, *Observer*, London, May 13, 1923.

20. From Richard Aldrich, *New York Times*, February 1, 1922.

21. The Ligeti Piano Etudes were composed in groups of I–VI (1985 as Book I), VII–XIV (1998–94 as Book II), and XV–XVII (1995–2001 as Book III); the discussion concerns only the first two books.

9

Glenn Gould, Autistic Savant

S. TIMOTHY MALONEY

Introduction

Canadian concert pianist Glenn Gould (1932–1982) quickly attained international prominence after the release of his first commercial recording in 1956.[1] Before the end of that decade, he had given recitals in major concert halls around the world, collaborated with elite conductors and orchestras on several continents, and established his pre-eminence as a Bach interpreter. He had also acquired a reputation as an eccentric who exhibited undisciplined deportment onstage, neglected his personal grooming and wardrobe, and habitually wore winter attire even in summer.

Although the intensity and iconoclastic freshness of Gould's playing have attracted millions of listeners worldwide for the past half-century, earning him posthumous cult status in some quarters, reactions during his life to aspects of his personality and behavior ranged from good-natured jokes to spiteful personal attacks. His many idiosyncrasies were rich fodder for journalists and caricaturists alike, especially in North America, where concert critics focused at least as much on his demeanor as on his extraordinary musical gifts.

While still a schoolboy in the 1940s, Gould was chided by Toronto critics for "incipient mannerisms" onstage (McCarthy 1947). By 1955, he was being routinely taken to task, and headlines such as the following random selection were not unusual:

"Wears Gloves At Piano ... But No Shoes" (*Toronto Telegram*, March 9, 1956)
"Gould Great, Antics Upsetting" (*Detroit Times*, March 16, 1956)
"Glenn Gould Writhes, Soars" (*Ottawa Citizen*, April 17, 1956)
"Mannerisms Mar Fine Gould Effort" (*Stratford Beacon*, July 10, 1956)
"Gould Fits—Suit Doesn't" (*Chicago American*, April 23, 1962)

Some critics were particularly harsh. A Toronto writer likened Gould's abnormally low seated position and the extra-musical movements and gestures he made at the keyboard to a combination of "the last act of Macbeth with an imitation of a proposal of marriage by a man who has just swallowed a fly" (Tumpane 1955).[2] After his first appearance with an American orchestra in 1956, the *Detroit Times* (see the second headline above) pointed out that "his behavior at the piano produces laughter in his audience," and asked, "Why do pianists feel that they can indulge in these fantastic emotional ecstasies …?" (Taylor 1956).

In April 1962, the *Chicago Daily News* reported: "Glenn Gould finally slouched onto the Orchestra Hall stage Sunday afternoon, after three cancellations … Seating himself … on a sawed-off, rickety relic of a chair that was held together with wires, the disheveled recitalist sang and stomped and conducted an invisible orchestra …" (Henahan 1962). The *Chicago American* went further (see the last headline above): "His appearance is careless. … His clothes don't fit, his hair needs cutting and grooming, he appears to have his trouser pockets stuffed with grapefruits, and walks like an impersonation of Henry Fonda impersonating the young Abe Lincoln" (Dettmer 1962).

Gould himself allowed, "Perhaps many of the complaints about my manner on the stage are justified. … [I]t is because I am in some kind of intense relationship to what is going on" (Roberts 1999, 193). "[The success of my first recording] launched me into the most difficult year I have ever faced. Up until that time I had not regarded … my eccentricities … as being of any particular note at all …. When I was suddenly made aware of this in about 1956, I became extremely self-conscious about everything I did" (ibid., 186).

In 1964, at age thirty-one, Gould ceased concertizing, complaining, "At live concerts I feel demeaned, like a vaudevillian" (Bester 1964, 152). Columbia Records producer Paul Myers recalls: "[Glenn] once privately admitted to me that one of the reasons for his decision to quit the concert stage was that he was tired of being regarded as a 'freak show.' He felt that too many members of the public came to see him rather than hear him and since his well-known mannerisms were unconscious, he could not change them" (Bergman 1999, 48).

Freak

Gould's "enfreakment" (Hevey 1992, 53) raises issues Rosemarie Garland-Thomson refers to variously as "spectacles of otherness," "discomforting dissonance," "exceptionality [seen] as anomaly," and ultimately as a "cultural contaminant" (Garland-Thomson 1997: 8, 12, 17, 33). She continues, "The extraordinary body [or individual] is nonconformity incarnate," with the "prototypical disabled figure [or eccentric] … often function[ing] as a lightning rod for the pity, fear, discomfort, guilt, or sense of normalcy of the reader [or audience member]" (ibid.: 44, 15).

When concert-goers snickered at Gould or journalists mocked him or conductors belittled his efforts,[3] they were demonstrating their inability to see beyond, let alone excuse or ignore, his behaviors. Expressed differently, critical response to Gould was "engulfed" by the stigmatic traits of his disability (ibid., 11). That engulfment is apparent in the caricature shown as Figure 9.1, which emphasizes Gould's unusual posture at the piano and his unkempt personal appearance.

Seclusion

After he stopped concertizing, Gould devoted the rest of his life to recording, writing, radio and television broadcasting, and films, none of which required public appearances. He also lived an increasingly hermitic existence, eventually communicating with all but a very few close colleagues strictly by telephone.

Even his withdrawal into "monastic seclusion" (Bester 1964, 156) was criticized. When he predictably skipped a reception to celebrate the launching of the film *Glenn Gould's Toronto* fifteen years after his last concert, he was castigated: "Gould may well be one of the world's greatest interpreters of Bach, yet he has always struck me as a particularly pretentious recluse, cursed with intellectual snobbery. Failing to show at last week's party in his honor at City Hall seemed just another example of the Greta Garbo syndrome being used as an excuse for poor manners" (Pennington 1979).

To date, Glenn Gould is the only "classical" musician to have relied exclusively on electronic and print media for a substantial portion of his career. In his biography of Gould, psychiatrist Peter Ostwald notes: "Glenn Gould gathers about him many timeless questions on that rare and astonishing phenomenon called genius" (Ostwald 1997, 14). Oliver Sacks, a much-published chronicler of unusual neurological disorders, expands on that comment, describing Gould as having "a transcendent artistic conscience and sensibility ... an immensely complex personality, wounded, constricted, damaged in some ways, but hugely creative and rich and wonderful in others" (Sacks 1998, 8). This is a vastly different picture of the pianist from the facile, petulant portraits painted by members of the popular press during his lifetime.

In what ways was Gould "wounded, constricted, [and] damaged?" Ostwald suggests that "some of the behavior he manifested later in childhood and during his adolescence ... does resemble a condition called Asperger Disease, which is a variant of autism" (Ostwald 1997, 42). Ill with cancer when he wrote the book and, in fact, deceased before it was published, Ostwald devoted only a few lines to the subject of autism, and proposed no other theories to explain Gould's many idiosyncrasies.

Ostwald's reference to autism paralleled suspicions I had entertained since performing and recording with Gould myself in 1982, but, not being a medical doctor and lacking expert validation for such a hypothesis, I had not followed up. Intrigued by the mention of Asperger's Syndrome (AS), I began to mine the ever-expanding Gould literature, the numerous published and broadcast interviews given by the pianist and people who worked with him, the many radio, television, and film productions he participated in, and his voluminous archival papers (which were under my care at the National Library of Canada 1988–2002) to discover whether the anecdotal evidence about his unusual behavior and lifestyle as an *adult* might support a posthumous determination of autism.

The notion is not universally accepted. Kevin Bazzana speaks for the doubters when he insists in his Gould biography, "So far I have not been persuaded that such a diagnosis [autism] really fits the biographical facts or is necessary for making sense of Gould" (Bazzana 2003, 5). Moreover, there are at least two other theories about him.

A Jungian psychologist, Lynne Walter, has diagnosed Gould's "obsessional, schizoid, and narcissistic qualities," as well as his self-professed "Puritanism," as a "Mixed Personality Disorder" (Walter 2000, 89). And in her "psychobiography" of Gould, a Freudian psychiatrist, Helen Mesaros, diagnoses Gould as having "recurrent depression overlapping with social phobia and with obsessive and

Figure 9.1 A typical caricature depicting Glenn Gould with long, uncombed hair, seated cross-legged on his low chair, wearing hat, scarf, fingerless gloves, and an oversized rumpled suit with the pocket stuffed with pill bottles. (Toronto Globe and Mail, February 13, 1970)

unrelenting hypochondria" (Mesaros 2000a, 88). Among the distinct neuroses and phobias she attributes to the pianist are the fear of germs, of flying, and of the dark, in addition to stage fright and separation anxiety. Mesaros has gone so far as to rule out any neurological basis for Gould's behavior, insisting "there isn't a chance that Gould had Asperger's disorder" (Mesaros 2000b, 24).

Who is right, or does any of this even matter? Some Gould fans find the dissection of their musical hero distasteful, but if his eccentric comportment, unusual lifestyle, and even aspects of his musical genius could be shown to originate in a single neurobiological condition, as opposed to being merely disparate manifestations of a high-strung, self-indulgent personality, would a reappraisal of his life and career not be in order?

Ostwald believes that "Gould's 'neurotic' mannerisms … were integral to his artistic personality. They were part of a behavioral style that he seemed to need for expressing what he felt about himself as a highly nervous creative artist, striving constantly to excel and to become the world's foremost pianist. He was special but not secure. He wanted people to notice his vulnerability as well as his genius" (Ostwald 1997, 102–03). But if Gould were autistic, there would likely be no volition involved. His "neurotic mannerisms" and "behavioral style" would be manifestations of his autism, possibly even *despite* any desire on his part to act otherwise.

Considering the advances made since the 1980s in the awareness and diagnosis of neurological disorders, and the growing body of knowledge about autism, genius, and savant gifts, the moment seems right to reconsider Glenn Gould's life to ensure that the historical record is accurate. This chapter examines through the lens of autism some of the anecdotal evidence about him that I have amassed.

Autism and Asperger's Syndrome

The word "autism" still conjures up images of youngsters lost in a world of their own, compulsively rocking back and forth, completely unable to communicate. This was the public face of autism until the 1980s, despite the fact that Hans Asperger, a Viennese pediatrician, first published his findings in 1944. To describe his young patients, he used the same term an American psychiatrist, Leo Kanner, had used in a paper published the previous year: "autistic" (from the Greek word for "self," *autos*). Whereas Kanner's subjects exemplified the extreme model above, Asperger's group had normal intelligence and language development, but showed deficiencies in social and communication skills, as well as some behaviors similar to those exhibited by Kanner's patients.

While Kanner's case studies describing what is now known as "classic autism" became widely known after World War II, Asperger's research on less profoundly affected children remained virtually unknown until the British psychiatrist Lorna Wing brought it to wider attention in 1981. Only since 1994 has AS been included in the American Psychiatric Association's

Diagnostic and Statistical Manual of Mental Disorders as part of a group of "pervasive developmental disorders" that share impairments in socialization, communication, and imagination.[4]

Today, it is generally conceded that "autism" applies to a broad spectrum of conditions ranging from the lower-functioning abilities of the most severe cases to the much greater capabilities of those with only "a dash of autism" (Frith 1991, 31–32). Although issues of taxonomy and diagnostic boundaries are still being debated, numerous experts agree that "Asperger's syndrome is part of the autistic continuum" (Wing 1991, 116). For the purposes of this chapter, AS will be considered a form of high-functioning autism (HFA).

Because the study of "disorders of empathy" (Gillberg 1992) like AS is still relatively new, with terms such as High Functioning Autism, Nonverbal Learning Disorder, Semantic-Pragmatic Disorder, and Asperger's Syndrome applied to similar sets of symptoms, and because the demarcation lines within the autistic spectrum cannot always be clearly determined, as of this writing there is still no universally accepted set of criteria for diagnosing AS or HFA.

Lorna Wing has published a table entitled "The Autistic Continuum," which codifies eight criteria she considers "essential for diagnosis" (Wing 1991, 112–13). Other experts, such as Christopher and Karina Gillberg (Gillberg 1991, 123) from Sweden, a Canadian group led by Peter Szatmari, (1989, 558) and Digby Tantam (1991, 149) in England, have each proposed smaller sets of criteria for the specific diagnosis of AS, most of which overlap with items in Wing's list. From these sources, as well as DSM-IV and the World Health Organization's *International Classification of Diseases* (ICD-10),[5] I have compiled a composite list of criteria for considering anecdotal evidence about possible manifestations of autism in Glenn Gould.

1. Impairment of Reciprocal Social Interaction
2. Non-Verbal Communication Problems
3. Unchanging Routines and Rituals
4. Fixations and Obsessive Interests
5. Speech and Language Idiosyncrasies
6. Abnormal Reactions to Sensory Stimuli
7. Motor Abnormalities
8. Mental Imaging and Feats of Memory
9. Savant Gifts
10. Late Onset and Chronic Health Problems

Caveat

The disability community challenges approaches that pathologize disability and channel it into medical categories. For example, Simi Linton argues that "the medicalized classification system and the use of diagnostic categories" create "distorted representations of disability" and "perpetuate stereotypes through the use of tools such as testing and diagnosis" (Linton 1998: 76, 4, 82). In Rosemarie Garland-Thomson's view, "pathologized difference is fraught with assumptions of deviance, patronizing relationships, and issues of control" (Garland-Thomson 1997, 37).

Alternatively, Garland-Thomson suggests "seeing disabled bodies [and, by extension, disabled people themselves] ... as extraordinary rather than abnormal," viewing them "as the entitled bearers of a fresh view of reality" (Garland-Thomson 1997: 137, 38). This echoes Hans Asperger, who noticed in his youthful subjects an "originality of thinking" and "a special clear-sightedness" that "can in favorable cases lead to exceptional achievements which others may never attain" (Asperger 1991: 54, 74). Indeed, most "Aspies" (a colloquial term used by the Asperger community itself) have normal-to-superior intelligence and some achieve distinction through their unique abilities to find new approaches to their fields of endeavor.

Temple Grandin, a well-known expert who is autistic herself, notes: "Family histories of high-functioning autistics often contain giftedness, anxiety or panic disorder, depression, food allergies, and learning disorders" (Grandin 1992, 113). A study conducted at the University of Iowa (Andreason 1987) showed that eighty percent of creative writers experience mood disorders, and a high percentage of artists, poets, and writers rely on medication to control their conditions (Grandin 1995, 178).

Another study at Iowa State University (Persson 1987) found "strong evidence that mathematical genius and giftedness are highly correlated with physical abnormalities" (Grandin 1995, 179). Grandin also notes the prevalence of left-handedness in people with high mathematical ability (ibid.). As it happens, Glenn Gould was left-handed and had a savant gift for math (discussed below). Grandin suggests: "It is likely that genius is an abnormality. If the genes that cause autism and other disorders such as manic-depression were eliminated, the world might be left to boring conformists with few creative ideas" (ibid., 178). As the ancient Greek and Roman writers, Aristotle and Seneca, recognized so long ago, genius and creativity seem to go hand in hand with madness and melancholy (Frith 1991, 32).

In light of the above, Garland-Thomson argues for "shift[ing] our conception of disability from pathology to identity" (Garland-Thomson 1997, 137), a proposition essentially seconded by Grandin: "If I could snap my fingers and be nonautistic, I would not—because then I wouldn't be me. Autism is part of who I am" (Grandin 1995, 16). To show that Glenn Gould was autistic, however, requires applying the diagnostic criteria listed above to aspects of his personality and behavior. The ultimate goal is to achieve deeper insights into his "complex personality" and "transcendent sensibility." With this understanding, we will proceed.

Was Glenn Gould Autistic?

Impairment of Reciprocal Social Interaction

Gould had problems fitting in at school, was often tutored privately, and never graduated from high school. "His fellow students certainly found him peculiar. ... [H]e took part in none of the usual pastimes of boys; I cannot remember a moment when he was not an outsider" (Fulford 1983, 61). Throughout his life, he formed few close friendships, most of which ended badly, and never married, though he had brief intimate relationships with several women.

He lacked personal warmth, was uncomfortable in groups, and had anger issues into adulthood. He occasionally displayed a lack of basic courtesies and even insensitive behavior. He was a hypochondriac who lived an unhealthy lifestyle ("he did zero exercise and he ate scrambled eggs every damn day") (Friedrich 1989, 318) and reacted poorly to criticism and contrary opinions. He was seen as naïve, "almost childlike in his personal life" (Bergman 1999, 48), lacking in common sense, and was considered a "supernarcissist" by one psychiatrist (Ostwald 1997, 197). He preferred solitude and the companionship of animals to human company, and was fascinated with machines and technology.

Gould was controlling, inflexible, pedantic, and, though wealthy, lived in austere surroundings, jokingly referring to himself as the "last Puritan" (Gould 1983, 91). His pedantry, extreme inflexibility, and "stubborn independence of mind" (Dutton 1983, 197) directly impacted significant aspects of his music-making, such as repertoire (most concertos and nineteenth-century works were anathema), piano sonority (he had a strange abhorrence of the sustaining pedal), tempos and articulations (played without regard for the composers' wishes), and pace: as appropriate as his insistence on "rhythmic propulsion" and "unyielding tempi" (Roberts 1999, 264) was for Bach, it was completely wrong-headed for Mozart. The anecdotal evidence shows that Gould had many of the impairments to reciprocal social interactions associated with high-functioning autism.

Non-Verbal Communication Problems

Besides neglecting his grooming and wardrobe, his surroundings and personal possessions were also in a permanent state of disarray. Onstage, he constantly rocked at the keyboard, mouthed the melodies and hummed or vocalized audibly, made conducting gestures when either hand was momentarily free, crossed his legs, "stomped" his feet, turned his body away from the audience, and generally exhibited atrocious posture and comportment. As we saw, such "exhibitionism" (Maley 1956b) outraged the critics and made audiences uncomfortable.

From boyhood on, he consistently overdressed, wearing overcoats, hats, scarves, gloves, and even galoshes in the heat of summer. He had difficulty making eye contact with people, and much preferred the telephone to face-to-face communication. He was unable to handle confrontation and emotional situations, and relied on handfuls of tranquilizers in his pockets to get him through the stressful occasions he could not avoid. He tended to interpret what people said too literally, and had difficulty appreciating many jokes, taking unusual offense at some. His own sense of humor was sophomoric and not always appreciated by others. This anecdotal evidence suggests that Gould had the same types of nonverbal communication problems as those experienced by autistics, most of them to an acute degree.

Unchanging Routines and Rituals

Gould's need for unchanging routines was considerable. He adapted poorly to the vagaries of travel and public concertizing, experiencing severe homesickness and developing real and imagined illnesses on tour, which led him to cancel many concerts. His diet, his choices of clothing colors and fabrics, even his record-listening and film-viewing habits were all extremely restricted and repetitious.

His need for repetitive rituals was also acute. "Gould had a repertoire of rituals and ritual objects in his concert-giving days. … They include[d] pre-performance soaking and massaging of the arms" in boiling hot water (Payzant 1978, 76). The hand-soaking became compulsive behavior required even for recording sessions that did not involve piano-playing. "The ritual objects included a small carpet under his feet, a bottle of Poland water at his side, numerous medications, and his battered, squeaky chair. This chair can be heard in most Gould recordings, and is as much a secondary trademark of his performance as his vocal noise" (ibid., 77).

Even after wear-and-tear had reduced the low folding chair his father had adapted for his use to a "rickety relic"—an empty wooden frame with legs and a back but no seat, held together by electrical tape, piano wire, and the glue and screws of many repairs—Gould stubbornly refused to abandon it. "He treated this chair … almost as a sacred object" (Ostwald 1997, 305). The anecdotal evidence clearly shows that Gould exhibited the "anxiously obsessive desire for the preservation of sameness" experienced by autistics (Wing 1991, 93).

Fixations and Obsessive Interests

Gould was a "workaholic" who focused obsessively on his musical projects to the exclusion of any real leisure pursuits. He toiled long hours, usually all through the night. Even as a child, "if Glenn ever did anything wrong that he had to be punished for, his mother would just shut the piano down and lock it. … That was far worse than any corporal punishment" (Tovell and Till 1985, 25). Focus and intensity were hallmarks of his performances: "On mike or on camera he work[ed] with an almost unimaginable intensity" (Payzant 1978, 48). "His concentration was relentless" (Littler 1967, 29).

He suffered chronic anxiety: "Gould was always tense, intense, and valium came to seem a necessity" (Friedrich 1989, 299). "[H]e couldn't sleep … his mind seemed to be always restless, probing" (ibid., 299). Gould admitted, "I have difficulty falling asleep unless I take a sedative" (Ostwald 1997, 28), which suggests that he was unable to relax due to hyperactivity or overwork.

The anecdotal evidence shows that Gould exhibited acute levels of the fixations, obsessive behaviors, anxiety, hyperactivity, and insomnia commonly associated with autism. He also compulsively collected meaningless sets of objects, including a large number of hotel and rental-car keys, another autistic trait.

Speech and Language Idiosyncrasies

"He's always been too old for his years and has few friends, none of them his own age …. In many ways Glenn was not like a child at all. Rather he was a wise little man" (Shenner 1956, 102). Gould and his pet topics dominated all conversations. From an early age, he had an uncontrollable compulsion to "lecture," exercised through his many record liner notes and magazine articles, his radio, TV, and film scripts, and his long, late-night telephone monologues. Although he was considered "one of the most articulate musical performers of the [twentieth] century" (Fulford 1983, 62), his language was stilted and his spelling poor.

His writings are also peppered with neologisms, for example, "contrapuntal radio," which involved overlapping the voices of documentary interviewees like the musical lines of a Bach partita, thereby creating "exchanges" and "scenes" between people who had, in fact, never met. He considered his novel manipulation of recorded voices every bit as creative as composing music. This is one example of the highly original approaches he brought to all his undertakings, an ability commonly found in high-functioning autistics.

Gould was also an inveterate mimic: "He was a gifted imitator of … facial expressions, speech mannerisms, foreign accents, and body movements …. [H]e loved to engage in playacting and make-believe with friends" (Ostwald 1997, 103).

The anecdotal evidence shows that Gould's speech and language idiosyncrasies were consistent with those associated with high-functioning autism, including monologues, "perseveration," verbal pyrotechnics, and coined words and expressions. He was also adept at mimicry, role-playing, and accents, additional talents commonly associated with high-functioning autism. Finally, as with Hans Asperger's so-called "little professors" (Asperger 1991), the teenaged Gould was later described, as "a wise little man" (Shenner 1956, 102) who had no friends his own age.

Abnormal Reactions to Sensory Stimuli

The oversized, loose-fitting clothes he always wore, the soft fabrics and foods he preferred, and his rigorous avoidance of physical contact with others, to the point of displaying a sign in his dressing room to discourage people from trying to shake his hand, would all be consistent with a general hypersensitivity to touch. That he also eschewed neckties, belts, and footwear (whenever possible), and left his collars and cuffs unbuttoned even when filming, likely indicates extreme discomfort wearing anything constricting, also consistent with touch hypersensitivity. His overdressing could be interpreted as an unusual intolerance to cold (rather than a phobia about germs, as has been suggested, though he had such a phobia), which would explain his craving for heat (the hand-soaking) and also fit the profile of hypersensitivity to touch. Of course, his over-dressing was an exaggerated response to the problem, as was soaking his hands in extremely hot water, but we saw already that compulsive behavior is typical of autism.

Considering his oft-stated unhappiness with sunny days, bright colors (especially primaries), and shiny surfaces, his insistence on darker colors (particularly gray and navy blue) for clothing and interior decorating, and the nocturnal schedule he followed from an early age, a hypersensitivity to light would seem a more logical conclusion than fear of the dark, especially as an adult.

Gould, who sweated profusely under his heavy clothing and hats, and reportedly bathed infrequently, appeared oblivious to his own body odor,[6] so it is likely that his sense of smell was either diminished or absent. He also had no sense of taste (Friedrich 1989, 295), another potential reason for the restricted bland diet he maintained.

There are several unusual aspects to Gould's auditory capabilities. He could differentiate between studio playbacks of Sony and Mitsubishi digital recorders, something none of the audio engineers could do (Friedrich 1989, 20). His hearing was so acute that he found ambient audience noises "a nuisance and a distraction" (Roberts 1999, 333), one possible reason behind his persistent vocalizing as he played. If he experienced the typical autistic inability to modulate auditory stimulation, he would have been unable to filter out audience noise without losing the sounds of his own piano-playing. In the context of his other sensory abnormalities, and considering that the concerts he gave unfailingly exhibited the highest standards of musical performance, this seems a more plausible explanation for his onstage discomfort than paralyzing stage fright.

When memorizing music, which he did by studying scores away from the piano, he purposely overwhelmed his hearing by placing a radio, record player, or television—or all three—right next to him with the volume turned up. Presumably the resulting bedlam blocked out other distractions, thereby helping him achieve the level of concentration he required for this activity. Note that they had to be loud, which may explain why coughing and rustling from audiences distracted him whereas a radio or TV blaring right next to him did not.

The above anecdotal evidence suggests overwhelmingly that Gould experienced acute abnormalities in his reactions to sensory stimuli, including hypersensitivity to touch, sight, and hearing, and hyposensitivity to smell and taste. Such abnormalities, which are consistent with those experienced by autistics, also provide a much more convincing explanation for Gould's unhappiness at school than does the notion of anxiety brought on by separation from his mother, which has been suggested. After all, he was away from her at the Royal Conservatory for much of each day over many years, but there is no anecdotal evidence whatsoever to suggest that he was ever unhappy there.

Motor Abnormalities

While exhibiting "almost miraculous" fine motor control at the piano (Ostwald 1997, 74), Gould had "atrocious" handwriting (Fulford 1983, 61), demonstrated a lesser ability to control gross motor functions such as catching balls and walking, and exhibited uncontrolled "stereotypies" such as body rocking and arm gestures. Body rocking, stereotypies gestures, an inelegant gait, and other gross motor idiosyncrasies exhibited by Gould are all autistic mannerisms. He was gauche and clumsy, his posture was "outlandish" from childhood (Fulford 1988, 37), and he was permanently stooped before the age of fifty. All of these characteristics are typical of AS.

Mental Imaging and Feats of Memory

Gould enjoyed total recall visually, aurally, and kinesthetically. He could create instant piano reductions of Wagner and Strauss operas from memory. He had a remarkable capacity for mental imaging, which he routinely used as a substitute for physical practice on the piano. Along with extraordinary kinesthetic (muscular) memory, however, he experienced an acute need for consistency of "tactile sensation" (e.g., piano action) (Ostwald 1997, 186–187) and key-width and -spacing (e.g., adjusting poorly to differences between piano, organ, and harpsichord keyboards) (Kazdin 1989, 130–31; Cott 1984, 48–49). This relates to our earlier discussion of Gould's adherence to unchanging routines.

Gould's feats of memory and visual thinking are consistent with the extraordinary acuity of short- and long-term memory and mental imaging routinely demonstrated by autistics. It is worth noting that visual thinkers are capable of absorbing large amounts of data quickly, but can experience "sequencing difficulties" (Sacks 1995, 259) that render them less adept at processing information involving multiple steps (for example, following directions to a friend's house or complicated plot twists in novels). Gould, who continually lost his way to his cousin's home in Oshawa, just east of Toronto, evidently had "sequencing" problems, and this aspect of autism may have played a critical role in shaping his repertoire preferences.

The music he excelled at was that of Bach and other polyphonists (such as Hindemith and Schoenberg), whose contrapuntal textures were ideal raw material for someone gifted at processing a lot of information rapidly (his ability to give each voice in a four-part fugue its own individual character was deemed "staggering" [Kaiser 1971, 148]). However, some of his most controversial recordings were of mainly homophonic music that evolved in a more episodic or sequential manner (for instance, the sonata and variation structures of Mozart and Beethoven), perhaps not ideal repertoire for someone who was less adept at sequential processing or for whom such material is simply not much of a challenge compared with the formidable task of controlling multiple lines of counterpoint simultaneously. He even disparaged the "autocratic" nature of the (treble-dominated) sonata as compared with the "mystic acquiescence" (equality of voices) in the fugue (Gould and Davis 1983: 282, 289).

Savant Gifts

Gould championed eighteenth- and twentieth-century contrapuntal repertoire yet he had such an intuitive grasp of musical style that, just as autistic savants quickly "know" the correct responses to complicated arithmetical problems or calendar calculations, he could, upon request, improvise brilliantly in the style of any composer named (Roberts 1999, 124; Friedrich 1989, 291; Ostwald 1997, 188; Berton 1997, 228–29). He perceived background patterns and structural features in compositions that other musicians did not always see (such as implied tempo relationships in the Brahms D-minor Piano Concerto [Maloney, 2007]), and built his interpretations around them.

Gould could perfectly sight-read at tempo any music put in front of him, including complex orchestral scores with instrumental lines in different transpositions. He could keep track of multiple conversations around him in restaurants as easily as he could play multiple musical lines simultaneously and give each its own special character. He could adroitly manage several sensory inputs and outputs simultaneously, and was amazingly adept at multitasking. He was also gifted in mathematics (he could perform instant mental calculations [Fulford 1983, 61; Bergman 1999, 63]), and excelled at finding or predicting trends in the stock market, making himself a small fortune in the process.[7] Such abilities are consistent with the savant gifts experienced by about ten percent of autistics (Grandin 1995, 46).

Late Onset and Chronic Health Problems

Gould's acute hypochondria notwithstanding, the anecdotal evidence shows that he had chronic health problems of the type that are now associated with autism, including allergies, recurrent upper-respiratory infections, perennial gastrointestinal complaints, anxiety, and insomnia. While the limited information available about his early childhood development does not appear to match the profile for classic autism, late-onset autism cannot automatically be ruled out in his case.

Conclusion

The critical mass of anecdotal evidence showing characteristics of autism in Glenn Gould, and the degree to which many of those traits were manifested in him, persuade me beyond a doubt that he was autistic. Far from deliberately flaunting odd behavior or courting controversy just to get attention and sell more recordings, Gould's many idiosyncrasies were the product of a disorder he probably did not even know existed, though he was surely very conscious of how different he was from so many others.

Autism is the solution to the perplexing riddle of Gould's existence, and is therefore arguably the fundamental story of his life. It provides a single logical answer to the "timeless questions" Peter Ostwald referred to, and leads us to a coherent understanding of both the man and the musician. Not only does it gather all his strange behavioral and lifestyle eccentricities into a unified *gestalt*, it also furnishes intriguing insights into important aspects of his music-making.

Ostwald suggests that Gould's "profound anxiety, schizoid insecurity, and personal eccentricity hampered enormously what might have been a far more productive career as a pianist, composer, conductor, and writer than it turned out to be" (Ostwald 1991, 23). But despite the social and sensory problems, the obsessions and compulsions, and the extreme inflexibility that impacted Gould's lifestyle and the perceptions of critics and concert-goers so profoundly, I would argue that his fine motor control, mental imaging, feats of memory, structural perceptions, omni-attentiveness, ability to think "outside the box," and other attributes contributed enormously to his many achievements.

Asperger's Syndrome gave him those gifts that in turn helped him forge a brilliant, multifaceted musical career. Without AS, he would not have been the distinctive musical genius we know as Glenn Gould. As with Temple Grandin, autism shaped Gould's worldview and molded his abilities. Asperger's Syndrome defined him as an autistic savant.

Notes

1. Bach, J.S., Goldberg Variations, Columbia LP No. ML5060.
2. All newspaper articles cited in this chapter can be found in Glenn Gould's archival papers in the music section of the Library and Archives Canada (LAC) in Ottawa. They were clipped from the papers in question many years ago, presumably by Gould's management. There are no page numbers on many of the clippings, and in a few cases the dates are also missing. A number of the newspapers have long since ceased publication and their archives are not available. In the bibliographic entries, "n.d." means "no date available" and "n.p." means "no page number available." Where possible, LAC archival document numbers have been given instead.
3. Leonard Bernstein disagreed so fundamentally with Gould's interpretation of the Brahms D-minor Piano Concerto that he issued a verbal disclaimer from the stage before their April 6, 1962 performance with the New York Philharmonic (see Bernstein 1983, 17–20).
4. "DSM-IV Criteria, Pervasive Developmental Disorders: 299.00 Autistic Disorder" *Diagnostic and Statistical Manual of Mental Disorders*, 4th edition (Washington, D.C.: American Psychiatric Association, 1994); available at www.autism-biomed.org/dsm-iv.htm, accessed December 4, 2005.
5. "Asperger's Disorder, European Description, F84.0 Childhood Autism [and] F84.5 Asperger's Syndrome," *International Classification of Diseases 10: Classification of Mental and Behavioural Disorders* (Geneva: World Health Organization, 1992), available at www. mentalhealth.com/icd/p22-ch07.html; accessed December 4, 2005.

6. Confirmed in personal communications between the author and several people who had also worked closely with Gould, including Peter Ostwald, Ezra Schabas, and Ray Roberts.
7. Despite his alleged "loose concern about money" (Kazdin 1989, 136), Gould left an estate worth about $750,000.

10
Using a Music-Theoretical Approach to Explore the Impact of Disability on Musical Development: A Case Study

ADAM OCKELFORD

Introduction

This chapter presents a preliminary exploration of how disability—in this case, congenital blindness—can impact on musical development using the music-theoretical approach to the cognition of musical structure set out by Ockelford (2002, 2004, 2005a, 2005b, 2006). The impact is shown to be twofold: direct, stemming from the effects of visual disability on auditory development—in particular the processing of musical sounds; and indirect, resulting from the attitudes of others to severe sensory loss and the confused expectations that can arise as a consequence. Hence, this chapter draws on both the medical and the social models of disability, aiming to fuse the two within an integrative paradigm as described, for example, by Seelman (2004).

A case-study method is adopted, in which a vocal improvisation by a four-and-a-half-year-old girl (called K here to protect her identity) with septo-optic dysplasia[1] that was previously videoed and transcribed (Ockelford et al. 2006), is analyzed in relation to two dimensions: (1) intrinsic coherence and expressivity; and (2) the influence of the contemporaneously improvised accompaniment. The identified implicative relationships connecting differing musical elements within and beyond K's improvisation offer a unique insight into her evolving musicality, provide evidence of how this may have been influenced by her congenital disability, and, it is suggested, may even serve as proxy measures of her social interaction in the context of music-making.

The findings bear upon a range of contemporary issues in music and disability studies, including the distinction between music education and therapy for children with disabilities (Ockelford 2000; Robertson 2000), the potential for exceptional musical development in the context of disability (Miller 1989; Treffert 2000; Ockelford and Pring 2005), and the significance of this exceptionality for a wider understanding of musical ability (Obler and Fein 1988). Moreover, it is anticipated that the new technique for analyzing improvised musical material with two participants or more will be of value in a range of therapeutic, educational, and music-analytical contexts.

Current Research into the Musicality of Children with Septo-Optic Dysplasia

An initial investigation into the musicality of children with septo-optic dysplasia was undertaken by Ockelford et al. (2006), who elicited the views of their parents and caregivers in the United Kingdom and the United States via a questionnaire. These accounts were contextualized through comparison with a further group of children, matched as far as possible by age and sex, with no known special educational needs. The findings of the study showed that, in the opinion of parents, blind children are significantly more likely than their fully sighted peers to have a particular interest in music and to find it important as a source of stimulation or comfort, for communication or for socialization or understanding or to mark out events in their daily routine. Moreover, it seems that they have a tendency to display exceptional musical abilities, including the possession of absolute pitch (AP)—the faculty of recognizing and reproducing notes in isolation from others. This capacity is extremely rare in Western populations as a whole, with a prevalence estimated at only 1 in 10,000 people (Takeuchi and Hulse 1993). Among those born with little or no sight, however, the position appears to be rather different. Welch (1988), for example, noted that twenty-two out of thirty-four blind children in special schools with which he came into contact had AP (65 percent), while Ockelford (1988) reported that nineteen out of fifty children (38 percent) in a London special school who were born blind or who had lost their sight shortly thereafter had unusually highly developed pitch-recognition abilities.[2]

With regard to those with septo-optic dysplasia, the findings of the 2006 survey are necessarily preliminary in nature, since they rely on indirect evidence of the children's musicality provided by others. The next step is to interrogate the musical production of some of these children directly, a research objective for which this chapter provides contributory evidence by providing an account and analysis of an interactive music session that K had with the author (hereafter AO).[3]

The Session with K

The session was originally intended to assess K's musical development and was triggered by her class teacher's observation that she particularly enjoyed singing and that, as far as the teacher was able to judge, her efforts appeared to be unusually advanced for a child of her age. It was known, too, that K had a small keyboard at home, which according to her parents kept her occupied for substantial periods of time even though she had never received any formal music instruction. What, then, were the scope and nature of her musical abilities and potential? And, more broadly, did K's musical development support the notion that some children with septo-optic dysplasia may display exceptional musicality?

The session began with AO suggesting that K might like to sing something, and she immediately set off unaccompanied with an up-tempo version of "Supercalifragilisticexpialidocious" from *Mary Poppins*. K's singing was characterized by a raucous enthusiasm. Despite the limitations of her vocal technique, which meant that her intonation was not always perfect, K's rendition had a secure tonal center (the key of D), which was established without a pitch reference. K evidently relished making music with someone else present, and she was happy to repeat the song with great gusto at an even faster tempo, this time with the piano in attendance.

Here, then, was a natural and uninhibited young performer who loved to make music and could communicate forcefully through sound. The fact that her rendition began recognizably in the key of D major[4] and remained in that key—notwithstanding the immaturity of her vocal production—indicated that K was very likely to have AP, lending support to previous findings that congenital blindness is a strong predictive factor in the development of absolute pitch perception, a positive musical corollary of this type of disability. In addition, K evinced a secure sense of rhythm that was flexible enough to accommodate different tempi. However, a number of issues remained to be resolved. For example, how effectively was K able to process harmony? Was she able to create her own music? And if so, at what level was she capable of assimilating and developing given material and fashioning this into a recognizable structure within a coherent stylistic framework? As her disability appeared to have had an impact on her perception of pitch, did its influence also extend to these other areas of musical functioning, directly or indirectly—for example, through constraints generated by the attitudes and expectations of others? And if so, could steps be taken to ensure that such barriers did not impede her future progress?

AO first sought to address these questions by suggesting that K make up a new song—perhaps about her pet dogs, Jack and Elisha.[5] Four chords—F major, D minor, G minor ninth, and C major—were presented on the piano with a gentle swing rhythm, and a simple vocal melody was added to set the scene. After only two iterations of the sequence, K took the lead and, against the continuing four-chord ostinato, made up a song that lasted for one and one-half minutes (see Figure 10.1).

This improvisatory approach, which was intended to be child led, arguably owed more to the thinking that typically underlies music therapy than that usually encountered in music education (see, e.g., Bruscia 1987, 1989). However, as Ockelford (2000) observes, music therapy and music education sessions for children with disabilities may well overlap a good deal in terms of approach and content, with the aims and objectives of the teacher or therapist accounting for the main differences between the two. Hence, although the session under discussion here took place within an educational context, the musical analyses that follow later in this chapter offer insights of potential interest to therapists too.

As the accompanist, AO's initial impression of this song was of an unfolding extemporization of startling moment-to-moment expressivity within a continuously evolving but coherent musical structure. Behind it, evidently, lay an active musical mind capable of creating new material intuitively, quickly, and confidently within a familiar style. Beyond these contemporaneous reactions, however, the taped record of the session made it possible to transcribe and to analyze K's efforts systematically in relation to a number of criteria, which enabled aspects of her musical development to be profiled and the possible impact of her disability on these to be gauged. The criteria were developed

Figure 10.1 K's improvisation on "I Have a Dog."

Figure 10.1 *Continued*

from the author's theory of how music intuitively makes sense and can convey meaning (Ockelford, 2005a, 2005b). An introduction to this zygonic theory follows.

Zygonic Theory: An Introduction

According to zygonic theory, musical coherence is based on a sense of derivation, whereby a given aspect of musical sound—a particular pitch, harmony, tonality, inter-onset interval, duration, or meter, for example—is felt to imitate another, something that typically occurs nonconsciously. Each of these features has the potential to induce a range of emotional responses, and the sense of derivation that exists between them enables a kind of abstract aesthetic narrative to be built up in the course of listening to a piece, rather like hearing a story devoid of concrete meaning.[6]

The cognition of derivation between musical elements is predicated on the presence of interperspective relationships[7]—cognitive constructs through which, it is hypothesized, percepts may be compared (cf. Krumhansl 1990, 3). Interperspective relationships may be regarded as forms of "link schemata" (Lakoff 1987, 283), which inhabit the mental space pertaining to music processing (Fauconnier 1994).[8] Such relationships potentially exist between any features of musical events. In most circumstances they are formulated unthinkingly, passing listeners by as a series of qualitative experiences. However, through metacognition, interperspective relationships may be captured conceptually and assigned values, commonly expressible as a difference or ratio.

Figure 10.2 shows interperspective relationships symbolized by an arrow with the letter I superimposed. Superscripts indicate the features concerned, each represented by its initial letter (P, pitch; O, onset). Relationships can be of different levels, with primary relationships potentially linking percepts directly, secondary relationships connecting primaries, and tertiary relationships comparing secondaries (Ockelford 2002). The level of a relationship is indicated by the appropriate subscript (here, 1 in each case). The values of the pitch relationships, shown near the arrowheads as −m3, have two components: polarity, which here is negative, showing that the intervals are descending; and magnitude, a minor third. Similarly, the values of the relationships of onset indicate both temporal polarity and magnitude, a dotted eighth note.[9]

Interperspective relationships through which imitation is cognized are deemed to be of a special type, termed *zygonic* (Ockelford 1991, 140–160).[10] Zygonic relationships, or *zygons*, are depicted using the letter Z. In Fig. 10.2, the primary zygonic relationship of duration, D, reflects the apparent derivation of the note-length used for the word "as" from that pertaining to the preceding "Jack." The secondary zygons of pitch and onset, indicated through the subscripts 2, show imitation at a more abstract, or intervallic, level. Observe the use of full arrowheads, which signify relationships between values that are the

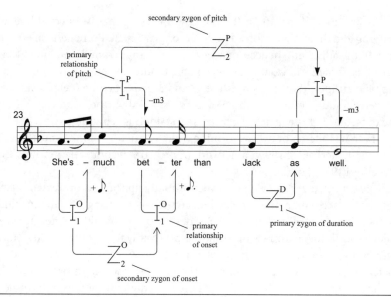

Figure 10.2 Zygonic analysis of mm. 23–24.

same. Half arrowheads are indicative of difference and are used in a zygonic context to show approximate imitation.[11]

This theoretical framework is used to analyze K's improvisation in relation to the two principal sources of material on which she was potentially able to draw: (1) the unfolding melody, as initiated by AO and subsequently taken up by K; and (2) the piano accompaniment provided by AO. The light these analyses shed on the relationship between K's musical abilities and her disability are considered in the course of the discussions that follow.

Analysis of K's Song

Internal Coherence and Expressivity

With regard to the improvised song melody, the first question to be addressed concerns its cogency: Does it make musical sense—and, if so, through what structural means? Zygonic theory holds that musical coherence requires at least one salient feature from each event to derive from another or others.[12] A full zygonic analysis of K's song, which is too extensive to be reproduced here,[13] shows that this is indeed the case, confirming the informal observation that successive notes do not pass by as isolated entities but sound logically connected to each other through similarities in pitch or rhythm that bind them together in the mind to form short melodic chunks. As is shown here, these chunks are themselves linked through various forms of sameness and similarity. Here, an analysis of K's first phrase suffices to illustrate the principles involved (see also Figure 10.2).

K starts by picking up on the E above middle C that AO's vocal line left hanging and that was reinforced in the accompaniment. From here, she moves back to the adjacent F in accordance with the change from dominant to tonic harmony, which she would have been able to anticipate from the same harmonic transition that spans measures 2 and 3. This opening melodic interval is a retrograde form of the ending of AO's last vocal phrase—showing K from the outset taking the material offered and stamping her authority on it. K's F proves to be the first of twelve, forming a pitch structure of the simplest kind, potentially derived through a network of primary zygonic relationships (see Ockelford 1993, 180 ff.).

This repeated series of notes, which initially appears to overextend itself against the accompanying ostinato harmonies—conflicting with the concluding dominant chord in the second half of measure 6—could be interpreted as a device for K to buy time while deciding which way to take the melody. However, analysis shows that the series of Fs grows organically from the preceding material, deriving from two sources: the pitches echo the initial repetitions of the melody, and the rhythm adopts the dotted-eighth-note–sixteenth-note pattern first heard in the second half of measure 2. Hence, K took two distinct elements from the opening phrases of the melody—supplied by AO—and fused them in her continuation, a form of musical development typical of many styles that simultaneously offers coherence and variety. K's forceful delivery of the repeated pitches adds to the sense that she is asserting her place in the partnership about to unfold: both musically and socially, building a foundation for the action to come.

This kicks off immediately: In the very next phrase (measure 7), there is a sense of release as K's melody springs up from the constraints of the opening repetitions using a new syncopated rhythm. Despite the feeling of things moving off in a new direction, both pitch and rhythm again derive logically from what has gone before: The dotted motive is once more pressed into service, and two similar ascending melodic intervals—from F to A and from A to C—were deployed to straddle the two phrases. This method of connecting chunks—through secondary zygonic relationships rather like using a musical ladder to link different ideas—is one K adopts a number of times—for example, between measures 16–17 and 22–23 (see Figure 10.3). Her other favored approach is to use a primary zygonic relationship—taking a pitch at or near the end of a phrase and using it to start the next: See, for example, the connections between phrases in measures 8, 18–19, and 20.

These two ways of connecting musical chunks are characteristic of many musical styles (Ockelford 2004). However, there is another way of linking segments: through the repetition, or variation, of chunks as a whole, arguably the most widespread of all music-structural techniques yet one K does not use. The nearest she gets to it is in measures 17–24, when a pattern of three descending pitches is successively transposed and varied, mirroring and enhancing the

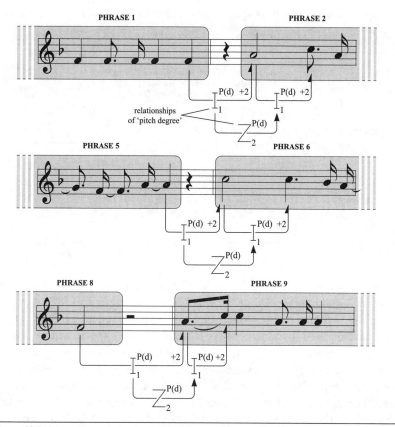

Figure 10.3 Connecting melodic chunks through secondary zygonic relationships.

rhetorical form of the verbal narrative at this point: "one for her biscuits, one for her water, and one for her meat" (see Figure 10.4). Exact transposition of the intervallic descent, which would have required a B-flat at the beginning of measure 19, appears to have been overwhelmed by K's desire for a convincing concord at this juncture, with the emphasis on the repeated word *one*. Thus, K demonstrates the intuitive ability to weigh up and to manage conflicting musical—and extramusical—demands and, in the midst of her improvisation, the capacity to select the option best suited to her expressive intentions.

Why is the commonplace method of repeating or varying chunks as a whole not utilized more? It may be a consequence of the improvised nature of the exercise that K was undertaking, in which building a coherent structure depended on remembering material that had just been made up at the same time as continuing with the creative process—which may well have interfered with the memories that had recently been formed. By intuitively adopting the approach of having each successive chunk pick up where the previous one left off, K made fewer demands on her memory and gave herself greater freedom

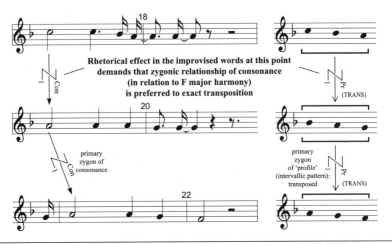

Figure 10.4 Linking melodic segments through the variation of chunks as a whole.

to follow her musical or verbal whim of the moment. However, the lack of motivic imitation may also be attributable to K's inexperience of interacting with other musicians. One could envisage that a skilled educator working with a precocious child like K would have focused on providing her with engaging musical experiences, sharing material in extemporized sessions of musical give and take—conversations in sound—in which ideas would be echoed back and forth between teacher and pupil, tacitly involving the imitation, variation, and transformation of motives and themes. Yet in common with all thirty-two children with septo-optic dysplasia in Ockelford et al. (2006), K had never had specialist music lessons. Ockelford, Welch, and Pring (2005) hypothesize that the lack of formal musical intervention in the lives of these young people may be accounted for by the unduly low expectations of their musical learning and achievement that their disability engenders in those around them. If this is true, then it could be argued that attitudes to K's disability had had a negative impact on aspects of her musical development up to this point.

A corollary of K's free-flowing approach in her improvisation is that there is no particular pattern to the links between chunks in her song: Though the moment-to-moment connections on the musical surface are convincing enough, there is no hierarchical arrangement of the segments—no deeper structural repetition or development. The climax, which occurs at the end of the improvisation, is signaled by a change of register and effected through a high, sustained tonic F (sung *fortissimo*) rather than occurring through a feeling of structural inevitability. Again, this may in part be due to her lack of experience in making music with others and so ultimately be attributable to attitudes to her disability. Nonetheless, K's song shows that she had grasped some of the key principles of how music—in the Western tonal vernacular of the early twenty-first century—is structured and that she could use these to create new tunes that would make sense to listeners. And the remarkable thing is that K developed this capacity with no intervention on the part of others—purely through being exposed to a range of music and through expressing herself by singing. Just as the great majority of people absorb the syntactical rules of their native language without conscious effort—simply by listening and trying things out for themselves—thereby acquiring the ability to create original but coherent and comprehensible linguistic utterances, so K evidently had done the same in the domain of music. Her intuitive awareness of certain elements of musical syntax within familiar styles enabled her to formulate new, stylistically authentic musical statements. Of course, this is not, in principle, exceptional; almost all young children make up songs that are coherent just by absorbing, copying, and extending what they hear (see, e.g., Moog 1976, 128–33; Hargreaves 1985, 60 ff.). It is the level of her achievement that, experience suggests, is so unusual; here we must confront the irony that lies at the heart of the relationship between her disability and her exceptional musical abilities. It is difficult to avoid the conclusion that K's disability was both directly responsible for her precocious aural, and subsequently musical, development and indirectly accounted for the fact that this potential had not been recognized, celebrated, challenged, or extended and, indeed, was in danger of being dissipated through neglect.[14]

Further evidence pertaining to these issues comes through considering the way in which the structural techniques K employed interacted with the accompaniment that was provided, and it is to this interaction that we next turn our attention.

Influence of the Accompaniment

The theory that musical structure stems from the derivation of material through imitation was used to gauge the impact of the accompaniment on K's creative efforts by assessing each note[15] in relation to its probable musical sources, which could be found either in AO's initial melodic thread (measures 1–4), the extemporized piano melody (equivalent to the uppermost RH notes), the LH ostinato bass, or K's vocal line.[16] For every note, up to ten zygonic relationships[17] were considered in relation to pitch, melodic interval, harmonic context, and rhythm. These were weighted as follows: Pitch scored 2 for exact repetition and 1 for the transfer of pitch class to a different octave; melodic interval scored 2 for identity, 1.5 for approximate imitation, and 1 for inversion or retrogression; harmonic context scored 2 for exact repetition, 1.5 for variation, 1 for transposition, and 0.5 for transposed variation; and rhythm scored 4 for identity, 3 for approximate derivation (including a change of relative location within the relevant metrical level), 2 for repetition of duration or inter-onset interval only, and 1 where the sole connection was the variation of duration or inter-onset interval. Since each aspect of every note could be considered to be derived from up to ten others, further weighting was necessary whereby each raw score of derivation strength was multiplied by a factor based on the theorized salience of the zygonic relationship concerned such that the sum of the factors pertaining to the given feature of a particular note was invariably 1.

For example, K's seventh pitch, labeled K7 in Figure 10.1, could be considered to derive from K6, K5, K4, AM13, K3, K2, AV12, AM11, AV11, and AM10—the order determined by their temporal adjacency to K7.[18] The pragmatic decision was made to separate each of the factors used to moderate the raw scores pertaining to a series such as this by a common difference (implying a linear decrease in the strength of their zygonic influence). In this case, with ten factors required, the values used to modify the raw derivation scores were 0.182, 0.164, 0.145, 0.127, 0.109, 0.091, 0.073, 0.055, 0.036, and 0.018, respectively. The result of applying these proportions to the raw scores was a series of derivation indices.

The indices for each feature were summed separately in relation to the material improvised by AO and K. The total potential derivation index for each note ranged between 0 and 10 from either of the two sources (AO or K). With regard to K7, the subtotals pertaining to AO- and K-derived material are as follows: Pitch has a derivation index of 0.618 from AO and 1.382 from K; melodic interval, 0.334 from AO and 1.666 from K; harmonic context, 1.335 from AO and 0.666 from K; and rhythm, 1.620 from AO and 2.136 from K. This yields a total derivation index of 3.907 from AO's material and 5.850 from K's. Given the maximum total derivation index of ten, the sum of these two figures (9.757) leaves a residue of 0.243, reflecting aspects of K7 that cannot be accounted for through derivation from other material in the song. This, then, is a measure of the originality of the event in question (K7) in relation to the improvisation up to that point.[19]

The usefulness of these figures in interpreting the relationship between AO's and K's contributions lies principally in the ratios between them—taken either as averages over a given period or in terms of event-by-event patterns of variation. For example, seventy percent of AO's production was generated from other of his own material, with a little under 13 percent deriving from K's input. In contrast, only 50 percent or so of K's melody is attributable to the emulation of her own efforts, with approximately 36 percent based on AO's introductory vocal melody and piano accompaniment. This is powerful evidence that, although improvising her own structurally and expressively coherent melody, K was able to attend to the piano accompaniment and—apparently without conscious effort—to take on board a range of presented musical ideas. Moreover, within the musical interaction that occurred, AO's influence on K was almost three times greater than K's impact on AO—a somewhat sobering statistic for a music educator who at the time felt he was providing a responsive foil for K's efforts. In fact, zygonic analysis indicates that the flow of musical ideas was largely from teacher to pupil. The derivation indices also enable us to track how the influence of one performer on another varied over time. For example, during K's first phrase (notes K1–K13), the derivation index from AO's material falls from 9.476 to 0.927, whose trend closely matches a linear descent ($R^2 = 0.8155$)—the principal exceptions being K9 and K10, where K introduces a rhythmic pattern similar to one used in AO's introduction (see Figure 10.5). This decline in K's use of AO's material through the phrase reflects K's increasing self-assertion (noted previously) and, as one would expect, is matched inversely by an increasing use of her own improvisation to generate further ideas.

Subsequent phrases show different derivational patterns that cannot be reported in detail here. However, the mean derivation indices pertaining to phrases are used to give an overview of trends at a deeper structural level. These show K drawing significantly on AO's material in her first phrase, less so in the second, and more again in the third and the fourth. Subsequently, there is a gradual decrease in AO's impact over phrases five to nine—the central part of K's improvisation with the descending sequence at its heart—during which K's efforts become ever more self-sufficient. In contrast, AO's influence is felt more strongly in K's tenth phrase, whose lack of verbal coherence suggests that K may have been running out of steam. Indeed, after rallying briefly in the eleventh phrase, K's creative flow almost completely dries up at the beginning of the twelfth, and she draws heavily on material in the accompaniment to sustain her vocal line, although in the concluding notes she finally wrests back the initiative. K's global pattern of derivation from AO, invariably lower than AO's derivation from K, is inversely related to it with a striking

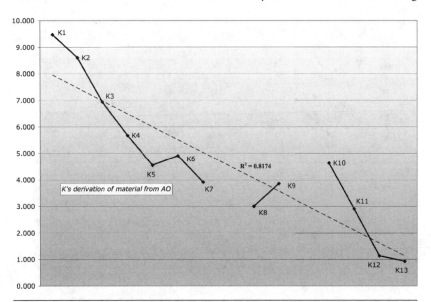

Figure 10.5 The influence of the accompaniment: the derivation of material through imitation.

consistency (82 percent). That is to say, during the improvisation as K chose to rely less on AO for material, AO tended to rely more on K and vice versa—perhaps through an intuitive desire on the part of one performer or both to ensure coherence in the improvised texture as a whole (see Figure 10.6).

Analyzing indices of originality reveals further issues of structural significance. For example, in K's events that had an originality index ≥ 0.25 (i.e., when a quarter or more of the material was derived other than from the improvisation (of which there are thirteen such events: K12, K14, K15, K17, K27, K28, K35, K49, K91, K92, K94, K103, and K104), her originality is most frequently expressed in the domain of harmonic context (in 62 percent of cases). On some occasions, this appears to be the result of K's melodic intent overriding the harmony provided (e.g., in the second half of measure 6 and at the end of measure 10), although her continuations make sense of these things in retrospect: As has already been observed, the repeated Fs in measure 6 serve as a springboard for the next phrase, whereas the F at the end of measure 10 is sustained to reach over into the F major harmony that starts the next sequence. However, at other times, rather than having arisen as a byproduct of melodic goals, K's harmonic originality seems to have been intrinsically motivated; see, for example, K27, where K's A-flat produces an astringent minor ninth chord on the supertonic bass provided. A further measure of K's harmonic creativity can be gleaned from the number of ways in which she melodizes a given harmony within the ostinato pattern. For example, K overlays the second chord in the sequence (which in AO's original version comprises a simple D minor harmony—D, F, A) at different times in the course of her

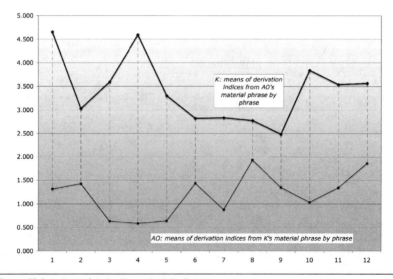

Figure 10.6 Indices of derivation and originality.

improvisation with D, F, G, A, B-flat, and C, using a range of melodic devices, described below.[20]

Despite the substantial impact of AO's improvisation on K's melody, the derivation is largely at a general level, whereby each feature almost invariably stems from a number of sources and the relationships concerned rarely have the salience to stand out from their coherence-creating neighbors and to acquire specific structural significance. There are exceptions, however, which function either through a series of relationships working in parallel or by prominent percepts being repeated in temporal apposition. For example, the syncopated rhythm first heard in the piano in measure 12 reappears in the vocal melody in measure 15—and then again in the piano in measure 24[21]—whereas from measure 30, K repeatedly derived A-flats and Fs from the accompaniment.

These findings reinforce the picture of K built up through the analysis of her improvised vocal line as an intuitive and unusually talented young musician but of one whose profile of musical development was uneven and idiosyncratic. Although she picked up very quickly on the ostinato AO provided—after only two iterations—and was able to improvise coherently and stylistically appropriately over its continuation, there was little if any direct emulation of the material provided, yet this is probably the most straightforward means of ensuring coherence in improvising with other musicians. Nor was there any direct borrowing from other pieces, although this technique is encountered widely in traditional jazz (see, e.g., Berliner 1994, 103 ff.).[22] Again, it seems reasonable to assert that this anomaly may partly be attributable to the contradictory impact of K's disability on her musicality, affecting it at once both positively and negatively.

Conclusion

In summary, an analysis was presented of a vocal melody that had been improvised against an ostinato piano accompaniment by a young girl with septo-optic dysplasia. The analysis employed a new music-theoretical technique rooted in cognitive science. The findings were used to gauge the impact of her disability on her musical development. Conclusions can be drawn in three main areas.

First, in relation to K's musical development, it is evident that within a familiar style she can grasp a repeating pattern of harmonies and create material that not only conforms to what is provided but that develops and extends it structurally and expressively. This shows exceptional musical development and reinforces the findings of previous research suggesting that congenital blindness may be a major contributory factor in such exceptionality. However, there is a lack of thematic correspondence between voice and accompaniment, certain common approaches to the logical connection of material are not used, and there is a concomitant absence of a deeper musical structure. These lacunae, it is argued, could well result from K's lack of music education, her early years notwithstanding. Indeed, a key finding of Ockelford et al. (2006) is that early intervention is essential, particularly for children who show signs of exceptional musical ability. It is suggested that the self-same disability that engendered K's precocious development may also have elicited unduly low expectations of her musical potential and may have deterred those around her from seeking appropriate tuition. Hence, although K has evidently achieved a great deal by dint of her own efforts, it is also clear that much more remains to be done and that she would benefit from working with a teacher willing to engage with her musical interests and with the capacity to work flexibly in extending her musical horizons. Thus, through appropriate support the barriers that her disability may have erected in the minds of others would be removed, and her musicality could continue to develop untrammeled.

Second, although it has been asserted that K's improvisation is indicative of exceptional musical ability, no comparative data are currently available to indicate objectively just how typical or unusual her musical development is in relation to what one might reasonably expect from a child of her age, with or without a visual disability. This is an area that should be tackled as a matter of urgency: The approach adopted in this chapter may offer one way forward; see below. Meantime, this study offers direct musical evidence in support of the hypothesis that exceptional musical ability may well be unusually prevalent in young children with septo-optic dysplasia (Ockelford 2003; Pring and Ockelford 2005) and more widely among youngsters with little or no vision (Miller and Ockelford 2005; Ockelford et al. 2006; Ockelford, Welch, and Pring 2005)—irrespective of other disabilities they may have (Ockelford 1998). The analysis undertaken here also supports the notion that the essential elements of advanced musical understanding, many of which are typically conceptualized and codified in the process of music education, can develop and thrive at a purely intuitive level (Ockelford and Pring 2005, 2007).[23] Thus, one enduring message for researchers and teachers alike is the capacity of the mind to absorb and intuitively utilize sophisticated musical strategies with no formal tuition at all. However, a second and equally important point is that if children—particularly those with complex mixtures of ability and disability—are not to be left music-developmentally stranded, then timely and expert intervention is essential.

Third, it appears that the zygonic approach may be of value in interrogating certain aspects of the ebb and flow of musical interaction involving two performers or more. Although labor-intensive at this stage, key elements in this type of analysis could be automated, leaving the researcher to check and to refine the data gathered using an appropriate computer program. The techniques set out in this chapter could be used more widely to support the assessment of certain aspects of children's music-making, informing the aggregation of a bank of comparative data that would enable individual efforts to be contextualized. This would benefit music therapists and educators seeking to evaluate the effect and effectiveness of their interactions with children with disabilities and other special needs. Indeed, the different and sometimes apparently conflicting aims of music teachers and therapists could be clarified and even resolved through adopting the common musical metalanguage that zygonic theory offers. Moreover, as music-analytical techniques such as those used here are further developed, it is interesting to postulate the extent to which the scrutiny of the purely musical elements of an improvisation with two people or more may shed light on aspects of broader personality and human relationships—including the capacity and willingness for imitation, resistance to change, and resilience—something of enormous potential value to both therapists and educators. Finally, and more broadly, the approach set out here may support the analysis of improvised forms in a range of genres, including jazz.

Notes

1. Septo-optic dysplasia is a rare condition that occurs in approximately 1 in 16,000 children. It is defined as a combination of optic nerve hypoplasia (i.e., absent or small optic nerves), pituitary abnormalities, and the absence of the septum pellucidum or corpus callosum—without which communication between areas of the mid-brain, such as the transfer of sensory information, is hampered. Among the likely effects of septo-optic dysplasia are visual impairment, hormonal problems, delayed development, behavioral difficulties, and obesity. The type and range of symptoms can vary from mild to very severe (Mehta and Dattani 2004). K is totally blind and does not have delayed development.
2. For comparison, Hamilton, Pascual-Leone, and Schlaug (2004) reported that 57 percent of blind musicians within a sample of twenty-one had AP.
3. At the time, I was working as a specialist music teacher in a school for visually impaired children in south London.
4. K was unaware of this or any other formal musical concepts or specialized terminology.
5. These names have been changed in the interest of preserving K's anonymity.
6. It is important to acknowledge that, in the case of K's song, words were present too, and although these are not the main focus of the discussion here, relevant points are noted in the context of the identified musical issues.
7. *Interperspective* is a term coined by Ockelford (1991) to mean between perspects—that is, perceived aspects—of music; it is used in contradistinction to the term *parameter*, which is reserved solely to refer to the physical attributes of sound. Hence, the perspect *pitch*, for example, most closely corresponds to the parameter *frequency*, though the connection between the two is far from straightforward (cf. Meyer 1967, 246).
8. For a discussion of interperspective relationships in the context of David Lewin's mathematically based theory of musical intervals and transformations, see Ockelford (2005a).
9. Observe that arrowheads may be open or filled—the former showing a link between single values and the latter indicating a compound connection within or between constants, typically values extended in time—implying a network of relationships that are the same. For a fuller explanation, see Ockelford (1999).
10. From the Greek term *zygon* meaning yoke, implying a union of two similar things.
11. Given the interdisciplinary nature of this chapter, it is particularly important to be clear about the status of zygonic relationships. They are hypothetical constructs intended to represent aspects of the typically subconscious cognitive processing that can be assumed to occur when we attend to, create, or imagine music—a supposition suggested by the structural regularities of pieces, which, as Bernstein (1976, 169) asserted, offer "a striking model of the human brain in action and as such, a model of how we think." Of course, the notion of a zygonic relationship can at best offer only a much-simplified version of certain cognitive events that may be stimulated by participation in musical activity. However, even though simplification is necessary to make headway in theoretical terms, it is important to bear in mind that the single concept of a zygon bequeaths a substantial perceptual

legacy with many possible manifestations not only potentially linking individual pitches, timbres, dynamics, durations, and inter-onset intervals but also prospectively existing between tonal regions, textures, processes, and forms that are the same; over different periods of perceived time; functioning reactively or proactively; and within the same and between different pieces, performances, and hearings. Given this variety, there is, of course, no suggestion that the one concept represents only a single aspect of cognitive processing. Hence, empirical evidence in support of the theory is likely to be drawn from a diversity of sources. Currently, for example, one can point to experiments in auditory processing, such as the continuity illusion summarized in Bregman (1990, 344 ff.) and work on expectation in a musical context, particularly that involving the perceptual restoration of omitted or obscured notes (for instance, DeWitt and Samuel 1990), to support the presence of proactive zygonic-type processes (Ockelford 1999, 123; 2006). General support exists for the theory too in the wide range of music-theoretical and analytical sources in which the fundamental importance of repetition in music is acknowledged. These are itemized in Ockelford (1999). Similar acknowledgments are made by Borthwick (1995) as a background to the exposition of his metatheoretical framework to which the notions of identity and nonidentity are central. Perhaps most pertinent of these to zygonic theory is Cone's (1987, 237) assertion made in relation to the derivation of musical material that "y is derived from x (y ← x), or, to use the active voice, x generates y (x → y), if y resembles x and y follows x. By 'resembles,' I mean 'sounds like.'"

12. That is not to say that to be coherent, K's improvisation should consist only of repetition. Through perceptual binding—the cognitive glue through which the different properties of an object cohere in the mind to form the notion of a single thing (see, e.g., Snyder 2000, 7)—and *Gestalt* perception—through which discrete events are reckoned to form larger wholes (see, e.g., Deutsch 1999)—sounds, or groups of sounds, may differ from each other in some respects while being the same in others. Hence, as is shown following, similarity and diversity work in parallel in the creation of musical material that is at once original and coherent.

13. Fuller presentations of data and their analysis are available in electronic form from the author.

14. As one mother of a twenty-three-year old in the 2006 septo-optic dysplasia survey stated, her son "could play the [piano and organ] well at four years old but never followed up, so lost a lot of his skills."

15. Hence, the analysis was as fine grained as it was practicable to make it. Longer pieces could be investigated using more substantial musical gestures as the primary unit of analysis.

16. This work was undertaken by AO, utilizing his intuitions as an experienced music analyst, performer, and educator. The principal disadvantage of this approach was the possibility of unconscious bias through idiosyncratic interpretation of the underlying structural relationships. The advantage was his intimate knowledge of the situation in question—in particular what was going through his mind as the accompanist. Future analyses along these lines could, though need not, be based more on the consensus of a number of people's views, depending on their purpose. Indeed, it is anticipated that a significant proportion of the analytical activity could be undertaken by computer through searching for combinations of similarity and salience through appropriate algorithms.

17. The number was chosen for pragmatic reasons—other analyses could involve more or fewer relationships per feature than this.

18. The ordering of these pitches is based on the grounds that, *ceteris paribus*, their temporal adjacency corresponds to their relative salience and therefore implicative strength. Factors that could impact on this assumption include the possibility of an event pertaining to a larger perceptual unit. Hence, it is thought that the bass note F at the beginning of measure 5, for example, more strongly derives from the bass notes at the beginning of measures 3 and 1, respectively, than the temporally more adjacent Fs in the vocal and piano melody lines—something reinforced through common and differing octaves, respectively.

19. The issue of material derived from other pieces is considered briefly in the third section of the analysis.

20. Similarly, although K's phrase lengths indicate her evident cognizance of the underlying harmonic structure, they are not bound by it, ranging in duration from two beats to nine.

Here the influence of the improvised words appears to have been particularly important. Moreover, in the manner of a mature musical dialogue, K sometimes left the piano to play on its own—notably in measures 11 and 12—partly to regroup her own thinking, no doubt, though nonetheless affording a convincing feeling of give and take.

21. The extent to which AO derives material from K—for example, in measures 28 and 35—is the subject of a separate investigation that seeks to gauge the balance of influence between the two parties and where the locus of control lies at any given point (Ockelford n.d.).

22. AO does borrow, however, quoting "Dream, Dream, Dream" by the Everly Brothers in measures 20–23.

23. K also shows us that, contrary to certain thinking, it is not necessary to know the names of notes to possess AP. For a discussion of a range of issues related to the current understanding of AP, see Deutsch, Henthorn, and Dolson (2004).

11
Melisma as Malady: Cavalli's *Il Giasone* (1649) and Opera's Earliest Stuttering Role

ANDREW OSTER

The opera stage is a prime locus for study of human disability. The sheer corporeality of opera's medium, fraught with singers' blaring vocal chords, heaving chests, and exaggerated body gestures, lays bare the human body's physicality and vulnerability as in no other performed genre of music. The physical demands of singing, coupled with dramaturgical concerns of staging, blocking, and oftentimes dance, render opera the most bodily of musical arts. Failure of the human body at the task of singing not only endangers the exigencies of live performance but also has been encoded into the genre in unique and profound ways. Hutcheon and Hutcheon (2000: 54–5, 74–9) noted audiences' incredulousness when disabled opera characters such as the hunchback Rigoletto, and the three crippled brothers in Richard Strauss's *Die Frau ohne Schatten*, are capable not only of physically commanding the stage but of singing ably and beautifully as well. Clark (2003) commented on the curious role of protagonist for the mute woman Fenella in Daniel Auber's 1828 opera *La muette de Portici*, despite her character never uttering a word. Her mere physical presence on stage localizes disability within the human body—in this case the vocal chords—as a permanent inability to sing.

Disability on the opera stage is no doubt largely a corporeal phenomenon, but what if disability were dematerialized and recast within the operatic voice? Such a strategy is consistent with recent trends in the field of disability studies, which aims to de-essentialize disability as an entirely physiological or medical construct. Musical—or operatic—disability would thus no longer solely be allocated to bodily markers such as Rigoletto's hunchback or Wotan's eye patch but would admit vocal impairment as well. The history of opera is full of musical settings that mimic aberrations or interruptions in standard vocal discourse: coughing, sneezing, humming, clearing one's throat, yawning, and the like.[1] These are all minor, passing instances of the voice's inability to communicate fluently. Perhaps the most debilitating of vocal disabilities is stuttering, the spasmodic repetition or prolongation of certain syllables of speech. Stuttering's place in the history of opera rests on a hand-ful of stuttering characters in well-known works from the past few centuries: the judge Don Curzio in Wolfgang Amadeus Mozart's *Le Nozze di Figaro*; Cochenille in Jacques Offenbach's *Les Contes d'Hoffmann*; Vašek in Bedřich Smetana's *The Bartered Bride*; and the eponymous Billy Budd in Benjamin Britten's opera (Vrticka 2000, 176–7). These latter-day roles, however, were preceded in manner and function by the most famous of seventeenth-century operatic stutterers: the courtier Demo in Francesco Cavalli's 1649 opera *Il Giasone*, the most frequently performed opera of the seventeenth century.[2]

Like Giuseppe Verdi's Rigoletto and Richard Wagner's Alberich, Demo has a physical impairment: He is a hunchback dwarf. This correlation between physical malformation and vocal impairment tends to fashion his person as uniquely disabled *vis à vis* Jason, Medea, Hercules, Jupiter, and the other mythically able characters with whom he shares the stage in *Il Giasone*. But instead of focusing on his physical disability, I'd like to consider the struggles he endures while speaking and singing. His speech condition, more so than his bodily impairment, suggests the most interesting implications for opera and for singing in general. As in aphasia, oral apraxia, and other neurological speech defects, the symptoms of stuttering can be lessened through recourse to music, via pitch or rhythm exercises (Keith and Aronson 1975).[3] Singing, when undertaken as a group exercise, yields the same positive results as when a stutterer reads or speaks in unison with others. Stutterers who lapse into repetition or delay (i.e., *block*) on certain spoken words have been shown to gain fluency when they sing the same words. Whether observed in real life or used as a therapeutical adjunct, the act of singing proves effective in overcom-ing stuttering. Music, and specifically song, facilitates fluency (Masura and Matejova 1975).[4]

In an operatic context, the therapeutic benefit of song is neither this straightforward nor advantageous. The conscious act of singing, of suspending narrative in a moment of aria, would seem to mitigate momentarily the effects of stuttering, yet Don Curzio, Cochenille, Vašek, and Billy Budd struggle with stuttering on nearly all planes of their vocal discourse. Certain stuttering characters, however, do show predilection toward song, perhaps aware of its therapeutic effects. Billy Budd, grilled by the overbearing master-at-arms John Claggart, responds that no, he cannot read, but "[he] can sing…" (Britten 1961). Apart from a single instance of phenomenal song, defined by Abbate (1991, 5) as "vocal performance that declares itself openly, singing that is heard by its singer [and] the auditors on stage," Billy Budd's unique vocal pro-file is marked by stuttering. The sea shanty Billy sings with his shipmates in act 1, scene 3 is this one instance in which Billy's confidence in the medium of song temporarily prevents his blocking. On the whole, the trope of stut-tering remains a persistent vocal marker that distinguishes his and other stuttering characters' discourse from that of their fellow characters. Singing, represented on the opera stage as aria, fails to destigmatize this fundamental vocal difference.

The consistency of these characters' symptoms results from gradual changes throughout the late eighteenth and nineteenth centuries in how composers staged musical narrative. By 1786, the year Mozart completed *Le Nozze di Figaro*, the previously clear stylistic demarcation between recitative and aria was becoming blurred. Subsequent treatments of stuttering on the opera stage do not strictly adhere to this fundamental formal dichotomy. As early as 1602, Giulio Caccini, composer and one of the first Florentine theoreticians of opera, defined recitative in the preface to his *Le nuove musiche* as the act of "speaking in music" (*in armonia favellare*) (Monson 2001). Aria, in turn, was recitative's more song-like corollary. At first little more than a point of repose amid dramatic action, aria was a platform for more emotional and subjective vocal discourse. But gradually, throughout the seventeenth century, stylistic differences between aria singing and recitative singing emerged. Aria vocal lines were at turns more melodic, lyrical, and eventually more virtuosic, than recitative. As such, aria becomes the singing in music counterpart to recitative's speaking in music. By 1649, the year Cavalli composed *Il Giasone* and outfitted the character Demo with his own speaking and singing voice, this stylistic contrast had reified into the two primary discursive modes of Baroque opera.[5]

Since in this reading recitative is tantamount to speaking in music, and aria to singing in music, it follows that Demo's moments of aria are devoid of stuttering—and this is largely the case. In recitative passages, on the other hand, his stilted, halting phrases struggle to maintain momentum, frequently suspending his words in mid-sentence. Despite momentary triumph over stuttering in his arias, however, his music never quite abandons its association with his speech condition. At the exact points in his aria when he suffers temporary relapses, his stuttering blocks are triggered not by the difficulty of syllabification but by musicorhetorical cues in Cavalli's orchestra. Imbedded within his aria's orchestral texture are a number of musical analogues to stuttering. These devices transmute stuttering's rhetorical hallmarks—repetition, suspension, and delay—into musical terms. In one of the earliest orchestral simulations of stuttering, Cavalli's strategic use of nonsequential repetition, orchestral vamps, and repeated V–VI bass motion creates momentary fits of orchestral stuttering that negate the therapeutic effect of Demo's song. Cavalli's seemingly intuitive understanding of the musical implications of stuttering in both aria and recitative approaches something of a theory of operatic stuttering, realized in the earliest and one of the best-known stuttering roles in the repertoire.

Demo's stuttering not only typifies his character musically but is also a key determinant of his character's dramatic function. His stuttering is routinely played for humor throughout *Il Giasone*, where it serves as a major source of comic relief. Consistent with many of today's cinematic portrayals of stuttering characters, Demo's condition is better suited to elicit laughs than to raise awareness of the difficulties of stuttering.[6] This is often also the case for deaf and blind cinematic characters, whose impairments are commonly cast in a comedic, not empathetic, light. Although it was a relative novelty on the opera stage, the comedic effect of Demo's stuttering had precedents in a number of contemporaneous performance traditions. Stuttering's dramaturgical function in seventeenth-century theater almost always served the cause of comedy, a function preserved in the operatic context of *Il Giasone*. Many of the comedic trappings of stuttering characters—repetitiveness, delay, long-windedness—resurface in Cavalli's opera in the guise of Demo. These shared mannerisms help usher the topos of stuttering from spoken theater to sung opera.

Demo's comedic portrayal eschews *Il Giasone*'s mythological origins and realigns the opera's plot and dialogue with more recent stage traditions. Apollonius of Rhodes' *Argonautica*, the original literary source of Jason's quest for the Golden Fleece, provided a familiar subject for many seventeenth-century Italian opera libretti. No fewer than thirteen operatic versions of the Argo myth date from Venetian theaters between 1642 and 1758 (Alm 1993). The *Argonautica*'s blend of adventure, unrequited love and the supernatural epitomized the plot conventions of the mid-century Venetian *dramma musicale*. In the case of *Il Giasone*, however, Apollonius' legend offered little more than a thematic point of departure. Cavalli's opera deviated most notably from the *Argonautica* in its borrowings from contemporary comedic stage traditions. Its unique fusion of myth and comedy, of high and low art, made it a common target of Arcadian critics, who in the late seventeenth and early eighteenth centuries sought to purify standards of poetry in opera libretti. Giovanni Maria Crescimbeni, writing in 1700, blamed *Il Giasone* for "the end of acting, and consequently, of true and good comedy as well as tragedy" (pp. 106–7; quoted in Rosand 1991, 275). Librettist Giacinto Andrea Cicognini, he believed, integrated the previously separate genres of comedy and tragedy into a single work, *Il Giasone*, through "mixing kings and heroes and other illustrious personages with buffoons and servants and the lowest men with unheard of monstrousness" (ibid.). Crescimbeni almost certainly refers to the character of Demo, a hunchback courtier at the court of Orestes, whom Cicognini fashioned with seemingly little function other than comic relief. Demo, together with Medea's elderly nurse Delfa, afford *Il Giasone* moments of levity lacking in Apollonius' epic.

In the still-nascent Venetian opera tradition of the 1640s, little precedent existed for the staging of a stuttering role, at least in the dozen years since publicly performed opera had taken root in the Republic. As is typical with the earliest existing opera sources, Cicognini's libretto and *argomento* to *Il Giasone* offer little detail as to the practicalities of performance. Demo's physical appearance, deportment, and staging remain at best mere conjecture. How might have Venetian costume designers and directors have fashioned his character? And would audiences have necessarily associated him with earlier dramatic conventions? Stuttering characters were fixtures of *seicento* comedic performance traditions, most notably in the Italian *commedia dell'arte*. The stuttering servant type Tartaglia (*stutterer* in Italian) was a frequent player on the *commedia* stage (Habermann 1995, 154). Not as archetypically roguish or as lazy as common stock valet characters Arlecchino, Pulcinella, or Scapino, Tartaglia's single defining trait was his stuttered speech. Iconographic documentation shows Tartaglia as rather corpulent, dressed in a green two-piece suit, cape, and ruffled collar. On his head he wore a tilted hat that left his forehead exposed, under which rested a large, cumbersome pair of glasses; he was not only myopic, but hearing impaired as well. His dramatic function consisted largely in heightening plot intrigue, although he was sometimes cast in the ostensibly respectable person of lawyer, apothecary, or judge (Oreglia 1968, 41). It is impossible to construe to what extent, if any, this image of the *commedia* stutterer translated into Demo's dwarf-like, hunchback physiognomy in Cicognini's libretto. The most obvious invocation would have involved outfitting Demo with eyeglasses, but *Il Giasone's* scant performance and reception history withholds knowledge of this and other performance details.

As a primarily improvised, nonliterary performance genre, the *commedia dell'arte* did not belong to an established textual canon or literary tradition. Actors merely enacted scenarios on a predetermined, hypothetical dramatic canvas. Tartaglia's comic identity, therefore, owed more to performative gestures and elements, such as his clown-like costume and stuttered speech, than to any given *commedia* text or body of works. But because Cicognini conceived the libretto to *Il Giasone* along more literary lines, drawing on his vast knowledge of French, Italian, and Spanish literature, Demo's comedic lineage extends beyond the purview of the *commedia dell'arte*. The dozens of libretti Cicognini authored for composers such as Cavalli, Benedetto Ferrari, Francesco Lucio, and Antonio Cesti were, as Ellen Rosand (1991, 268) writes, "more varied, more individualized, and poetically more sophisticated than those of his Venetian contemporaries." They stood out especially "by their mixture of comic and serious characters—even the permeation of serious elements by comedy—and for the dramatic impact of the poetry itself" (ibid.). Cicognini's unique literary style was particularly colored through his familiarity with Spanish theater, honed through his many translations and adaptations of the *comedias* of Tirso de Molina (1571–1648) and Pedro Calderón (1600–c. 1681) (Glixon 2001, 835). Cicognini also frequently turned to Spanish playwrights' *comedias* as models for his own comedic writings.

The Spanish *comedia* of the *siglo de oro* (c. 1600–1700) shared a set of conventions not dissimilar to the Italian *commedia dell'arte*, which had made significant inroads in the Iberian Peninsula by the mid-sixteenth century. Servant types resembling Arlechino, Pulcinella, Tartaglia, and others resurfaced in Spanish *comedias* in the guise of the stock character *gracioso*, or *bobo*. The slow-witted *gracioso* servant was a composite of nearly all the traits of his Italian *commedia* forerunners, including laziness, corpulence, amorousness, and drunkenness (Kinter 1978, 17–20). Though primarily serving the purpose of comic relief, the Spanish *bobo* often showed a more baneful side as well. Three archetypes of mischievous male servants existed in seventeenth-century Spanish *comedias*: (1) the scornful rogue; (2) the intriguer; and (3) the critical commentator (Heidenreich 1962, 53–86). Cicognini's portrayal of Demo draws on traits of the scornful rogue (act 1, scene 6) and intrigue-prone servant (act 2, scene 6) in particular. Despite his propensity for mischief, stuttering remains the *sine qua non* of Demo's persona and lends him something of the slapstick humor associated with the *gracioso*.

Cicognini's literary studies in Florence would have acquainted him with current French comedy as well, including the early works of Pierre Corneille (1606–84) and Jean-Baptiste Molière (1622–73). French authors were likewise apt to people comic scenarios with stock servant types and other character remnants of the *commedia dell'arte*. Typical ranks of servants in their works included valets, knaves, confidants, servants, chambermaids, and female attendants (Léman 1975, 51–61). As with their Spanish counterparts, these roles often did little to advance the play's plotline but were justified mainly through their comic exploits. The thrust of their comedic persona involved what Michel Léman (1975, 221–86) deems their essential "impropriety" (*l'inconvenance*), for a well-mannered and proper servant simply failed to serve the cause of comic relief. The gaucherie of servant characters cut across many parameters, chief among them the domains of character, decorum and manners, love, and language (ibid.).

Of the aforementioned four categories of social interaction, impropriety in the realm of language suggests the strongest kinship with the character of Demo and with his stuttering. Unlike the *commedia dell'arte* tradition, in which stuttered speech was indelibly associated with the single person of Tartaglia, seventeenth-century Spanish and French comedies employed stuttering as an *ad hoc* comedic device, applied to numerous servant roles and comic situations. Profanity, long-windedness, interruptions, amorous language, and colloquialism all counted as examples of servants' unsuitable use of language (Léman 1975, 259–77). Stuttering characters exhibited many of these vocal vices, but their manner of spoken discourse was obviously flawed as well. Their double impropriety is best explained in connection to the literary notion of *fantasie verbale*. Léman (1975, 278) writes that:

> more than profanities, loquacity, rhetorical excesses, or colloquialisms, *fantasie verbale* seems to constitute the most favored form of servants' liberty in matters of language. Liberty is in this sense the refutation of beautiful language and the return to condemned popular usages; but,

what's more, it is the refusal of all usage [of language]. It represents verbal invention, *the feel of words for themselves.*[7]

Although Léman does not explicitly include stuttering within his definition of *fantasie verbale*, the practice clearly displayed the very symptoms he cites: excessive enumeration, jargon, repetition, and gibberish (ibid.). These vocal devices rendered language especially opaque and abstract so as to deny it its inherent semantic potential. Under *fantasie verbale*, nonsignifying utterances replace actual words as the raw materials of speech. In Demo's frequent fits of stuttering, his repetition of empty, nonsignifying syllables compromises the semantic clarity of his language, blurring his words into an inscrutable gloss of gibberish.

In the attempt to locate the topos of the stuttering servant within seventeenth-century performance and literary traditions, I have thus far deflected attention away from the genre of opera. Ample precedent for the character type existed in spoken theater, such as *commedia dell'arte* stage conventions and the French and Spanish comedic literature of the age. In contrast, occurrence of a stuttering character on Venetian opera stages of the 1640s was something of a novelty, especially considering the recent origins of the genre. The character type's gradual transition from spoken theater to sung performance, however, bespoke factors greater than the burgeoning medium of opera. Demo's discourse of stuttering belongs to a large-scale mannerist current in *seicento* musical theater toward the detachment of language from reality. Theorized by such prominent *letterati* as Giovannbattista Marino and Camillo Pellegrino, the "semantic loss" of Baroque language proffered a striking reinterpretation of the five-part division of classical rhetoric: *inventio, dispositio, elocutio, pronuntiatio,* and *actio* (Calcagno 2000, 8–9).[8] In this sense, *elocutio* (verbal delivery) takes on extra significance: How something is expressed becomes almost as vital as what is expressed. In the context of opera, the raw, sonorous qualities of the human voice both substitute and compensate for the representational void of pure singing. The mere presence of the "living voice," writes Stefano Guazzo in 1574, often trumps the effective content of the sung word. The "sound of words," he writes, "has the force to make seem that which it is not, or more than it is" (quoted in Calcagno 2000, 15).

One manifestation of this crisis of Baroque language was a preponderance of verbal figures of repetition, listing, and enumeration. Use of these devices substituted the innate semantic meaning of words with raw sonic potential. This rupture between signifier and signified was perhaps nowhere greater than in the abundance of birdsong imagery in mid-century operas and madrigals. The ancient Greek myth of Procne and Philomela, in which two sisters are transformed into a nightingale and swallow, proved especially fertile to librettists and composers alike (Calcagno 2000, 30). Other constructions that privileged the sounding sensuality of the human voice over its encoded verbal content included onomatopoeia, laughter, crying, echo, and, of course, stuttering. Through the stark opposition of sound and meaning, of signifier and signified, *fantasie verbale* is translated into musical terms. Repeated, meaningless syllables—not words—become the raw materials of singing.

Fantasie verbale, transplanted onto the operatic voice, is not unlike melisma—a passage of several notes sung to a single syllable of text. The identical recurring syllables found in crying, echo, and stuttering, when distributed among a single or various musical pitches, resemble the syntax of melisma. Though more associated with the *bel canto* idiom of eighteenth-century Italian opera, countless melismatic passages mark Cavalli's scores of the 1640s.[9] Assigned mostly to soprano roles, sung melismata signals not so much a dearth, but a surplus, of expressiveness and emotion. In Carolyn Abbate's (1991, 10) words, melismatic vocalise becomes a powerful "voice-object" that draws the listener's attention "away from words, plot, character, and even from the music as it resides in the orchestra." To compensate for its break with representation—words, plot, character, and so forth—the voice-object takes on an intensified, melismatic mode of expression. During the earliest decades of opera, vocal melismata exerted the same destructive effect on the sung voice that *fantasie verbale* wrought on speech. It destroyed language by splitting words and by separating syllable from syllable, much in the same manner that verbal invention wreaked havoc on traditional language usage in the theater.

Although repeated, empty syllabification was a verbal hallmark of servant characters in seventeenth-century theater, the same gambit resurfaced in markedly different roles in the opera house. Melismatic vocal writing occurs most prominently throughout the seventeenth century in passages for women, as a token of lyrical virtuosity. Rodolfo Celletti (1991, 8) writes that throughout seventeenth-century opera, "the acrobatics of virtuoso passages rule[d] out male voices (baritone–tenor or bass) as being too harsh and crude in sound for a type of singing that called for agility, flexibility, nuance, and a pellucid and languorous tone." The stylized, inherently virtuosic quality of melismata was an undeniable emblem of virtuosity, but it also came to embrace another altogether: cacophony. More harrowing than enticing, more disconcerting than soothing, the undesirable corollary to the voice's semantic loss was its syntactical unfettering. Seventeenth-century theoreticians of music were duly heedful of the voice's tendency to go awry. Giovannbattista Marino, writing in 1614, asked, "Who does not know that the voice—indistinct, inarticulate, and signifying nothing—is itself imperfect? And [who does not know] that that which resounds without considerate expression of word and concept is not music, but rather bestial howling?" (Marino 1960, 332; quoted in Calcagno 2000, 38). His harsh dismissal of singing that fails to reconcile sound and word would seem to apply to Demo's stuttering as well. In Marino's estimation, Demo is more than merely long winded and inarticulate; his mode of discourse is cast as somehow subhuman, below the human capacity for verbal communication. The distinctiveness of Demo's vocal idiom does not go unnoticed by other characters. "What strange sounds!" Orestes exclaims to Demo in act 1, scene 6 (Cicognini 1988, 79). "I thought you were calling a dog!" (1.6.10-11)

If we continue with the equation of spoken stuttering with sung melisma, the very same musical device that evinces suavity, seduction, and virtuosity in heroic female characters renders Demo verbally incapacitated. Both patterns of language—stuttering and melisma—are deviations from accepted norms of verbal syntax. But in Demo's case, his condition clearly stands outside accepted vocal syntax as well, as defined and heard in the opera house. His stuttering may thus be seen as an alternate, impaired melisma: related to, yet inherently at odds with, the lyrical vocalise of female eloquence. Demo's peculiar brand of coloratura posits his voice as singularly *other* amid more conventional, *bel canto* melismatic song. Only in his arias, through the conscious act of singing, does Demo temporarily overcome this stigma and acquire a more fluent and normalized vocal discourse.

Act 2, scene 10 of *Il Giasone* finds Demo giving chase to Jason and the Argonauts, who have fled Colchis with Medea and the Golden Fleece in tow. Demo's boat is shipwrecked in a violent storm. His cries of help attract Orestes' attention, who swims to his rescue and saves him from drowning. The opening lines of Demo's recitative are as follows (Cicognini, 1988, 153):

DEMO	Soccorso, aiuto, ò là!	DEMO	Save me, help! You there!
	Io moro, oimè, pietà!		I'm dying, o woe, for pity's sake!
ORESTES	Qual voce verso il lido	ORESTES	What bellowing from the shore
	Mi ferisce l'udito?		Assails my ears?
DEMO	O onde scellerate	DEMO	O villainous waves,
	Così, m'assassinate?		Do you want to murder me?
ORESTES	Rinforzano le strida –	ORESTES	The shouting grows louder –
	Ma già comparve un		but there's a swimmer
	Nuotatore a terra.		being washed up on the shore.
DEMO	Oimè, son morto, oimè	DEMO	O me, I'm dead, o woe
	Me … me … meschino!		Mi … mi … miserable me!
			(2.10.1-9)

Figure 11.1 is Cavalli's musical setting of Demo's initial two lines, in which he frantically implores Orestes for help.[10] After five measures of bright D major pleas for help, the G minor harmony and meter change in measure 6 trigger a more tragic vein, as Demo's thoughts turn to the threat of death. By measure 9 he begins to block on the word *pietà*, which he does not fully articulate until the final measure. When he at last utters the complete word, he immediately repeats it, as if to confirm its meaning. Cavalli's text setting here is strikingly

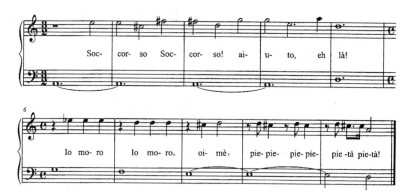

Figure 11.1 Demo frantically implores Orestes for help. (Demo's recitative, Act II, scene x)

consistent with traditional patterns of clonic stuttering, a type characterized by consecutive broken syllables and word repetition (Vrticka 2000, 174). Words that begin with a hard consonant, such as *pietà*, are typical stumbling blocks for the stutterer. Rarely do syllables or words beginning with vowels (e.g., *aiuto, ò, Io, oimè*) pose difficulties. Demo's final word, "pietà!," assumes the emotive highpoint of this sentence. As both noun and interjection, the word is not only a greater signifier of meaning than any pronoun, conjunction, or preposition could ever be but also carries more subjective meaning (Bloodstein 1993, 75–6).[11] No longer trying to attract Orestes's attention, Demo candidly laments the gravity of his predicament and almost certain death. Speech researchers believe that, somewhat ironically, the words on which stutterers most often block are the very words they consider the most important or critical (Bloodstein 1993). For this reason, the true extent of Demo's desperation—"for pity's sake!"—is betrayed through his stuttering lapse at this juncture.

Like Cicognini's (1988) text setting, Cavalli's harmonic and rhythmic treatment of these measures shows a keen awareness of the logic of stuttering. After failing to attract Orestes' attention in measures 1–5, Demo anticipates his own death over a descending tetrachord (G–F–E–D) bass sequence beginning in measure 6. Demo's lament is momentarily cut short in measures 8–10, as the bass descent idles on the note E. The sustained E causes a short hypermetric expansion of the stepwise bass lament: The otherwise four-measure sequence is expanded to five, since the next and final note of the tetrachord (D) is not reached until measure 10. After the G minor sonority of measures 6 and 7, the sustained E in measures 8–10 suggests an applied dominant to the key of A major. Instead, the passage seems to resettle into G minor and ends with a half cadence on D. Closure, however, is anything but emphatic. The sustained bass E of measures 8–10 resolves by way of a feeble whole-step descent into D. Demo's vocal line likewise fails to provide a strong sense of closure. His two notes of C-sharp in measure 10, instead of resolving upward to D, drop to A, in a clear violation of seventeenth-century standards of counterpoint. Extended phrase rhythm, inconclusive voice leading, and weak, stepwise harmonic motion combine to lessen the impact of the cadence in measure 10.

Demo's words at this point bear the same rhetorical inconclusiveness and ambiguity as Cavalli's harmonic setting. As of measure 9, when Demo begins to falter on *pietà*, the listener already has enough knowledge to infer his meaning. Five ensuing iterations of "pie–" all but confirm that only the word *pietà* could be eluding him. His eventual articulation of the word proves as unemphatic to the listener as the half cadence on D. Indeed, Demo's completion of the word is not nearly as interesting as when—or if—he will ever finish his sentence. In this passage of recitative, Cavalli's musical setting draws on the idiosyncrasies of stuttered speech for its harmonic design and pacing.

Figure 11.2 sets the final two lines of the scene, when Demo again cries out, "O me, I'm dead, o woe; mi–mi–miserable me!" (2.10.9) After measure 1 establishes the key of D major, a prolonged descending sequence comes to rest in measure 10 on a dominant chord, which resolves into the tonic in measure 12. As expected, Demo at some point lapses into a stutter—this time on the word *oimè* in measure 5. His eleven-fold repetition of the syllable *mè* coincides with the orchestra's meandering, wayward sequence. Appearing to head nowhere, the bass finally stagnates on A in measure 10, which through the addition of C-sharp and G assumes the undeniable function of dominant seventh chord. The chord's added duration and weight summons a tonic much more momentous than the mere throwaway gesture in Figure 11.1. Their differences are obvious: Figure 11.2's cadence is authentic, whereas Figure 11.1's is a half cadence. But textual concerns also play a part here as well. The closing cadence seems all the more prominent because it helps distinguish among the three consecutive *mè* syllables in the text. The line "Oimè, me meschino!" (O woe, miserable me) strings together a trio of audibly indistinguishable *me* syllables. The emphatic final cadence ends the illusion of stuttering by signaling the end

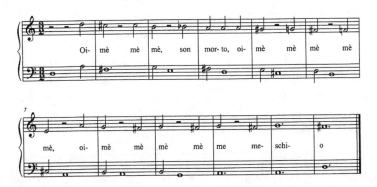

Figure 11.2 Demo again cries out: "O me, I'm dead, o woe; mi–mi–miserable me!" (Demo's recitative, Act II, scene x)

of one word and the beginning of the next. By the downbeat of measure 10, at the latest, Demo leaves the word *oimè* behind and utters *me* and *meschino*. This cunning play on words brings about semantic clarity at the last possible moment, after the direction and meaning of Demo's sentence had seemed otherwise irrefutable. As such, the strong cadential motion in measures 10–12 warns against the kind of passive listening usually permitted in the context of stuttering. The powerful harmonic impact of the final cadence is synchronized with Demo's sudden syntactical about-face.

Figure 11.1 and Figure 11.2 demonstrate the extent to which recitative accompaniment, through rhythmic expansion, voice leading, and cadential motion, conforms to stuttering's inherent rhetorical constraints. By adjusting the rate of harmonic rhythm, Cavalli replicates the stilted, variable trajectory of Demo's speech. In his two arias, in contrast, Demo's vocal pace gains in speed, as his stuttering gives way to newfound fluency. Musical cues, in turn, no longer flow hand in hand with Demo's speech but instead cut against it. Orchestral agents of stuttering—nonsequential repetition, orchestral vamps, and deceptive cadences—interrupt Demo's fluency, driving him into temporary blocking spells.

Demo's act 2, scene 7 aria is a G major vendetta piece in which he spitefully swears to a life of chastity, the first strophe of which is presented in Fig. 11.3 (Cicognini 1988, 139):

1	*Con arti e con lusinghe*	With artfulness, with wiles
	donne, se vi credete	you women, if you think
	di farmi innamorar, voi	to beguile me, you deceive
	v'ingannate affé:	yourselves, in faith:
	Queste bellezze mie voglio per me!	My beauty is reserved for me alone!
5	*Se ben penare*	Though I see you
	languire,	languish,
	crepare,	suffer,
	morire,	repine,
10	*io vi vedrò*	die,
	mai mi innamorerò.	I'll never fall in love.
	Nò, nò, nò, nò, nò, nò	No, no, no, no, no, no
	non lo sperate affé	don't set your hopes on it, in faith:
	Queste bellezze mie voglio per me!	My beauty is reserved for me alone!

Demo is nowhere more eloquent than in this aria. He manages to articulate the first three lines of text in their entirety without dissecting words into syllables. A few telltale symptoms of stuttering persist, however: He struggles briefly

Figure 11.3 Demo spitefully swears to a life of chastity. (Demo's aria, Act II, scene vii)

with the syllable *mai* in measures 16–17, but this amounts to only a fleeting interruption in an otherwise fluent singing style. The recurring "Nò nò nò nò nò nò" in measure 18, on the other hand, cannot be linked to Demo's stuttering per se. Such interjections were often sung in quick succession for dramatic effect, even by nonstuttering characters. Demo's repetition of the syllable *vo* at the end of measure 8 comes immediately after a small-scale harmonic progression (I–IV–V–I) is curtailed by V–VI (D–E) motion in the bass. The same four-note pattern in measure 8 vamps onward until measure 12, when a descending fifth (D–G) finally makes good on the cadence. Cavalli's use of this device is most intense in measures 8–12 and 20–24, each instance of which contains four consecutive interrupted progressions. While the orchestra vamps seemingly indefinitely, Demo stumbles on the word fragment *vo*. These passages of harmonic suspension seem so striking because Cavalli very rarely uses V–VI bass motion elsewhere throughout *Il Giasone*.[12] The three-fold repetition of this bass pattern postpones harmonic closure. Demo's song loses its syntactical thrust exactly in this moment of harmonic stasis, in limbo between dominant and tonic. Only on reaching the cadence in measure 12 does Demo complete his sentence and thereupon repeats "per me!" three times to affirm his meaning.

As a clonic stutterer, Demo tends to repeat not only syllables but entire words as well. He is tripped up on the words *voi v'ingannate* in measures 4–7. He sings these same words three times and same pitches (B–C-sharp–D–E–A) twice, until the D major chord in measure 7 finally breaks his pattern. A similar block occurs simultaneously in the orchestra, albeit involving different pitches (A–B–C-sharp–D–G). The awkward redundancy of these staggered, repeating motifs strikes one as quite unorthodox. One would expect each five-note motif to be sequenced, as in almost all other examples of small-scale melodic imitation in Cavalli's music. Instead, each is simply repeated verbatim. The overwhelming sense of stagnation of these four measures is nothing if not another musical metaphor for stuttering. Indeed, it is no accident that Demo's first relapse into stuttering in this aria—on the words *voi v'ingannate*—coincides with this passage of redundant, nonsequential imitation.

There is no greater showcase of vocal ability in Baroque opera than aria. Composers and singers came to translate an aria text's inherent means of expression into a number of artistic liberties, including greater lyricism, vocal ornamentation, and melisma. In aria, the affective and acoustic qualities of the human voice are paramount, perhaps even more so than declamation of text. Sound, as it were, trumps text. In the case of Demo's stuttering, however, the obverse relationship between word and sonority applies. In aria, not only does fluent text declamation become a possibility for Demo, but the word also regains its primacy *vis à vis* sound: For the first time, what Demo sings becomes more significant than how he sings it. Thanks to the therapeutic act of pure singing, Demo at last manages to overcome his stuttering. Yet, as demonstrated in Figure 11.3, his newfound fluency is fleeting at best, as a host of harmonic and structural agents of stuttering surface in the orchestra and trigger relapses. Much as Demo's hunched back persists in defining him physically ("If you look at me closely, from behind and from the front, on my shoulders my name is written!") (1.6.18–20), the onus of stuttering endures in some form throughout his vocal idiom. No amount of pure song can permanently erase the effects of his vocal impairment.

Notes

1. The choir in Adolphe Adam's *Le Postillon de Lonjumeau* sings as if coughing; Mustaffa in Gioacchino Rossini's *L'Italiana in Algeri* and Lazuli in Emmanuel Chabrier's *L'Étoile* sneeze; Papageno in Wolfgang Amadeus Mozart's *Die Zauberflöte* hums; Despina §(disguised as a notary) clears her throat repeatedly in Mozart's *Così fan tutte*; and Svegliato in Giovanni Paisiello's *Barbiere di Siviglia* yawns (Vrticka 2000, 173).

2. Demo's significance owes not only to *Il Giasone*'s enduring popularity but also to the character's primacy among operatic stuttering roles. Demo's is the earliest major stuttering character acknowledged by current opera scholarship.

3. Melodic intonation therapy (MIT) and other techniques of music therapy have proven useful in rehabilitating patients with speech and motor speech defects. See Keith and Aronson (1975, 483–88); Albert, Sparks, and Helm (1973, 130–1).

4. Singing alone or singing in connection with motions in group therapy sessions have yielded high rates of fluency among stutterers. One study reports that 92 percent of stuttering children acquire fluency while engaged in song (Masura and Matejova 1975, 220–9).

5. Rosand (1991, 276) wrote, "In *Giasone* the definitive separation of aria and recitative was finally achieved. Cicognini's standard means of distinguishing them persisted until the end of the century: strophicism and/or *versi misurati* meant aria; *versi sciolti*, recitative."

6. More recent cinematic examples of stuttering being played for comic effect include actor Austin Pendleton's portrayal of the stuttering public defender in *My Cousin Vinny* (Jonathan Lynn, 1992) and Adam Sandler's character Bobby Boucher in *The Waterboy* (Frank Coraci, 1998). Actor Michael Palin's portrayal of Ken Pile, the stuttering animal rights activist, in *A Fish Called Wanda* (Charles Crichton, 1988) is somewhat more ambiguous in its comedic effect. Whereas Jamie Lee Curtis's character attempts to understand him in spite of his severe speech condition, Kevin Kline's Otto mocks him mercilessly. If there is humor in this exchange, it is discomforting at best: In fact, the National Stuttering Project petitioned Metro Goldwyn Mayer to have this scene removed from the film (see Kuster 2005).

7. Author's translation (with italics added) of the original French: "Mieux que le parler cru, la loquacité, l'excès rhétorique et l'usage fréquent de termes familiers ou de locutions proverbiales et populaires, la fantaisie verbale nous paraît constituer la forme la plus poussée de cette liberté des serviteurs en matière de langage. La liberté, c'est le refus du beau langage, le retour aux usages populaires condamnés, mais c'est, plus encore, le refus de tout usage, l'invention verbale, le goût des mots pour eux–mêmes."

8. For explanation of the term *semantic loss*, see Ferroni and Quondam (1973, 216; quoted in Calcagno 2000, 8–9). I am indebted to Calcagno's dissertation in the following discussion of Baroque era language. See also Calcagno (2003).

9. Rosand (1971, 217) identified an abundance of melismatic writing in *La virtù de' strali d'Amore* (1643) and *Ormindo* (1644).

10. All musical examples are transcribed by the author from *Il Giasone*'s original 1649 manuscript. See Cavalli (1649).

11. In addition to nouns and interjections, adjectives, verbs, and adverbs are especially important keys to an utterance's meaning yet are more frequently stuttered than less essential parts of grammar (see Bloodstein 1993, 75–6).

12. Throughout act 1, for example, V–VI bass motion occurs only in a few instances: once in scene 2, twice in scene 10, and once in scene 13.

12

The Organ of the Soul: Voice, Damage, and Affect

LAURIE STRAS

O, How wonderful is the human voice! It is indeed the organ of the soul!
The intellect of man sits enthroned visibly upon his forehead and in his
eye, and the heart of man is written upon his countenance. But the soul
reveals itself in the voice only.

Henry Wadsworth Longfellow, *Hyperion*

Laboravi clamans raucae factae sunt fauces meae. In the King James
version of the Old Testament, the third verse of Psalm 68/69 reads, "I am
weary of my crying: my throat is dried." Yet a more accurate translation from
the Vulgate would be, "I have labored, crying out; my [vocal] cords are made
hoarse [raucous]." The forceful, involuntary and bodily expression of emotion
through voice, especially when combined with the muscular constriction and
hormonal surges of the acute stress response, can disturb the delicate tissues
of the pharynx and larynx, thereby altering and disrupting their functionality,
much as would happen if the throat were inflamed by infection or damaged by
injury or illness.[1]

The disrupted voice conveys meaning even before it conveys language; in
Western cultures we hear disruption as pathology, in both the current and
obsolete meanings of the word: it is indicative of passions, suffering, disease,
malfunction, abnormality. We hear it, too, as the result of labor—the physical
trace of an agent working on the body, a measure of the body's cumulative
experience of extrinsic (environmental) or intrinsic (entropic) forces. Time
and trauma take their toll on the voice, and although we are left to imagine, discover, or construct a context for the disruption—is this person a heavy
smoker? Has that person been shouting? Is she going through the hormonal
changes of aging? Is he gripped by psychic terror?—we are certain there is
more being communicated by the voice than the words it speaks.

As this essay appears under the banner of disability studies in music, the
reader may already be wondering what hoarseness can possibly have to with
the overarching topic. In most circumstances, we would probably not consider

vocal disruption a disability per se unless the voice had permanently and completely failed. And yet one of the fundamental issues of debate throughout the medical, sociological, and philosophical literature on disability is the accurate definition of *disability* and its normally concomitant term *impairment*. Historically, and for many still today, disabilities are equivalent to impairments: "those *variations* [sic] in the structure, function and workings of bodies which, in Western culture, are medically defined as significant abnormalities or pathologies" (Thomas 1999, 8).

This equivalence underlies the medical model of disability, which, although not inescapably so, is frequently essentialist in its deployment. The social model, however, encourages impairment to be viewed contextually; disability is then defined as a construction, the result of social barriers or restrictions experienced by the impaired person. Integrating both social and medical models can sometimes be the most practical way to assess the degree of a person's disability.[2] So, in the case of the voice, the significance of vocal disruption or damage to an individual will be in proportion to his or her reliance on vocal function for daily activity, and the more significant it is, the more disabled that person may be seen to be if afflicted by vocal pathology.

Notwithstanding such apparent reason, problems arise the minute a wider context is invoked. In the Western art music tradition the voice is trained, like an athlete's body, to maximize both achievement and endurance while simultaneously avoiding either accidental or long-term damage. Undamaged voices are valued, and a singer whose voice is perceived to be damaged can, at the very least, expect that perception to be remarked upon as a detriment. Surgery, therapy, and retraining may be recommended and pursued, but if the perception of impairment remains, likely as not the singer will need to find an alternative career.

In Western popular music, however, a rather different situation obtains. Many of the voices that have shaped the sound of popular singing have been characterized by audible evidence of damage to the vocal tract. The damaged voice continues to be accepted, even preferred, in many genres within popular music, to the point of optimum levels of damage appearing suitable for different types of singing: the gravel-voice of the rock singer is not interchangeable with the subtle hoarseness of the jazz vocalist. Many singers have learned to simulate or manipulate damage in the voice, so further revealing the affective value of the sound; and in a reversal of what might be considered normate associations, damage here seems to be linked with concepts of authority, authenticity, and integrity.

My own experience as a singer serves to illustrate the paradox. After some years of training to be a classical singer, an internationally respected teacher told me that the musculature of my tongue was too large in relation to my vocal tract for me ever to be able to produce a "pure" sound, devoid of breathy overtones. So convinced was she that I would never overcome the disadvantage, she recommended that I alter my career intentions to singing in popular styles. Nonetheless, I was soon advised by the bandleader who took me on that I needed to "toughen up" in order both to sing with an appropriate sound and range, and to be able to work the long hours of a nightclub singer; this, I was told, could be achieved only through what I had previously been taught to regard as vocal abuse. So, with the aid of Triple-A Spray ("Armour! Antiseptic! Anaesthetic!"), I sang past the pain, loudly and hard on a nightly basis, until I literally spat blood into the dressing-room sink. Clearly, in medical terms I was willfully damaging my body and almost perversely employing a medication that was intended to help the body repair the injury I was striving to create. But it worked. Soon I had both the breathiness caused by my innate physical qualities and a tonal burr caused by the thickening and scarring of my vocal folds; consequently, at the end of the engagement the bandleader congratulated me on how well I had developed. Now, twenty years on, I am told that I have slight, but permanent, vocal damage—damage that does not prevent me from doing anything (except, perhaps, resuming a career I understood I was physically unsuited to, anyway), but damage nonetheless.

This short story may be anecdotal, but it bridges both sides of the essentialist/constructionist debate in defining disability and impairment. In the admittedly tiny sphere of Western classical singing, I was labeled as essentially impaired by virtue of a naturally occurring variation in my bodily structure, to the point that I believed I could not participate in the activities of that community at the level I desired. Yet outside that sphere the variation had no effect on my life, and once within the sphere of popular singing it was positively enabling. Furthermore, in order to increase my body's potential value in the new culture, I actively produced in myself a medically defined pathology, an acquired impairment, engaging in a practice that (in classical singing terms) could only be regarded as self-harm. My case, and I would hazard also the cases of many other singers engaged in popular music, might suggest that vocal damage has acquired the status of a culturally inscribed desirable mutilation, at least partially analogous to tattooing or body piercings. Singers who simulate vocal damage are donning metaphorical clip-on earrings—but why?

Concepts of mutilation and disorder link disability theory with trauma theory, and both have provided useful hermeneutics for analyzing cultural uses of damage. Trauma theory applied to screen studies suggests that such representations in film might help to heal the spectators' individual and collective traumas, thereby "mitigat[ing] traumatized isolation and creat[ing] empathy with the sufferings of others in the present" (Radstone 2001, 192). Are we then to infer that, to some audiences, the damaged singing voice facilitates empathy and identification between performer and listener? Moreover, trauma typically forces a disjunction between body and voice (as the bearer of narrative), but the integration and healing of trauma is achieved through reestablishing narrative, through giving voice to the trauma. Nonetheless, the disrupted singing voice cannot help but tell of trauma, for the damage leaves its traces at sublinguistic levels—it is not a structural part of the vocal narrative, but it is still "essential" to the voice. This essay begins an examination of why and how damage signifies in the singing voice, how it is valued (or not), and how a marker of corporeal impairment, normally a site of cultural anxiety, might also act as a catalyst for anxiety's release.

At first glance, the question of why art music on the whole rejects vocal disruption and damage could be seen to hinge simply upon technical or aesthetic considerations. It could be assumed that the damaged voice will not be able to operate with agility and control, and is therefore unsuitable for the performance of an exacting repertoire, yet this notion is disproved by countless jazz, gospel, and even rock singers for whom virtuosic display is an essential component of their singing. Nor can a damaged voice be assumed not to be a beautiful voice. Reviewers and critics who describe Maria Callas's voice near the end of her career as being "in tatters" are also liable to regard her late performances as being among her most beautiful, and her most moving. But in that assessment is revealed a more powerful consequence of hearing damage in a voice—it connects the listener inescapably with the body of the performer, and the emotion in the performance is communicated as a testimony of personal experience rather than as an expression or invocation of the idea of emotion. The singer is no longer just a conduit for the composer's musical intentions and the poet's literary ones, but a person whose own flesh speaks its history wordlessly through the voice itself.

It is perhaps this fundamental materiality that Roland Barthes (1990) attempts to pinpoint in his term the *grain* of the voice. His essay, although often quoted, especially by scholars who seek a vocabulary to discuss vocal quality in popular music, remains problematic for some (Potter 1998). Nevertheless, it isolates an issue that, by its very nature, defies language: that of the transmission of affect by what Teresa Brennan (2003, 141 and throughout) calls "fleshly codes," the sublingual communication and entrainment of bodily affective states through the nonvisual senses.[3]

Barthes (1990, 295) rejects singers for whom the technical and intellectual approaches to song overwhelm and obscure the physical realities of the vocal production, preferring instead those voices in which the body can be heard "speaking in its mother language." Brennan (2003, 138–148) uses similar distinctions to separate the listener's—or, more accurately, the recipient's—methods of comprehension or assimilation. The "slow I" understands only through the logical, learned processes of language, but the "fast I" receives another's affective state through the instantaneous communicative channels of the senses. Neither Barthes nor Brennan is overly concerned with the singer's personal history and identity, however. Barthes uses the example of a nameless bass of the Russian Orthodox Church as a voice that has grain but no discernible identity; Brennan's ultimate thesis is that human beings are much less individually motivated than we might think, but are rather susceptible to affective entrainment at levels we barely understand or can even acknowledge.[4]

The so-called supremacy of the score and the composer in the appreciation and criticism of Western art music, combined with modes of listening that privilege the complex languages of technique, performance practice, and compositional style over the immediacy of Brennan's (2003) fleshly codes, suggests a reason why voices that admit too readily of bodily experience—damaged voices, in other words—are regarded as unfit for purpose. Vocal materiality is "an object of *jouissance*, and this intrusion of *jouissance* into language subverts the signifying action of the spoken words ... From this standpoint, whatever might interfere with meaning is necessarily proscribed, beginning with the reintroduction of vocal materiality and the *jouissance* connected to it" (Poizat 1992, 103).

Yet, returning to Maria Callas as an example, there are clearly situations in which the body can speak with a disrupted voice and remain valid for at least a section of the art music audience. Callas, of course, had an already established reputation as an artist, but when her voice began to fail, for many she became "the object of the most brutal criticism" (Poizat 1992, 94). Nevertheless, her vocal deterioration (in pathological terms) was seen by her loyal fans as an inevitable outcome of physical self-abuse brought on by the pressures of stardom, and thus a manifestation of psychological trauma. No matter that the damage is now considered to be primarily the result of an idiosyncratic technique, Callas's public persona as tragic heroine allowed, and continues to allow, her audience to connect a personal history with an otherwise indeterminate sound of damage. The notion lends verisimilitude to her performances, but it also engages with the logic of a narrative so that her singing can be evaluated through the rhetoric of heroic struggle.

Rosemarie Garland-Thomson (2001, 339) proposes that visual images of the disabled invoke certain rhetorical constructions, including a rhetoric of wonder; such an analysis can be applied to the receptions of Callas's late performances that pit her musicianship against her impairment and conclude that the musicianship wins the day: "At this stage in her life, Callas's voice was in tatters, but even lacking her earlier vocal riches, she extracts every grain of almost unbearable expressivity contained in the score" (Seletzky 2004, 600). One might also see a parallel rhetoric at work, which Garland-Thomson labels *benevolence*, in which the disabled body evokes pity and concern. For other listeners, it is perhaps the foregrounding of her vocal materiality that opens the door for the blurring of personal boundaries, for the failure of the signifying order, for identification and catharsis. Evan Eisenberg (1987, 38–41) and Michel Poizat (1992, 26) both report fans reacting to Callas's recordings by being emotionally overwhelmed; Eisenberg's subject goes so far as to lip sync with his records, assuming the diva's voice and identity in order to express and to make sense of his emotional response to the performance.[5]

The relationship between audience and singer is clearly central to the discussion of the different ways damage is perceived in the singing voice. In linguistics, vocal difference, perceived as accent, is a signifier for regional or cultural difference; like vocal disruption, it is also a means by which materiality is highlighted. The question for the singer is whether damage is considered, and by whom, as an indicator of difference or congruence. Hoarseness, however temporary and caused either by infection or by prolonged exertion of the vocal folds (through crying or shouting), is a common enough event to humans that the listener is able to construe the sound through personal experience. Furthermore, regardless of its pathology, unless the singer is known to the listener, the disruption need not be heard as permanent—the listener can fantasize as to whether the singer is simply suffering a lack of sleep or a particularly bad sore throat rather than being irrevocably "othered" through permanent damage. But whereas the artistic intention may be to "dress our impulses in aesthetic coverings so that, vicariously and at a safe remove, we can satisfy our ... desires" (Walrod 2005, 137), through bypassing linguistic signification and opening up the channels of affect, vocal disruption can bring the artist and the performance over the acceptable boundaries that distance them from the listener. This transgression can precipitate catharsis and even healing for the traumatized, who may resonate bodily with the raw feelings discerned in the singer's damaged voice. Indeed, Teresa Brennan (2003, 200–1, note 17) insists that corporeal affective communication is essential to the healing of trauma: "Personal consciousness can learn from trauma and expand itself. But it cannot release itself without the intervention of one of the strange tongues of the body."

Expanding on Sigmund Freud's reference to Torquato Tasso's *Gerusalemme liberata*, Cathy Caruth's insightful writing on trauma highlights the role of the voice. Freud (1991, 293) cites Tancred's hallucination in the wood—hearing the dead Clorinda's voice emanating from a wound opening up in the tree he has just struck—as an illustration of the experience and reexperience of trauma.[6] Caruth (1996, 8) hears the voice in the wound not only as the voice of the othered self—referring to the psychic doubling that characterizes trauma—but literally as the voice of another, validating the hearing of another's trauma as a means of healing one's own: "We can also read the address of the voice here, not as the story of the individual in relation to the events of his own past, but as the story of the way in which one's own trauma is tied up with the trauma of another, the way in which trauma may lead, therefore, to the encounter with another, through the very possibility and surprise of listening to another's wound." There is, of course, a problem in reconciling the collapse of identity that occurs in the catharsis effected by a performance with the construction of personal narratives attached to the performer, such as those that surround Callas. Yet one may see such narratives as the means to erect the temporal boundaries of something akin to what the psychoanalyst Donald Winnicott (1971, 71) called "the holding environment;" a place where we may enter between internal and external reality, where we may safely play in order to make sense of our relationship with the world.

Undoubtedly the process of catharsis—defined as a relieving of pent-up or previously inaccessible emotions—can be initiated by listening to music, and scholars and critics frequently use the term when writing about the experience of listening to opera. The term also crops up relatively frequently in writing about the blues, particularly in relation to the performers themselves. Yet, as ethnomusicologist Harriet Ottenheimer (1979) notes, the blues singers she studied rarely, if ever, recognized catharsis as part of the process of either singing or listening to the blues. Instead, she identified the evocation or creation of the "blue" feeling in the audience or, alternatively, matching the mood of a listener who was already "feeling blue" as being the most desirable outcomes of blues performance (ibid., 79–83).[7] The reported conversations with the singers describe a process that strongly resembles Brennan's (2003) affective entrainment, in which it is necessary for the singer actively to be experiencing a feeling—either summoned or unbidden—to transmit that same feeling to the listeners: "All I know is if I feel it, you got it. It's a contagious thing ... I can't give it to you less'n I feel it" (ibid., 81).

Damaged voices abound in the blues canon; indeed the very sound of the blues singer has been defined by voices in which physical suffering is almost palpable. The early singers were called *shouters* for good reason; in the words of a Harlem medic, they "wore themselves ragged trying to rise above the inattentive din of conversation, and soon, literally, yelled themselves hoarse; eventually they lost whatever music there was in their voices and acquired that throaty roughness which is so frequent among blues singers, and which, though admired as characteristically African, is as a matter of fact nothing but a form of chronic laryngitis" (Fisher 1999, 62).

Although this overt disruption is still a feature of blues singing and of those rock styles derived from blues, around the turn of the 1930s a subtler form of damage began to be heard in American popular voices. "Singers' nodules"—areas of coarsening on the vocal folds—when mild enough and when the singer is otherwise in good health, can create moderate disruption in the folds' operation, altering the voice's tone but without causing it to fail completely. Blues singer-turned-popular-performer Ethel Waters attempted to keep her voice unaffected by long hours of singing in undesirable environments, but over ten years into her career—at turn of the 1930s—she was obliged to have surgery to have her nodules removed (Waters 1992, 210–13).

Two of the other seminal voices in jazz and popular singing, Connie Boswell and Bing Crosby, were also altered by throat problems. Boswell underwent an operation in her late teens before she became an international star, but Crosby refused to submit to surgery. In all three voices, especially those of Waters and Crosby (both of whom had already recorded a substantial catalogue before their vocal pathologies fully emerged) there is a perceptible burr made more apparent to the audience through the new intimacy of the electric microphone. Together with the permanently hoarse Louis Armstrong, Crosby, Waters, and Boswell formed a quartet of vocal icons for a generation or more of Western popular singers.

This is not to suggest that the acceptability of vocal damage in the popular singing voice is due to the agency of four individuals; it is simply to highlight the synchronicity that, at a point when technology made it possible to sing quietly, the moderately damaged voice came into its own. Crosby's circumstances show that even though the development of the damage was unintentional, creating what he called "the effect of a lad with his voice changing singing into a rain barrel," once there it became vital (Trippett 1977, 106). When in 1933 Paramount Pictures had Crosby's voice insured for $100,000, the insurers Lloyd's of London put a clause into the policy that insisted Crosby not undertake corrective surgery lest he compromise the husky quality the nodule created, which was considered to be essential to his "vocal charm" (Giddins 2001, 270). Yet the disruption created by the pathologized vocal tract is not a fixed quality, even in the same voice; when his nodule became inflamed through illness or overwork Crosby could become so hoarse that he could not sing. Nevertheless, a rest remedy was considered sufficient to him—lost revenue from cancelled engagements was preferable to the loss of his vocal personality.[8]

Crosby, however, may well have been able to carry the damage more easily as a male singer; as in the many other ways in which the female body can voluntarily, if violently, be denaturalized, Waters and Boswell may have felt under more pressure to have corrective surgery in order to conform to—or to return to—a more acceptably female, unpathologized sound: Boswell had her nodules removed before she became a star, presumably to ensure her future as a singer.[9] There may even have been a racialized element to the reception of the damaged voice that Waters was trying to circumvent: the Harlem medic's evaluation of black voices quoted earlier occurs in the context of comments on Waters's original approach to singing—that she did not "yell herself hoarse." Such a reading opens the door for further considerations of a more contemporary racialized concept of purity of vocal sound, or its lack. White blues singers who model themselves on black singers—for instance, Janis Joplin on Bessie Smith, or Joe Cocker on Ray Charles—are instantly recognizable by the roughness of their vocal tone, acquired and nurtured as appropriate to the genre. And perhaps not surprisingly, the considerable damage in Cocker's voice has been described in terms of disability and impairment: in 1969, *Life Magazine* called it "the voice of all those blind criers and crazy beggars and maimed men who summon up a strength we'll never know to bawl out their souls in the streets" (Bean 2004, 73).

The attendant dangers of throat surgery for a singer who suffers vocal damage unwillingly should not be underestimated. Another iconic voice of the twentieth century, that of Julie Andrews, was "lost" as a result of complications during an operation to remove a nodule; she settled her malpractice suit against the surgeons out of court but was reported to have needed extensive counseling to come to terms with her new changed self. Andrews' case exemplifies an acquired disability construed as loss; it is difficult for her audience to hear her recent performance of "song-speech" without mentally referring to what her voice had been before the operation, and comparing the "damaged Julie" to the "whole Julie." When she attempted a few bars of "The Rain In Spain" while hosting a New York AIDS benefit in 2000, the audience gave her a standing ovation, perhaps moved by the quality of her voice, but certainly moved by what they saw as her courage in the face of suffering. It is unlikely, however, that the audience would have reacted the way they did had Andrews' voice, and indeed Andrews herself, not already been completely objectified with a distinct cultural significance—purity, innocence, wholeness, goodness—constructed through her status as a child star and more importantly through her most famous roles, Maria von Trapp and Mary Poppins. The surgery had left her with a voice whose qualities signified none of these things—in fact, quite the opposite. The randomness and suddenness of Andrews' loss is also significant—a classically defined trauma—so her damaged voice becomes a powerful symbol to a society suffering from "insidious trauma," that is, a society that is forced to recognize its proximity to traumatic events and their arbitrariness that threaten to afflict any individual at any time (Brown 1995). Note that Andrews sang only momentarily; a sustained performance, while likely to have been a physical impossibility, would also have been unbearably uncomfortable for the audience.

Although Andrews consented to the operation, the resulting damage was clearly not her fault, a fact that gains impact because she had originally sought surgery to remedy an impairment; the psychic trauma suffered was as a result of the voice being lost. Such could not be said of Judy Garland, another child star who carried her career into adulthood. Like Callas, the damage in Garland's voice was emblematic of her chaotic and troubled life—in a reversal of Andrews' situation, the voice was "lost" as a result of psychic and physical trauma, in many ways self-induced (although the mythology of the Hollywood victim looms large here, too). Garland's 1964 performance of "Over The Rainbow," during a concert given at the London Palladium with her daughter, Liza Minnelli, is, and was, a painful experience.[10] The voice cracks, wavers, and fails in both tone and pitch; the song is sung more or less at full belt all the way through, as there is no appreciable dynamic range left to exploit. And yet the physical—and for all we know psychic—pain heard in the singer's voice was felt positively by the audience, judging by the remarkable, rapturous reception at the end of the performance.[11] Furthermore, those present at the concert still recall the experience with wonder and sentiment (I use the word in its full "feeling/hearing/perceiving" sense); for example, one spectator acknowledged that although Garland could no longer hit the high notes, the performance was the most moving thing she felt she had ever heard.[12]

Listeners are drawn to pity and to marvel at Garland, the singer with the "broken" voice, but her extraordinary status as a star and the alien nature of the public deterioration of her lifestyle allow enough distance that the trauma the voice evokes can be witnessed in safety: "We can be spectators, titillated by the thrill of risk, safe behind our imaginary psychic barriers; or we can watch in horror as trauma happens to others but reassure ourselves that we are not next" (Brown 1995, 108). The original audience appears not to have experienced the mood matching of the blues performance, for its reaction was joyous; we may surmise that the effect of the performance was indeed beneficial, if not positively cathartic, for whatever pain may have been conjured in the listeners was clearly relieved by the end of the song.

Trauma theorists emphasize that representations of trauma must necessarily lack narrative, and it is the reestablishment of narrative that ultimately leads to integration and closure. In film, trauma is frequently invoked by fragmentation of images—all the elements of a story with little to bind them; the disrupted voice is also a fragmented voice. Yet the linking of the singer's history with the sublinguistic sound of trauma in the voice pulls the narrative together for the listener, the singer's personal tragedies providing an interpretative framework for the "slow I." Perhaps this is why the late Eva Cassidy's own performance of "Over the Rainbow" became one of the most unexpected and bizarre marketing successes of 2001. Friends say she was suffering from a cold the night it was recorded live, which accounts for the mild disruption in the voice. However, the hindsight that she was terminally ill—albeit unaware of being so—as she sang gives the listener a reason to hear that disruption as perhaps more than just a cold, its affective weight magnified and intensified by the knowledge of her premature demise. And as with Callas and Garland, listeners to Eva Cassidy's recordings from that night regularly report being moved to tears, as the audience was (Burley and Maitland 2001, 110–13).

Without extensive, structured analysis—both objective and subjective—of the effects of damage on the way a voice is heard and perceived, it is impossible to come to any hard and fast conclusions as to why some audiences value vocal disruption while others reject it. Yet Brennan's (2003) insights into the transmission of affect may offer some clues as to how this marker of impairment might assist in the creation of a positive balance of emotion for the audience. Brennan insists that there are two ways of forming personal identity: through projected judgments (which are inextricably bound up with the affects of others) or through maintaining "the sense of a distinct identity by discernment ... an openness to the distinct being who is sheltering behind the common ego, in oneself and others alike" (p. 134). "Only then," she says, "can one attend to one's own sensations and feeling for the other, by sensing what is not oneself, and noting, as well as feeling, when one falls back on the negative affects" (ibid.).

When listening to the damaged voice we are susceptible, through the agency of Brennan's (2003) fleshly codes, to the negative affect it transmits; we recognize bodily dysfunction sublinguistically and therefore quite apart from the logic of the performance itself, and yet we are aware—regardless of whether that awareness is suspended for the duration of the performance—that the affect that works upon us is part of a performance. The boundaries between singer and listener, however blurred during the singing, are snapped back into place as the song or aria finishes. The whole experience is a rehearsal for dealing with affect as it assails us in our daily lives: For Brennan (2003, 135), "negative affects are brought to a stop when ... resist[ed] without violence." Noting, or attending to, the equilibrium achieved by being able to experience another's pain, anger, or despair, even when entrained into deep identification but ultimately without having to take it personally, equips the listener with the tools for transforming negative affects in the real world.

Acknowledgments

I would like to thank friends who have read earlier versions of this essay and who have generously offered advice, information, and the benefit of their experience: Nicola Dibben, Don Greig, Mitchell Morris, John Potter, Deborah Roberts, Robynn Stilwell, and Pete Thomas. I am particularly indebted to Beverley Lomer and Karen Randell for introducing me to the work of Teresa Brennan and Cathy Caruth.

Notes

1. "[U]nder certain circumstances ... the vocal folds may crash together unevenly, their edges being corrugated and unmatched, rubbing against each other and producing a sound which sounds broken, frictional, rough and discontinuous. These broken sounds are referred to as disrupted" (Newham 1998, 49).
2. The World Health Organization's *International Classification of Functioning, Disability and Health* (ICFDH) attempts to reconcile the medical and social models for disability in a new paradigm, the biopsychosocial model (World Health Organization 2002). It proposes that disability is an "outcome of interactions between health conditions (diseases, disorders and injuries) and contextual [environmental and personal] factors ... Disability therefore involves dysfunctioning at one or more of these ... levels: impairments, activity limitations and participation restrictions," where impairments are "problems in body function or structure such as a significant deviation or loss" (p. 10).
3. Brennan (2003, 9) defines *entrainment* as "the form of transmission whereby people become alike ... a process whereby one person's or one group's nervous and hormonal systems are brought into alignment with another's." Brennan's work, curtailed by her death during the copyediting stage of her book, developed her arguments on the transmission of affect through the olfactory sense, although it is clear that sound is also implicated. She mentions that the word *sentir* and its cognates in Romance languages mean both "to feel" (both touch and emotion) and "to smell"; they do, of course, also mean "to hear" and "to perceive." Essential to Brennan's hypothesis is that affect is transmitted as feeling, not as emotion, and that it is discerned rather than understood.
4. In Lacanian terms, it is precisely this suppression of vocal materiality by signification that constitutes the development of the Self's relationship with the Other. See Poizat (1992).

5. Eisenberg's subject is gay, and his response to Callas exemplifies the "opera queen" practices described by Morris (1993, 190): "The ability to invent and sustain intense personal revelation is typical of the characters that the great divas play. These are invoked to justify emotional states in everyday life, and, conversely, personal experience is brought to bear on their interpretation."

6. The passage occurs in *Canto Tredecisimo, 41–3.*

7. Although why and how negative mood matching in a performance is perceived as positive or beneficial remains open to debate, empirical research may provide support for the phenomenon. Peretz's (2001, 124) work on neural correlates and musical emotion refers to two independent studies, one that "sees similarities in the emotional 'chills' evoked by sad music and those engendered by 'distress calls' of young children and animals;" the other which implicates the septum, "a region [of the brain] typically associated with pleasure, in emotional 'chills' for self-selected music."

8. One should also remember that Crosby's style of singing was not universally admired. McCracken (1999, 381) cites an article in *Musical America* from the 1930s in which a voice teacher described crooning as "a perversion of the natural production of the voice" and "extremely injurious."

9. Garland-Thomson (1997) has noted the similarities between the ways in which beautification processes and disability configure the female body.

10. A recording of the concert is available on Curb Records, *Judy Garland and Liza Minnelli: Together* (Curb D2-77585, 1993).

11. This essay is not the place to debate how the vicissitudes of stardom are made manifest, yet one might read Garland's performance at this concert in the same way Barthes (1993, 105) reads *La Dame aux camélias*: "She sees that she suffers, but imagines no remedy which is not parasitic to her own suffering; she knows herself to be an object but cannot think of any destination for herself other than that of ornament in the museum of the masters."

12. The circumstances of the concert, and the audience reaction to it, were described by Paul Gambaccini in an episode of his BBC Radio 4 series, "For One Night Only," first broadcast January 11, 2005.

Part III
Composing Disability Musically

13

Les chansons des fous: On the Edge of Madness with Alkan

L. POUNDIE BURSTEIN

Many celebrated composers have a reputation for being unconventional or eccentric. But even in such company, Charles-Valentin Alkan (1813–1888) stands out. As Alan Ridout put it, Alkan "chose to live in a way that in no sense could be described as normal. His fantasy life was more important to him …. Alkan would have composed quite differently, though possibly as effectively, had he not been cursed, or blessed, with such a strong obsessional neurosis" (Smith 1987, v). Such a characterization, which directly relates his idiosyncratic musical style to his reputedly abnormal personality, is by no means uncommon in discussions of Alkan and his music. Indeed, it seems that for many, the image of Alkan's music is tightly bound up with that of a "mad" composer.[1]

The notion of the mad artist, of course, has been a popular and enduring one.[2] The characterization of madness in art is not a benign one, however, for it can lead to unfortunate distortions. In particular, it can wrongly suggest that the emotions and qualities associated with eccentric artworks are held only by an isolated segment of society rather than ones shared to some extent by everybody. Yet all people have a certain degree of unwarranted fears, obsessions, and anxieties. Similarly, all artists can express such things through their creations, which in turn can speak to experiences with which everyone can empathize. At what point of severity or frequency these qualities warrant a classification of madness is not absolute but is rather one that varies according to culture.[3] For instance, whether a certain degree of a fear of heights represents a normal survival mechanism or a case of acrophobia will differ for a Sherpa mountaineer on the one hand and an Iowa farmer on the other. Likewise, the presence of madness in a work of music must be considered in light of stylistic and generic norms; what is commonplace in a composition of one style might well come across as sounding mad within another.

This certainly seems to be the case with Alkan's music. Although some of the oddities of his pieces may readily be found in the works of others, especially from later eras, it is their abundance within their stylistic context that has led many to regard Alkan's music as being somewhat mad. For the most part,

Alkan's compositions are actually rather conventional. The basic harmonic, melodic, and formal language of his music largely is similar to that of other composers from his time. But although firmly ensconced within the Romantic style, many of his works nevertheless have features so notably odd that they seem to come from a different world. Alkan's detractors—of whom there are several—criticize his music for its wild excesses, inconsistencies, and bizarre features.[4] On the other hand, many of Alkan's devotees admire his music for the very same reasons.

The most notorious aspect of his music is its extraordinary demand for virtuosity. Even compared to other virtuoso works of the nineteenth century, Alkan's piano writing is incredibly challenging, demanding "a physical, mental and moral staying power beyond that required for any other music of the period" (Smith 1987, 245). It is not merely that his pieces are difficult, but that the difficulties arrive unceasingly over the course of unusually lengthy pieces.[5] In works of other composers, the virtuoso passages are usually saved to reinforce the emotional climax. Alkan, on the other hand, often starts his compositions at a frighteningly difficult level and either maintains this level throughout or else heightens the complications even further, far beyond a point that would seem reasonable. This is true not only of his etudes but also even of many of his pieces in genres where virtuosity would normally be considered inappropriate, such as his *Sonatine*, Op. 61, which is hardly the short and simple piece its title would suggest.

Extremely virtuosic works of other composers tend to highlight the ability of the performer to transcend the limitations of the body. Such pieces ideally involve a public display of this transcendence, thereby allowing the performer to assert a sense of individual freedom to an audience.[6] Yet Alkan's virtuosic works are curiously cerebral and private. As Hugh McDonald (2001, 378) notes, Alkan "wrote not as a pianist with a keyboard before him but with the cerebral exactness of someone for whom the notation is more important than the sound."

If anything, Alkan's virtuosic pieces are so replete with self-imposed obstacles as to emphasize arbitrary limitations imposed on the body. Such is the case, for instance, with his *Three Etudes for Piano*, Op. 76, for left hand alone, right hand alone, and both hands together, respectively. Not surprisingly, despite their monumental power, these monstrously difficult etudes are rarely performed—especially as a unit—so that they exist practically as abstract thought games. Even Alkan only rarely played his works in public, so his pieces can hardly be regarded as vehicles meant to enhance his own career as a performer (Schilling 1986, 83–102). And in certain of his works, the difficulties are such that they must remain hidden from view. This is the case in the four-part fughetta for feet alone from his *Twelve Etudes for pedal-piano or organ* (see Figure 13.1). The nature of this etude's medium naturally prevents audiences from witnessing the hardships its performer must endure.

Figure 13.1 Twelve Etudes for pedal-piano or organ (for feet alone), No. 4, mm. 1–8

As a result, far from being allowed a public display of freedom the organist must struggle in private with the peculiar requirements of this work.

Alkan's music brashly deviates from the norms of its style in other ways as well. Several of his works that are not virtuosic go to the other extreme by exhibiting a Satie-like simplicity (as in his Prelude Op. 13, No. 21). Alkan frequently exploits the registral limits of the piano, having both extremely high and extremely low notes sound at the same time, often in thick chords, so as to produce odd-sounding sonorities. Extremism also may be witnessed in the great length of a number of his works, as well as the extent to which Alkan maintains a single mood, texture, or idea to the point of sounding obsessive.

For instance, consider his Prelude Op. 31, No. 8, subtitled "La chanson de la folle au bord de la mer" ("The song of the madwoman by the seashore"). The title character of this prelude is depicted by an obsessionally repetitive, sometimes harsh melody in an extremely high register (see Figure 13.2). This melody is contrasted by uncannily low, thick chords in the accompaniment, which illustrate the steady crashing of the waves to which the madwoman sings her lonely song. That they are meant to portray the actions of a madwoman only partly explains the abnormal sonorities and repetitiveness found in this piece, since these features may be found in many of Alkan's other works. This is true even in compositions that have no suggestive programmatic title, such as his Etude Op. 39, No. 4, which likewise exploits the outer registers of the piano in an uncanny fashion.

Alkan's harmonies likewise tend toward extremes. Although his tonal language is mostly rather conservative, his music nonetheless often features strikingly daring modulations (as in the nearly atonal *Les Enharmoniques*, Op. 63, No. 41), exotic scales (as in the entirely Lydian *Allegro Barbaro*, Op. 35, No. 5, and the octatonic scales in the finale of the *Grande Sonate*, Op. 33), and shockingly dissonant sonorities (as in the tone clusters excerpted in Figure 13.3A). Another notable eccentricity of Alkan's music may be found in its use of rapid changes in mood. In many of his works, a furious section is

Figure 13.2 Prelude in G-flat Major, Op. 31, No. 8, "La chanson de la folle au bord de la mer," mm. 11–31.

suddenly followed by a simple and naive theme, or vice versa. Rapid starts, stops, and violent outbursts are likewise quite common in Alkan's oeuvre (as in the excerpt of Figure 13.3B, where a jovial passage is suddenly interrupted by out-of-meter chordal blasts).

Perhaps the strangest aspect of Alkan's music, however, may be found in its narrative layout. Although Alkan often uses standard forms, many of his compositions nevertheless exhibit an unusual narrative shape. The standard procedure in most tonal works involves the introduction of a disruptive element early on, after which this disruptive element is confronted so that it is either overcome, reconciled, or else succumbed to.[7] In much of Alkan's music, on the other hand, the disruptive element simply exists: It either is introduced late in the composition, is sustained throughout, or else otherwise remains somehow unchanged, as though oblivious to its environment.

Consider his Prelude Op. 38, No. 2, subtitled "Fa." Although this piece is in A minor, until the last six bars the pitch F is struck on every eighth note, a total of 406 times in a row. At the outset of the piece, the pitch F is an irritant that clashes with the fifth of the tonic chord (see Figure 13.4A). As the prelude modulates through various keys, the F at times becomes less bothersome (as when the piece turns toward B-flat major in measures 60 ff.) and at times

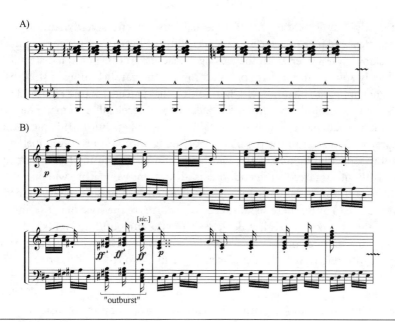

Figure 13.3 Excerpts from two Etudes: (A) Etude in E-flat Major, Op. 35, No. 7, mm. 45–46; (B) Etude in A Minor, Op. 39, No. 1 ("Comme le vent"), mm. 184–95.

Figure 13.4 Excerpts from Prelude in A Minor, Op. 38, No. 2, "Fa": (A) mm. 1–8; (B) mm. 133–41.

absolutely intrusive and even nonsensical (as at the tonicization of C major in measures 84–5). But through it all, the pitch F steadfastly remains. Even at the end of the piece, the F continues to be asserted in an utterly baffling fashion (see Figure 13.4B). This weirdly reiterated F does not achieve heroic victory or suffer tragic reversal, nor is it changed in any manner; it simply persists, as though insensible to the changing surroundings.

Alkan's Prelude Op. 31, No. 12, in G-flat major, presents another such eccentric narrative framework. Despite its diatonicism, this prelude sounds extremely fragile, owing to its repeated quintuplets, soft dynamics, and complete avoidance of a perfect cadence. Nothing overturns the work's tentative stability, however, until the closing measures. At this point, a disruption suddenly appears in the form of a shift toward the parallel minor, a shift that does not appear to be prompted by anything that precedes it (see Figure 13.5). It is not uncommon for a minor key piece to end heroically in a major key or for a major key piece to end tragically in a minor key. But in this piece the unprepared motion to the parallel minor, along with an unresolved melodic leading tonic highlighted by this chromatic motion, enters and leaves quickly and without fanfare. In the end, one is almost left wondering whether this shift toward minor actually took place or whether it was simply imagined: The motion to minor here so far exceeds the norms of the style that it seems to represent a break from reality, detached from the surrounding events.

For one more example of a work in which disruptive elements enter and depart with relatively little fuss, consider the finale to Alkan's *Grande Sonate*, Op. 33, subtitled "50 ans: Prométhée Enchaîné." After a tonally vague opening, the piece introduces a hymn-like theme in G-sharp minor that modulates toward its relative major, with chromaticisms increasing in intensity as the expected cadence in B major approaches (see Figure 13.6). This cadence is

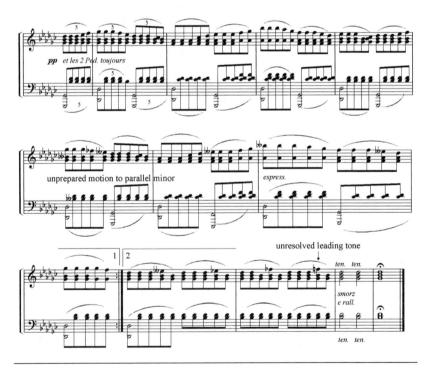

Figure 13.5 Prelude in G-flat Major, Op. 31, No. 12, "J'étais endormie, mais mon coeur veillait" ("Though I Slumbered, My Heart was Awake"), mm. 19–28.

Figure 13.6 *Grande Sonate*, Op. 33, iv: "50 ans: Prométhée Enchaîné, mm. 1–24.

thwarted in measure 16, however, by a sudden deceptive motion to G major. During the next passage the G natural is prolonged, as though frozen in horror. But much as it enters suddenly, so the G natural departs suddenly as well: In measure 21, the motion to B major resumes almost effortlessly, as if the nightmarish intrusion of the G natural in measures 16–20 had never taken place. Such alternations of simple diatonic themes with eerie, shocking tonal diversions continue throughout the movement. Again, unlike in the works of most other composers, the disruptive elements here are never purged or reconciled to their surroundings. As with the bound Prometheus of the movement's subtitle, who must endure his suffering without hope of escape through freedom or death, there is never a sense that these chromatic disturbances will overpower or be overpowered, but rather that they are destined to be endured without hope of redemption.

The larger, multimovement framework of the sonata likewise is highly unusual. The opening movement, subtitled "20 ans," is maniacal from its very first bar, with wild technical demands, cross-rhythms, and rapid modulations throughout. A brief respite arrives only in the middle, where a lyrical theme enters, but by the end of the movement even this lyrical theme gets caught up in the frenzied excitement. The second movement, "30 ans: Quasi Faust," is schizoid, with wild shifts of sections, moods, registers, dynamics, and keys; it climaxes with a jaw-dropping eight-part fugue, in which three of the fugal voices are doubled in octaves. The ravishing third movement, "40 ans: un heureux ménage," is much calmer, although it does boast certain Alkanesque excesses, particularly regarding the length as it sustains certain textures and moods. The third movement is in the key of G major, and its tonal point of furthest remove is G-sharp minor. This tonal relationship is reversed in the finale, which is in G-sharp minor with G major treated as a disruptive, distant key (see Figure. 13.6).[8] The last movement is perhaps the darkest finale of any piano sonata from the nineteenth century; it is practically as depressed as the first movement is manic.

The program implied by the subtitles of the movements in this sonata is a surprisingly bitter one. As these subtitles suggest, the sonata charts the course through four decades of a protagonist, who is introduced in the first movement as a twenty-year-old youth filled with exuberance. By the end of the sonata, however, the hopes of the opening movement appear to be dashed, as the protagonist seems almost incapacitated by world-weariness. Curiously, the dark finale does not portray someone who is extremely aged, as one might expect, but rather someone who is merely fifty years old. Evidently, the implied narrator who relates the tale expressed by this sonata holds an extremely pessimistic and depressed view of life.

Here, as in many of his works, it does not seem that Alkan is simply representing or depicting madness at arm's length. This might have been the case if the odd moments of his compositions were separated from the more staid passages by being segregated within distinct sections. In such a scenario, it would be as though the strange passages were being winked at, while the compositional voice behind the music stands apart, at a safe distance from the oddities. In Alkan's music, however, the bizarre-sounding moments and straightforward moments frequently intermingle with one another. Often, a passage by Alkan that boasts a stirring Romantic harmonic progression is the same one that forcefully features an odd-sounding sonority, strange technical demand, or eccentric narrative layout. As such, much of his music—like his *Grande Sonate*, Op. 33—suggests the direct presence of a mad persona underlying the music. That is, features of his music so strikingly clash with the norms of its style that his music seems to directly express the emotions of one who would be coded by society as being mad.

As always, however, care should be taken not to confuse the musical persona with the actual composer.[9] For instance, that a happy-sounding piece should project a happy persona by no means indicates that the composer was necessarily in a good mood when the piece was composed. Likewise, that a mad persona underlies much of Alkan's music by no means indicates that the composer himself had any mental or emotional problems.

Yet, as seen in the quotation at the beginning of this essay, some have found it hard to resist relating the persona behind Alkan's music to the composer himself. Even some of his most ardent admirers have suggested that Alkan's unconventional compositional approach is a musical manifestation of the composer's personality. The following statements, all from leading advocates of Alkan, are typical:

> Everything about Alkan is strange; his life, his death, his music and its fate during his life and after his death (Lewenthal 1964, 1).
>
> Alkan's enigmatic character [is] reflected in his music. … He dressed in a severe, old-fashioned, somewhat clerical manner, discouraged visitors and went out rarely. … He had few friends … was nervous in public and pathologically worried about his health, even though it was good (MacDonald 2001, 377).
>
> In his revealing study of creative motivation, *The Dynamics of Creation*, Anthony Storr describes traits of the obsessional personality … With Alkan these characteristics, exacerbated no doubt by his isolation, are carried to the edge of fanaticism. … At the heart of Alkan's creativity there is also this fierce obsessional control … his obsession with a specific idea can border on the pathological (Smith 1987, 244–5).[10]

These statements suggest that Alkan had severe mental or emotional problems. But is such an assumption justified?

Let us consider Alkan's biography in its broad outlines.[11] Alkan entered the Paris Conservatory at an early age, where he was celebrated as an astounding prodigy. By his early twenties he became recognized as one of the great piano virtuosos of his time. He was greatly admired by most of the leading musicians of Paris; Franz Liszt reportedly claimed that Alkan "had the finest technique of anyone he knew" (Murdoch 1935, 232–3). Alkan's subsequent career did not live up to its early promise, however. He never gave a concert tour and hardly ever performed or even visited cities outside of Paris. From ages twenty-six to sixty he performed in only a handful of concerts, and for many years he completely avoided the concert stage, including a twenty-year hiatus from 1853 to 1873. He shunned not only performing but also people in general, preferring to stay home translating the Bible and composing. Visitors to his home were repeatedly turned away, and he even lost a chance at receiving the coveted Legion of Honor by rebuffing the award committee every time they came to meet with him. He also suffered from various physical illnesses, real or imagined, and apparently had trouble relating to his servants, turning down over fifty applicants before he could find a replacement for a housekeeper who left him in 1861. Not surprisingly, Alkan was considered an obscure, mysterious figure long before he died.

Do these events indeed indicate that his anxieties and obsessions seriously impeded Alkan's ability to function within his society? If he had been a hermit or a farmer in a remote village, his actions would have been quite normal. Within his own social setting as a leading piano virtuoso, however, his actions do come across as highly unusual. Certainly, they are not inconsistent with a diagnosis that Alkan was a hypochondriac whose irrational fears and agoraphobia destroyed his chances for outstanding wealth, fame, and success. And if this were true, it would indeed be possible that his mental condition had an impact on the idiosyncratic nature of his music.

On the other hand, perhaps his behavior had perfectly reasonable explanations. Perhaps he simply did not enjoy performing; perhaps he was too busy with his scholarly and compositional activities to entertain guests. Maybe he was not a hypochondriac but really did suffer from physical ailments. As a religious Jew living in Paris in the mid-1800s, it is not surprising that Alkan would acquire a reputation among his contemporaries as an eccentric, and it is quite possible that his isolation from society was a reaction to anti-Semitism. For all we know, Alkan should more properly be characterized not as mad but rather as a modest, sober, and dedicated musician who chose to eschew the vanities of a stage career to commit himself to composition and religious studies.[12]

In sum, it might well be that Alkan did not put his life into his music but rather that the public has put his music into his life. In actuality, little is known about Alkan's character, personality, or mental condition. Nevertheless, the fragments of his biography that survive allow one to piece together a story about his life, and that this story so often is framed as a tale of a madman seems prompted more by the transgressive nature of his compositions than by any solid evidence that survives concerning his existence.

The event of Alkan's life story that seems to have been most skewed to match the qualities perceived in his music is his death. The tale of Alkan's death has been retold countless times; it is by far the most celebrated aspect of his biography. However, despite their notoriety, his final hours are surprisingly unremarkable: At age seventy-four, Alkan fell down in his house and was unable to get up until discovered hours later by his housekeeper. Weakened from his ordeal, the frail, elderly man died later that day. Although this tale is rather humdrum, it has become twisted over the years into something much more sensational. According to the legend surrounding Alkan's death, he was *crushed* to death by a falling bookcase. Though only tangentially related to the actual facts, this story nonetheless does capture something of Alkan's myth, for it has seemed fitting to some that a composer of such mad pieces should not only have had a mad life but a mad death as well.[13]

Alkan's music has a kind of split personality. In certain ways, it is quite conservative, conforming to the stylistic norms of his time and culture. In other ways, however, it is so shockingly unconventional and excessive as to suggest the compositional voice of one who is an outcast from society. But it would be misleading to thereby suggest that the emotions expressed by his music are ones experienced by only a small number of people. Although the intensity and frequency of such features vary from person to person, qualities such as obsessiveness, extreme mood swings, and erratic and unsocial behavior are experienced by all. Perhaps more so than almost any other composer of his time, Alkan explored facets of life that many have stigmatized as emblematic of madness. As such, his music helps give voice to an important part of the shared human condition.

Notes

1. The term *madness* refers to mental and emotional behavior that radically fails to conform to the norms and expectations of one's society, behavior now typically medicalized as mental or emotional illness, bipolar disorder, schizophrenia, neurosis, and the like. The celebrated discussion in Foucault (1961) situates the classification *madness* as part of a societal power play that first developed in seventeenth-century France. As others have since noted, however, the bracketing of certain members of society as having mental disorders has long existed in a wide variety of cultures (see, e.g., Roth and Kroll 1986).
2. Becker (1978) provides an overview of concepts that have been put forth regarding the connection between madness and genius, along with a list of fifty-four works written from 1836 to 1949 that address this issue, pro or con. Other discussions on this matter include Storr (1988), Jamison (1993), Eysenck (1995), Hershman and Leib (1998), Claridge (1998), and Nettle (2001). Studies that explicitly explore the connection between musicians—such as Carlo Gesualdo, George Frideric Handel, Wolfgang Amadeus Mozart, Ludwig van Beethoven, and Robert Schumann—and their purported mental or emotional problems include Slater and Mayer (1959, 1960), Trethowan (1977), and Ober (1973, 80–93); see also Davies (1989), Storr (1972), Hershman and Leib (1988), and Shoham (2003). Dissenting voices that question the connection between creativity and madness may be found in Kessel (1989), Rothenberg (1990), and Schlesinger (2002).
3. A cogent discussion of the role of society in determining the boundaries of mental illness and madness may be found in Horwitz (2002). That societal values serve as chief determinants in the categorization of a disability is of course a central theme of disability studies, and this is as valid for the classification of mental and emotional disabilities as it is for physical disabilities.
4. For instance, in Bouyer (1903, 276), Alkan's music is depicted as "dense, strange, bizarre, inconsistent" ("touffu, curieux, bizarre, inégal"). Similarly, in a more recent review, Lloyd (1996, 29) stated that "opinion remains divided over whether [Alkan's works] are radically inventive or merely naive, eccentric and grotesquely overblown salon pieces...In far too much of [his] music, the lack of convincing melodic invention and sudden alternations of whimsy, sentiment and bombast rapidly become tiresome."
5. As noted in Luguenot and Martin (1991, 188), "Alkan seems to have anticipated the recommendation of Neuhaus: 'Fast, loud, and for a long time.' And we should add: to the extreme limits psychologically." ("Alkan semble avoir devancé la recommendation de Neuhaus: 'Vite, fort, longtemps.' Ajoutons: jusq'aux extrêmes limites psychologiques.")
6. The interconnection of virtuosity, freedom, and public display is discussed in Samson (2003, 76–7).

7. See Straus (2006), which traces such narratives in music by Beethoven and Franz Schubert, linking them to Arnold Schoenberg's concept of the "tonal problem."
8. Various other motivic connections linking the movements of this sonata are discussed at length in François-Sappey (1991b, 95–128).
9. The distinction between composer and persona is discussed most famously in Cone (1974).
10. The reference is to Storr (1972), which discusses composers with obsessive–compulsive disorders and manic–depressive temperaments. The popular press often is less tactful when discussing Alkan. For instance, in praising the composer Yungkans (2004) crudely states that "Alkan was one of the certified wackos of classical music. ... Hearing [his] etudes in one sitting made me think of a variation of the oft-quoted phrase about Glenn Gould. In Alkan's case, that genius is definitely a nut."
11. The following summary is based on information found in standard writings on Alkan, such as Smith (1976), Schilling (1986), and François-Sappey (1991a).
12. See comments in Schilling (1986, 81–2). Also, compare with discussions in Frosch (1987, 1990a, 1990b), which question the validity of the alleged mental problems of Beethoven, Handel, and Mozart, respectively.
13. Another element of the Alkan myth involved in the story of his death is the suggestion of his religious devotion (or perhaps even fanaticism?), since invariably it is claimed that it was the Jewish Talmud he was trying to pull out of the bookcase at the time of the accident. This detail underlines the very preposterousness of the story, because it is never explained how anybody could tell from among a pile of fallen books that it was the Talmud Alkan was grabbing for, nor does it make sense that such a frequently consulted book of his should have been placed at an awkward spot on the bookshelf. For an extended discussion and criticism of the legend surrounding Alkan's death, see Macdonald (1973, 1988).

14
Finding Autism in the Compositions of a 19th-Century Prodigy: Reconsidering "Blind Tom" Wiggins

STEPHANIE JENSEN-MOULTON

Introduction to Thomas Wiggins ("Blind Tom")

In 1849, the fourteenth child of Black slaves Charity Greene and Mungo Wiggins was born blind. The following year, five members of the Wiggins family—both parents, two boys, and a baby—were sold to the wealthy and well-educated Bethune family in Georgia. The Wiggins' baby son, Tom, clearly disabled, was thrown in at no charge with the purchase of the mother and father (Southall 1979). This free item—a blind, mentally incompetent child—soon became one of the most famous and well-paid personages of nineteenth-century stage entertainment. Thomas Greene Wiggins'[1] legendary career as a pianist is a rich site for the exploration of disability as a contributing factor to cultural production.

Wiggins approached the piano, without training, and played one of the Bethune daughters' most difficult pieces at the age of four. General James Neil Bethune saw a financial opportunity and brought Wiggins to the concert stage by age eight. The first public appearance of "Blind Tom" took place on October 7, 1857, in Temperance Hall in Columbus, Georgia (Southall 1979). A review in the *Columbus Enquirer* from October 13, 1857, notes that Wiggins was advertised as an "eight year old genius, without benefit of instruction, yet capable of performing the most difficult works by Beethoven, Mozart, Herz, and others of equal reputation" and that he performed "to the satisfaction of an appreciative and fashionable audience" (Southall 1999). A Southern audience, in the midst of antebellum anti-black sentiment, devoured this type of entertainment. Not only was Wiggins a spectacular pianist for a boy of eight years, but he also provided the type of stage show that was crucial to a justification of black subjugation and enslavement. Wiggins also sang and made circular motions with his hands while he played, which added to the spectacle (Southall 1979).

Bethune capitalized on Wiggins' remarkable memory in his construction of the stage act. In addition to a recital of works ranging from parlor songs of Wiggins' own composition to works by Frédéric Chopin and Louis Gottschalk, he took requests from the audience and played them backward, simultaneously, or with his back turned to the piano. Bethune then invited challengers to the stage, who played a piece and then asked Wiggins to repeat it immediately, which he did perfectly. Typically, these challengers would purposefully make a mistake in their renditions, expecting Wiggins to play the piece as originally written, therefore proving that he already knew the piece. True to his reputation, Wiggins could reliably play pieces exactly as they were played for him and could copy any mistakes to the note. Add to this Wiggins' propensity for speaking about himself in the third person, his tendency to leap up from the piano and pace wildly around the stage between numbers, and his repetition of bodily motions and gestures, and Bethune had essentially created a one-man freak show in the style of P.T. Barnum. He soon sold the act to a manager named Perry Oliver for a cool $15,000; Oliver then cleared over $50,000 exhibiting Wiggins (Southall 1979).

Through this management, as well as through the Bethunes' manipulation of post-bellum custodial loopholes, Wiggins provided income for his plantation masters and their descendents for the duration of his life. Three trials concerning Wiggins' custody occurred between 1865 and 1886. Each trial revolved around three central issues: Wiggins' legal status (i.e., slave or free Black), his mental state (i.e., competent or incompetent), and his potential as income earner for the appointed guardian. Custody not only in the first two trials was granted to Bethune, with whom Wiggins toured extensively not only in the United States but also in Europe and Canada. Wiggins' 1866 concerts in London alone cleared $100,000 for his managers. Wiggins continued to tour after his custody was granted to Bethune's estranged daughter-in-law, Eliza Stutzbach. He commanded large audiences throughout his life, up until just three years before his death in 1909 (Southall 1999).

Understanding Wiggins and his role in nineteenth-century American musical life requires an acknowledgment of the full spectrum of his disabilities, both physical and cognitive. Contemporary accounts universally acknowledge his blindness, but his cognitive disability is either disputed or difficult to quantify; secondary sources colored by racism, political bias, or desire for financial gain further cloud the issue. Though his principal biographer, Geneva Southall, addresses Wiggins' blindness, she does not attempt to reconcile his musical career with his probable autism. Southall's goals to legitimize Blind Tom and to bring his music into a canon of Black composers are clear in this statement from the introduction to Southall's (1999, xvi) third volume: "Of course Blind Tom was eccentric. ... But to what extent was this encouraged by prejudice, blindness [figurative], social isolation, and his coaching? Unlike the instances of others, this seems not to have been an affectation. It was probably an absence of discipline (which is a nuance of education)." Neither Wiggins' supposed eccentricity nor his lack of education accounted for the well-documented court hearings regarding his custody in his later years. A merely uneducated or undisciplined individual, even if blind, might not require full-time care into middle age, suggesting that Wiggins was not just blind but multiply disabled. Given that all three of these trials incorporated testimony about Wiggins' mental state, I conclude that his cognitive difference was significant and falls in line with autistic spectrum behaviors.

Because of Wiggins' precarious position as a Black performer born into slavery, any conception of him as an "idiot" reinforced the stereotypes about blacks that were most valued by racist patrons. Documentation of Wiggins' disabilities was mediated either by the press or by General Bethune. As Adrienne Asch (2004, 17) states, "arguably, the most important prong of any definition of disability is that of being 'regarded' as impaired." Yet an understanding of Wiggins' autistic behaviors leads to a greater understanding of his music. Previous writings on Wiggins have not provided detailed readings of his compositions, and the lack of any customary primary sources other than Wiggins' music underscores the need for musical analysis. This chapter examines cultural and musicological issues primarily surrounding Wiggins' "Battle of Manassas," as well as his "Variations on 'When This Cruel War Is Over'" and "Wellenklänge," through the lens of his multiple disabilities.

Perceiving Blind Tom: Cultural Constructions of Race and Disability

Setting out to prove that Wiggins was autistic through a kind of historical diagnosis would be nearly impossible, given that the term *autism* did not even come into use until the mid-twentieth century. Based on the accounts of Wiggins' amazing repertory and descriptions of his stage persona, one can only conjecture that he was an autistic savant. A performer who could memorize so rapidly and accurately, who could call up remote tunes from his vast repertory of memorized pieces, yet who exhibited particular patterns of speech and communication delay as well as repeated gestures and sounds would likely fall somewhere on the autistic spectrum of behavior. To deny that Wiggins possessed characteristics in line with a cognitive disability such as autism erases a significant aspect of the person and betrays a desire for an American narrative of disability transcended, problems overcome. Rather, Wiggins' autism is central to his personal identity and to his modes of musical composition and performance. An understanding of his cognitive disability is therefore intimately linked to a deeper analysis of his works.

The physical disability of blindness and the cognitive differences associated with autism carry different social and societal meanings. Although blindness might disable an individual, it generally did not carry with it any judgment about a person's intelligence, as a cognitive disability might. Testimony from the custody trials surrounding Wiggins provides some clues into the actual and perceived patterns of behavior that suggest his cognitive difference. In an 1865 article, one reporter from the *Cincinnati Gazette* of July 20, 1865, noted, "When we first saw Tom he was twisting himself in every imaginable attitude, hopping around on one foot and his head bent down nearly to the ground resembling in nearly every gesture the movements of the monkey much more than a human being. When playing or listening to music he seems to be under something like a mesmeric influence, and is sometimes so excited and agitated as to tremble from head to foot as if suffering from intense pain" (quoted in Southall 1979, 48). The racist overtones in this article and in the following review—replete with language of superstition and bodily instinct—bring to mind the sheet-music covers from blackface minstrel tunes, depicting blacks with exaggeratedly long arms and big mouths, often suggestive of apes. Yet Wiggins was not a minstrel performer but rather a concert pianist. His gestures and posturings, though probably exaggerated in the previous quotation, were likely well outside the realm of the normative. Another account from the first custody trial describes his speech as "crude, hesitant, and sometimes indirect" (Southall 1979, 56). A later review from 1892 describes Wiggins' behavior in his hotel during a tour:

> He rarely sat down, and presumably by way of satisfying an instinct for bodily exercise he occasionally danced about the room, poising his bulky body first upon one foot and then upon the other, and now and then bending over the foot board of his bed end putting his great big head hard and rapidly against the mattress (quoted in Southall 1999, 53).

Whereas other disabled performers of the period such as Tom Thumb and Blind Boone were made partners in their own enterprises, Wiggins' physical attitudes and difficulty with speech made a manager a necessity. One cannot fully understand to what extent these managers—General Bethune, Perry Oliver, and Eliza Stutzbach Bethune—encouraged or cultivated the physical manifestations of Wiggins' disabilities. What is certain is that these proclivities contributed to a cultural construction as a mentally impaired individual.

Several problems with the information available on Thomas Wiggins surface immediately. First, the existence of typical primary sources—journals and letters written by Wiggins, for example—is highly unlikely. The combination of his blindness, enslavement, and probable autism posed a triple threat to his potential to receive education; since Wiggins never attended school, it is unlikely that he could read or write—at least in any conventional way. Authorship presents a particular problem in regard to Wiggins' compositions. Blind composers have certainly existed in the past, but one must pose the question: How exactly does the music from the mind of a blind nineteenth-century composer reach the page and then go into print? The case is complicated further by the potential for exploitation due to Wiggins' cognitive disability. If indeed he composed over 100 original pieces, how did they reach the public eye and ear? The testimony of one of Wiggins' teachers, Dr. Joseph Poznan-sky, reveals vaguely that his various teachers served as scribes for his original works (Southall 1999), but the transmission of the material to the teachers is highly questionable. One of his teachers' names often appears prominently on Wiggins' sheet-music covers, with the name Blind Tom either in parentheses or absent altogether and replaced by a pen name. One of Wiggins' pen names, Prof. W. F. Raymond, masks Wiggins' disability by taking on the persona of a professor; another, François Sexalise, aligns him with a white, European compositional tradition.

One of the main sources for the narrative of Wiggins' early life is the 1967 biographical article written by Norbonne T. N. Robinson. As Southall (1999, 76) noted, "Since the writer was a grandson of General Bethune, and had written from the orally transmitted information as given from the Bethunes themselves, the author's statements will understandably be biased in favor of his relatives." As a result, Wiggins' early life and initial forays into musical activity are difficult to document. Anecdotal evidence presented by Charity Wiggins in the context of custody trials and the oral history passed through generations of Bethunes are the best sources available thus far. Secondary sources, in particular articles from newspapers, also pose problems of bias. Civil War-era media, clearly divided on issues of race, could have easily used reviews and coverage of Wiggins' performances and activities as vehicles for propaganda and the dissemination of pro-slavery or abolitionist ideologies. General Bethune was a celebrated pro-slavery journalist and would have been expert at the manipulation of information for public consumption. In sum, when Wiggins did speak for himself, his words were mediated by someone else; likewise, any documentation of his disabilities was handled by others. His music is the only primary source where Wiggins and his autism may be found relatively unmediated.

Blind Tom in Aural Space: "The Battle of Manassas"

In his "Battle of Manassas," Wiggins brings an important Civil War battle into his own understanding through a musical transcription of the event, using seven melodies—six borrowed and one original. This composition, with its use of pastiche and onomatopoetic imitation, reflects Wiggins' unique world-view and brings to light specific characteristics of composition that relate directly to autistic-spectrum interests and behaviors such as echolalia (i.e., immediate and exact repetition of heard speech) and repetition of one sound or task. When these modes of thought become music, the publisher and editor attempt to mediate them to shield the public from the embarrassment of the performance indications; these are quite well suited to Wiggins but perhaps not to nineteenth-century American social mores.

Given the questions of authorship, musical style, and primary sources out-lined already, Wiggins' descriptive pieces for solo piano—including imitations of a guitar, a music box, and a sewing machine—represent the repertory most likely to bear his authorship and to reveal his elusive persona.[2] Arguably Wiggins' most famous work, "The Battle of Manassas" easily falls into the descriptive category. The North's Battle of Bull Run is known in the South as the Battle of Manassas, hence the title of Wiggins' piece. This battle, one of the first of the Civil War, took place within mere miles of Washington, D.C., and proved to be a barometer of the way the war would progress: slowly, violently, and with an unpredictable outcome. Unlike other pieces attributed to Blind Tom, this piece contains specific, programmatic indications at the start of each section. Here, he is featured as the composer by the name of Blind Tom instead of as one of his other previously mentioned pseudonyms. Also unique to this piece is the lengthy note preceding the musical score.

General Bethune wrote the introductory note, which contains an introduction to the thematic material found in the piece as well as the circumstances under which it was composed: "Soon after the battle [of Manassas] occurred, I happened to a very serious accident which kept me in Nashville for several months.[3] Tom was often in my room. Every little paragraph about the battle was discussed in various forms for a week or more. He heard this thing read of and talked of, and after hearing it for ten days he took his seat at the Piano and produced what he will now play for you; and when asked what that was he was playing, his reply was, that it was his Battle of Manassas" (Wiggins 1866). The note states that Wiggins' piece will illustrate both Confederate and Union armies approaching the battle site, with the tune "The Girl I Left Behind Me"[4] representing the South and "Dixie" representing the North. (Only later would "Dixie" be appropriated as symbolic of Southern ideology.[5]) Then, Wiggins would:

> represent the eve of battle by a very soft sweet melody, then the clattering of arms and accoutrements, the war trumpet of Beauregard and then McDowell's in the distance, like an echo of the first. He will represent the firing of the cannon to Yankee Doodle, Marseillaise Hymn, Star Spangled Banner, Dixie, and the arrival of the train of cars containing Gen. Kirby Smith's reinforcements; which you will all recollect was very valuable to Gen. Beauregard upon that occasion after the arrival of which, the fighting will grow more severe, and then retreat (ibid).

It is likely that Bethune gave this sort of introduction when Wiggins played the piece in public, though Bethune indicated earlier in this document that Wiggins would sometimes introduce the piece himself in this fashion: "Tom will now play for you his Battle of Manassas. This is a piece of his own conception of a battle" (Wiggins 1866).

Wiggins' musical language might be considered his first language, as he began to play piano before he could speak (Southall 1979). Autistic children often create interior worlds that they find much more interesting than the real world on the exterior. As these individuals grow in language and in experience, they often use their unique interior landscapes to comprehend situations occurring on the outside that can be difficult to understand as well as frightening. Even pretending to be an inanimate object can be comforting, and fantastic and detailed imaginings that border on real events are not uncommon among the autistic (Attwood 1998). Thus, Wiggins' assimilation of this major event in American history into his unique mode of expression, more musical than verbal, falls directly in line with autistic-spectrum behaviors.

The piece itself, illustrative of Wiggins' unique understanding and assimilation of this historical event, is in the form of a musical pastiche. Musical transitions are few and far between, and the composer restricted himself to a small number of related key areas in spite of the piece's use of seven different melodies. Six of the seven melodies are familiar patriotic tunes—patriotic generally defined according to the listener's sympathies. Only one of these appears to be an original theme composed by Wiggins; the "soft sweet melody" referred to in the introductory note as his conception of the "eve of battle" stands alone as an example of Wiggins' thematic creativity in the piece as a whole. Figure 14.1 charts the tonal, onomatopoetic, and thematic progression of the piece and traces the appearance of the seven melodies.

The top line of Figure 14.1 outlines major sections of the piece, as well as its general organization. Sections A, A', and A" all share the same upward rumbling figure in the low bass register of the piano. These sections are also devoid of chords in either part but rather convey the sound of the fife over a drone or over a drum. They do not share the same melody. In fact, three different melodies appear in this fife and drum format: first, the Confederate army's theme

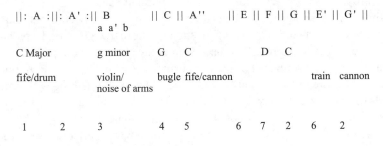

1= "The Girl I Left Behind Me" –Southern army's theme
2= "Dixie"—theme for the Northern army
3= Original "soft sweet" theme descriptive of the "eve of battle"
4= Bugle call in both G and C
5= "Yankee Doodle"
6= "La Marseillaise"
7= "The Star-Spangled Banner"

Figure 14.1 Schematic diagram of formal, tonal, imitative, and melodic organization in "The Battle of Manassas."

song—at least according to Wiggins—and then, "The Girl I Left Behind Me" warbles in piccolo register, with a starting pitch of C7. The high, thin tones of the right-hand melody stand in stark contrast to the repeated grace-note bass figure that unfailingly lands on C2 in all of the A-type sections. After two statements of the Southern army's theme, the next melody is introduced without even a pause.[6] Also written in piccolo—fife, in this case—register, the Northern army's theme, "Dixie," hovers above the percussive, repetitive bass figure on C. This melody, too, is repeated twice with no change in harmonic underpinnings. Despite the static harmonic rhythm, the composer does indicate that the dynamics should very gradually increase from *ppp* to an eventual *ff* at the end of section A' to illustrate the closing in of the respective armies on the place of impending battle (see Figure 14.2).

The arrival of Section B marks the first occurrence of any harmonic change in the piece whatsoever.[7] The preceding A and A' sections have each been repeated, and now, after a pause, an intimate G minor melody begins. For the first time, the melody is heard in vocal register, and its soprano-range tones, seen in Figure 14.2, are reminiscent of a violin solo's long, quivering lines. A new registral closeness reinforces the introspective quality of the melody itself, accompanied by arpeggiated chords in the left hand until B minor, where the right hand takes over the role of harmonizing. This passage is noted in the score as the indicator of the "noise of arms and accoutrements" at the camp. In the B minor section, the right hand shimmers in tremolo thirds and fourths while the left hand sobs out a descending passage that leads to the D minor dominant of the next key area, G major. After a brief rest, a bugle call in G major indicates General McDowell's trumpets in the distance; the same call transposed into C major follows directly without pause.

The third fife and drum section, labeled A'' in my schematic, utilizes "Yankee Doodle" as a theme and once again employs the high register of the piano. This time, however, the bass is composed not only of low Cs with grace notes but also of the first sounds of the cannon firing, as seen in Figure 14.3. A footnote in the score indicates that "the Cannon is played by striking with both hands (if both are at liberty; if not, with the left hand alone) and with the flat of the hand, as many notes as possible, and with as much force as possible, at the bass of the piano." Though this type of action makes perfect sense in the

Figure 14.2 Transition from A' to B, with registral shift toward the vocal and away from the rumbling bass.

Figure 14.3 Cannon fire in the left hand as transitional material between two patriotic tunes.

context of a battle piece, this technique was quite new to the concert stage and presages the use of the piano's capacity for other sounds in U.S. composition.

As stated earlier, the third of the A fife themes occurs at this point in the piece, with the new addition of cannon noise played by flat hands in the bass register. This return of the bass motive reasserts C as the tonal center for the piece. When the fife completes its melody, two strikes of the cannon are indicated, bringing the listener into the first statement of the "Marseillaise," which is also punctuated by cannon fire in the left hand. Following a perfect cadence in C major and three cannon strikes, as seen in Figure 14.3, no transitional material appears to carry the listener into D major for the "Star-Spangled Banner." The treatment of the future American anthem is quite different from the march-like chord leaps of the Marseillaise and features arpeggiated chords and *messa di voce* dynamic swells. The melody, though arranged less aggressively, is still prone to bouts of cannon fire in the left hand.

The cannon fires, and the music moves suddenly—again, without any transition—back to C major with a quick reprise of "Dixie" in the fife and drum style. Just as shortly, the "Marseillaise" returns—section E' of Figure 14.1—but this time with a vocal "chu chu chu" accompaniment and train whistle on high C, as seen in Figure 14.4. As shown on the schematic of imitative sounds in

Figure 14.4 Vocal imitation of a train.

Figure 14.1, until this moment in the piece, all of the onomatopoetic sounds have been made using the piano. Suddenly, the pianist is asked to "chu chu" like a train and to manufacture a screeching whistle on high C. The publishers undoubtedly understood that these sounds might deter the performer from continuing with the piece. A footnote in the score regarding these vocal sounds indicates that the noises were outside of normative pianistic decorum: "This 'chu chu,' (imitating the noise of the engine) also the subsequent 'Whistle' Tom makes with his mouth. Those of our players who may desire to add the exercise of their vocal organs to that of their fingers for their friends' amusement, can do the same; but the piece is complete without" (Wiggins 1866). If the composer of the piece is indeed Thomas Wiggins, as I argue here, it would be more accurate to state that the piece is *incomplete* without the vocal sounds. Because Wiggins had—and has—not yet commanded respect as a composer in his own right, apologetic footnotes permit, even promote, performances of his works in a lesser form.

Not only were the sounds essential to Wiggins' performance, but they were also sonic outlets for his heightened awareness of the world of sound so crucial to this blind and autistic person. Individuals with autism are often hyperaware of sound to the point that they experience discomfort or fear or, in Wiggins' case, extreme pleasure. His mother recounted his capacity for vocal imitation: "If he heard a chicken crow before he was a year old he would make the same noise. If he heard a dog bark, he would bark. And if he heard a bird sing he would try to sing. He would try to follow any noise that pleased him, so we had to watch him. … But he would get away from us. And it was when he got away once that his music talent was found out" (quoted in Southall 1983, 255). The written-in sound of the train reinforces the probability that Wiggins is the composer of the piece. This footnote in the score, not to mention the opening paragraphs for "The Battle of Manassas," is a method of socially and economically motivated apologies for the actions of disabled individuals that become embarrassments to society. Thus, the instructions to whistle like a train and "chu chu" should be as essential to authentic performance as any other sonic element of the piece.

The next section begins to bring the piece to a close with an increased use of pedal and the appearance of numerous cannon bombs in the left hand. First, the now-familiar "Marseillaise" appears in a louder, more intense incarnation of its former self, still in the tonic key of C major. But it is "Dixie" that Wiggins chooses for his coda and most florid octave work. Perhaps because this battle is acknowledged as a surprise Confederate victory, Wiggins may have meant this raucous "Dixie" as a musicosymbolic appropriation of the Union's flag. The South has taken possession of the North's tune, and the victory is theirs, right at home in the tonic key and without apology. The musical gesture is prescient, considering the subsequent evolution of "Dixie" as a Southern anthem.

Composed by an individual for whom verbal description was more problematic than verbal imitation, "The Battle of Manassas" represents the unique creation of a musical pastiche under the rubric of the Battle of Bull Run. A related nineteenth-century musical genre is the panorama piece. Visual panoramas were extremely popular during and after the Civil War and would attract large numbers of people to view scenes from biblical lands to cityscapes to the American West (Miller 1996). Precursors of film, these panoramas would appear in specially constructed buildings, and often music would accompany a viewer's walk through the scenes. The panoramas could be rolled up easily and taken on tour for exhibition at a price; owners of panoramas might also sell them for exorbitant amounts of money. A relative of the panorama, the cyclorama, was a moving painting that depicted a battle scene; this subgenre of the panorama was also popular during and after the Civil War. Some music used to accompany the panorama viewings was composed specifically for the event, and some pieces were selected from preexistent repertory. Wiggins' "Battle of Manassas" might be understood as musical analogue to the visual panoramas of battle scenes; each event passes by in an aural frame of sorts without a need for transitional moments. Yet, the general awkwardness of Wiggins' transitional moments in music may have made this genre, as well as that of the theme and variations examined following, appealing to this composer.

Wiggins' musical understanding of the battle also reflects General Bethune's heavy Confederate ideological influence, enabling the listener to gain greater insight into Wiggins' unique cognitive make-up. As an oppressed slave, for whom a Northern victory would signal his liberation, his interpretation of this important battle might have been expected to be quite different. Instead, Wiggins' lighthearted composition creates a pastiche of six patriotic tunes, reflective not of his blindness but perhaps of his other disability. If artistic production is a site of resistance, how does "The Battle of Manassas" fit in?

Perhaps Wiggins' understanding of events, like that of many blind individuals, is in terms of the aural and tactile, heightened by his nearly obsessive emphasis on understanding sound as an event and, additionally, a spatial one.[8] It is only natural that Wiggins should try to assimilate this defining point in the war via his most effective means of communication: music. Rather than participating in what might have been a challenging interpersonal conversation, he may have decided to make sense of the battle in musical terms, which he could better control. In neurologist Oliver Sacks' account of his meeting with a blind man whose vision had been partially restored after forty years of blindness, he states: "The cortex of an early blinded adult ... has already become highly adapted to organizing perceptions in time and not in space" (1995, 140). Any use of the tactile occurs in time, which makes the analogy with playing music quite natural since music also occurs in time. The spatial and tonal world of the piano, so deeply familiar to Wiggins, would be a much more logical site for his assimilation of the event than in the realm of words, which he may have found confusing. His frequent use of the third person to refer to himself is indicative of Wiggins' discomfort with the verbal and social. As Sacks states, "aloneness [is] the cardinal feature of autism…this lack of contact was only in regard to people; objects, by contrast, might be normally enjoyed" (ibid., 190).

Another common feature of autistic spectrum behavior is an obsessive interest in a particular subject, so all-consuming that it crowds out most other interests.[9] This type of obsession can take its form in a prodigious talent, as is probably the case with Wiggins and his unbelievable pianistic skill. But autistic individuals also enjoy repetition to the point that individuals with nonautistic cognitive processes may find the repetition uninteresting or even unnerving. In the words of autistic writer Donna Williams, "The constant change of most things never gave me any chance to prepare myself for them. Because of this I found pleasure and comfort in doing the same things over and over again" (1992, 39). Leo Kanner, the first scientist to use the term *autism,* notes that one of the defining features of autism is an obsessive reliance on sameness "in the form of repetitive movements and noises" (quoted in Sacks 1995, 190). If indeed Wiggins had become obsessed with the actual Battle of Manassas, as the score note indicates, the composition of a piano piece would enable him to relive the battle on his own aural, social, and spatial terms. In addition, Wiggins would have the chance to repeat his performance of the piece countless times in many different venues, an experience not necessarily relished by other nineteenth-century touring performers.[10]

Blind Tom in Print: "When This Cruel War Is Over" and "*Wellenklänge*"

Blind Tom Wiggins' "Variations on 'When This Cruel War Is Over'" provides another example of his capacity to write pieces devoid of typical Romantic-era transitional material. This tendency reinforces the argument that Wiggins' compositions bear the mark of a different kind of cognitive function, and one related to elements of autistic behavior and creativity. It is quite possible that with a supposed repertory of over 7,000 pieces, Wiggins' conception of music and composition was as sectionalized as his thought.

On the inside of the score, one finds a set of three variations on a popular Civil War tune of 1863 by Henry Tucker, "When This Cruel War Is Over," set off by an introduction and statement of the theme. The first page is a B-flat major introduction in the style of a fanfare; after a *sforzando* dominant seventh chord, a full-measure decending run leads to a *fortissimo* octave F in the left hand. Wiggins has come close to transitional material between sections in spite of the rests following. Then, for the first statement of the theme, we find ourselves squarely in B-flat major. The tune, consisting of two parallel periods, stays precisely within tonal bounds. The section ends in B-flat, and after a moment of rest, the performer must leap into the first of three variations. Each contains significant exercise for the pianist's fingers, like a Frédéric Chopin or Franz Liszt etude (Bellman 2000). The challenge in the first variation is the repetition of thirds and fourths in the right hand, in accordance with the tune and at a quick pace. Each variation stands alone and without transitional material.[11]

The second variation features right-hand sextuplets and the theme in the left hand. The pattern only breaks to become more complex from a technical perspective, but, also less interesting musically; now, the pianist must play Hanonesque scales with the right hand while the left hand performs the melody, eventually returning to the initial treatment of the theme. The third variation reveals an even more repetitive yet technically challenging section reminiscent of Gottschalk's piece "The Banjo." In Gottschalk's work, the pianist's fingers must rapidly repeat the same notes to create the aural sensation of a banjo playing. Yet Wiggins does not explain his repetitive passage by means of any image; it is simply repetition. Tonally, however, this movement is the only one that reaches beyond the grasp of B-flat major, as it delves into G-flat for the first part of this variation. The transition back to B-flat, seen in Figure 14.5, is signaled awkwardly by an A diminished triad; the A-natural in the high register serves as a leading tone back to the tonal world of B-flat-major, where the piece will come to its final resting place.

Wiggins' name is found on pieces outside the theme and variations and descriptive genres, and it is noteworthy that his stylistic choices are consistent through his other repertory. Even apart from the more sectionalized genres examined already, the transitional material and repetitive gestures remain part of Wiggins' compositional vocabulary. His 1882 "*Wellenklänge* (Voice of the Waves)," a parlor waltz comparable to a Chopin Mazurka in style, bears the pseudonym François Sexalise but also bears the stylistic signatures of its parenthetical composer, Blind Tom. On the sheet-music cover, shown in Figure 14.6, the hierarchy of pseudonym and actual composer is evident. After an introduction and the statement of four themes, each of which is repeated exactly after its first statement, the work reaches a perfect cadence on G-flat major. Suddenly, the listener is reminded that G-flat is quite far from the waltz's original key of A-flat major. See in Figure 14.7 how, without warning or transitional assistance, we crash back into the octave A-flats of the initial A-flat major introduction, which is then repeated in full before a new statement of the first two themes.

The finale, which contains the same material twice in rapid succession, follows the general pattern of the piece: written out repeats of the exact same thematic material, without ornamentation or any change in harmonic underpinnings. Far from a typical Romantic parlor waltz, Wiggins' is an exercise in comforting repetition, even at the expense of logical harmonic transitions and the potential for elaboration.

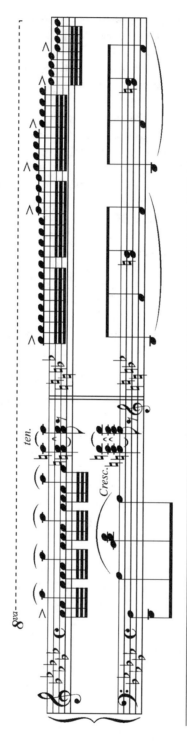

Figure 14.5 Transition between Variation 3 and closing material in "Variations on 'When this Cruel War is Over.'"

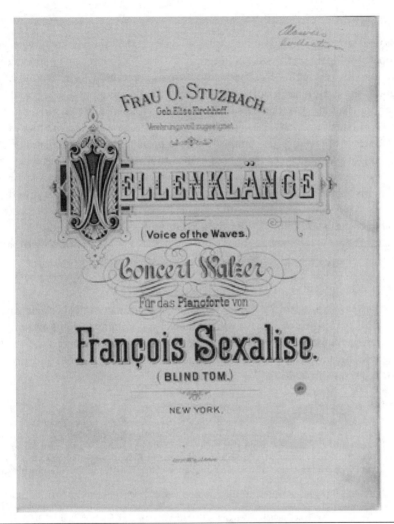

Figure 14.6 Sheet music cover featuring Blind Tom's pseudonym, dedicated to his guardian, Eliza Stuzbach. (http://scriptorium.lib.duke.edu/dynaweb/sheetmusic/1860–1869)

Figure 14.7 Cadence in G-flat major, followed by the start of repeated opening material in A-flat major, from "Wellenklänge (Voice of the Waves)."

Conclusion

Thomas Greene Wiggins' compositions provide rich sources for investigation of the world of a gifted and multiply disabled composer and pianist. The complexity of Wiggins' worldview and its manipulation by those around him render the examination of his life extremely challenging but also intriguing. I argue that the awkwardness of transitional moments in Wiggins' music, the tendency to repeat tunes and figures in a unique way, and the modes of imitation employed in his compositions can be viewed as symptomatic of his autism. In addition, given the problems of authorship discussed here, the presence of autistic mannerisms within Wiggins' music would argue in favor of Wiggins himself as the composer. Any attempt to downplay his cognitive disability could only overshadow the absolute individuality of this composer's voice. Wiggins' disability brings these compositions to a new level of importance: They are not only his own works, but they are also our only primary source.

Acknowledgments

I wish to express thanks to John Graziano for helpful comments on an early draft of the chapter, to Adrienne Fried Block for her many insights and information on panoramas, to Neil Lerner for clear and careful editing, and, above all, to Joe Straus, without whose tireless advice and mentoring the study would not have come to fruition.

Notes

1. I have chosen to refer to Thomas Bethune Wiggins as *Wiggins* throughout the paper. Though he is best known as Blind Tom, this stage name not only lets his visual impairment subsume his identity but also renders him inferior to other composers in the power structures of Western art music. The use of the name Bethune not only reinscribes Wiggins' status as a slave but also renders discussion of his relationship with his slave owners confusing.
2. A typical program offered by Blind Tom would include vocal and pianistic imitations (Southall 1999).
3. Bethune was disabled, using two canes to walk with his cork leg (Southall 1979).
4. In Wiggins' concerts, he would often be asked to play two tunes at once while singing a third, in the manner of Wolfgang Amadeus Mozart's courtly tricks. His sung tune was often "The Girl I Left Behind Me."
5. For a bibliography, Web links, a historical recording, and a detailed discussion of the issues surrounding Dan Emmett's "Dixie," see National Public Radio Morning Edition, "Dixie," November 11, 2002, http://www.npr.org/programs/morning/features/patc/dixie/.
6. John Davis's 1999 recording of "The Battle of Manassas" adds a pause between the two sections where there is no musical indication for one, a decision that adds to the aural comprehension of a melody change but that also detracts from the sense of overlap perhaps intended by the composer.
7. Figure 14.2 details the B section more than the others by using small letters to indicate smaller formal changes. This does not imply that the other sections of the piece indicated by capital letters do not also have smaller formal considerations. Because every other section of the piece is based on popular melody, the structure of the piece in those sections with borrowed melodies follows the relatively well-known structure of those melodies.
8. Kleege (1999) detailed this type of spatial understanding in her explanations of the psychokinesthetic effects of living as a blind person.

9. These special interests often involve transportation and, even more frequently, trains (Attwood 1998).
10. Gottschalk, for example, felt wearied by his own extensive touring schedule (Hitchcock 1988).
11. Though the genre of theme and variations may not lend itself to extensive transitional material, Henri Herz's 1848 piece "The Last Rose of Summer (with an introduction and brilliant variations for the pianoforte)" does include transitions between his variations. It is otherwise quite similar in style to a Wiggins piece.

15

Beyond Abnormality — Dis/ability and Music's Metamorphic Subjectivities

MARIANNE KIELIAN-GILBERT

Momma related times without end, and without any show of emotion, how Uncle Willie had been dropped when he was three years old by a woman who was minding him. ... She felt it necessary to explain over and over again to those who knew the story by heart that he wasn't "born that way."

In our society, where two-legged, two-armed strong Black men were able at best to eke out only the necessities of life, Uncle Willie, with his starched shirts, shined shoes and shelves full of food, was the whipping boy and butt of jokes of the underemployed and underpaid. Fate not only disabled him but laid a double-tiered barrier in his path. He was also proud and sensitive. Therefore he couldn't pretend that he wasn't crippled, nor could he deceive himself that people were not repelled by his defect.

Only once in all the years of trying not to watch him, I saw him pretend to himself and others that he wasn't lame.

Maya Angelou, *I Know Why the Caged Bird Sings*, p. 9

Claiming Dis/ability

Maya Angelou's Uncle Willie was proud, sensitive, yet disabled by society in a "life not worth living."[1] Not in control, not able to pretend, and sensitive to this knowledge of his condition, he had starched shirts, shined shoes, and shelves full of food but was the whipping boy for underpaid and underemployed others. Ensnared in this "ghetto," he could not pretend otherwise, nor could he escape the voyeurism and revulsion of others. He was mired in the material and social fixity of disability.

The *dis/abilities* of lived experience include multiple abilities and disabilities.[2] How might these matter in music experience and understanding? What might be the implications for music and musical experience of turning attention away from the voyeurisms of the disabled–abled or abnormal–normal binaries and toward the potential—and musical—sociality of multiple and varied abilities? Changing one's conceptions and orientations also has the potential to effect changes in social, cultural, and economic configurations.

Writing this essay has been a process of stasis, struggle, and movement, opening to dis/abilities of others in and outside my circle of experience and myself. Music—and writing—figure these processes, but often not explicitly or directly. Can I critique my abled and disabled conditions and orientations as changing? Can I imagine how I have felt or might feel in situations when or if I am differently abled? How can one speak of these things, and how do they matter? Things of tangibly experiential realms—apprehensions secret or painfully visible, whispered or shouted or unspoken—of loss, fear, denial, struggle, aspiration, and striving?

> There is this white wall, above which the sky
>   creates itself—
> Infinite, green, utterly untouchable.
> Angles swim in it, and the stars, in indifference also.
> They are my medium.
> The sun dissolves on this wall, bleeding its lights.

Sylvia Plath, Apprehensions *(1962), from first poem*
in **Winter Trees**, *1972, first stanza*

Shulamit Ran's 1979 composition, *Apprehensions*, is a musical setting of the poem of the same name by Sylvia Plath. In her setting of Plath's poem, Ran presents metamorphically changing atonal repetitions to differentiate the musically expressive intensities and orientations of a metamorphosis through "colors" white, grey, red, and black:

> What immediately struck me upon reading [*Apprehensions* by Sylvia Plath] was what I perceived of as the musical suggestiveness of the poem's central idea and formal plan: in four stanzas, the colors white, gray, red and black are used as a metaphor for the metamorphosis of a state of mind. ... The overall shape of a gradual ascent to a horrific climax culminating in a steep fall was one I found myself drawn to enormously, leading me to treat the work as a kind of a "mini-opera," consisting of three "acts," or movements followed by an "aftermath," or an epilogue. Toward that end, I added a clarinet (to me an instrument which can be closely linked to the human voice), as a kind of "alter ego" to the more conventional pairing of voice and piano.[3]

In this powerful and compelling work, the contradictions (madness) of temporal variability confront the disability (fixity) of repetition. Ran explores the paradox of being and becoming, of never going back in time in relation to the idea that as things change, they also remain the same. Contradictions of times (orientations) and emotional colors (intensities and conditions) bring the continually changing and the inevitably returning together with ever-present and ever-changing emotional filters—"colors." In Ran's view, "music…has the unique power to reconcile and be expressive of both."[4]

Ran's *Apprehensions* wrestles with the contradictions of moving dramatically and musically through different forms of relationality as against depictions of madness as abnormality. Apprehensions are feelings of anxiety, actions of seizing upon or grasping. The "grasp" of the intellect carries the psychic cost of conception and intellection—the anticipation, perhaps chiefly of things adverse. The grasping with the mind exacts a psychic cost on the subject. Apprehension, however, is also potentially a movement toward knowledge, the awareness of being materially in and of an ever-changing world. Responding creates an effect, potentially open-ended in interaction and movement. In Ran's setting of the first verse, the poem accumulates (apprehends) the physical and experiential specificities of "becoming music"—putting into (inter)play different physical states ranging from spoken text, half-spoken text, text-poem in scansion, and *Sprechstimme* (speech-song), to song and wordless vocalise. Such actualizing through differentiating and exploring intermediary states can be suggestive for moving music and music analysis outside a logic of fixed identity. Metamorphic becoming shifts from concerns of identity and identification to the expressive intensities and processes of becoming other.

The realities of lived human experience include multiple abilities and dis/abilities. Under the "bounds of normalcy," the "abnormal" could not be aligned with the rational; it was screened and contained as madness and denied a connection to the sociality and potentiality of varied ability.[5] Nicholas Mirzoeff (1995, 58) describes how deafness was imported into "the screen" of disability in the nineteenth century: "Such framing was necessary if the invisibility of deafness was to become visible." This framing has also encouraged "long-lasting and complex analogies" between conditions of disability, deafness, and madness and restrictions of race, gender, age, and ethnicity (ibid., 63).[6] Ideologies of difference render these conditions visible, dis-eased, deviant, and germed, as for example in nineteenth-century connections of deafness and insanity (ibid., 56) or in the contested cultural spaces of drinking fountains and toilets before the civil rights movement. The resulting visibility and dis-ease disables people as socially outcast and intolerable and thus also invisible, unable to participate in or to shape their future becoming. The ideological screen of disability is thus one of social exclusion and isolation, *removing possibilities of social interaction and expression* in concrete material conditions.

One of the implications of restriction is the relation of fixity to disability, both as an experiential dimension of a drastic restriction of mobility and as an experiential content of disability in one form or another. In contrast, metamorphic becoming, or being in motion, allows for the notion of *dis/abilities* as contingent potentials, as potentially physically and organically transformative and evolving, in contrast with being varied or developed.

It is one thing to think about disability as if a traveler in a foreign or exotic country, however, and quite another in a potentially metamorphic encounter that is irreducible to oneself (Irigaray 2001, 29). Even though it is impossible to put oneself in the place of someone else, especially someone in pain, it is possible to imagine oneself as dis/abled *in relation to* them, and it is important to do so. Rematerializing oneself in relation to another is potentially metamorphic. The compassionate and empathetic exchange of positionality changes the relational dynamics and the terms of criticism. As both possibility and illusion, empathy is a kind of encountering in which someone or something can affect and be affected by another while also remaining distinct. Though these encounters and exchanges may tread dangerously close to appropriation, they are crucial to metamorphic exchange and empowerment. In this sense, dis/ability *enables* experience and allows us to listen and hear from alternate positions and in different registers of the social and material. Temple Grandin (2005; see also Klinkenborg 2005) draws on her condition of autistic dis/ability to reconnect humans with animals by imagining and describing experience from "their" perspectives. "Becoming animal," she enables us to understand in our potential and metamorphic relations to her that we are "becoming animals," that is, without replacing, substituting, resembling or repeating, or diminishing her or her experience.

Musical becoming, metamorphic transforming, is a particular way of expressing and materializing the movements between multiple conditions and identities, between abilities and dis/abilities. By refiguring the other in the self, the self in the other without hierarchy, difference registers as relational potential. Such relationality registers those aspects of difference and interiority of another person—that acknowledged sensing that "that person is not me."[7] The logic of identity, recognition (resemblance), and repetition is inadequate and restrictive in life and in music and is problematic in figuring the temporal nature of encountering another and transforming oneself. Becoming is encountering, being in motion in the temporality of another.

Rather than locating music's expression of dis/ability solely in a mimesis or mimicry of society's lack of engagement with physical disability or solely in extremes of musical madness and hyper-abnormality, I want to consider the implications of hearing or listening of, or for, musical subjectivity as *dis/abled*, and thus materially and immaterially incomplete, partial, contingent, and expressive. The explorations of this essay thus consider *dis/ability* in relation to music's potential to metamorphically transform condition and orientation in flow and movement.

Drawing from the work of disability studies—opening *dis/ability* to the social—is a reminder of those differences, material and social, that interact in and transmute experience. It is the reminder that we never have a complete picture. *Dis/ability* renders music incomplete, in flux and with potential, socially and materially contingent, mixing aesthetic and social sensibilities, sparking encounters, and desiring and metamorphically transforming subjectivities. Music is a particular medium and experience capable of realizing social and relational potential or movement between multiple conditions and identities. Music renders dis/ability emergent and expressive. We begin to figure subjectivities of dis/ability; we begin to figure multiple and varied abilities and a *dis/abled* construction of the social by which we can experience anew.[8]

Is There No Way Out of the Mind? Music and Metamorphic Subjectivities

> A gray wall now, clawed and bloody.
> Is there no way out of the mind?
> Steps at my back spiral into a well.
> There are no trees or birds in this world,
> There is only a sourness.
>
> **Plath, *Apprehensions*, second stanza**

The experiential aspects of trauma, progressive illness, and chronic disability play out in complex combinations of emotions (e.g., loss, frustration, anger) and in relation to a complex of medical and care needs. Experientially disability can stem from a physical *condition* that creates negative evaluation or negative self constructs or from the *orientations* of a "damaged self" arising from a lack of control, choice, or empowerment (Magee 2002; MacDonald, Hargreaves, and Miell 2002). That is, the screen of disability can work as condition or orientation and can be heightened by their complicated interconnections. The self-inflicted physical blindness of Oedipus may be an expression of his social blindness. In turn, his physical blindness may allow him to re-experience and "sight" the social or suggest that he continues in the grip of the gods. Connections between condition and orientation are not causally or necessarily related; they cannot be justified in loose association or conceptual slippage. Notably, they take their force in situations of choice and empowerment rather than, or in contrast to, loss of control or lack of choice.

Recognizing the potential and power of constructing knowledge and participating in cultural representation, Simi Linton (1985, 5) speaks of cultural narratives newly emerging from "the foundation of a clearly identified disabled community":

> The cultural narrative of this community incorporates a fair share of adversity and it is also, and significantly, an account of a world negotiated *from the vantage point of the atypical*. Although the dominant culture describes that atypical experience as deficit and loss, the disabled community's narrative recounts it in more complex ways. The cultural

stuff of the community is the creative response to atypical experience, the adaptive maneuvers through a world configured for nondisabled people. The material that binds us is the art of finding one another, of identifying and naming disability in a world reluctant to discuss it, and of unearthing historically and culturally significant material that relates to our experience.

These orientations could include sensitivities to the temporal experience of before or after, especially in relation to acquiring disability; to effects of physical or psychic treatment, such as rehabilitation or nonrecovery; to negotiating or transcending material or physical experience, especially in the context of loss, that is, going outside or beyond the conditions one faces; or to empowering through knowledge construction or through making and participating in cultural expression.

Benjamin Boretz noted that how we choose to understand and express music is also social action (quoted in Kielian-Gilbert 2005). Adapting the "Theatres of Madness" of Susan Jahoda (1995),[9] I present several musical examples by Elvis Presley, Joseph Haydn, Anton Webern, and Shulamit Ran in resonant juxtaposition to expose the contingent nature of listening and analytical observation, questioning the scientific nature of observation and suggesting the implications of metamorphic processes of encountering: temporally and materially changing forms, internalizing, expressing, embodying, interacting, transcending or releasing, and being in motion.

Elvis and Forrest: Dis/ability as Contingent Becoming

The 1994 film *Forrest Gump* (Robert Zemekis) presents the accidental encounters of developmentally and mentally dis/abled Forrest with some of the most important people and events in America from the late 1950s through the 1970s.[10] In a chance (contingent) encounter with the not-yet famous Elvis Presley, Forrest, a youngster in leg braces, dances to the music as Elvis plays his guitar. In the next scene, Forrest and his mother see "that funny little walk" on the television in Elvis's performance on the Ed Sullivan show in 1956. Forrest may not realize the significance of his connections to Elvis's walk—of his "becoming Elvis" and Elvis "becoming him"—but through his mother's eyes we do. The film presents a chance to refigure this encounter and our potential connections to it in a process not only of turning the tables but also of sensing their contingency, notably made possible through exchanges of *dis/ability*.

Reliving Elvis Presley's rendition of "Hound Dog" requires the madness of incorporating the physical and temporal correlates of musical encounters and the rhetoric that expresses their particular material or lived realities. Robert Fink (1998, 169) notes that Elvis's "gyrations" in "Hound Dog" began as "a witty multiracial piece of signifyin' humor, troping off white overreactions to black sexual innuendo" and contrasts Elvis's performance with that of Big Mama

Thornton in 1953. Music's contingent encounters embody the cultural potential of subjectivities as interactive, potentially and metamorphically in flux.

*Haydn, String Quartet in D minor, Op. 76, No. 2 ("Fifths," Hob. III:
76), I, Allegro, Measures 1–17: Dis/ability as Metamorphic Potential*

The assertiveness of the pattern of perfect fifths at the opening of the movement seems to announce the fixity of its substance as evidently prior and resistant to change and thus in contrast to the composed ideas (see Figure 15.1A).[11] As self-propelling agents, fifths can multiply and proliferate within or outside a tonal sphere, for example, in tonal or exact (real) imitation.

Theorizing the experience of *dis/ability* in music is in part to rethink the fixity of material perceptions by hearing and listening for metamorphic potentials, that is, for unanticipated and changing character or substance interacting and in motion with surrounding material. As fixed, those articulated fifths, opening the performance in apparent disregard of their surroundings, behave as if without potential and thus disable changing interactions with the instrumental lines.

How might one refocus a listening toward the potential of moving between the fifth patterns and surrounding materials and of expressing the interactions of structural–material levels? The opening of the *Allegro* embodies contradictory structural tendencies: the scale-degree setting of the Violin 1 line is apparently melodically closed (D minor: $\hat{5}$–$\hat{1}$–$\hat{2}$–$\hat{5}$) but is, potentially and problematically, harmonically open (i–V) in relation to the melodic-harmonic patterns of measures 3–4. Even before the shift—unprepared?—to the tonal region of F major at measure 13, the status of the initial fifths' presentation as fixed or malleable, motive or theme, melody or bass, closed or open, resistant to influence or influential, or suggestive of contrapuntal or harmonic origins opens to question. In measures 13 and following, new scale-degree orientations for the double-fifth pattern emerge (F major: $\hat{1}$–$\hat{4}$–$\hat{5}$–$\hat{1}$), sounding implications of harmonic rather than melodic function, yet the melodic openness and proliferation of fifths (measures 15ff.) through contrapuntal imitation undo the fixity of thematic versus formal conventions and of textural-contrapuntal versus harmonic priorities (see Figure 15.1B).[12] Such material potentials of action and relationship contradict aesthetic perceptions of distance and immobilizing priority, potentially enabling forms of the *other*. The *dis/abilities* of the alternate lines thus express and assert their metamorphic potentials, undoing their muteness in the face of the apparently unbending fifths.

*Anton Webern, Four Pieces for Violin and Piano, Op. 7 (1910), No. 3,
"Sehr langsam": Dis/ability as Metaphoric and Contingent Transcendence*

Characterizing works from Anton Webern's second period, Theodor Adorno (1999, 92) described Webern's tendencies toward "absolute lyricism" and "the pure sonority of the object, without an alien remainder that refuses to be assimilated" (p. 93). Adorno construed "the lack of violence," namely,

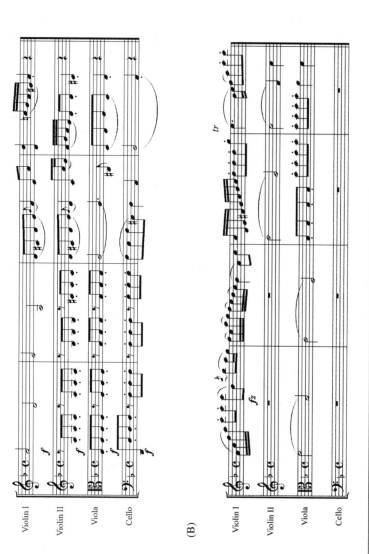

Figure 15.1 Joseph Haydn, String Quartet in D minor, Op. 76, no. 2, I: (A) mm. 1–4; (B) mm. 13–16.

as "the absence of the composer as sovereign subject" (p. 101). How might one listen to Webern's Op. 7, No. 3, "Sehr langsam" in relation to Adorno's descriptions of its "absolute expression" (p. 99)? "The pure sound to which the subject is drawn as its vehicle of expression is freed from the violence that the shaping subject otherwise inflicts on the material" (p. 98).

This music and its listeners let go of the "violence" that subjectivity inflicts on the material. Engaging this music and its absorption of subjectivity in ongoing compositional differentiation, one might follow, say, unfoldings of its twelve-note chromatic. Transcending or releasing any attempt to apprehend a series of twelve pitch elements as fixed—or disabled or captured—the sounds eschew the fixing of patterns and elements; temporal unfoldings overlap and move. Performing this listening and hearing is both misleading and highly suggestive of an unfolding and folding twelve-note chromatic succession of overlapping and recurring intimations of trichords (see the shaded areas in Figure 15.2).[13] This music experience seeks sonic individuation and differentiation. At the end of the piece, the rumbling of sound in the low register of the piano sublimates the last note of the chromatic succession, G!, rendering that note-sound "barely audible" ("*kaum hörbar*").

> The absolute transitory, the toneless beating of wings, as it were, becomes in his music the faintest, but most persistent, seal of hope. Disappearance, an ephemerality that fixes on nothing that exists anymore, or even that objectifies itself, becomes the refuge of a defenseless eternity (Adorno 1999, 105).

These intimations are metamorphically expressed in music-sound: chromatic tones individuate, unfolding continually changing trichordal groupings. These trichordal associations overlap and embody each other, metamorphically connecting to subsequent patterns. They distribute relative to the piano and violin such that neither part dominates the other: for example, E-flat–C-sharp–D, piano, measures 4–5, embodied later in the piano, C-sharp–E-flat–D, in measures 6–7; and the first four notes A–B-flat–A-flat–E-flat, measures 1–4, embodied in the last set, B-flat–A–A-flat–E-flat, in measures 9–11. Other metamorphic expressions may be sensed, such as the sonic associations of the major-minor third sonorities of the piano in measures 7–8 and in measures 12–14 or between the registral and sonic exchanging of A3 in measures 1–3 (violin), with A4 in measure 4 (piano), A3 in measures 6–8 (violin), and A4 in measures 10–11 (piano). In this relationally changing world, *dis/ability* approaches communion or communal subjectivity through a contingent transcendence, i.e., by escaping objectification.

How might such changing sonic worlds impact our own or shape our changing positions? Can we learn from them? Or do we inadvertently seek ways to curtail potentials?[14] Webern wrote the *Slow Movement for String Quartet* (1905) early in his apprenticeship with Arnold Schoenberg (roughly 1904–10) and before the first of his published (numbered) works in 1908. Listening to

Figure 15.2 Anton Webern, Four Pieces for Violin and Piano, Op. 7, no. 3, "Sehr langsam."

and hearing the difference of the changing tonal character and directional qualities of this earlier work suggest not only that analysts have tended to disable (to isolate and ignore) its tonality in relation to his later atonal and serial works[15] but also that apprehending Webern's Op. 7, No. 3 is a matter of listening and hearing differently and with extension, as Adorno (1999, 98) suggested:

> [T]his threefold pianissimo, this almost inaudible sound, is nothing but the threatening shadow of an infinitely remote and infinitely powerful din. This was the sound of the rumble of artillery from Verdun in 1916 …

the falling leaf becomes the harbinger of catastrophes to come (98) ... a reduction of what is heard that makes use of silence to create space for subtle differentiation (99).

In a different turn, the cultural conditions of deafness and disability as lack or absence turn inward toward the madness of inner voices and interior worlds. By excluding the differently abled, disability haunts the abled community. If madness makes possible suspensions of rationality—via abnormalities mental and physical or via conditions of deformity, disfigurement, and freakishness—rationality is also haunted and framed by what it excludes.

Connections between disability and dis/abled subjectivity such as madness are long standing. Repressed fears feed conditions of hysteria. From the Greek *hystera*, "of the womb," the etymological connections associate hysteria with the female or feminine, wild and unchecked excitability, anxieties, and dysfunctional outbreaks of uncontrolled feeling and paranoia. The notion of hysteria ties fear to conditions of the female body with its seemingly extreme emotional states. Notably these fears are expressed in sound—in incomprehensible outpourings of cries, noises, unintelligible speech, wild singing, laughter, and muttering, or in sublimated expressions, such as Edvard Munch's woodcut *Cry/Scream* (1893). Music-sound can thus become, or index, corporeal deviance, excess, and absence, internalized fragility, or divine contact.[16]

As these examples suggest, musical portrayals of the abnormal as dis/abled align with cultural emotional extremes (e.g., madness, danger, anxiety) or the potential formative possibilities of unrestricted intertextuality, the contingencies of experience, and the seeming non-logic of disjunction and disassociation. What are the implications of experiencing a musical portrayal of madness from a position of normality or from experiential interpretive positions of multiple *dis/abilities*? The examples take up these questions from the musically metamorphic potentials of temporal-material interplay (e.g., Haydn), temporal-material release (e.g., Webern), or contingent becoming (e.g., Forrest/Elvis, Ran). The philosophical and methodological dispositions that support these interpretations involve expressing music's relationality or sociality in terms of temporally changing potentials, musically metamorphic processes, and unanticipated or contingent relationships.

Shulamit Ran, *Apprehensions* (1979) for Voice, Clarinet and Piano: Dis/ability as Metamorphic and Contingent Embodiment

> This red wall winces continually:
> A red fist, opening and closing,
> Two grey, papery bags—
> This is what I am made of, this, and a terror
> Of being wheeled off under crosses and a rain of pieties.
>
> *Plath,* **Apprehensions,** *third stanza*

Ran's musical setting of the third stanza of Sylvia Plath's poem *Apprehensions* encompasses the musical, dramatic, and emotional climax of the "opera." This stanza suggests pairs of actions and conditions, connected by association or disassociation (see lines 1–2 and 3–5). Textual processes of identification (i.e., moments of recognition: "this is what I am made of") follow those of motion ("winces continually," "opening and closing"). Identification and recognition, however, can both direct and limit; the terrors or securities of fixity, limitation, and restriction or of movement, freedom, and unlimited potential are unknown. What of their dangers or potentials?

The opening vocal evocation of the third stanza dramatically refigures the opening vocal line of Ran's setting of the first stanza. Subsequently the vocal line of the third stanza winces (alternating G-sharp5–G5), echoed and elaborated in the piano (A-flat5–G5) and clarinet (as the alter ego of the voice, G5–G-sharp5).[17] In contrast, the opening disjunct evocation of the piano returns twice more, varied in response to the vocal cry ("This red wall"), each time also incorporating five iterated pulsed sounds, also presented by the clarinet figure at rehearsal B shown in Figure 15.3. In the music that accompanies this clarinet figure, the ending idea of the opening piano evocation segues into the disjunct chordal evocation pattern and ostinati cycles in the clarinet and piano at rehearsal D, where "wincing" patterns of voice, piano, and clarinet—previously an octave higher, G5–G-sharp5—shift to the voice in a lower register, G4–G-sharp4 (see Figure 15.4). This shift both links and metaphorically transforms the musical wincing in the vocal stutter at rehearsal D: "red," G4, versus "wall," G-sharp4. The metamorphic process is one of continual overlap, accumulation, and resonance: In effect the bodies of clarinet and piano (of the opening) speak back through the grain of the soprano voice.

From rehearsal C to F, each timbral configuration of voice, clarinet, and piano operates in its own sphere, articulating overlapping periods and cycling and recycling ostinato-like patterns increasing in intensity—see the clarinet's dissonant period length of seven eighths against the piano's six in Figure 15.4. The seeming static, nonchanging quality of these periods is broken locally by the stutters now wincing in the patterning of the intermittent staccato gestures in the heightened mutterings of the voice.[18]

The third piano evocation at rehearsal H, not shown, initiates a still longer span of cyclic activity at rehearsal I (see clarinet in Figure 15.5), at which point the earlier stutter patterns of the voice from rehearsal D (Figure 15.4) shift to the piano. The piano becomes the backdrop for the dramatic outburst of the

Figure 15.3 Shulamit Ran, *Apprehensions* (1979) for voice, clarinet, and piano, III, clarinet figure at Rehearsal B.

Figure 15.4 Shulamit Ran, *Apprehensions*, Rehearsal D.

Figure 15.5 Shulamit Ran, *Apprehensions*, after Rehearsal I.

clarinet at rehearsal I (Figure 15.5), and its subsequent subsiding—gently, less loud—at rehearsal J, not shown. At rehearsal I, the clarinet dramatically extends the registral shifting that the voice has attempted, while the piano assimilates the stuttering abilities of the voice, extending and metamorphically transforming its character in relation to previous and subsequent patterns: Both piano and clarinet strikingly extend and refigure *dis/abilities*. These embodiments recast the earlier vocal stuttering, dramatically externalizing and outfolding as clarinet alter ego and internalizing and infolding as piano obsession.

After rehearsal L (see Figure 15.6), listeners encounter for the first time an unforeseen textual double or counterpart, the textual rendering of a previously sounding musical statement in the piano: an aural "encounter." As the clarinet doubles the voice a tritone higher,[19] they render, with "a sense of urgency," the first occurrences of textual patterns, each of which present at least five phonemes, "what I am made of": "(two) grey papery bags," "two papery bags," and "this, and a terror." That is, the phrases, "grey papery bags" and "two papery bags" express the pattern of the five-pulsed equally spaced musical iterations that had ended the piano evocation—iterations up to this point that had no text (see Figure 15.3 and the patterns added at the bottom of Figure 15.6). The piano thus—retrospectively—portends the virtual textual expressions of the five iterated pulses as vocalized text. Music becomes or is made of text, which becomes or is made of music, in as yet unthought and unforeseen futures.

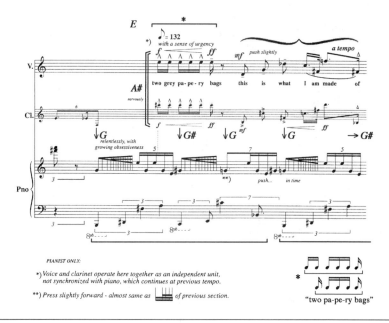

Figure 15.6 Shulamit Ran, *Apprehensions*, before Rehearsal L.

The piano now embodies the patterns of the vocal stutter in its period constructions. Evocation and iteration becomes stutter; stutter becomes evocation and iteration. In this metamorphic exchange one is experienced in—and resonates in and in relation to—the others and vice versa: Note the significance of the plural *others* in this characterization. Condition and orientation intimately socialize—metonymic and metaphoric, materially social and socially material.

These encounters, or exchanges and metaphoric transformations and embodiments, continue and multiply at a new level of intensity at rehearsal P, not shown, in the deliberateness and grotesqueness of a death march. Again the soprano sings "Two grey papery bags" (E-flat4–G-flat4–D4–F4–C5–E-flat5 or E-flat6) textually and vocally rendering and embodying the previous gawkish clarinet ostinato from rehearsal C–D, which had been subsequently transferred to the bass of the piano at rehearsal F. These processes of embodiment accumulate and culminate in the outflow of the march-like section that concludes the composition—great resonant sounds that still evoke an element of beauty.

Shulamit Ran thus musically explores the borders of madness in relation to the limits, possibilities, and potentials of embodiment (infolding and outfolding): How much can a musical psyche take in and embody without an imploding of values or extend without fissuring subjectivity?

Listening In/Listening Out

On a black wall, unidentifiable birds
Swivel their heads and cry.
There is no talk of immortality among these!
Cold blanks approach us:
They move in a hurry.

Plath, Apprehensions, *final stanza*

Disability is an ever-potential identification, close and threatening to us. Unspoken anxieties, degrees of vulnerability, and feelings of terror and hopelessness accompany its constructions.[20] Disability is something we will experience: People with dis/abilities make up the largest minority group in the United States, with over forty to fifty million individuals.[21]

The tyrannies of ableism have often been compared to the oppressive structures (and the "logic") of whiteness as the assumed or unquestioned background of race, of the masculine as the universal gender, or of the heterosexual as the norm for judging sexual difference. Such hegemonic structures, whether operating on individual, institutional, cultural, or metaphysical levels, depend on their silenced others for their definition at the same time that they construct the subordinate categories and displace the agency and viability of those in that category. Frames of power, unquestioned and uncritiqued, become normative and simultaneously oppressive and exclusive of difference. The supportive structures of whiteness represent racelessness, masculine universals assume genderless neutrality, and compulsory heterosexuality stands for sexually normative behavior.[22] Disability studies fights these tyrannies of the *same* and the negative constraints of structural rigidity.

Disability studies (see, e.g., Garland-Thomson 1997; Davis 1995) have brought new and valuable perspectives to scholarship and the workplace. This area of study activates the voices of the disabled and asserts their active roles in constructing knowledge and participating in cultural representation, refigures notions of dis/ability and dis/figurement, and enables cultural and knowledge production. Its theories have led to more and better networking, support, visibility, and political agency for persons with disabilities. In contrast to the recent climates that have produced Enron, Wal-Mart, or Halliburton (i.e., military industry), the movements of civil rights, different waves of feminism, and disability rights point to another America and figure principles of social justice crucial to the growing worldwide interconnectedness of the over six billion people on planet Earth. Music and music scholarship cannot be immune to social impulses or to the intellectual and material challenges and issues of conditions and orientations of dis/ability. As the constraints of old logic fall away or prove increasingly inadequate, new models confront the implications and consequences of bodily and psychic specificity. Beyond facts and standard research, dis/ability sounds and refigures music, and music has similar potential for refiguring dis/ability.

The realities of lived experience in the social and material specificities of gender, dis/ability, race, age, ethnicity, and class resist reduction. To encapsulate them in life or in music risks losing them to meaninglessness and social ineffectiveness.

Listening for, hearing, and theorizing dis/ability in music, and vice versa, present choices: for temporal metamorphic becoming, listening for and hearing music as changing, responding to, embodying and expressing material and virtual relational potentials. The process of vivifying (apprehending) experience has to do with bringing the aesthetic and the material together in the sparks of unfamiliarity, contingency, and unforeseen connections that underlie their potential interactions. The crux is to allow the play of forces and in particular to recognize the capacity of material or physical and psychic specificity to create, to direct, and to nuance the aesthetic—to make it real. Acknowledging the multiple social relationalities that develop out of difference, interiority, and *dis/ability* is crucial to experiencing, describing, and deepening our understanding of music. And just as striking, the changing relationalities that music articulates and makes possible can voice new relational configurations and transform the socialities of lived experience, for which interiority as difference is crucial to our survival, to our metamorphic becoming, and to our as yet unthought futures.

Notes

1. This phrase is referenced in the title of Proctor (1995), "The Destruction of 'Lives Not Worth Living'": "By the late '30s, German medical science had constructed an elaborate world view equating mental infirmity, moral depravity, criminality, and racial impurity" (p. 181).
2. I italicize *dis/ability* at times to suggest the positive potential of acknowledging multiple abilities and disabilities.
3. Shulamit Ran, composer's note to the published score of *Apprehensions* (Israel Music Institute, Tel-Aviv, Israel, 1984).
4. Ran stated in Briscoe (1997, 263), "In recent years, I find myself progressively more drawn by the idea, and the ramifications, of a formal return in a piece of music yet, at the same time, moving onward. As in life, one can never go back in time. There is no such thing as a real recapitulation. What has happened in the intervening time has altered things irrevocably. Pitted against this reality is an equally compelling statement, namely, the more things change, the more they remain the same. The cyclical versus the inevitability of the flow of time are two major currents at the source of all of life and nature. Music, I believe, has the unique power to reconcile and be expressive of both."
5. According to Davis (1995, 24), the terms *normal* and *normalized* date from the mid-nineteenth century. A normative class began to control the bounds and myths of "normalcy," segregating and rendering mad the sociality and potentiality of dis/ability: that which could not be claimed needed to be contained. In contrast, see Canguilhem (1991, 246, quoted in Mirzoeff 1995, 54): "Between 1759, the date of the first appearance of the word *normal*, and 1834, the date of the first appearance of the word *normalized*, a normative class conquered the power to identify ... the function of social norms, whose content it determined, with the use that that class made of them."
6. "For the deaf, for the African, and for women, originality was a category from which they were excluded by definition, reinforcing the long-lasting and complex analogies between these three groups, which had originated in the myth [cultural site] of the harem" (Mirzoeff

1995, 63). "The use of sign language by deaf and hearing people became a mutually reinforcing indicator of pathology" (ibid., 60).

7. "But is my existence not protected by your irreducibility?" (Irigaray 2001, 9) "In us, sen-
sible nature and the spirit become in-stance by remaining within their own singularity
and grow through the risk of an exchange with what is irreducible to oneself" (ibid., 29).
These orientations draw from the critical ideas of Irigaray (2001), Braidotti (2002), and
Grosz (1999), after Deleuze (1994).

8. Dowsett (2000, 37) argued in similar terms for "the formative action of the body-in-sex,
this time deeply embedded within a relationality that encodes sensation. This account
must reinsert the relational into an investigation of sex as embodied yet not lose the body-
in-sex inside relationality."

9. Jahoda (1995, 253) presented a series of images of physical disability in juxtaposition and
collage format, pairing and layering various source materials in visual "theatres of madness." Madness ensues in the interstices and dislocations of the images, in their pointing up "relations that overdetermine the internalization of oppression and, in turn, the
degrees of complicity and resistance to that oppression" (ibid.).

10. *Forrest Gump*, videorecording, directed by Robert Zemekis (1995 [originally released as
a motion picture in 1994]; Hollywood, CA: Paramount Pictures, 2001). The references to
particular performances are crucial to the significance of temporal experience and performance as experientially concrete and expressive, as opposed to abstract.

11. My discussion of this Haydn quartet takes as its point of departure a recorded performance by the Takács String Quartet, *Haydn Quartets* (1988), CD, London, 421 360–2.

12. Eschewing music as directly mimetic of society, Theodor Adorno located a critical register of the musically social in its dialectical relations with the "conceptual autonomy" of
art (see Subotnik 1991, 25). For Adorno, human subjectivity is expressive of a contingent
and dialectical relationship between individual freedom and form as a possible locus of
"external reality" (23). For a description of the unexpectedness of the later F-minor passage of measures 32ff., see Dubiel 1992.

13. My discussion of this piece is related to its performance by Gidon Kremer (violin) and
Oleg Maisenberg (piano), *Complete Webern* (2000, CD, Deutsche Grammophon, 457 637-2
[457 638-2–457 643-2]). I thank Chun Fang Bettina Hahn for her help in formatting the
musical examples for this essay.

14. Theory is often motivated and preceded by self-identification and interest; openness to
these orientations connects theory to the social. An earlier version of this paper linked
the analytical approaches to particular experiences to suggest that music may be felt or
conceptually related to lived experience.

15. Thanks to Nery Rodriguez, Indiana University, for reminding me of this piece and how
music analysts have tended to ignore it in relation to Webern's later atonal and serial works.

16. See Metzer's (2003, 74–104) chapter 3, titled "Madness," and McClary (2002) for related
discussions of the portrayal of madness in music and the cultural fascination with madness and female excess. Metzer described conditions of madness in music as "suffering
from reminiscences," and "hysteria as a morass of reminiscence and delusion" (p. 77).
On madness as the excess and promiscuity of intertextual reference that disrupts and
deforms musical-social logic, see Welten (1996) and Williams (2000) on *Eight Songs for a
Mad King (1971)* by Peter Maxwell Davies. Madness has also been regarded as a locus of
contact with the divine: Was Joan of Arc, perhaps a schizophrenic in our terms, hearing
the voices of divine beings?

17. This song (Ran 1984) is recorded on *Music of Shulamit Ran* (1991, CRI, CD 609 CRI), with
Judith Nicosia (soprano), Laura Flax (clarinet), and Alan Feinberg (piano). Please note that
the clarinet part (in A) sounds a minor third lower than written.

18. In contrast, the poetic text "opening and closing" is set, ironically, and respectively, by
the non-mimetic whole-tone neighbor-note and ascending stepwise patterns following
rehearsal G.

19. At Rehearsal P, this same process occurs to cycle and exchange "two grey papery bags"
as a textual and vocal rendering or embodiment and infolding of the previous gawkish
clarinet ostinato from Rehearsal C–D (also transferred to the piano at Rehearsal F).

20. "Whites do not worry about becoming black; men don't worry about becoming women.
Disability, however, is always a potential status" (Gordon and Rosenblum 2001, 16; cited
in Smith 2004, 8).

21. Definitions of disability are contingent and are matters of social construction and debate. See the Disability Statistics Center online: "Although the 2000 Census long form and the Census Supplementary Surveys used the same set of questions to measure disability, the 2000 Census counted a much higher number of people with disabilities. The 2000 Census counted 49.8 million people with disabilities, or 19.3% of the civilian non-institutionalized population aged 5 and over. However, the Census Supplementary Surveys show that only 39.6 million people have disabilities, or 15.6% of the population." <http://dsc.ucsf.edu/main.php?name=resources> Section 504 of The Americans with Disabilities Act of 1990 (ADA) is a civil rights law that prohibits certain forms of discrimination on the basis of a disability. A person has a disability if he or she (1) has a physical or mental impairment that substantially limits a major life activity; (2) has had a physical or mental impairment that substantially limits a major life activity; or (3) is regarded as having a disability by others. Major life activities include walking, seeing, hearing, speaking, breathing, learning, working, caring for oneself, and performing manual tasks. The disability need only substantially limit one major activity for the person to be eligible.

22. For work that aligns the social mapping of disability to the "landscape of race," see Smith (2004). For related work on music and difference, see Solie (1993) and Agawu (2003).

16
Mental Illness and Musical Metaphor in the First Movement of Hector Berlioz's *Symphonie fantastique*

STEPHEN RODGERS

Berlioz and Eccentricity

In the introduction to his translation of Hector Berlioz's memoirs, David Cairns writes, "Today ... the characteristics that once made [Berlioz's music] bizarrely unconventional ... are once again quite natural; his originality, without having lost its vividness, no longer seems eccentric" (Berlioz 2002, xi). Cairns is right, in that anyone who studies Berlioz's music with the care and attention it deserves will learn that many of the all-too-common characterizations of it do not hold true: It is formless, slapdash, so strange as to elude comprehension, and resistant to analysis. Berlioz is understood better now than ever before, so students of his work are less likely to throw up their hands or, worse, to cast aspersions when his music does not behave as expected. Few today would rail so strongly against the "singular perversity" and "technical deficiencies" of Berlioz's music or would argue that the first movement of the *Symphonie fantastique* "simply breaks with all the fundamental rules of the art, and that not with the iconoclasm of a reformer, but with the awkwardness of a tyro," as W.H. Hadow (1904, 313) did in the early part of the last century. Thanks to the great strides made by the "new Berliozians" in the 1990s[1] and the even newer Berliozians in the past few years, Berlioz is now beginning to be seen as the true craftsman he was—a heady and exuberant craftsman, to be sure, but more mindfully experimental than "bizarrely unconventional."

But does his originality really no longer seem eccentric? Is anyone really in a position to deem Berlioz's works fully comprehensible? Berlioz, it now seems clear, was not clumsy and unschooled. He did not compose in the careless, white heat of inspiration, without thought for balance and design. The pace and construction of his music mattered dearly to him, evidenced not least by the extensive revisions he made to his scores. Yet it is hard to escape the fact that much of his music continues to confound us even after we have gotten to know it well. Many of his works in fact confound us as if by design.

This chapter focuses on Berlioz's most famous and famously confounding form: the *Symphonie fantastique*'s first movement. Its peculiarities are, *pace* Hadow, not a sign of Berlioz's inability to handle large-scale form. Still less, however, can they be regarded as uneccentric. They can be neither dismissed as the products of recklessness nor happily subsumed under a sonata-form paradigm in an effort to show that the movement is unified and fully coherent. This piece, like so many of Berlioz's, traffics in a gray area between coherence and incoherence.

Even more, in distorting certain formal and tonal conventions, the *Symphonie fantastique* raises the possibility that musical deformations can represent human deformations—that disability can be, as it were, written into music. I place my discussion of the movement in the context of disability studies not only because it radically deforms the conventions of sonata form but also because its program about a lovesick artist maniacally obsessed with an idealized woman resonates with a type of mental illness widely discussed by French psychiatrists of Berlioz's time and well known among the public. Berlioz's disorienting form is, I will argue, a musical metaphor for the mania experienced by the *jeune musicien* of the symphony's program.

The word *deformation* is borrowed from James Hepokoski and Warren Darcy, whose Sonata Theory focuses on how individual works interact with what they call "reasonably ascertainable, flexible generic norms" (Hepokoski and Darcy 1997, 116) conventions that can be modified and distorted to particular aesthetic effect.[2] Hepokoski and Darcy (2006, 614–615) assert that the term *deformation,* as they use it, retains none of its familiar, conventional meaning or implications:

> While we do intend "deformation" to imply a strain and distortion of the norm—the composer's application of uncommon creative force toward the production of a singular aesthetic effect—we do not use this term in its looser, more colloquial sense, one that might connote a negative sense of aesthetic defectiveness, imperfection, or ugliness…Within our system, "deformation" is only a technical term referring to a striking way of stretching or overriding a norm.

But as Straus (2006, 130) notes, it is difficult to ignore the conventional meaning of *deformation* when applying the term to music:

> The term "deformation," like any theoretical concept, has a history and a resonance that are impossible to escape entirely. Indeed, from a certain point of view (not Hepokoski and Darcy's point of view) their use of the term deformation simply makes explicit what is already implicit in any conformational theory of musical form: a musical form, understood as a normative container, is a metaphorical human body, and thus formal deformations can be understood as bodily disfigurements.

Musical forms, Straus argues, "may be understood to be metaphorically about normal and deviant bodies, and thus to participate in the construction of the culture and history of disability" (Straus 2006, 131).

In following Straus (2006) and adopting Hepokoski and Darcy's (2006) concept of deformation, but attaching to it certain connotations unintended by them, I am not departing from the basic premise of their theory: Works of music can profitably be viewed as being in dialogue with certain generic conventions, and part of a work's expressive meaning lies in how it modifies and sometimes even disrupts those conventions. What is suggested here is that with a composer like Berlioz ample reason can be found to extend the notion of purely musical deformation into the realm of physical—and, in the case of the *Fantastique*, mental—deformations and thereby to posit that a deformational musical form can behave like a disabled body. The *Symphonie fantastique* is, after all, not Berlioz's only work that calls to mind notions of mental disorder. Themes of mania and madness appear remarkably often in the written stories, titles, evocative headings, and texts of Berlioz's music: in the title to the scherzo from *Roméo et Juliette*, *La Reine Mab*, which makes reference to Mercutio's speech about the charms and dangers of the subconscious and the creature that slips nightly into men's minds as they sleep; in the network of associations surrounding the *Roi Lear* overture, a work about a king who steadily loses his mind; and in the text to Berlioz's song, *La Mort d'Ophélie*, which describes Ophelia's gradual descent into madness and the swirling torrent that sucks her under.

The first movement of the *Fantastique* is also not the only work of Berlioz to radically distort formal conventions. Each of the pieces mentioned previously features a form that likewise evokes the disorder implied by its "extramusical" context. A great deal can be learned from the terms Hadow (1904) used to describe Berlioz's style: perversity, deficiency, awkwardness. However overstated these descriptors may seem today and however much he used them to demonstrate Berlioz's shortcomings as a composer, they cannot be dismissed as irrelevant. Berlioz's music is not defective and ugly, but there is something awkward—even at times perverse—about his forms. Those awkward features should not be regarded as faults that should have been corrected by Berlioz—or, for that matter, problems that can be explained away by music analysts—but rather as indicators of the extreme psychological states that works like the *Symphonie fantastique* conjure up by artfully, not haphazardly, distorting musical norms.

A distinction is often made within the field of disability studies between *impairment* and *disability*, or between what Rosemarie Garland-Thomson (1997, 6) called "disability as an absolute, inferior state and a personal misfortune" and "disability as a representation, a cultural interpretation of physical transformation or configuration." If this distinction is transferred from the sphere of human abnormality to that of musical abnormality, an allowance can be made that the deformations of the *Fantastique*'s first-movement form do not make it absolutely inferior; they are only interpreted that way by a critic like Hadow (1904). The peculiar "configuration" of the work (to borrow Garland-Thomson's word) could just as well be viewed as productive and essential to how it functions, something that cannot and should not be remedied.

This is to say that an analysis of how the symphony evokes mental illness can benefit from the sociocultural view of disability promoted by current disability theory, which addresses the many ways disability can be construed and experienced, as opposed to a biological and medical view, which, in the words of Alan Gartner and Tom Joe (1987, 205), inappropriately characterizes disabled people as "sick, helpless, invalid." If we grant that the first movement of the *Fantastique* is in many ways a musical embodiment of human disability, then we also need to grant that its "disability" need not be regarded as a feature that makes it less than another, better formed work, but different from it. The movement's bizarre form, in other words, need not be corrected but rather coped with or "accommodated," to use Straus's (2006, 170) word from a discussion of the "tonally problematic" G-flat in Franz Schubert's Piano Sonata in B-flat, D. 960, which likewise cannot be overcome compositionally or fully normalized by the music analyst.

To quote Oliver Sacks (1995, xviii) writing about patients with extraordinary neurological conditions, it may be necessary to redefine concepts like *health* and *disease,* "to see them in terms of the ability of an organism [or, in this case, an artwork] to create a new organization and order, one that fits its special, altered disposition and needs, rather than in terms of a rigidly defined 'norm.'" The rest of this chapter is devoted to exploring the "altered disposition" of the *Fantastique*'s first movement and the psychological meanings attached to it.

Mental Illness and the Symphony's Program

On April 16, 1830, Berlioz sketched out the program to the *Symphonie fantastique* in a letter to his close friend Humbert Ferrand and then added these lines:

> Now, my friend, this is how I have woven my novel, or rather my history, whose hero you will have no difficulty in recognizing …I conceive of an artist, gifted with a lively imagination, who, in that state of soul which Chateaubriand so admirably depicted in *René*, sees for the first time a woman who realizes the ideal of beauty and fascination that his heart has so long invoked. By a strange quirk, the image of the loved one never appears before the mind's eye without its corresponding musical idea, in which he finds a quality of grace and nobility similar to that which he attributes to the beloved object. This double obsession [*idée fixe*] pursues him unceasingly. That is the reason for the constant appearance, in every movement of the symphony, of the main melody of the first allegro (Cairns 1999, 359; translated from Berlioz 1975, 318–20).

The first draft of the program found in this letter is strikingly similar to the subsequent versions that appear with the symphony's score, particularly in its characterization of the malady that affects the symphony's protagonist. In the Ferrand letter Berlioz writes about the first movement's "intimations of passion; aimless daydreams; frenzied passion with all its bursts of tenderness, jealousy, rage, alarm, etc., etc.," which in the 1845 version printed with the first corrected edition of the full score has become "a state of dreamy melancholy, interrupted by several fits of aimless joy, ... delirious passion, with its impulses of rage and jealousy, its returning moments of tenderness, its tears, and its religious solace" (Berlioz 1972, 218).

Even more, the language Berlioz uses in all versions of the program to describe his hero's mental and physical condition strongly resembles the language he uses to describe his own condition when he conceived and composed the symphony. Consider the following two passages. The first comes from another letter to Ferrand, written on February 6, 1830; it recounts Berlioz's devastation on seeing Harriet Smithson leave Paris for London in 1830, three years after he saw her play Ophelia in *Hamlet* and fell madly in love with her, but still two years before they would meet. The second is from a letter to Berlioz's father, written thirteen days later:

> I have just plunged back into the anguish of an endless, uncontrollable passion without motive, without object. She is still in London, and yet I feel her about me; all my memories awake and combine to rend me. I listen to the beating of my heart, its pulsations shake me like the pounding pistons ... I was on the point of beginning my big symphony ..., in which the course of my infernal passion is to be depicted; I have the whole thing in my head, but I can write nothing (Cairns 1999, 356-57; translated from Berlioz 1975, 306).

> I wish I could also find a specific to calm the feverish excitement which so often torments me; but I shall never find it, it comes from the way I am made ... Often I experience the most extraordinary impressions, of which nothing can give an idea; nervous exaltation is no doubt the cause, but the effect is like that of opium ... Well, this imaginary world [*ce monde fantastique*] is still part of me, and has grown by the addition of all the new impressions that I experience as my life goes on; it's become a real malady [*c'est devenue une véritable maladie*]. Sometimes I can scarcely endure this mental or physical pain (I can't separate the two) (Cairns 1999, 357–8; translated from Berlioz 1975, 309–13).

Debates continue about how much the *jeune musicien* of the *Symphonie fantastique* should be regarded as Berlioz's alter ego. Yet when scouring Berlioz's correspondence, many letters like these can be found, rife with descriptions of that alluring and tormenting *monde fantastique* into which Berlioz plunged himself on first seeing Harriet Smithson, making it difficult not to conclude that he channeled his physical and mental malady into the work and its program—that he transformed his "history" into his "novel."

But what was the nature of that malady? Was it the product of Berlioz's melancholic spirit, of a self-absorption and hypersensitivity of the kind found in Johann Wolfgang von Goethe's *Werther* and François René Chateaubriand's *René?* It was indeed. Berlioz refers to Chateaubriand in the draft of the program and its later versions, encouraging us to relate Chateaubriand's *vague des passions* (that quintessentially Romantic form of melancholy in which a young imagination feeds on its own desires), Berlioz's travails, and the symphony that gives them voice.[3] But the condition described in the *Symphonie fantastique* extends even beyond the *vague des passions* and into the realm of a definable mental illness. Berlioz's symphony participates in a web of relations that are not just aesthetic and personal but also pathological.

Francesca Brittan (2006) makes this argument in her essay "Berlioz and the Pathological Fantastic: Melancholy, Monomania, and Romantic Autobiography," which fundamentally reshapes the understanding of what Berlioz's *idée fixe* is all about and whence it comes. Drawing on a wealth of literary, musical, journalistic, and medical works written in and around the time Berlioz composed his symphony, she argues that "[f]ar from new, then, Berlioz's amorous obsession resonates with a host of earlier fictional fetishes. Although I do not suggest that he knew all of the *idées fixes* cited here, it is clear that his symphony participated in an existing tradition of literary 'fixations' – obsessions that reached well beyond general romantic attachment into the realm of clinical disorder" (ibid., 214). Her argument need not be rehearsed here, but its most salient points should be mentioned, at least insofar as they relate to the preceding discussion of disability.

Late eighteenth- and early nineteenth-century France, Brittan (2006) claims, witnessed a growing fascination with mental health. Doctor-psychiatrists explored the connections between the impressions of the imagination and the physical sensations transmitted by the nervous system. Mental disorders were defined with a new level of precision and were referred to extensively in medical and legal literature as well as in popular culture. Central among the doctor-psychiatrists of the early nineteenth century was Étienne Esquirol, who theorized a new mental illness called *monomania*, first identified around 1810 and later defined and classified in an 1819 paper published in the *Dictionnaire des sciences médicales* (1819). Monomaniacs, writes Brittan, were "consumed by one thought, idea, or plan of action, a state of mental fixation producing an 'energetic' effect while also causing 'nervous exaltation,' 'illusions,' feverish thought patterns and—in advanced cases—hallucinations, convulsions, and disturbing dreams. Sufferers might also experience melancholic symptoms, the frustration of their desires leading to depression, despair, and sorrowful withdrawal" (Brittan 2006, 221).[4]

One form of monomania—and Esquirol enumerated many, including theomania and monomania from drunkenness—was what he called *erotic monomania*.[5] Erotomaniacs were overtaken by monomaniacal passion for mythical characters, imaginary creatures, or—important for our purposes—women they had never met but nonetheless idealized. The afflicted were, in Esquirol's words, "pursued both night and day by the same thoughts and affections" (Esquirol 1838, 341; trans. Brittan, 2006), drawn toward an unattainable and largely imagined *idée fixe*. "While contemplating its often imaginary perfections," he writes (in what could just as well be a diagnosis of Berlioz's state), "they are thrown into ecstasies. Despairing in its absence, the look of this class of patients is dejected; their complexion becomes pale; their features change; sleep and appetite are lost. They are restless, thoughtful, greatly depressed in mind, agitated, irritable and passionate" (ibid.).

Esquirol's writings were influential in medical circles. By 1826, Brittan (2006) notes, monomania was the most common diagnosis assigned to patients entering the mental hospital Charenton.[6] The malady he identified also captured the public's imagination. Mental illness and psychiatric theory were fashionable topics of conversation in Parisian salons, and in time references to monomaniacal fixation began to appear widely in journalism, fiction, and art. Brittan's conclusion—which, however bold, seems unassailable—is that when Berlioz gave to his *jeune musicien* the symptoms of monomania, "he was not describing a vague or imaginary nervous disorder, but a *maladie morale* [mental illness] that would have been easily identifiable by many of those in the concert-going public.... Indeed, it could well be that Berlioz was constructing his own erotic disorder and that of his 'fantastic' protagonist according to the detailed descriptions of manic fixation saturating scientific and journalistic writing of the period" (Brittan 2006, 222–23).

Musical Representations of Mania

Brittan's essay establishes that the program to the *Symphonie fantastique* can be discussed within the context of disability, as it has been defined by Straus—a "culturally stigmatized bodily difference," where "bodily" refers to a range of physical and mental differences, including mental illness (Straus 2006, 119). By directing attention to "obsessive illness and its reconfiguration in the program of the *Fantastique*" (Brittan 2006, 219), Brittan demonstrates that Berlioz created a protagonist in his own image who was not just in love but in fact was mentally disturbed according to the terms and diagnoses of the day. What, then, is an effective way to build on her findings and to explore how that obsessive illness is reconfigured in the *music* of the *Fantastique*?

Humanities scholars have considered how aspects of disability can be felt in literature, art, drama, and film, but studies of how music can represent disability are rare, save of course Straus (2006) as well as the essays in this volume. Another notable exception is a recent article by Michael Davidson,

"Concerto for the Left Hand: Disability (in the) Arts," that challenges us to imagine how a "disability aesthetic" might deal with not only thematic but also formal questions—how, in his words, such an aesthetic might be a "frame for engaging disability at levels beyond the mimetic" (2005, 615).[7] One way of considering how the first movement of the *Symphonie fantastique* engages disability at the level of musical form is to ask how the symptoms of mono-mania might find their musical counterparts in formal processes. Doing so provides a way out of the bind of trying to match up the musical events of Berlioz's symphony with the extramusical events of its program—a rather "mimetic" approach taken by many who analyze Berlioz's music. In fact, as Berlioz stressed again and again throughout his writing, a piece of music does not follow its program in such a literal fashion; nor does the program follow the music. The music is what he would call a *metaphore* or *analogie* for its program. It presents a musical image that arouses passions and emotions comparable to those implied by its program.[8] Garland-Thomson (1997, 5) has written persuasively about "social narratives of bodily difference." By exten-sion, the first movement of the *Symphonie fantastique* might be considered a musical narrative of bodily difference, but one that need not parallel Berlioz's programmatic, or personal, narrative because it has its own means of repre-sentation distinct from those of language.

In sketching out those means, I will for the sake of clarity highlight three symptoms of monomania, as evident in Esquirol's and Berlioz's writings, and then consider how they might be manifested musically. The first symptom is an obsession with an ever-recurring *idée fixe* ("being pursued both night and day by the same thoughts and affections" as Esquirol puts it, or being haunted by a "double obsession which pursues him unceasingly," as Berlioz writes in his April letter to Ferrand, both quoted above). The second is a tendency to vacillate from a state of joy to one of despair, depending on whether the sufferer believes the object of his desire is within reach or not—recall Berlioz's sudden grief on seeing Harriet Smithson leave for London; a mere glance in his direc-tion, meaningless to her but all the world to him, could just as quickly send him into a spell of ecstasy. The third is a lavishing of devotion on a character that is largely self-created. Harriet Smithson, though of course a real woman, is in Berlioz's mind his Ophelia, more fictional than actual, as are the fixa-tions of Esquirol's monomaniacs. These are of course not the only symptoms of monomania, and I do not mean to imply that Berlioz sat down with the idea of translating these three into musical terms. But laying them out like this is a convenient way to speculate about how our listening experience bears strik-ing similarities to the emotional experience of Berlioz's afflicted hero—how, in other words, the movement presents not so much the events of his love story as the quality of his affliction.

The first part of my analysis, "Obsession," focuses on the movement's varied-repetitive large-scale form, as well as its sonata-like features, and the changes the *idée fixe* undergoes. The persistence of the protagonist's obsession and the delirium it gradually induces are reflected musically in the obsessive repetition of the *idée fixe* and its step-by-step delyricization. The second part, "Vacillation," shows how the movement's many thematic cycles are bounded by sections vastly different in style and affect and how these contrasts suggest the emotional extremes between which the artist swings. And the third part, "Self-Creation," shows how these sections, however different they may seem, are generated from similar musical materials, much as the *jeune musicien*'s beloved and the delight and anguish of his relationship with her are the products of a delusional imagination.

Obsession

All who study the first movement of the *Symphonie fantastique*—and probably all who hear it performed—will note that it is driven by the repetition of the *idée fixe*. What is perhaps less immediately apparent, and what has not been discussed by many analysts, is that the first statement of the theme initiates a wave of multiple themes, which itself is repeated and varied as the movement progresses. The *idée fixe* is the impulse that sets these waves in motion. It appears five times prominently throughout the movement, as the first element in a series of thematic cycles. Figure 16.1 shows the first several measures of the *idée fixe* melody as it appears at the beginning of these five cycles. Figure 16.2 presents an overview of the movement's form that takes into account how the movement's initial three-theme pattern (here called a rotation) changes, sometimes considerably, over the course of the movement.[9] The details of this diagram will be discussed in greater detail in what follows. At the moment, it is most important to note the many repetitions of the *idée fixe*—here labeled P—and the variations to the thematic pattern it initiates (P–TR–S). Those variations sometimes involve the omission of one or more sections (TR or S) and sometimes the addition of a new section (X). The added X sections, more harmonically than thematically distinctive, are the famous passages based on parallel first-inversion triads. The third X section (measures 358 and following) is overlaid with fragments of the *idée fixe*, a later addition to the score by Berlioz—hence X/P in Figure 16.2.[10]

The sonata-form labels popularized by Hepokoski and Darcy (2006) should also be noted. P, TR, and S refer, respectively, to the primary theme, transition, and secondary theme of a sonata form. The movement's sonata features will be addressed in a moment, but for now the focus is solely on the rotational presentation of its themes. Hepokoski (1993) coined the concept of *rotational form* in a monograph on Jean Sibelius's Symphony No. 5, and he and Darcy (1994, 1997, 2001) have used it to characterize certain recursive forms by Gustav Mahler, Richard Wagner, Anton Bruckner, and Giacomo Puccini, among others. It is also central to their discussions of late eighteenth-century sonata forms. Rotational forms involve the presentation of what Hepokoski

Figure 16.1 Five main statements of the *idée fixe*.

(1993, 25) terms a *referential statement* of contrasting and differentiated ideas—here, P–TR–S—which is "elastically treated" in later rotations. In an essay that discusses the *Tristan* prelude's constant repetition and variation of formal units, Robert Morgan (2000) used the term *circular form* to describe a comparable formal phenomenon. Although Hepokoski's and Morgan's terminology and aims differ, their characterizations of this varied-repetitive formal process are strikingly similar.[11]

It is easy to imagine why a rotational or circular model such as this would lend itself to the evocation of monomaniacal fixation and would suit Berlioz's programmatic ends. The repeated thematic waves triggered by the *idée fixe* suggest the relentlessness of the artist's passion for his beloved; he returns again and again to her image, just as the movement's rotations return again and again to the *idée fixe*. The variation to those waves over time—and particularly to their initial element, the *idée fixe*—suggests the progress of that passion; her

Introduction	m. 1			
Rotation 1	72	111	150	
	P	**TR**	**S**	
	I		V	
Rotation 2	166	191	198	
	P	**S**	**X**	
	V	I		
Rotation 3	232	291	311	358
	P	**TR**	**S**	**X/P**
	V	V	iii---I	
Rotation 4	410	439	451	461
	P	**X** interruption **P**		**X** int.
	I			
Rotation 5	491			
	P			
	I			

Figure 16.2 Formal diagram of the first movement.

image changes as his obsession grows more intense, just as the musical rotations change as they are repeated.

Why then does Berlioz reference the conventions of sonata form? And how does he distort its conventions to heighten the form's circularity? Debates about whether the movement is a sonata form at all persist to the present day, and with good reason. Rushton (2001, 258), for instance, writes, "If Berlioz's first movement, read as sonata form, appears inadequate, it could be the result of a wrong reading rather than any flaw in music which possesses convictions even in its composed hesitations." In fact, sonata form does seem rather inadequate. The movement can only very uncomfortably be squeezed into a normative sonata mold. But a great deal can be learned by recognizing how Berlioz invokes sonata form without necessarily embracing it. Rushton had it right: Berlioz composes hesitation into this music, and sonata form is one of the objects of that hesitation.

The music exhibits certain normative sonata-form characteristics that should be taken into account. The exposition is repeated—a later revision by Berlioz but nonetheless evidence of sonata-like thinking (Berlioz 1972, 201)—and it is in two parts, with a caesura before the S theme. A long introduction precedes the allegro, the standard for Berlioz's sonata forms. And the key structure moves from the tonic to the dominant before the repeat of the exposition, into more distant realms thereafter, and back to the tonic by the end.

The movement also shows signs of the symmetry noted first by Robert Schumann (1971, 230) and developed by Edward T. Cone (1971, 251). Both see the piece as an arched sonata form with the primary and secondary themes reversed in the recapitulation.[12] A version of Cone's diagram is reproduced in

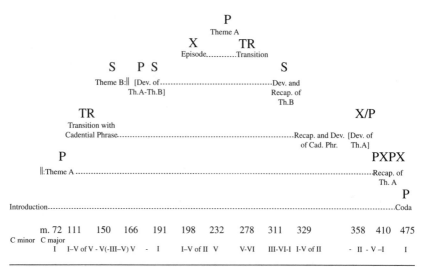

Figure 16.3 Cone's diagram of the movement's form (with my thematic labels overlaid).

Figure 16.3, with my thematic labels overlaid.[13] The arch form can be heard in performance as much as it can be gleaned off the page: in the clamorous return of the *idée fixe* in C major in measure 410 (Cone's recapitulation) that makes another statement of the secondary theme impossible or at least unnecessary; in the vast stretch of G major in the middle of the form (measures 232 and following) that counterbalances the C major sections on either side of it (measures 72, 410); and even in the concluding section (Cone's coda) that matches the introduction in mood, if not in length, with its lyricism and quietness.

But, in truth, this piece is too idiosyncratic to fit nicely into either a standard sonata-form model or a neat symmetrical scheme like Cone's (1971). It is perhaps best viewed as a sonata contorted in such a way as to become maddeningly reiterative and also to suggest a degree of long-range symmetry. Berlioz has written a tangled, hybrid form with competing impulses and above all an overriding varied-repetitive drive, which vividly evokes the riots of a mind "pursued both night and day by the same thoughts and affections," to quote Esquirol again (Esquirol 1838, 341; trans. Brittan, 2006).[14] The formal deformations create a musical image that excites sensations comparable to the physical and mental sensations symptomatic of monomania: confusion, restlessness, internal conflict, and escalating obsession.

The movement's uncommon repetitiveness is brought into relief by its most deformational feature with respect to sonata form, a long G major section in the middle of the form (measure 232), a curious circus carousel variant of the *idée fixe* that hollows out the form and calls into question conventional notions of development and recapitulation. The G major section begins too weakly to be called a recapitulation; plus, it is in the "wrong" key.[15] Yet it does send strong signals of return. It is plainly no mere developmental diversion, either. Berlioz was not averse to hollowing out his development sections with long and even static themes,[16] and he does not seem to have subscribed to the idea that there ought to be a strong opposition between development and recapitulation. That said, nowhere else does he fill apparently developmental space with a full statement of a movement's main theme. Nowhere else does a development sound so much like a re-beginning.

If the G major section seems too much like a varied restatement of the *idée fixe* to be called merely developmental, the tonic statement of the *idée fixe* in measure 410 seems too much like a further varied restatement to be called merely recapitulatory. C major is of course stated as boldly as can be—but almost too boldly. Nineteenth-century symphonists were no strangers to the climactic, clamorous recapitulation, yet Berlioz's sounds out of character—too hectic, feverish, unstable in its overresolution. Moreover, unlike the previous full statements of the *idée fixe* in C major and G major, it does not reach its end. It is interrupted twice by the X section and cannot muster the strength to produce an authentic cadence.

What these sections are called is less important than how their functions are regarded. If names must be given, the G major section could be called a development that sounds somewhat like a recapitulation and the C major return a recapitulation that sounds somewhat like a coda, particularly considering what has come before it. Figure 16.4, which places over Figure 16.1 the sonata-form labels *exposition, development, recapitulation,* and *coda,* attempts to capture this ambiguity.

The rhetoric of sonata form is called up, but mixed with it is an even stronger rhetoric of what Rushton (2000) called *strophic elaboration.*[17] That elaboration occurs in three broad arcs: a first that presents the main theme and passes through a section that behaves very much like a typical development (rotations 1 and 2); a second that, if not a full-fledged recapitulation, is nonetheless a full-scale return (rotation 3); and a third that bombastically reiterates the theme, followed by a "religious" reflection on it (rotations 4 and 5).

The variation to the movement's rotations is signaled most obviously by the variation to the *idée fixe* itself. Because that theme is unequivocally connected to the object of the protagonist's infatuation, its transformation can by extension be linked to the evolution of his passion for his beloved. What happens to the *idée fixe* as a musical idea, in short, reflects what happens to it as a mental idea. The theme is progressively constrained and its lyricism sapped; its aspect changes, from what might be called alluring to addling, in accordance with the intensification of the monomaniac's malady and of his pursuit of the woman he cannot have.[18] The theme's transformation is most apparent when examining its three equally weighted appearances at the beginning of rotations 1, 3, and 4.

Introduction   m. 1

Exposition
Rotation 1   72   111   150
              P   **TR**   **S**
              I   V

Development
Rotation 2   166   191   198
              P   **S**   **X**
              V   I

Development cont.? / Recap?
Rotation 3   232   291   311   358
              P   **TR**   **S**   **X/P**
              V   V   iii---I

Recap? / Coda?
Rotation 4   410   439   451   461
              P   **X** interruption **P**   **X** int.
              I

Coda
Rotation 5   491
              P
              I

Figure 16.4 Sonata-form overlay.

In the exposition, the *idée fixe* is a strain of pure melody without accompaniment and seemingly without meter, or, at least with an ambiguous meter. Figure 16.5 indicates how the meter and downbeats of the opening measures can be heard in various ways. Not every option is equally feasible, of course, and each depends on the perceived length of the opening whole note. All, though, are in the air, and without harmonic or rhythmic support it is difficult on a first pass to hear the bar lines as they are written—or to hear that there are bar lines at all.

In later appearances of the *idée fixe* the harmonic and rhythmic structure is more rigidly defined and the theme thereby more restrained. At the beginning of rotation 3, the melody is identical to that of rotation 1 (if anything, it is sweeter, marked *dolce* and played now by woodwinds). Its setting, however, is not. The steady eighth-note accompaniment and the heavy tonic pedal restrict the theme's movement from the outset. By measure 410 the *idée fixe* is completely hemmed in, and its lyricism has vanished. It is played twice as fast and double forte, amidst the first *tutti* in the whole movement. Its phrase structure is also normalized and compressed, the five- and seven-measure phrases of measures 72 and following becoming four-measure phrases in measures 410 and following.[19]

Such normalization comes at a cost. The *idée fixe* can no longer sing and unfurl on its own to reach its own end. We should be wary of overspecifying

Figure 16.5 Competing metrical patterns in mm. 72–79.

a programmatic interpretation of this process. It is difficult to say whether the *idée fixe* grows more threatening, more impure, or more unyielding, or whether the artist makes it so for all his fixating on it. Short of tying the theme's transformation to a particular sequence of events in the movement's programmatic scenario, however, we can contemplate how the process by which the theme metamorphoses, indeed ossifies, is analogous to the process by which the beloved's image does the same. The *jeune musicien*'s descent into madness implied by the movement's program—in which he is ever more disabled by the mania that afflicts him, his elation turns to insane anxiety, and a tantalizing, free-floating image is transformed into something threatening—is reflected in the progressive restriction and normalization of the theme that represents the woman he loves.

Vacillation

The shift between pleasure and pain to which Esquirol (1838) and Berlioz (1972) alluded finds its musical counterpart in the progression from stable to unstable formal areas—namely, P and X, respectively—over the course of several of the movement's rotations. The melodious *idée fixe* sections and the chaotic, athematic X sections that frame these rotations are seemingly opposites. The P sections are harmonically grounded and closed: Every one of them, save those at the beginning of rotations 2 and 4, ends with some sort of cadence; they are sounded in stable key areas, normally the tonic and the dominant; and they are generally songful, no matter how much their songfulness diminishes over time. The X sections, on the contrary, are as unhinged as anything Berlioz or any other mid-nineteenth-century composer ever wrote: Devoid of melody and harmonic functionality, they are musical depictions of delirium.

Interestingly, the connection between these unstable section endings and stable beginnings grows stronger as the movement unfolds; the elation and depression evoked by P and X gradually coalesce.[20] As the *idée fixe* is constricted, so is the scope of the cycles it generates—not in terms of actual,

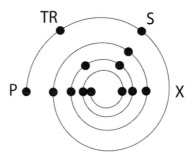

Figure 16.6 Movement's spiral form.

temporal distance—the middle rotation, number 3, is by far the longest—but in terms of what might be called the musical distance between the cycle's outer elements. At first, the contrast between the two elements is great. A grand pause separates the X section at the end of rotation 2 from P of rotation 3 (see fig. 16.4 for reference). In measure 358 the *idée fixe* is sounded amidst the X section's sliding first-inversion chords, bringing X and P into even closer contact. In rotation 4, P and X effectively become one, as the X section twice interrupts P in measures 439 and 461, and its strangeness infiltrates P's structure, leading it astray and preventing it from reaching completion.

The form of the movement is thus as much spiral as circular. If the musical distance each cycle travels is drawn as an arc, then as P and X move closer together musically that distance gets progressively smaller, as does, of course, the distance between each cycle. In Figure 16.6 the upper arcs represent the course of each cycle and the lower arcs the passage from one cycle to another.[21] Each dot represents a pass through the stations marked along the outside of the circle—P, TR, S, and X. Where there is no dot—as for example at the end of the first rotation at point X—that station is not passed through.

This spiral is as fitting an image as any for the whirlwind of back-and-forth emotions that overcomes the symphony's protagonist and Berlioz himself. These wild oscillations are central to the programmatic narrative of the first movement (with its "delirious passion, with its impulses of rage and jealousy, its returning moments of tenderness, its tears, and its religious solace"[22]) and also to the mental illness characterized by Esquirol. Berlioz's pursuit of Harriet Smithson is likewise a tale of extreme highs and lows. His letters show us a man whose hopes are fueled and crushed by the smallest turn of events: by the news given him by her agent that if Berlioz loves her, he can wait a few months to see her, which Berlioz interprets as a sign of interest; by the fact that he receives no replies to the many letters he sends her, which puts him in ruins; by the prospect of having his *Waverley* overture performed at a concert that also features her in a staging of the love scene from *Romeo and Juliet*, which thrills him to no end; by the sight of her rehearsing the tomb scene before the concert, which makes him flee the theater with a cry. Again, it is not necessary to draw a one-to-one correspondence between a musical event and a nonmusical one (e.g., at this point in the score the artist is spurned by his beloved, at this point he flees from her) to establish an intimate relationship between a musical procedure—oscillating between two contrasting musical ideas, ever faster and faster—and a mental–physical act—alternating ever more wildly between joy and despair.

Self-Creation

If the spiral in Figure 16.6 continued, it would presumably bring P and X so near each other that they would be practically indistinguishable. The ecstasy and grief of love, the hope of possessing what one desires and the torture of not being able to, the thing one covets and the intoxicating need to covet it—however the emotional extremes typical of this disability are characterized, each of these would join fully with the other. However, for the monomaniac the ideal of beauty and the passions it inspires are concoctions of a troubled mind. Everything—object and subject, pleasure and pain, hope and dejection—stems from the same source. Berlioz's tempestuous relationship with Harriet Smithson, as he perceives it while he is writing his symphony, is a fiction, as is indeed the entire *monde fantastique* he has created for himself.[23]

Berlioz translates the self-creative aspect of this mental illness into something musical and richly metaphorical by building the *idée fixe* and its polar opposite, the jarring X section, from the same raw material. From the outset, the two sections are joined even before they begin to spiral together. Figure 16.7 presents a reduction of each X section, highlighting the parallel first-inversion triads that underlie them: Although the third X section properly begins in measure 358, at the retransition to the recapitulation in C major, the passage of chromatically rising first-inversion triads does not begin until measure 369. The slurs in this example simply indicate the extent of each upward or downward slide.

Figure 16.8 presents a Schenkerian analysis of the *idée fixe* as it appears in the exposition. The defining elements of the X sections—sixths and chromatic lines—are present in the *idée fixe* as well, albeit in a more tonally rooted and lyrical context. The theme is structured around an ascending sixth-span (E–C) filled in chromatically. That sixth is in fact the same sixth heard at the beginning of the first X section in measure 198. Now, to be fair, the long ascending sixth that stretches across the *idée fixe* does not contain every chromatic pitch between E and C; A-flat and B-flat are properly neighbors, not members of the line itself that receive strong harmonic support. But a chromatic rise is apparent nonetheless, particularly because A-flat and B-flat are metrically and rhythmically accented.

The relationship between P and X hardly seems coincidental, and it is aurally perceptible, not just analytically demonstrable. Yet it has only been alluded to

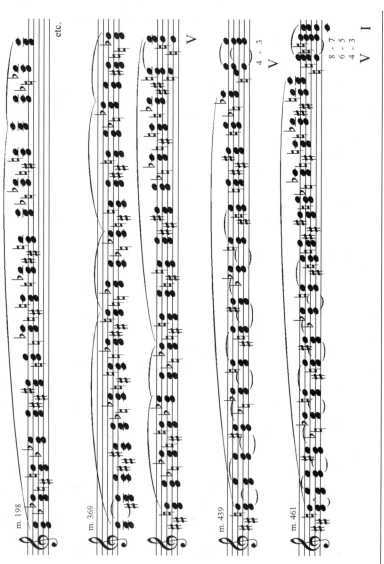

Figure 16.7 Chromatically rising and falling first-inversion chords in the X sections.

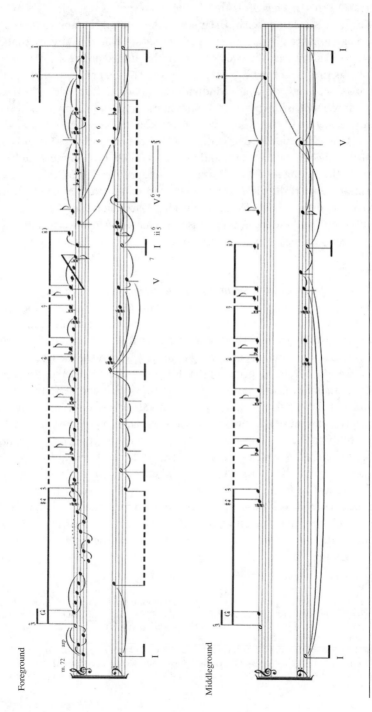

Figure 16.8 Schenkerian analysis of the *idée fixe*.

in print.[24] What it suggests is that P and X are not as opposite as they first appear. The distress induced by the image of the beloved contains something of that image, and the image, however pure it may seem at first, already contains the madness it spawns. The two are inextricably linked before the drama even begins—as they ought to be. Nicholas Cook (1987, 292) argued, after all, that Berlioz's symphony portrays "an individual's moods and fantasies"; the drama of the movement is the product of one man's mind, so it only makes sense that the elements in that drama would resemble one another. At base, all of the movement's sections are related. The *idée fixe* finds its image not only in X but also in the secondary theme and in Cone's (1971, 251–2) lyrical "cadential phrase"—the glimmer of a fully lyrical secondary theme that the truncated exposition never really gives us—as well as in the theme that is intertwined with the fragments of the *idée fixe* in the long X section leading up to measure 410. Each one of these musical ideas is the same self-generated phantom in a different shape, illusions of a tortured mind.

Epilogue

The first movement of the *Symphonie fantastique*, as noted previously, is not Berlioz's only work that betrays a preoccupation with mental illness. The earlier analysis, however preliminary, suggests that the movement can be productively read as a musical narrative of bodily difference, to return to Garland-Thomson's (1997) formulation, and that in reading it this way we can ascribe special meaning to its unique musical form. Yet that Berlioz's other disordered pieces (e.g., *La Reine Mab, Roi Lear*) do not feature programs that can be so thoroughly grounded in a discourse of pathology need not deter us from considering how they, too, employ musical metaphors of madness, mania, melancholy, and the like. As disability studies and music theory begin to come together, one of the tasks will be to determine which bodies of music would most benefit from the lessons disability scholars have to teach us—where our analytical methodologies can be not just be hitched to new theories but transformed by them. Berlioz, with his disarming eccentricity, which is so often misunderstood and stigmatized, and his abiding interest in expanding the limits of musical expressivity to include the sorts of extreme and abnormal states discussed here, seems as good a starting point as any.

Notes

1. *New Berliozians* include such scholars as Peter Bloom, David Cairns, Hugh MacDonald, Ian Kemp, Julian Rushton, and Katharine Kolb Reeve, each of whom contributed essays to the volume *Berlioz Studies* (Bloom 1992), a work that was instrumental in re-igniting a scholarly interest in Berlioz's life and work.
2. Their "Sonata Theory" is expounded most fully in *Elements of Sonata Theory: Norms, Types, and Deformations in the Late-Eighteenth-Century Sonata* (Hepokoski and Darcy, 2006). See also Hepokoski (2002a, 2002c) for discussions and applications of the theory.

3. Cairns (1999, 56) called Chateaubriand's *Génie du Christianisme* nothing less than "the primer of early French Romanticism," and it was certainly that for Berlioz. Berlioz would have encountered Chateaubriand's texts in his teens and reveled not least in their evocations of one of his favorite poets, Virgil. His fervor for Chateaubriand was, like all his passions, long-lasting, and it had a direct impact on his conception and composition of the *Symphonie fantastique*. Indeed, the symptoms of Chateaubriand's *vague des passions*, as evident in *Génie* and *René*, are similar to those of Esquirol's mental malady (outlined below), and seem also to make their imprint to some degree on the music of the symphony. The mania characterized by Esquirol, however, is perhaps the best rubric under which to look at the *Symphonie fantastique*'s first movement, if only because the *vague des passions* would seem to represent the searching melancholy of youth, without anything yet to fixate upon, whereas Esquirol's mania is defined by its obsession with a particular object of desire—an *idée fixe*.

4. As Brittan notes (2006, 221, fn 43), these are the symptoms described in a later treatise by Esquirol, *Des maladies mentales: considérées sous les rapports médical, hygiénique et médico-légal*, (1838, 1–4), which consolidates his earlier writings on monomania. Translations from this treatise in the present essay are taken from Brittan (2006).

5. These categories appear in Esquirol's early writings but are most clearly defined in Esquirol (1838).

6. Charenton was founded in 1645 by the Frères de la Charité in Charenton-Saint-Maurice, France. The Marquis de Sade was held there until his death in 1814, as was Jérôme-Joseph de Momigny, who died at the asylum in 1842. Today the hospital is called Esquirol Hospital, after Étienne Esquirol who directed it in the nineteenth century.

7. The number of scholars who have written about representations of disability in works of art is far too great for me to be able to provide an exhaustive list. In addition to the articles mentioned already, the following studies were of particular use to me in preparing this essay: Garland-Thomson (1997), Kriegel (1987), Kent (1987), Longmore (1987), Davis (1997a), Mitchell (1997), Uprety (1997), and Shakespeare (1999).

8. For Berlioz's views on this matter and others relating to music's relationship to the world of ideas and images, see Berlioz (1971). Rodgers (2005) drew on recent theories of musical metaphor, as well as on Berlioz's own writings on the topic and those of late eighteenth-century thinkers who influenced him, and argued that his forms are best construed as musical processes that reflect but do not replicate the dramatic and psychological processes implied by their programs.

9. In my analysis of the movement I number the measures according to the *New Berlioz Edition* (Berlioz 1972). These numbers do not correspond to those in Cone's *Norton Critical Score* (Cone 1971). Cone counted the two measures of the exposition's first ending; the *New Berlioz Edition* did not.

10. I regard each restatement of the *idée fixe* as the onset of a new rotation, so long as a substantial and clearly delineated section of new material separates it from a previous statement. The first X interruption section in rotation 4 is so brief that when P returns in measure 451 it sounds less like a new rotation than the continuation of an old one—hence P–X–P–X in rotation 4. Measures 491 and following I call a new rotation since the most important tonic PAC in the movement separates them from the music of the previous rotation.

11. My chapter is heavily indebted to the work of Hepokoski (1993) and Morgan (2000), as is my dissertation (Rodgers 2005), which shows how Berlioz used rotational form to evoke not only the mania of the *Symphonie fantastique*'s *jeune musicien* but also the impassioned goodbyes of young lovers in the *Scène d'amour* from *Roméo et Juliette* (1839), the spell cast by Mephistopheles' sylphs in *La Damnation de Faust* (1845–46) as they dance round and round Faust and lull him into a trance, and the wayward, homeward journey of marching pilgrims in *Harold en Italie* (1834). *La Mort d'Ophélie* (1842) is also a circular form, with successively elaborative strophes—a stunning evocation of her spiraling physical and mental collapse.

For discussions of rotational form see especially Hepokoski and Darcy (2006, Appendix 2), Hepokoski (1993, 23–6, 58–84; 1996; 2001; 2002b; 2004), and Darcy (1994; 1997, 256–77; 2001). For a more extended treatment of the various meanings of the terms *rotational form* and *circular form*, as well as comments by Berliozians about the varied-repetitive nature of his musical forms, see Rodgers (2005, 22–30).

12. The term *arched sonata form* is actually used only by Cone (1971, 251). Schumann (1971, 230) described the allegro as a "wide-arching whole," but he meant the same thing.

13. I have also corrected Cone's measure numbers so that they correspond to those in the *New Berlioz Edition* (Berlioz 1972).

14. Jean-Pierre Bartoli, who has emerged as the foremost Berlioz analyst in France, notes as well that the first movement of the *Fantastique* is a "hybride" of sonata form and varied-repetition form—what he calls *rondo avec un refrain évolutif* (2003, 200). See also Bartoli (1995) for further discussions of the *Symphonie fantastique*.

15. This was not originally the case. Berlioz made several changes to the autograph score between 1830 and 1833, by which time it seems to have assumed essentially the same shape as the published full score of 1845. Among these was the substitution of measures 185–234 for a longer passage of ninety-three measures. Much of the original music is lost, but we know it ended with a V^6_5 of G major rather than a V^6_5 of D—in other words, one notch too far away from the tonic rather than two (see Berlioz 1972, 202–3).

16. The F minor overture to *Les Francs-juges* (1826) is an example, with its static development that contains a near wholesale appearance of S in E-flat major.

17. Rushton (2000, 47) rightly called strophic elaboration "one of Berlioz's lifelong preoccupations."

18. Banks (1984, 39) argued that over the course of the entire symphony the "role of the *idée fixe* is successively reduced in significance." I make a similar argument about its main occurrences in this movement alone—not so much that the theme's significance is reduced as that its lyricism is. In a way, the arc of the theme itself—pure lyricism giving way little by little to fever—is mirrored in the course of the theme's long-range cyclic elaboration.

19. Cook (1987, 286) noted this as well, commenting that the C major version of the *idée fixe* is now "integrated into a fully symphonic texture, with its characteristic irregularities of metre and tempo all ironed out."

20. My discussion of the coalescence of P and X, particularly as it relates to how Berlioz brings the end of X and the beginning of P closer and closer together, owes a great deal to Christian Berger's excellent analysis of the movement. He devotes a considerable portion of his commentary to the "zwei Arten der Satzgestaltung": "Thema" and "Entwicklung." These two modes are exemplified by P and X (see Berger 1983, 51–2).

21. I have made the bottom arcs roughly as long as the upper ones, even though of course the number of measures within a given cycle is naturally larger than the number of measures between cycles, because, again, I am interested more in the musical distance traveled, not the temporal distance.

22. The line comes from the first corrected edition of the printed full score (1845).

23. Raby (1982, 104) expressed a similar idea in his biography of Harriet Smithson when he wrote that Berlioz, in his mad quest for her heart, "was playing all the parts in this imaginary scenario." Brittan also elaborates on this point in her essay: "His passion is directed toward a fictional, and therefore unattainable, character" (Brittan 2006, 224).

24. Cook (1987, 292, n. 1) noted that the *idée fixe* is linked to other sections of the movement in that it "outlines a stepped ascent with intermediate falls."

17

Inversional Balance and the "Normal" Body in the Music of Arnold Schoenberg and Anton Webern

JOSEPH N. STRAUS

Inversional symmetry and the sense of harmonic balance it creates play a central role in the free atonal music of Arnold Schoenberg and Anton Webern, written between 1908 and the outbreak of World War I. In some ways, inversional symmetry comes to function in this music in a manner analogous to key in tonal music: a systematic way of regulating the relationships among the tones, a normative principle of pitch organization. And, as with any normative principle, inversional symmetry may be subject to deviation and disruption.

The free atonal music of Schoenberg and Webern often engages a three-part narrative that involves the establishment, disruption, and reestablishment of a normative symmetry. This narrative may be present only in part: Pieces may unfold without any significant disruption of symmetry, or their symmetry may be disrupted and never reestablished, or a sense of symmetry may gradually emerge without ever having been clearly established in the first place. The initial sense of balance may be precarious, the disruption not vividly marked, the structural response not notably violent, and the resolution not entirely definitive.

In all of these situations, the interplay between a normative symmetry and abnormal disruptions can be usefully understood in relation to the cultural construction of disability. In all of the literature on musical symmetry, there is an emphasis on balance, on the physical sense of symmetrical balance around a fulcrum, of a body in a physically balanced state. In this context, deviations from inversional symmetry are felt as physical disruptions that unbalance the musical body—that create the threat or the reality of a disability—which the music must then deal with in some way. Inversional symmetry and symmetrical balance thus create the possibility for musical narratives that depend on a contrast of normative and non-normative bodily states. This body of music is typically understood as pure abstraction, devoid of cultural or social meaning. Through its reliance on inversional symmetry, however, this music both reflects and participates in the cultural and social construction of disability.[1]

Figure 17.1 presents three openings that both establish and challenge a sense of inversional balance and symmetry. Webern's Bagatelle, Op. 9, No. 5 (1911-13) (Fig. 17.1A) begins in a state of perfect pitch symmetry around D4.[2] Indeed, for the first four measures the notes of the piece simply wedge outward from that central tone, thus vividly establishing a normative sense of inversional balance: C-sharp4 is balanced against D-sharp4, C4 against E4, B3 against F4, and B-flat3 against G-flat4. The balance is disrupted in measure 5 by the viola's C5, the highest and—although marked *pianissimo*—the loudest note in the piece so far. It thus takes on a special rhetorical charge and sense of urgency: To maintain the sense of balance around D, that C must find its inversional partner E, and preferably E3, which would maintain the pitch symmetry. Until then, the music gives a sense of being off balance, its initial symmetry impaired.

The sense of symmetry around D waxes and wanes over the course of the piece and several E arrivals present themselves. E3 does arrive at the very end of the piece, but the final chord contradicts rather than confirms the original D symmetry. The narrative of the piece is thus one of balance established, disrupted, and only partially and equivocally restored: The abnormal is never fully normalized.

The second of Webern's Movements for String Quartet, Op. 5 (1909) (Fig. 17.1B) begins in a similar state of inversional symmetry and balance. The axis of symmetry is D (or A-flat), with every note balanced by its inversional

Figure 17.1 (A) Webern, Bagatelle for String Quartet, Op. 9, No. 5; (B) Webern, Movement for String Quartet, Op. 5, No. 2;(C) Schoenberg, "Valse de Chopin" from *Pierrot Lunaire.*

partner: G with A, B with F, and A-flat and D with themselves. The arrival of C-sharp signals a forceful disruption of the symmetry. Rhetorically marked as a melodic highpoint under a fermata, the C-sharp has no inversional partner, thus creating a musical gesture of passionate seeking: The C-sharp seeks to balance itself with an E-flat.[3]

The music that follows offers various E-flat arrivals, but none is fully satisfactory. At the end of the piece, however, C-sharp does return—and within a fully symmetrical structure. The final chord, with C-sharp now once again under a fermata, is arranged symmetrically in pitch: A balances E, and the low C balances the fermata C-sharp. C-sharp is now fully and satisfactorily balanced by C whereas it was never successfully balanced by E-flat, despite repeated attempts. The basic narrative structure of balance established, disrupted, and then restored still shapes the piece, but with a twist: The balance restored at the end is not exactly the same as the one disrupted at the beginning. In this music, the forces of normal and abnormal, balance and imbalance, symmetry and asymmetry, and ability and disability are evenly matched.

The opening of the "Valse de Chopin" from Schoenberg's *Pierrot Lunaire* (1912) (Fig. 17.1C) projects a strong sense of symmetry—actual pitch symmetry—around A3. In the first four beats of the piece eight different pitch classes can be heard. These are arranged symmetrically around A3, with one significant exception: D-sharp5 has no inversional partner to balance it. The desired pitch would be D-sharp2, three octaves below the unpartnered D-sharp5.

In the music that immediately follows, both the sense of A symmetry and of D-sharp5 as a rhetorically charged challenge to it are intensified. The aggregate of all twelve pitch classes is heard repeatedly in this piece, which also moves rapidly to fill out the entire pitch space from its lowest to its highest note. As the music moves toward its close, there are two fleeting iterations of E-flat2 (measures 32–33), and then, as the first line of text returns, E-flat is stated prominently on the downbeats of three successive measures. This emphatic gesture is nearly, but not quite, symmetrical around D-sharp5, the original problematic note. So the long-delayed E-flat arrives in conjunction with the inconclusive assertion of D-sharp5 as a symmetrical center. In its engagement with inversional symmetry, this piece thus leads to an ambiguous conclusion.

The issues of symmetry and balance and of bodily integrity and disability posed by the music of "Valse de Chopin" resonate also with its text, explicitly concerned as it is with disease. The text, by Albert Giraud, likens a diseased body to a disturbing piece of music. The first line of the text, with its disruptive "drop of [tubercular] blood on the sick man's lip" ("*Wie ein blasser Tropfen Bluts/Färbt die Lippen einer Kranken*") is thus associated musically with the disruption of inversional balance and the ultimate failure of the music to restore it.

Like Schoenberg and Webern's free atonal music itself, the theoretical traditions that have grown up around it have also been preoccupied with inversional symmetry and balance. Those traditions may be said to begin with Schoenberg himself. For Schoenberg, a tonic in a tonal piece and an inversional axis in an atonal piece are both capable of inducing a musical sense of harmonious balance, and in analogous ways: As David Lewin (1968, 2–3) observes, "The 'balance' of the total chromatic induced by the functioning of such an inversion was treated by Schoenberg, throughout his career, as something quite analogous to the balance induced by a tonal center ... [Schoenberg] conceived of a 'tonic' as a fulcrum about which all else balanced. ... Indeed, the widely used term 'tonal *center*' implicitly suggests exactly such a notion."⁴

For Schoenberg, who operated within the organicist tradition, a piece of music is analogous to a human body and as such is susceptible to non-normative stigmatized states—that is, disabilities such as imbalance. The normative and desirable bodily state, or balance, is understood in relation to a non-normative and undesirable state, or imbalance. And even though imbalance may be understood as desirable in many contexts, permitting forward motion both of human bodies and musical works, if excessive and uncontained and if incapable of normalization, imbalance may become disabling.

Schoenberg believed that musical works typically begin in a normative state of balance, which is disrupted by the imbalance of what he called a *problem*. Schoenberg was generally concerned with *tonal problems* (i.e., with threats to tonality), and his descriptions generally assume the presence of a major or minor key. Nonetheless, his language is sufficiently general that it can be extended to the disruptions of an atonal symmetry as well.

Every tone which is added to a beginning tone makes the meaning of that tone doubtful. If, for instance, G follows after C, the ear may not be sure whether this expresses C major or G major, or even F major or E minor; and the addition of other tones may or may not clarify this problem. In this manner there is produced a state of unrest or imbalance which grows throughout most of the piece and is enforced further by similar functions of the rhythm. The method by which balance is restored seems to me the real *idea* of the composition (Schoenberg 1984b, 122–3).

Every succession of tones produces unrest, conflict, problems... Every musical form can be considered as an attempt to treat this unrest either by halting or limiting it, or by solving the problem (Schoenberg 1967, 102).

Over the course of a work, the tonal problem must be solved, and this solution involves normalizing an abnormal bodily state: Rest is reattained, and balance is restored. Indeed, for Schoenberg the tonal problem provides the essential motivation for the musical drama—the crux of the narrative.

To extrapolate a bit from Schoenberg's own metaphorical language, it might be said that the tonal problem creates the nonnormative and stigmatized bodily states of imbalance and unrest. In that sense, Schoenberg's tonal problem is a concept deeply bound up with disability, both with its threat and its actuality. For Schoenberg, musical works are bodies; like bodies, they must strive to maintain their integrity and normativity in the face of the threat of disfigurement and disability.

From this point of view, the free atonal works discussed with respect to Figure 17.1 can be understood as musical bodies with potentially disabling problems. The C in Webern's Bagatelle, the C-sharp in Webern's Movement for String Quartet, and the D-sharp in Schoenberg's "Valse de Chopin" are all rhetorically charged notes that challenge and disrupt a prevailing inversional symmetry. Narratively, they are a problem to be solved, an abnormal element to be normalized, a disability to be remediated or rehabilitated. In each case, however, the musical response to the problem is ambiguous. In traditional tonal music, including particularly the music of Ludwig van Beethoven, tonal problems are often solved in a triumphant blaze—think, for example, of the Eroica Symphony's rectification of the troubling C-sharp of the opening theme of the first movement in its recapitulation and coda.[5] Schoenberg and Webern, however, have a different way of dealing with problematic disruptions of the normative scheme. Their music offers narrative engagement with issues of disability, but without the promise that the disability can be overcome, much less in a heroic manner. An initial symmetry, once lost, proves difficult or impossible to reattain. The music may express a concomitant sense of regret and loss but, at least in the pieces discussed with reference to Figure 17.1, the affective context is more one of melancholy recollection than bitterness or anger. Rather, this music offers a vision of the acceptance and accommodation of bodily difference.

A similar interest in inversional symmetry established, challenged, and possibly regained underpins a number of more recent theoretical traditions that have grown up around Schoenberg and Webern's free atonal music, including particularly the work of David Lewin. Lewin has consistently argued that pitch or pitch-class inversion has the potential for inducing a sense of musical balance: One group of notes is symmetrically balanced against another around some central note or notes. The resulting balance can be felt as an ideal, stable, harmonious state, explicitly analogous to the physical balance of the normal, nondisabled human body. The balance can be disrupted, but the disruption may set in motion a musical effort to restore the balance. For Lewin, then, disruptions of balance are similar in effect to Schoenberg's tonal problem—disturbances in the musical flow, deviations from the norm, potentially disabling conditions that the music must either cure or accommodate in some way.

For Lewin (1982-83, 1987, 1993, 1997), inversion can not only create a static sense of balance among musical elements but also can supply motivation for musical movement. Notes may be understood to "search" for their absent inversional partners, and such a search may be resolved, in the manner of a dissonance resolving to a consonance, when the absent partner appears. When two harmonies are nearly but not quite related by inversion, the music may convey a sense of urgent desire to repair the fault and to create true symmetry. Under such circumstances, a state of imbalance may be experienced as a defect, which the musical body may seek to recuperate. Indeed, the musical discourse of certain pieces may be understood as a series of efforts to reestablish or to create a sense of inversional balance and symmetry.

In Lewin's writing, two complexes of metaphors have clustered around inversional symmetry. The first imagines the state of inversional balance as a harmonious ideal, one that can be challenged, disrupted, or obscured, and possibly reestablished. The second has to do with the desire imputed to musical tones to find their inversional partners. When a sense of inversional balance has been established, Lewin (1982–83, 1987, 1993, 1997) imagined that isolated notes may be heard to seek their counterparts on the other side of the axis. Musical lusts, urges, and desires (Lewin's terms) are always directed toward the creation or restoration of balance—in this particular compositional context, symmetrical balance is the desired state, and notes seek that state. And the two metaphors are closely related: The desire of individual tones to form inversional partnerships is a manifestation of a more global musical interest in establishing, or reestablishing, inversional balance.

To grasp the full impact of these metaphors, it is important not to overlook their physicality—their origins in bodily experience. Most people have bodies that are symmetrical and depend on that symmetry for the maintenance of physical balance. If the symmetry is disrupted, the resulting loss of balance may be experienced as challenging, disruptive, frightening, and potentially catastrophic. The persistence of imbalance may be experienced as a disabling condition, a mobility impairment that prevents normal, smooth navigation through the world. In that situation, a person's physical experience of asymmetry and imbalance in his or her own body may be like Lewin's experience of asymmetry and imbalance in the music of Schoenberg and Webern: a problem to be solved, a restoration and recuperation to be desired, a disability to be overcome. It is revealing, however, that Schoenberg and Webern's free atonal music so often resists straightforward narratives of overcoming. Rather, their music is expressive of a more open, accepting attitude toward disability—it creates an artistic space within which disability can be accepted and accommodated.

The subtle narratives of disability embedded in the free atonal music of Schoenberg and Webern intersect in complex and interesting ways with two other related cultural categories: the *grotesque* and the *degenerate*, which are themselves intertwined.[6] A surprising number of early modernist musical works, including Schoenberg's *Pierrot Lunaire*, reveal a pervasive preoccupation with common grotesque features, including disease, deformity, and disability (see, e.g., the separate settings by Franz Schreker and Alexander Zemlinsky of Oscar Wilde's *Birthday of the Infanta*, with its central figure of a hunchbacked dwarf). This tendency is even more pronounced in the visual arts, where an interest in the grotesque, including the deformation and distortion of the human form, is a defining characteristic.

> Images gathered under the grotesque rubric include those that combine unlike things in order to challenge established realities or construct new ones; those that deform or decompose things; and those that are metamorphic. ... Grotesque describes the aberration from ideal form or from accepted convention, to create the misshapen, ugly, exaggerated, or even formless. This type runs the gamut from the deliberate exaggerations of caricature, to the unintended aberrations, accidents, and failures of the everyday world represented in realist imagery, to the dissolution of bodies, forms, and categories. ... The grotesque permeates modern imagery, acting as *punctum* to the ideals of enlightened progress and universality and to the hubris of modernist dreams of transcendence over the living world (Connelly 2003, 2, 6).[7]

The paintings of Oskar Kokoschka and Richard Gerstl, for example, both close associates of Schoenberg's, frequently involve distortions of the human form that invoke the tradition of the grotesque. In this, they exemplify a pronounced trend in artistic Expressionism toward extreme emotional and bodily states.

The artistic tradition of the grotesque frequently involves depictions of people with disabilities: "One of the ways that visual images of the disabled have been appropriated into the modernist and postmodernist aesthetic is through the concept of the 'grotesque' ...While the term *grotesque* has had a history of being associated with [a] counterhegemonic notion of people's aesthetics and the inherent power of the masses, what the term has failed to liberate is the notion of actual bodies as grotesque. There is a thin line between the grotesque and the disabled" (Davis 1997b, 64).

Schoenberg's own paintings, particularly the well-known series called "Gazes," involve severe deformities and distortions of the human face and thus engage the grotesque directly. One of the most persistent distortions involves unbalancing the symmetry of the two eyes. In the frequently reproduced "Green Self-Portrait" (1910), for example, much of the face is dematerialized in favor of a vivid representation of the eyes, and these are strikingly asymmetrical. These asymmetrical depictions of the human form are related to the musical asymmetries discussed above: in both cases the body—physical or musical—is thrown off balance, and some of the resulting artistic energy resides in the tension between a normative state of symmetrical balance and a challenge to normativity posed by asymmetry and imbalance.

Asymmetry, whether in music or in painting, would have been understood by Schoenberg and his contemporaries as an outward mark of degeneracy—a politically charged, pseudoscientific term typically used to condemn aspects of modern life and art. Here is part of a description by Nordau (1993, 16–18) in his widely circulated treatise on *Degeneration* (1892) of the physical symptoms, the disabling abnormalities, associated with degeneracy:

> Degeneracy betrays itself among men in certain physical characteristics, which are denominated "stigmata," or brandmarks. ... Such stigmata consist of deformities, multiple and stunted growths in the first line of asymmetry, the unequal development of the two halves of the face and cranium. ... In the mental development of degenerates, we meet with the same irregularity that we have observed in their physical growth. The asymmetry of face and cranium finds, as it were, its counterpart in their mental faculties. Some of the latter are completely stunted, others morbidly exaggerated.

Asymmetry—as a deviation from a normative state of symmetry, a deformation of a form—is where the cultural traditions of the grotesque and the degenerate intersect most forcefully with disability. Far from rejecting bodily asymmetries and the degeneracy they were understood to suggest, Schoenberg and Webern's music embraces them. In its acceptance of musical asymmetry and its willingness to forego the narrative restoration of a normative symmetry, this music accepts and accommodates the kinds of bodily differences that were culturally marked as grotesque or degenerate.

Music by Schoenberg and Webern, insofar as it expressly grapples with the stigmatizing deformity of asymmetry, becomes an artistic means for arousing and channeling anxiety about disability. The musical body, like the human body, is a fragile thing. The tonal musical body is particularly subject to puncture wounds—the diatonic container is permeable, subject to chromatic intrusions. The atonal musical body is subject to mobility impairments—its sense of balance imperiled—and to deforming asymmetries. In this sense, disability and anxiety about disability appear to be central to musical modernism, at least in its free atonal Viennese variety.

It is a historical irony that Schoenberg and Webern's free atonal music was written at a point when people with actual deformities, disfigurations, and mobility impairments had been rendered largely invisible by institutions designed simultaneously to sequester and to serve them (Stiker 2000). Neither composer had any direct experience with physical disability, nor was it a prominent part of their world, apart from aestheticized representations of the grotesque in the arts. Their music encodes and responds to an anxiety about disability but does so largely in the abstract.

Amid the Great War and its immediate aftermath, however, Schoenberg and Webern, like all citizens of Europe, found that disability had become a pervasive part of their daily lives. Suddenly, the streets of Vienna—like those of other European capitals—were full of wounded war veterans with physical impairments and deformities of all kinds. And amid the economic chaos that attended the end of the war, the effects of poverty and starvation on the bodies of their fellow citizens, particularly children, would have been unavoidable as well.[8]

In the same period, during and immediately after the war, both Schoenberg and Webern fell silent as composers. Their prewar music was concerned to some degree with representations of the human body and with narratives of bodily disability. Perhaps their silence was due, in part, to their search for an appropriate artistic response to a new sense of the human body, one sharply inflected by direct experience of disability on a large scale. Some contemporary visual artists, like George Grosz and Otto Dix, responded with direct representations of war wounded. Schoenberg and Webern appear to have responded in precisely the opposite way. In their prewar music, disability enters the musical body in the form of asymmetry, posing a challenge to a normative symmetry. Within these free atonal works, normative symmetry once unsettled is not usually reestablished in any definitive way, and to that extent these works may be understood as accommodating of bodily difference. In their postwar music, both composers adopt twelve-tone, serial styles that remain fundamentally concerned with inversional balance and symmetry but that approach them in a quite different way. Though the prewar music accommodated asymmetry, the postwar twelve-tone music banishes it, at least from the deeper levels of structure.

In Webern's twelve-tone music, the normative polyphonic combination involves series-forms related by inversion. Literal symmetries in pitch space typically reinforce the underlying symmetry of pitch class. Instead of the flexible interaction of symmetry and asymmetry typical of the free, atonal music, inversional symmetry and balance seem to permeate the entire musical fabric from top to bottom and from beginning to end without any serious challenge or need for accommodation.[9]

The hallmark of Schoenberg's mature twelve-tone music is *hexachordal inversional combinatoriality*, in which a series form is combined with its inversion such that "the inversion of the first six tones, the antecedent, should not produce a repetition of one of these six tones, but should bring forth the hitherto unused six tones of the chromatic scale. Thus, the consequent of the basic set, the tones 7 to 12, comprises the tones of this inversion, but, of course, in a different order" (Schoenberg 1984a, 225). In Schoenberg's twelve-tone music, the surface is often asymmetrical in striking ways, but the inversional symmetry of the underlying twelve-tone structure is guaranteed in advance.[10]

I suggest here that the dramatic shift in the social and visual landscape of wartime and postwar Vienna may have been among the factors that gave rise to the twelve-tone idea, which for Schoenberg and Webern is fundamentally concerned with inversional balance and inversional symmetry. As one of its central achievements, the method of composing with twelve tones establishes a secure harmonic framework grounded in inversional symmetry and balance. Typically in a twelve-tone piece by Schoenberg or Webern, the sense of inversional balance is far more pervasive and far more stable than in their free atonal music. The sense of balance in their twelve-tone music is explicit, fundamental, and unimpaired.

When people with physical disabilities were largely invisible to them, Schoenberg and Webern wrote music that explored extremes of asymmetry and imbalance and generally refused explicit solutions to the tonal problem, rebalancing of the unbalanced, normalization of the abnormal. When people with physical disabilities become an everyday part of the visual landscape, with an attendant rise in social and cultural anxiety about disability, Schoenberg and Webern responded with a musical language that guaranteed stable balance and that virtually banished the possibility of lingering asymmetry. In this sense, in the twelve-tone idea can be seen an extreme avoidance reaction to the threat of deforming asymmetry and imbalance, now made shockingly real in everyday life.

Notes

1. Scherzinger (1997) makes a similar argument about the role of inversional symmetry in dissolving traditional gender binaries embodied in the major-minor duality of traditional tonality and related pitch-class inversion to a contemporary interest in sexual inversion.
2. The initial symmetry in this piece is noted by Antokoletz (1984), Morgan (1992), and Stoecker (2003).
3. Lewin (1982–83) is the source for much of this discussion, including the idea that the C-sharp seeks an appropriate, E-flat to maintain the inversional balance established in the opening. See also Archibald (1972), which describes the power of symmetry in this piece to create a situation in which "we expect near-symmetries to become completed" (p. 159) and in which "we expect completion of symmetrical groupings when there seems to be an imbalance" (p. 160).
4. Lewin (1968) relates the idea of inversion also to other tonal theorists who invoke the concept of balance, including Jean-Philippe Rameau, for whom dominant and subdominant are balanced symmetrically around a tonic, and Hugo Riemann, whose harmonic dualism imagined a major and minor triad generated symmetrically above and below a root. The role of inversional symmetry in dualist theories of tonal harmony and in early theories of atonal music is explored in Bernstein (1993).
5. See Straus (2006) for a discussion of tonal problems and their solution in the music of Beethoven and Franz Schubert in relation to the history of disability. See also Cone (1982) for his related concept of the *promissory note*.
6. For a history of the concept of the grotesque and its role in twentieth-century opera, see Fullerton (2005). Draughon (2003, 390) described the waltz, the ostensible genre of Schoenberg's "Valse de Chopin," as a locus for the grotesque and the degenerate and further described the close linkage between degeneracy and disability on the one hand and femaleness and Jewishness on the other: "At the turn of the century, this rural-urban polarity was intimately bound with ideologies of gender, the body, and decadence. While the *Stadtmensch's* body came to be regarded as a potential carrier of a feminized, urban degeneracy, the ideology of *Korperkultur* (body culture) proposed a cure for this degeneracy in an idealized chaste and rural male body." On the role of the waltz in Schoenberg's music as "a parody of its former self" and as "signifying horror," see Cherlin (1998, 593).

7. For additional discussions of the grotesque in the visual arts and music, see Powell (1974), Schorske (1981), and Sheinberg (2000).

8. The extensive disability, deformity, and disfigurement brought about by the Great War and its immediate aftermath have been thoroughly documented (see Whalen 1984; Cohen 2001; Gerber 2000; Healy 2004; Boyer 1995).

9. For one among many published descriptions of the role of inversional symmetry in Webern's twelve-tone music, see Bailey (1991).

10. On the relationship in Schoenberg's twelve-tone music between underlying pitch-class symmetrical twelve-tone structures and their often asymmetrical realization in pitch space, see Cherlin (1991) and Peles (2004). As Peles observed, "The system itself is also defined at so abstract a level that it need not be—and in Schoenberg's music usually is not—associated with explicit foreground symmetry, or repetition of other obvious sorts. Instead, a maximumly asymmetrical and non-repetitive surface will typically play itself out against the backdrop of a maximumly symmetrical abstract succession" (p. 61).

References

Abbate, Carolyn. 1991. *Unsung Voices*. Princeton: Princeton University Press.

Adorno, Theodor W. 1999. "Anton von Webern." In *Sound Figures (Klangfiguren)*, trans. Rodney Livingstone, 91–105. Stanford: Stanford University Press.

Agawu, Kofi V. 2003. *Representing African Music: Postcolonial Notes, Queries, Positions*. New York: Routledge.

AIDS Quilt Songbook. 1993. Score. London: Boosey & Hawkes.

AIDS Quilt Songbook. 1994. CD. Harmonia Mundi HMU 907602.

Albert, M. L., R. W. Sparks, and N. A. Helm. 1973. "Melodic Intonation Therapy for Aphasia." *Archives of Neurology* 29: 130–1.

Alm, Irene. 1993. *Catalogue of Venetian Opera Libretti at the University of California, Los Angeles*. Berkeley: University of California Press.

Altman, Rick. 1987. *The American Film Musical*. Bloomington: Indiana University Press.

Alvin, J. 1975. *Music Therapy for the Autistic Child*. London: Oxford University Press. Available at http://www.questia.com.

American Psychiatric Association (APA). 1994. "DSM-IV Criteria, Pervasive Developmental Disorders: 299.00 Autistic Disorder." In *Diagnostic and Statistical Manual of Mental Disorders*. 4th ed. Washington, DC: American Psychiatric Association. Available at http://www.autism-biomed.org/dsm-iv.htm.

Andreason, N. C. 1987. "Creativity and Mental Illness Prevalence Rates in Writers and First-Degree Relatives." *American Journal of Psychiatry* 144: 1288–92.

Angelou, Maya. 1969. *I Know Why the Caged Bird Sings*. New York: Bantam.

Anon. 1918. *Songs the Soldiers and Sailors Sing*. New York: Feist.

Ansen, David. 2000. "Light and 'Dark.'" *Newsweek*, September 25, 66.

Antokoletz, Elliott. 1984. *The Music of Bartók: A Study of Tonality and Progression in Twentieth-Century Music*. Berkeley: University of California Press.

Archibald, Bruce. 1972. "Some Thoughts on Symmetry in Early Webern, Op. 5, No. 2." *Perspectives of New Music* 10(2): 159–63.

Arell, Ruth. 1950. "Defects into Dividends." *Music Journal* 8: 28–30, 32–3.

Asch, Adrienne. 2004. "Critical Race Theory, Feminism, and Disability: Reflections on Social Injustice and Personal Identity." In *Gendering Disability*, Ed. Bonnie G. Smith and Beth Hutchison, 9–44. New Brunswick, NJ: Rutgers University Press.

Asperger, Hans. 1991. "'Autistic Psychopathy' in Childhood." Trans. and annot. Uta Frith. In *Autism and Asperger Syndrome*, Ed. Uta Frith, 37–92. Cambridge: Cambridge University Press.

Attinello, Paul. 1992. "Just Deal with It." Review of *Take It and Leave It: Aspects of Being Ill* by Renate Rubinstein." *Positive Living, Newsletter of AIDS Project Los Angeles* 1(6): 10

———. 2000. "Music and AIDS: Some Interesting Works." *GLSG Newsletter* 10(1): 4–6: 10.

———. 2004. "Music and AIDS." *The Queer Encyclopedia of Music, Dance, and Musical Theater*, Ed. Claude Summers. San Francisco: Cleis Press. Available at http://www.glbtq.com.

———. 2006. "Closeness and Distance: Songs about AIDS." In *Queering the Popular Pitch*, Ed. Sheila Whitely and Jennifer Rycenga, 221–31. New York: Routledge.

Attwood, Tony. 1998. *Asperger's Syndrome: A Guide for Parents and Professionals*. London: Jessica Kingsley Publishers.

Autism Network International. n.d. "What is Autism?" http://www.ani.autistics.org/definitions.html.

Autism Society Canada. n.d. http://www.autismsocietycanada.ca/asd_research/asc_initiatives/index_e.html.

Autism Society of America. n.d. http://www.autism-society.org.

Avins, Styra. 1997. *Johannes Brahms: Life and Letters*. Trans. Josef Eisinger and Styra Avins. Oxford: Oxford University Press.

Bailey, Kathryn. 1991. *The Twelve-Note Music of Anton Webern*. Cambridge: Cambridge University Press.

Baker, B. 1982. "The Use of Music with Autistic Children." *Journal of Psychosocial Nursing and Mental Health Services* 20(4): 31–4.

Bamberger, J. 1986. "Cognitive Issues in the Development of Musically Gifted Children." In *Conceptions of Giftedness*, Ed. R. Sternberg and J. Davidson, 388–413. New York: Cambridge University Press.

Banks, Paul. 1984. "Coherence and Diversity in the *Symphonie fantastique*." *19th-Century Music* 8(1): 37–43.

Baron-Cohen, Simon. 2000. "Is Autism Necessarily a Disability?" *Development and Psychopathology* 12: 489–500.

Barrier, Michael. 1999. *Hollywood Cartoons: American Animation In Its Golden Age*. New York: Oxford University Press.

Barthes, Roland. 1990. "The Grain of the Voice." In *On Record: Rock, Pop and the Written Word*, Ed. Simon Frith and Andrew Goodwin, 293–300. New York: Routledge.

———. 1993. *Mythologies*. Trans. Annette Lavers. London: Vintage.

Bartoli, Jean-Pierre. 1995. "Forme narrative et principes du developpement musical dans la *Symphonie fantastique* de Berlioz." *Musurgia: Analyse et pratique musicales* 2(1): 25–50.

———. 2003. "Forme symphonique." In *Dictionnaire Berlioz*, Ed. Pierre Citron and Cécile Reynaud, 199–201. Paris: Fayard.

Barton, Justin. n.d. "Thoughts, Bodies, and Intensive Cartography." Chap. 2 in *Autism*. http://www.cinestatic.com/trans-mat/Barton/IC2s2.htm.

Bunt, Leslie. n.d. "Music Therapy." In *Grove Music Online*, ed. L. Macy. http://www.grovemusic.com/shared/views/article.html?from=search&session_search_id=784735154&hitnum=1&section=music.19453.

Bazzana, Kevin. 2003. *Wondrous Strange: The Life and Art of Glenn Gould*. Toronto: McClelland & Stewart.

Bean, J. P. 2004. *Joe Cocker—With a Little Help from My Friends—The Authorized Biography*. London: Virgin.

Beast with Five Fingers Papers. Warner Brothers Archives. Los Angeles: University of Southern California.

Becker, George. 1978. *The Mad Genius Controversy*. Beverly Hills: Sage Publications.

Bellman, Jonathan. 2000. "Chopin and His Imitators: Noted Emulations of the 'True Style' of Performance." *19th-Century Music* 24(2): 149–60.

Berger, Christian. 1983. *Phantastik als Konstruktion: Hector Berlioz' "Symphonie fantastique."* Kassel: Bärenreiter.

Bergman, Rhona. 1999. *The Idea of Gould*. Philadelphia: Lev Publishing.

Berliner, Paul F. 1994. *Thinking in Jazz: The Infinite Art of Improvisation*. Chicago: University of Chicago Press.

Berlioz, Hector. 1971. "On Imitation in Music (1837)." In *Berlioz: Fantastic Symphony*, Ed. Edward T. Cone, 36–46. New York and London: W.W. Norton.

———. 1972. *Hector Berlioz: New Edition of the Complete Works*. Gen. Ed. Hugh Macdonald. Vol. 16: *Symphonie fantastique*, Ed. Nicholas Temperley. Kassel: Bärenreiter.

———. 1975. *Correspondance générale de Hector Berlioz*. Gen. Ed. Pierre Citron. Vol. 1: 1803–32, Ed. Pierre Citron. Paris: Flammarion.

———. 2002. *The Memoirs of Hector Berlioz*. Trans. and Ed. David Cairns. New York and Toronto: Knopf.

Bernstein, David. 1993. "Symmetry and Symmetrical Inversion in Turn-of-the-Century Theory and Practice." In *Music Theory and the Exploration of the Past*, Ed. Christopher Hatch and David Bernstein, 377–408. Chicago: University of Chicago Press.

Bernstein, Leonard. 1976. *The Unanswered Question*. Cambridge, MA: Harvard University Press.

———. 1983. "The Truth about a Legend." In *Glenn Gould Variations*, Ed. John McGreevy, 17–22. Toronto: Macmillan of Canada.

Berton, Pierre. 1959. "Boy at a Piano Breaking all the Rules." *Toronto Daily Star*, January 8, sec. 2, 1.

———. 1997. *The Last Good Year: 1967*. Toronto: Doubleday Canada Ltd.

Bester, Alfred. 1964. "The Zany Genius of Glenn Gould." *Holiday Magazine* 35(4): 150–6.

Blanc, Mel, and Philip Bashe. 1988. *That's Not All Folks!* New York: Warner Books.

Bloodstein, Oliver. 1993. *Stuttering: The Search for a Cause and a Cure*. Boston: Allyn and Bacon.

———. 1995. *A Handbook on Stuttering*. 5th ed. San Diego: Singular Publishing Group.

Bloom, Peter, ed. 1992. *Berlioz Studies*. Cambridge: Cambridge University Press.
———. 2000. *The Cambridge Companion to Berlioz*. Cambridge: Cambridge University Press.
Bluemel, C. S. 1913. *Stammering and Cognate Defects of Speech: Vol. I: The Psychology of Stammering*. New York: G.E. Stechert.
Bonnel, A., L. Mottron, I. Peretz, M. Trudel, E. Gallun, and A. M. Bonnel. 2000. "Enhanced Pitch Sensitivity in Individuals with Autism: A Signal Detection Analysis." *Journal of Cognitive Neuroscience* 15(2): 226–35.
Bordman, Gerald. 1992. *American Musical Theatre, A Chronicle*. 2d ed. New York: Oxford University Press.
Borthwick, Alan. 1995. *Music Theory and Analysis: The Limitations of Logic*. New York: Garland.
Bouyer, Raymond. 1903. "A propos du 'Festin d'Esope.'" *Le Ménestrel* 69(35): 276-7.
Boyer, John. 1995. *Culture and Political Crisis in Vienna: Christian Socialism in Power, 1897-1918*. Chicago: University of Chicago Press.
Braidotti, Rosi. 2002. *Metamorphoses: Towards a Materialist Theory of Becoming*. Cambridge: Polity Press.
Bregman, Albert S. 1990. *Auditory Scene Analysis: The Perceptual Organization of Sound*. Cambridge, MA: MIT Press.
Brennan, Teresa. 2003. *The Transmission of Affect*. Ithaca: Cornell University Press.
Briscoe, James R. 1997. "Shulamit Ran." In *Contemporary Anthology of Music by Women*, Ed. James R. Briscoe, 260-3. Bloomington: Indiana University Press.
Brittan, Francesca. 2006. "Berlioz and the Pathological Fantastic: Melancholy, Monomania, and Romantic Autobiography." *19th-Century Music* 29(3): 211-39.
Britten, Benjamin. 1961. *Billy Budd*. Score. Libretto by E. M. Forster and Eric Crozier. London: Boosey & Hawkes.
Brown, Laura. S. 1995. "Not Outside the Range: One Feminist Perspective on Psychic Trauma." In *Trauma: Explorations in Memory*, Ed. Cathy Caruth, 100-12. Baltimore: Johns Hopkins University Press.
Brown, W. A., K. Cammuso, H. Sachs, et al. 2003. "Autism-Related Language, Personality, and Cognition in People with Absolute Pitch: Results of a Preliminary Study." *Journal of Autism and Developmental Disorders* 33(2): 163-7.
Bruscia, Kenneth E. 1987. *Improvisational Models of Music Therapy*. Springfield, IL: Charles C. Thomas.
———. 1989. *Defining Music Therapy*. Spring City, PA: Spring House Books.
Buhler, James. 2001. "Analytical and Interpretive Approaches II: Analysing Interactions of Music and Film." In *Film Music: Critical Approaches*, Ed. K. J. Donnelly, 39-61. New York: Continuum.
Burley, Rob, and Jonathan Maitland. 2001. *Songbird*. London: Orion.
Cairns, David. 1999. *Berlioz 1803-1832: The Making of an Artist*. Berkeley: University of California Press.
Calcagno, Mauro. 2000. "Staging Musical Discourses in Seventeenth-Century Venice: Francesco Cavalli's *Eliogabalo* (1667)." Ph.D. diss., Yale University.
———. 2003. "Signifying Nothing: On the Aesthetics of Pure Voice in Early Venetian Opera." *The Journal of Musicology* 20 (4): 461–497.
Canguilhem, Georges. 1991. *The Normal and the Pathological*. Trans. Carolyn R. Fawcett. New York: Zone.
Caruth, Cathy. 1996. *Unclaimed Experience: Trauma, Narrative, and History*. Baltimore: Johns Hopkins University Press.
Cavalli, Francesco. 1649. *Il Giasone*. MS (microfilm). Contarini Collection. Biblioteca nazionale marciana. Venice.
Celletti, Rodolfo. 1991. *A History of Bel Canto*. Trans. Frederick Fuller. Oxford: Clarendon Press.
Chateaubriand, François. 1951. *Atala, René*. Ed. Phyllis Crump. Manchester: Manchester University Press.
———. 1966. *Génie du Christianisme*. Vol. 1. Paris: Garnier-Flammarion.
Cherlin, Michael. 1991. "Dramaturgy and Mirror Imagery in Schoenberg's *Moses und Aron*: Two Paradigmatic Interval Palindromes." *Perspectives of New Music* 29(2): 50–71.
———. 1998. "Memory and Rhetorical Trope in Schoenberg's String Trio." *Journal of the American Musicological Society* 51(3): 559–602.
Cicognini, Giacinto Andrea. 1988. *Il Giasone*. CD. Trans. Derek Yeld. Cond. René Jacobs. Arles: Harmonia Mundi 901282.84.

Cizmic, Maria. 2004. *Performing Pain: Music and Trauma in 1970s and 80s Eastern Europe.* Ph.D. diss., University of California, Los Angeles.

Claridge, Gordon. 1998. *Creativity and Madness: Clues from Modern Psychiatric Diagnosis.* Oxford: Oxford University Press.

Clark, Maribeth. 2003. "The Body and the Voice in *La muette de Portici.*" *19th-Century Music* 27: 116–31.

Clifton, John. 2001. "Autism and Jazz." Paper presented to the Guelph Jazz Festival Colloquium, Guelph, Ontario, Canada. Available at http://www.ont-autism.uoguelph.ca/Jazz.PDF.

Cohen, Deborah. 2001. *The War Come Home: Disabled Veterans in Britain and Germany, 1914–1939.* Berkeley: University of California Press.

Cohen, Leonard. 1988. "Everybody Knows." *I'm Your Man.* CD. Columbia (Sony) 460642 2.

Collister, Ron. 1956. "Wears Gloves at Piano...But No Shoes." *Toronto Telegram*, March 9: n.p. Document 1979-20, 41, 10, 17, Glenn Gould Papers, Music Section, Library and Archives Canada, Ottawa.

Cone, Edward T., Ed. 1971. *Berlioz: Fantastic Symphony.* New York: W.W. Norton.

———. 1974. *The Composers Voice.* Berkeley: University of California Press.

———. 1982. "Schubert's Promissory Note: An Exercise in Musical Hermeneutics." *19th-Century Music* 5(3): 233–41.

———. 1987. "On Derivation: Syntax and Rhetoric." *Music Analysis* 6: 237–55.

Connelly, Frances, Ed. 2003. *Modern Art and the Grotesque.* Cambridge: Cambridge University Press.

Cook, Nicholas. 1987. *A Guide to Musical Analysis.* London: J.M. Dent & Sons.

Cott, Jonathan. 1984. *Conversations with Glenn Gould.* Boston: Little, Brown.

Couser, G. Thomas. 1997. *Recovering Bodies: Illness, Disability, and Life Writing.* Madison: University of Wisconsin Press.

Covert, Colin. 2000. "Tragic Magic." *Star Tribune*, October 6, 27.

Crawford, Richard. 2001. *America's Musical Life: A History.* New York: W.W. Norton.

Crescimbeni, Giovanni Maria. 1700. *La bellezza della vulgar poesia.* Rome: Buagni.

Crimp, Douglas. 1988. *AIDS: Cultural Analysis, Cultural Activism.* Cambridge, MA: MIT Press.

Crutchfield, Susan. 2001. "The Noble Ruined Body: Blindness and Visual Prosthetics in Three Science Fiction Films." In *Screening Disability*, Ed. Anthony Enns and Christopher R. Smit, 135–50. Lanham, MD: University Press of America.

Curtis, James. 1982. *James Whale.* Metuchen, NJ: Scarecrow.

Darcy, Warren. 1994. "The Metaphysics of Annihilation: Wagner, Schopenhauer, and the Ending of the Ring." *Music Theory Spectrum* 16(1): 1–40.

———. 1997. "Bruckner's Sonata Deformations." In *Bruckner Studies*, Ed. Timothy L. Jackson and Paul Hawkshaw, 256–77. Cambridge: Cambridge University Press.

———. 2001. "Rotational Form, Teleological Genesis, and Fantasy-Projection in the Slow Movement of Mahler's Sixth Symphony." *19th-Century Music* 25(1): 49–74.

Davidson, Michael. 2005. "Concerto for the Left Hand: Disability (in the) Arts." *PMLA* 120(2): 615–19.

Davies, Peter. 1989. *Mozart in Person: His Character and Health.* New York: Greenwood Press.

Davis, Lennard J. 1995. *Enforcing Normalcy: Disability, Deafness, and the Body.* New York: Verso.

———. 1997a. "Constructing Normalcy: The Bell Curve, the Novel, and the Invention of the Disabled Body in the Nineteenth Century." In *The Disability Studies Reader*, Ed. Lennard J. Davis, 9–28. New York: Routledge.

———. 1997b. "Nude Venuses, Medusa's Body, and Phantom Limbs: Disability and Visuality." In *The Body and Physical Difference*, Ed. David Mitchell and Sharon Snyder, 51–70. Ann Arbor: University of Michigan Press.

———. 2002. *Bending over Backwards: Disability, Dismodernism and Other Difficult Positions.* New York: New York University Press.

Dekker, Martijn. n.d. "On Our Own Terms: Emerging Autistic Culture." http://trainland.tripod.com/martijn.htm.

Deleuze, Gilles. 1994. *Difference and Repetition.* New York: Columbia University Press.

Deshaze, Mary K. 2003. "Fractured Bodies: Women's Cancer and Feminist Theater." *National Women's Studies Association Journal* 15(2):1–26.

Dettmer, Roger. 1962. "Gould Fits—Suit Doesn't." *Chicago's American*, April 23: n.p. Document 1979-20, 41, 41, 11, Glenn Gould Papers, Music Section, Library and Archives Canada, Ottawa.

Deutsch, Diana. 1999. "Grouping Mechanisms in Music." In *The Psychology of Music*, 2d ed., Ed. Diana Deutsch, 299–348. New York: Academic Press.

Deutsch, Diana, Trevor Henthorn, and Mark Dolson. 2004. "Absolute Pitch, Speech, and Tone Language: Some Experiments and a Proposed Framework." *Music Perception* 21(3): 339–56.

DeWitt, L.A. and A.G. Samuel. 1990. "The Role of Knowledge-Based Expectations In Music Perception: Evidence From Musical Restoration." *Journal of Experimental Psychology: General* 119: 123–44.

Diagnostic and Statistical Manual of Mental Disorders IV. 1994. Washington, DC: American Psychiatric Association.

Disability Statistics Center. n.d. http://dsc.ucsf.edu/main.php?name=resources.

Doane, Mary Ann. 1987. *The Desire to Desire: The Woman's Film of the 1940s*. Bloomington: Indiana University Press.

Dorn, Mike, Carol Marfisi, Lydia Pecteau, et al. 2005. "Disability Studies: Temple U." http://disstud.blogspot.com/2005/09/disability-blogs-roundup-katrina.html.

Dowsett, Gary W. 2000. "Bodyplay: Corporeality in a Discursive Silence." In *Framing the Sexual Subject: The Politics of Gender, Sexuality, and Power*, Ed. Richard G. Parker, 29–45. Berkeley: University of California Press.

Draughon, Francesca. 2003. "Dance of Decadence: Class, Gender, and Modernity in the Scherzo of Mahler's Ninth Symphony." *Journal of Musicology* 20(3): 388–413.

Dubiel, Joseph. 1992. "Senses of Sense-Making." *Perspectives of New Music* 30(1): 210–21.

Dutton, Dennis. 1983. "Ecstasy of Glenn Gould II." In *Glenn Gould Variations*, Ed. John McGreevy, 191–8. Toronto: Macmillan of Canada.

Eads, Martha Greene. 2002. "Unwitting Redemption in Margaret Edson's *W;t*." *Christianity and Literature* 51(2): 241–56.

Edel, Theodore. 1994. *Piano Music for One Hand*. Bloomington: Indiana University Press.

Edson, Margaret. 1999. *W;t*. New York: Faber & Faber.

———. 2001. *W;t*. DVD, VHS. Dir. Mike Nichols. With Emma Thompson. New York: Home Box Office.

Eisenberg, Evan. 1987. *The Recording Angel*. New York: McGraw-Hill.

Elkins, James. 1996. *The Object Stares Back: On the Nature of Seeing*. New York: Harcourt.

Elliker, Calvin. 1996. "Sheet Music Special Issues: Formats and Functions." *Notes* 53(1): 9–17.

———. 1999. "Toward a Definition of Sheet Music." *Notes* 55(4): 835–59.

Esquirol, Étienne. 1819. "Monomania." In *Dictionnaire des sciences medicales*. Vol. 34 (1819), 117–22.

———. 1838. *Des maladies mentales: considérées sous les rapports médical, hygiénique et médico-légal*. 2 vols. Paris: Ballière.

Euper, J. A. 1968. "Early Infantile Autism." In *Music in Therapy*, Ed. E. T. Gaston, 181–90. New York: Macmillan.

Ewing, Tom. 2005. "can we talk about autism and music?" (bulletin board, 2005) http://ilx.wh3rd.net/thread.php?msgid=6084353.

Eysenck, H. J. 1995. *Genius: The Natural History of Creativity*. Cambridge: Cambridge University Press.

Fauconnier, Gilles. 1994. *Mental Spaces: Aspects of Meaning Construction in Natural Language*. Cambridge: Cambridge University Press.

Felman, Shoshana, and Dori Laub, M.D. 1992. *Testimony: Crises of Witnessing in Literature, Psychoanalysis, and History*. New York: Routledge.

Ferroni, Giulio, and Amedeo Quondam. 1973. *La "locuzione artificiosa": Teoria ed esperienza della lirica a Napoli nell'eta del Manierismo*. Rome: Bulzoni.

Feuer, Jane. 1982. *The Hollywood Musical*. Bloomington: Indiana University Press.

Fink, Robert. 1998. "Elvis Everywhere: Musicology and Popular Music Studies at the Twilight of the Canon." *American Music* 16(2): 135–79.

Finn, William. 1990. *March of the Falsettos* and *Falsettoland*. CD. DRG Records 22600.

Fisher, Rudolf. 1999. "The Caucasian Storms Harlem." In *Keeping Time: Readings in Jazz History*, Ed. Robert Walser, 60–5. Oxford: Oxford University Press.

Flindell, E. Fred. 1971. "Paul Wittgenstein (1887–1961): Patron and Pianist." *Music Review* 32: 107–27.

Flinn, Caryl. 1992. *Strains of Utopia: Gender, Nostalgia, and Hollywood Film Music*. Princeton: Princeton University Press.

Foucault, Michel. 1961. *La Folie et la Déraison*. Paris: Librarie Plon.

François-Sappey, Brigitte, Ed. 1991a. *Charles Valentin Alkan*. Paris: Fayad.

————. 1991b. "Grande Sonate op. 33 'Les quatre ages': Un destin musical." In François-Sappey, 1991a, 95–128.

Frank, Arthur W. 1995. *The Wounded Storyteller: Body, Illness, and Ethics*. Chicago: University of Chicago Press.

Freleng, Friz. 1994. *Animation: The Art of Friz Freleng*. Vol. 1. With David Weber. Newport Beach, CA: Donovan.

Freud, Sigmund. 1991. *Beyond the Pleasure Principle* [1921]. Reprinted in *On Metapsychology: The Theory of Psychoanalysis: "Beyond the Pleasure Principle," "The Ego and the Id" and Other Works*. Vol. 11 of *The Pelican Freud Library Series*, Ed. Angela Richards, 269–338. London: Penguin.

Friedrich, Otto. 1989. *Glenn Gould: A Life and Variations*. Toronto: Lester & Orpen Denys.

Frith, Uta. 1991. "Asperger and His Syndrome." In *Autism and Asperger's Syndrome*, Ed. Uta Frith, 1–36. Cambridge: Cambridge University Press.

Frosch, William. 1987. "Moods, Madness, and Music—I—Major Affective Disease and Musical Creativity." *Comparative Psychiatry* 28: 315–22.

————. 1990a."Moods, Madness, and Music—II—Was Handel Insane?" *Musical Quarterly* 74(1): 31–56.

————. 1990b. "Review of *Mozart in Person: His Character and Health*, by Peter J. Davies." *Musical Quarterly* 74(1): 170–3.

Fulford, Robert. 1983. "Growing Up Gould." In *Glenn Gould Variations*, Ed. John McGreevy, 57–63. Toronto: Macmillan of Canada.

————. 1988. *Best Seat in the House: Memoirs of a Lucky Man*. Toronto: Collins.

Fullerton, Graeme. 2005. "The Grotesque in 20th-Century Opera." Ph.D. diss., City University of New York.

Garber, Marjorie. 1992. *Vested Interests: Cross-Dressing and Cultural Anxiety*. New York: Routledge.

Garland-Thomson, Rosemarie. 1997. *Extraordinary Bodies: Figuring Physical Disability in American Culture and Literature*. New York: Columbia University Press.

————. 2001. "Seeing the Disabled: Visual Rhetorics of Disability in Popular Photography." In *The New Disability History: American Perspectives*, Ed. Paul Longmore and Laurie Umansky, 335–74. New York: New York University Press.

————. 2004. "Integrating Disability, Transforming Feminist Theory." In *Gendering Disability*, Ed. Bonnie G. Smith and Beth Hutchison, 73–103. New Brunswick, NJ: Rutgers University Press.

Garrett, Charles Hiroshi. 2004. "Chinatown, Whose Chinatown? Defining America's Borders with Musical Orientalism." *Journal of the American Musicological Society* 57(1): 119–73.

Gartner, Alan and Tom Joe, eds. 1987. *Images of the Disabled, Disabling Images*. New York: Praeger.

Gerber, David, Ed. 2000. *Disabled Veterans in History*. Ann Arbor: University of Michigan Press.

Giddins, Gary. 2001. *Bing Crosby: A Pocketful of Dreams: The Early Years, 1903–1940*. Boston: Little, Brown.

Gilbert, Douglas. 1940. *American Vaudeville: Its Life and Times*. New York: Whittlesey House.

Gillberg, Christopher. 1991. "Clinical and Neurobiological Aspects in Six Family Studies of Asperger's Syndrome." In *Autism and Asperger's Syndrome*, Ed. Uta Frith, 122–46. Cambridge: Cambridge University Press.

————. 1992. "Autism and Autistic-Like Conditions: Subclasses among Disorders of Empathy." *Journal of Child Psychology and Psychiatry and Allied Disciplines* 33(5): 813–42.

Gillingham, Gail. 1988. *Autism: Handle with Care*. 3rd ed. Tacit Publications.

Gilmore, Leigh. 2001. *The Limits of Autobiography: Trauma and Testimony*. Ithaca: Cornell University Press.

Glixon, Beth L. 2001. "Giacinto Andrea Cicognini." In *The New Grove Dictionary of Music and Musicians*, Vol. 5., 2d ed., Ed. Stanley Sadie and John Tyrrell, 835–6. London: Macmillan.

Gorbman, Claudia. 1987. *Unheard Melodies: Narrative Film Music*. Bloomington: Indiana University Press.

Gordon, B., and K. Rosenblum. 2001. "Bringing Disability into the Sociological Frame: A Comparison of Disability with Race, Sex, and Sexual Orientation Statuses." *Disability and Society* 16: 5–19.

Górecki, H. 1992. Symphony No. 3 ("Symphony of Sorrowful Songs"). Score. London: Boosey & Hawkes.

Gould, Glenn. 1983. "Toronto." In *Glenn Gould Variations*, Ed. John McGreevy, 85–92. Toronto: Macmillan of Canada.

Gould, Glenn, and Curtis Davis. 1983. "The Well-Tempered Listener." In *Glenn Gould Variations*, Ed. John McGreevy, 275–94. Toronto: Macmillan of Canada.

Gracyk, Tim. 2000. *Popular American Recording Pioneers, 1895–1925*. With Frank Hoffman. New York: Haworth Press.

Grandin, Temple. 1986. *Emergence; Labeled Autistic*. New York: Warner Books.

———. 1992. "An Inside View of Autism." In *High-Functioning Individuals with Autism*, Ed. Eric Schopler and Gary Mesibov, 105–26. New York: Plenum Press.

———. 1995. *Thinking in Pictures and Other Reports from My Life with Autism*. New York: Doubleday.

———. 2005. *Animals in Translation: Using the Mysteries of Autism to Decode Animal Behavior*. With Catherine Johnson. New York: Scribner.

Graziano, John. 1991. "Music in William Randolph Hearst's *New York Journal*." *Notes* 48(2): 383–424.

Grimley, Daniel. 2005. "Hidden Places: Hyper-realism in Björk's *Vespertine* and *Dancer in the Dark*." *Twentieth-Century Music* 2(1): 37–52.

Grosz, Elizabeth. 1999. "Thinking of the New: Of Futures yet Unthought." In *Becomings: Explorations in Time, Memory, and Futures*, Ed. Elizabeth Grosz, 15–28. Ithaca, NY: Cornell University Press.

Guthmann, Edward. 2001. "Björk Dazzling in 'Dancer.'" *San Francisco Chronicle*, March 23, C8.

Habermann, Gustav. 1995. "Die Commedia dell'arte und das Stottern auf der Bühne." *Sprache—Stimme—Gehör* 19: 152–6.

Hadow, W. H. 1904. "Berlioz." In *A Dictionary of Music and Musicians*. 2d ed. Ed. J. A. Fuller Maitland, 305–10. New York: Macmillan.

Hamilton, Roy H., Alvaro Pascual-Leone, and Gottfried Schlaug. 2004. "Absolute Pitch in Blind Musicians." *NeuroReport* 15(5): 803–6.

Haraway, Donna J. 1991a. "A Cyborg Manifesto: Science, Technology, and Socialist-Feminism in the Late Twentieth Century." In *Simians, Cyborgs, and Women*, Ed. Donna J. Haraway, 149–81. New York: Routledge.

———. 1991b. "'Gender' for a Marxist Dictionary: The Sexual Politics of a Word." In *Simians, Cyborgs, and Women*, Ed. Donna J. Haraway, 127–48. New York: Routledge.

Hargreaves, David. 1985. *The Developmental Psychology of Music*. Cambridge: Cambridge University Press.

Harris, Charles K. 1906. *How to Write a Popular Song*. New York: Charles K. Harris.

———. 1926. *After the Ball: Forty Years of Melody*. New York: Frank-Maurice, Inc.

Harvey, William Fryer. 1919. "The Beast with Five Fingers." *New Decameron*. Vol. 1. Oxford: Blackwell.

Hawkins, Anne Hunsaker. 1999. *Reconstructing Illness: Studies in Pathography*. 2d ed. West Lafayette, IN: Purdue University Press.

Healy, Maureen. 2004. *Vienna and the Fall of the Hapsburg Empire: Total War and Everyday Life in World War I*. Cambridge: Cambridge University Press.

Heartbeats: New Songs from Minnesota for the AIDS Quilt Songbook. 1994. CD. Innova 500.

Heaton, P. 2003. "Pitch Memory, Labeling and Disembedding in Autism." *Journal of Child Psychiatry and Psychology* 44(4): 543–51.

Heaton, P., B. Hermelin, and L. Pring. 1999. "Can Children with Autistic Spectrum Disorders Perceive Affect in Music? An Experimental Investigation." *Psychological Medicine* 29(6): 1405–10.

Heaton, P., L. Pring, and B. Hermelin. 2001. "Musical Processing in High Functioning Children with Autism." *Biological Foundations of Music: Annals of the New York Academy of Sciences* 930: 433–44.

Heidenreich, Helmut. 1962. "Figuren und Komik in den spanischen 'Entremeses' des goldenen Zeitalters." Ph.D. diss., Ludwig–Maximilians–Universität zu München.

Helman, Alicja. 1999. "Women in Kieślowski's Late Films." In *Lucid Dreams: The Films of Krzysztof Kieślowski*. Ed. and trans. Paul Coates, 116–35. Wiltshire: Flicks Books.

Henderson, George, and Willie V. Bryan. 1984. *Psychosocial Aspects of Disability*. Springfield, IL: Charles C. Thomas.

Henahan, Don. 1962. "The Eyes Have it in Gould Recital—Show Obscures Music." Chicago Daily News, April 23: n.p. Document 1979-20, 41, 41, 13, Glenn Gould Papers, Music Section, Library and Archives Canada, Ottawa.

Hepokoski, James. 1993. *Sibelius: Symphony No. 5*. Cambridge: Cambridge University Press.

————. 1996. "The Essence of Sibelius: Creation Myths and Rotational Cycles in *Luonnotar*." In *The Sibelius Companion*, Ed. Glenda Dawn Goss, 121–46. Westport, CT: Greenwood.

————. 2001. "Rotations, Sketches, and the Sixth Symphony." In *Sibelius Studies*, Ed. Timothy L. Jackson and Veijo Murtomäki, 322–51. Cambridge: Cambridge University Press.

————. 2002a. "Back and Forth from Egmont: Beethoven, Mozart, and the Nonresolving Recapitulation." *19th-Century Music* 15(2–3): 127–54.

————. 2002b. "Beethoven Reception: The Symphonic Tradition." In *The Cambridge History of Nineteenth-Century Music*, Ed. Jim Samson, 424–59. Cambridge: Cambridge University Press.

————. 2002c. "Beyond the Sonata Principle." *Journal of the American Musicological Society* 55(1): 91–154.

————. 2004. "Structure, Implication, and the End of *Suor Angelica*." *Studi pucciniani* 3: 241–64.

Hepokoski, James, and Warren Darcy. 1997. "The Medial Caesura and its Role in the Eighteenth-Century Sonata Exposition." *Music Theory Spectrum* 19(2): 115–54.

————. 2006. *Elements of Sonata Theory: Norms, Types, and Deformations in the Late-Eighteenth-Century Sonata*. New York: Oxford University Press.

Herman, Judith Lewis, M.D. 1992. *Trauma and Recovery*. New York: HarperCollins Publishers.

Hershman, D. Jablow, and Julien Leib. 1998. *Manic Depression and Creativity*. Amherst, NY: Prometheus Books.

Hevey, David. 1992. *The Creatures Time Forgot: Photography and Disability Imagery*. New York: Routledge.

Hitchcock, H. Wiley. 1988. *Music in the United States: A Historical Introduction*. Englewood Cliffs, NJ: Prentice Hall.

Horwitz, Allan. 2002. *Creating Mental Illness*. Chicago: University of Chicago Press.

Howard, Luke. 1998. "Motherhood, Billboard, and the Holocaust: Perceptions and Receptions of Górecki's Symphony No. 3." *Musical Quarterly* 82(1): 82–130.

Hutcheon, Linda, and Michael Hutcheon. 2000. *Bodily Charm: Living Opera*. Lincoln: University of Nebraska Press.

Insdorf, Annette. 1999. *Double Lives, Second Chances: The Cinema of Krzysztof Kiéslowski*. New York: Hyperion.

————. 2003. "Commentary." *Krzysztof Kiéslowski's Three Colors: Blue, White and Red*. three-disc DVD collection. Dir. Krzysztof Kiéslowski. Hollywood, CA: Miramax Home Entertainment.

Irigaray, Luce. 2001. *To Be Two (Essere due)*. Trans. Monique M. Rhodes and Marco F. Cocito-Monoc. New York: Routledge.

Jahoda, Susan. 1995. "Theatres of Madness." In *Deviant Bodies: Critical Perspectives on Difference in Science and Popular Culture*, Ed. Jennifer Terry and Jacqueline Urla, 251–76. Bloomington: Indiana University Press.

Jamison, Kay. 1993. *Touched with Fire: Manic Depressive Illness and the Artistic Temperament*. New York: Free Press.

Jasen, David A. 1988. *Tin Pan Alley: The Composers, the Songs, the Performers and Their Times*. New York: Donald I. Fine.

Kaiser, Joachim. 1971. *Great Pianists of Our Time*. London: George Allen & Unwin.

Kalinak, Kathryn. 1992. *Settling the Score: Music and the Classical Hollywood Film*. Madison: University of Wisconsin Press.

Katrina. n.d. "Disability Studies: Temple U." http://disstud.blogspot.com/2005/09/disability-blogs-roundup-katrina.html.

Kazdin, Andrew. 1989. *Glenn Gould at Work: Creative Lying*. New York: E. P. Dutton.

Keith, Robert L., and Arnold E. Aronson. 1975. "Singing as Therapy for Apraxia of Speech and Aphasia: Report of a Case." *Brain and Language* 2: 483–8.

Kent, Deborah. 1987. "Disabled Women: Portraits in Fiction and Drama." In Gartner and Joe, 1987, 47–64.

Kessel, Niel. 1989. "Genius and Mental Disorder: A History of Ideas Concerning Their Conjunction." In *Genius: The History of an Idea*, Ed. Penelope Murray, 196–212. Oxford: Basil Blackwell.

Kickasola, Joseph G. 2004. *The Films of Krzysztof Kiéslowski: The Liminal Image*. New York: Continuum.

Kielian-Gilbert, Marianne. 2005. "*Meta-Variations* and the Art of Engaging Music." *Perspectives of New Music* 43(2): 6–34.

Kiéslowski, Krzysztof. 2003. "Krzysztof Kiéslowski's Cinema Lesson." *Krzysztof Kiéslowski's Three Colors: Blue, White and Red*. Three-disc DVD collection. Dir. Krzysztof Kiéslowski. Hollywood, CA: Miramax Home Entertainment.

Kinter, Barbara. 1978. *Die Figur des Gracioso im spanischem Theater des 17. Jahrhunderts*. München: Wilhelm Fink Verlag.

Kirkeby, Per. 2001. "Audio Commentary by Artist Per Kirkeby." *Dancer in the Dark*. Dir. by Lars von Trier. New Line Home Entertainment DVD.

Kirshenblatt-Gimblett, Barbara. 1998. *Destination Culture: Tourism, Museums, Heritage*. Berkeley: University of California Press.

Klaver, Elizabeth. 2004. "A Mind–Body–Flesh Problem: The Case of Margaret Edson's *W;t*." *Contemporary Literature* 45(5): 659–83.

Kleege, Georgina. 1999. *Sight Unseen*. New Haven: Yale University Press.

Klein, Michael. 1989. *Poets for Life: Seventy-Six Poets Respond to AIDS*. New York: Crown.

Klinkenborg, Verlyn. 2005. "What Do Animals Think?" Review of *Animals in Translation: Using the Mysteries of Autism to Decode Animal Behavior*, by Temple Grandin. *Discover* 26(5): 46–53.

Kriegel, Leonard. 1987. "The Cripple in Literature." In Gartner and Joe, 1987, 31–46.

Kristeva, Julia. 1982. *Powers of Horror: An Essay on Abjection*. New York: Columbia University Press.

Krumhansl, Carol. 1990. *Cognitive Foundations of Musical Pitch*. New York: Oxford University Press.

Kuster, Judith Maginnis. 2005. *The Stuttering Homepage*. Mankato, MN: Minnesota State University. Available at http://www.mnsu.edu/comdis/kuster.

Lakoff, George. 1987. *Women, Fire, and Dangerous Things: What Categories Reveal about the Mind*. Chicago: University of Chicago Press.

Larson, Jonathan. 1996. *Rent*. CD. Dreamworks DRMD2-50003.

Larson, Randall D. 1997. "Review of *The Lost Patrol / Virginia City / The Beast with Five Fingers*." *Soundtrack!* 16(61): 18–9.

Lawrence, Amy. 1991. *Echo and Narcissus: Women's Voices in Classical Hollywood Cinema*. Berkeley: University of California Press.

Lee, Colin. 1996. *Music at the Edge: The Music Therapy Experiences of a Musician with AIDS*. New York: Routledge.

Léman, Michel. 1975. *Les valets et les servants dans le théâtre comique en France de 1610 à 1700*. Cannes: C.E.L.

Lerner, Neil. 2001. "Copland's Music of Wide Open Spaces: Surveying the Pastoral Trope in Hollywood." *Musical Quarterly* 85(1): 477–515.

Levy, Lester. 1967. *Grace Notes in American History: Popular Sheet Music from 1820 to 1900*. Norman: University of Oklahoma Press.

———. 1971. *Flashes of Merriment: A Century of Humorous Songs in America, 1805–1905*. Norman: University of Oklahoma Press.

———. 1975. *"Give Me Yesterday": American History in Song, 1890–1920*. Norman: University of Oklahoma Press.

———. 1976. *Picture the Songs: Lithographs from the Sheet Music of Nineteenth-Century America*. Baltimore: Johns Hopkins University Press.

Lewenthal, Raymond. 1964. "Preface." In *The Piano Music of Alkan*, v-xx. New York: Schirmer.

Lewin, David. 1968. "Inversional Balance as an Organizing Force in Schoenberg's Music and Thought." *Perspectives of New Music* 6(2): 1–21.

———. 1982–83. "Transformational Techniques in Atonal and Other Music Theories." *Perspectives of New Music* 21: 312–71.

———. 1987. *Generalized Musical Intervals and Transformations*. New Haven: Yale University Press.

———. 1993. *Musical Form and Transformation: 4 Analytic Essays*. New Haven: Yale University Press.

———. 1997. "Some Notes on *Pierrot Lunaire*." In *Music Theory in Concept and Practice*, Ed. James Baker, David Beach, and Jonathan Bernard, 433–58. Rochester, NY: University of Rochester Press.

Lewis, Al. 1935. *From Rhymes to Riches*. New York: Donaldson, Douglas & Gumble.

Linton, Simi. 1998. *Claiming Disability: Knowledge and Identity*. New York: New York University Press.

Littler, William. 1967. "Glenn Gould: The Pianist has Turned Radio Producer and Is Fashioning His Own Far-Out Documentary on—Who Would Have Guessed It?—the Canadian North." *Toronto Star*, December 23, 29.

Lloyd, William. 1996. "Somewhere in Chingford." *Musical Times* 137: 29.

Longmore, Paul K. 1987. "Screening Stereotypes: Images of Disabled People in Television and Motion Pictures." In Gartner and Joe, 1987, 65–78.

———. 2001. "Screening Stereotypes: Images of Disabled People." In *Screening Disability*, Ed. Anthony Enns and Christopher R. Smit, 1–18. Lanham, MD: University Press of America.

Lorde, Audre. 1980. *The Cancer Journals*. San Francisco: aunt lute books.

Lott, Eric. 1993. *Love and Theft: Blackface Minstrelsy and the American Working Class*. New York: Oxford University Press.

Lubet, Alex. 2004. "Tunes of Impairment: An Ethnomusicology of Disability." *Review of Disability Studies* 1(1): 133–56.

Luguenot, François, and Laurent Martin. 1991. "Interpréter Alkan." In *Charles Valentin Alkan*, Ed. Brigitte François-Sappey, 171-89. Paris: Fayad.

Lyall, Sarah. 2001. "For 'Wit,' Emma Thompson Supplies a Wit of Her Own." *New York Times*, March 18, late edition, sec. 2.

MacDonald, Hugh. 1973. "The Death of Alkan." *Musical Times* 114: 25.

———. 1988. "More on Alkan's Death." *Musical Times* 117: 118–20.

———. 2001. "Alkan, Charles Valentin." In *The New Grove Dictionary of Music and Musicians*, Vol. 1, Ed. Stanley Sadie and John Tyrell, 377–80. London: Macmillan.

MacDonald, Raymond A. R., David J. Hargreaves, and Dorothy Miell, eds. 2002. *Musical Identities*. New York: Oxford University Press.

Magee, Wendy L. 2002. "Disability and Identity in Music Therapy." In MacDonald et al., 2002, 179–97.

Maley, S. Roy. 1956a. "Gould's Debut with Symphony Scores Hit." *Winnipeg Tribune*, January 14: n.p. Unnumbered Glenn Gould "vertical" file, Music Section, Library and Archives Canada, Ottawa.

———. 1956b. "Triumph of Season Scored by Gould." *Winnipeg Tribune*, December 14, 33.

Maloney, S. Timothy. 2007. "Glenn Gould and Richard Wagner." In *New Millennium Wagner Studies: Essays in Music and Culture*, Ed. Mathew Bribitzer-Stull and Alex Lubet, forthcoming. New York: Palgrave MacMillan.

Marino, Giovannbattista. 1960. *La Musica, in Dicerie Sacre e La Strage de gl'Innocenti*. Ed. Giovanni Pozzi. Torrino: Einaudi.

Marks, Edward B. 1934. *They All Sang: From Pastor to Rudy Valleé*. New York: Viking Press.

Marks, Martin. 1996. "Music, Drama, Warner Brothers: The Cases of *Casablanca* and *The Maltese Falcon*." *Michigan Quarterly Review* 35(1): 112–42.

Marmorstein, Gary. 1997. *Hollywood Rhapsody: Movie Music and Its Makers, 1900 to 1975*. New York: Schirmer Books.

Marsh, Charity, and Melissa West. 2003. "The Nature/Technology Binary Opposition Dismantled in the Music of Madonna and Björk." In *Music and Technoculture*, Ed. Rene T. A. Lysloff and Leslie C. Gay, 182–203. Middletown, CT: Wesleyan University Press.

Martini, Adrienne. 1999. "Playwright in Spite of Herself." *American Theater* 16(8): 22–5.

Masura, S., and Z. Matejova. 1975. "Musiktherapie bei Stotterern." In *Orff–Schulwerk und Therapie: Therapeutische Komponenten in der elementaren Musik– und Bewegungserziehung*, Ed. Hans Wolfgart, 220–9. Berlin: Carl Marhold Verlagsbuchhandlung.

McClary, Susan. 2002. *Feminine Endings: Music, Gender, and Sexuality*. Minneapolis MN: University of Minnesota Press.

McCarthy, Pearl. 1947. "School Concert Program Pleases, Heinze Conducts." *Toronto Globe and Mail*, January 15: n.p. Document 1979-20, 41, 3, 2, Glenn Gould Papers, Music Section, Library and Archives Canada, Ottawa.

McCracken, Allison. 1999. "'God's Gift to Us Girls': Crooning, Gender and the Re-creation of American Popular Song, 1928–1933." *American Music* 17(4): 365–95.

Mehta, Ameeta, and Mehul Dattani. 2004. "Clinical Aspects of Septo-Optic Dysplasia." *Eye Contact* 38: 5–7.

Mesaros, Helen. 2000a. "Aspects of Glenn Gould: Glenn Gould and the Doctors." *Glenn Gould* 6(2): 86–8.

———. 2000b. "Did Glenn Gould Have a Form of Autism?" *Medical Post*, May 9, 24–5.

Metzer, David. 2003. *Quotation and Cultural Meaning in Twentieth-Century Music*. New York: Cambridge University Press.

Meyer, Leonard. 1967. *Music, the Arts, and Ideas*. Chicago: University of Chicago Press.

Michener, Wendy. 1956. "Mannerisms Mar Fine Gould Effort." *Stratford Beacon*, July 10: n.p. Document 1979-20, 41, 11, 23, Glenn Gould Papers, Music Section, Library and Archives Canada, Ottawa.

Miller, Angela. 1996. "The Panorama, the Cinema, and the Emergence of the Spectacular." *Wide Angle* 18(2): 34–69.

Miller, Leon. 1989. *Musical Savants: Exceptional Skill in the Mentally Retarded*. Hillsdale, NJ: Lawrence Erlbaum Associates.

Miller, Olga, and Adam Ockelford. 2005. *Visual Needs*. London: Continuum.

Mirzoeff, Nicholas. 1995. "Framed: The Deaf in the Harem." In *Deviant Bodies: Critical Perspectives On Difference in Science and Popular Culture*, Ed. Jennifer Terry and Jacqueline Urla, 49–77. Bloomington: Indiana University Press.

Mitchell, David. 1997. "Modernist Freaks and Postmodernist Geeks." In *The Disability Studies Reader*, Ed. Lennard J. Davis, 348–65. New York: Routledge.

Mitchell, David T., and Sharon L. Snyder. 2000. *Narrative Prosthesis: Disability and the Dependencies of Discourse*. Ann Arbor: University of Michigan Press.

Moldenhauer, Hans. 1979. *Anton von Webern, A Chronicle of His Life and Work*. New York: Knopf.

Monson, Dale. 2001. "Recitative." In *The New Grove Dictionary of Music and Musicians*, Vol. 21, 2d ed., Ed. Stanley Sadie and John Tyrrell, 1–6. London: Macmillan.

Moog, Helmut. 1976. *The Musical Experience of the Pre-School Child*. Trans. C. Clarke. London: Schott.

Moore, Allan F. 2005. "The Persona-Environment Relation in Recorded Song." *Music Theory Online* 11(4): 1–21. Available at http://www.societymusictheory.org/mto/issues/.

Morgan, Robert. 1992. *Anthology of Twentieth-Century Music*. New York: Norton.

———. 2000. "Circular Form in the *Tristan* Prelude." *Journal of the American Musicological Society* 53(1): 69–104.

Morris, Mitchell. 1993. "Reading as an Opera Queen." In *Musicology and Difference: Gender and Sexuality in Music Scholarship*, Ed. Ruth Solie, 184–200. Berkeley: University of California Press.

Murdoch, William. 1935. *Chopin: His Life*. New York: Macmillan.

Nettl, Bruno. 1983. *The Study of Ethnomusicology: Twenty-Nine Issues and Concepts*. Urbana: University of Illinois.

Nettle, Daniel. 2001. *Strong Imagination: Madness, Creativity and Human Nature*. Oxford: Oxford University Press.

Newham, Paul. 1998. *Therapeutic Voicework: Principles and Practice for the Use of Singing as a Therapy*. Gateshead: Athenaeum Press.

Nordau, Max. 1993. *Degeneration*. Trans. George L. Mosse. Lincoln: University of Nebraska Press.

Norden, Martin F. 1994. *The Cinema of Isolation*. New Brunswick, NJ: Rutgers University Press.

———. 2001. "The Hollywood Discourse on Disability: Some Personal Reflections." In *Screening Disability*, Ed. Anthony Enns and Christopher R. Smit, 19–30. Lanham, MD: University Press of America.

Ober, William. 1973. "Carlo Gesualdo, Prince of Verona: Murder, Madrigals, and Masochism." *Bulletin of the New York Academy of Medicine* 49: 634–45.

Obler, Loraine, and Deborah Fein. 1988. *The Exceptional Brain: Neuropsychology of Talent and Special Abilities*. New York: Guilford Press.

Ockelford, Adam. 1988. "Some Observations Concerning the Musical Education of Blind Children and Those with Additional Handicaps." Paper presented at the 32nd Conference of the Society for Research in Psychology of Music and Music Education (now "SEMPRE"), at the University of Reading.

———. 1991. "The Role of Repetition in Perceived Musical Structures." In *Representing Musical Structure*, Ed. Peter Howell, Robert West, and Ian Cross, 129–60. London: Academic Press.

———. 1993. "A Theory Concerning the Cognition of Order in Music." Ph.D. diss. The University of London.

———. 1998. *Music Moves: Music in the Education of Children and Young People Who Are Visually Impaired and Have Learning Difficulties*. London: Royal National Institute for the Blind.

———. 1999. *The Cognition of Order in Music: A Metacognitive Study*. London: Roehampton Institute.

———. 2000. "Music in the Education of Children with Severe or Profound Learning Difficulties: Issues in Current UK Provision, a New Conceptual Framework, and Proposals for Research." *Psychology of Music* 28(2): 197–217.

———. 2002. "The Magical Number Two, Plus or Minus One: Some Limits on Our Capacity for Processing Musical Information." *Musicæ Scientiæ* 6(2): 177–215.

———. 2003. "Focus on Music." *Focal Points* 2(3): 1-2. Available at http://www.wisconsinmedicalsociety.org/savant/sodarticle.pdf.

———. 2004. "On Similarity, Derivation and the Cognition of Musical Structure." *Psychology of Music* 32(1): 23–74.

———. 2005a. *Repetition in Music: Theoretical and Metatheoretical Perspectives*. Aldershot: Ashgate.

———. 2005b. "Relating Musical Structure and Content to Aesthetic Response: A Model and Analysis of Beethoven's Piano Sonata Op. 110." *Journal of the Royal Musical Association* 130(1): 74–118.

———. 2006. "Implication and Expectation in Music: A Zygonic Model." *Psychology of Music* 34(4): 81–142.

———. n.d. "Quantifying interaction and influence in musical improvisation with two participants or more." Unpublished paper.

Ockelford, Adam, and Linda Pring. 2005. "Learning and Creativity in a Prodigious Musical Savant." *International Congress Series* 1282: 903–7.

———. 2007. *Exploring the Exceptional Musical Abilities of Derek Paravicini*. London: Royal National Institute of the Blind.

Ockelford, Adam, Graham Welch, and Linda Pring. 2005. "Musical interests and abilities of children with septo-optic dysplasia." *International Congress Series* 1282: 894–97.

Ockelford, Adam, Linda Pring, Graham Welch, and Darold Treffert. 2006. *Focus on Music: Exploring the Musical Interests and Abilities of Blind and Partially-Sighted Children with Septo-Optic Dysplasia*. London: Institute of Education.

Oreglia, Giacomo. 1968. *The Commedia Dell'arte*. Trans. Lovett F. Edwards. London: Methuen.

Ostertag, Bob. 1994. *Fear No Love*. CD. Disk Union AVAN 041.

Ostertag, Bob. n. d. http://bobostertag.com/.

Ostwald, Peter. 1991. "Some Personal Reminiscences." *Bulletin of the International Glenn Gould Society* 15/16 8(1–2): 23–8.

———. 1997. *Glenn Gould: The Ecstasy and Tragedy of Genius*. New York: W.W. Norton.

Ottenheimer, Harriet. 1979. "Catharsis, Communication, and Evocation: Alternative Views of the Sociopsychological Functions of Blues Singing." *Ethnomusicology* 23(1): 75–86.

Payzant, Geoffrey. 1978. *Glenn Gould: Music and Mind*. Toronto: Van Nostrand Reinhold.

Peles, Steven. 2004. "'Ist Alles Eins': Schoenberg and Symmetry." *Music Theory Spectrum* 26(1): 57–86.

Pennington, Bob. 1979. "Gould Discovers his Home Town." *Toronto Sun*, September 27: n.p. Document 1979-20, 43, 11, 16, Glenn Gould Papers, Music Section, Library and Archives Canada, Ottawa.

Peretz, Isabelle. 2001. "Listen to the Brain: A Biological Perspective on Musical Emotions." In *Music and Emotion: Theory and Research*, Ed. P. N. Juslin and J. A. Sloboda, 105–34. Oxford: Oxford University Press.

Persson, Camilla Benbour. 1987. "Possible Biological Correlations of Precocious Mathematical Reasoning Ability." *Trends in Neuroscience* 10: 17–20.

Philadelphia. 1993. CD. Columbia/Tristar Studios.

Pick, Daniel. 1989. *Faces of Degeneration: A European Disorder, c. 1848–c. 1918*. Cambridge: Cambridge University Press.

Plath, Sylvia. 1972. "Apprehensions (1962)." In *Winter Trees*, 3. New York: Harper & Row.

Poizat, Michel. 1992. *The Angel's Cry: Beyond the Pleasure Principle in Opera*. Ithaca: Cornell University Press.

Potter, John. 1998. *Vocal Authority: Singing Style and Ideology*. Cambridge: Cambridge University Press.

Powell, Nicholas. 1974. *The Sacred Spring: The Arts in Vienna, 1898–1918*. New York: Graphic Society.

Preisner, Zbigniew. 1993. *Bleu: Bande Originale Du Film*. CD. Virgin Movie Music 39027.

Pring, Linda, and Adam Ockelford. 2005. "Children with Septo-Optic Dysplasia—Musical Interests, Abilities and Provision: The Results of a Parental Survey." *British Journal of Visual Impairment* 23(2): 58–66.

Proctor, Robert N. 1995. "The Destruction of 'Lives Not Worth Living.'" In *Deviant Bodies: Critical Perspectives On Difference in Science and Popular Culture*, Ed. Jennifer Terry and Jacqueline Urla, 170–96. Bloomington: Indiana University Press.

Raby, Peter. 1982. *Fair Ophelia: A Life of Harriet Smithson Berlioz*. Cambridge: Cambridge University Press.

Radstone, Suzannah. 2001. "Special Debate: Trauma and Screen Studies." *Screen* 42(2): 188–216.

Ran, Shulamit. 1984. *Apprehensions* (1979). Score. Tel-Aviv: Israel Music Institute; King of Prussia, PA: Theodore Presser.

———. 1991. *Music of Shulamit Ran*. CD 609 CRI.

Reed, Lou. 1989. "Halloween." *New York*. CD. Sire 9 25829-2.

Roberts, John P. L., Ed. 1999. *The Art of Glenn Gould: Reflections of a Musical Genius*. Toronto: Malcolm Lester Books.

Robertson, James. 2000. "An Educational Model for Music Therapy: The Case for a Continuum." *British Journal of Music Therapy* 14(1): 41–6.

Rodgers, Stephen. 2005. "Circular Form as Metaphor in the Music of Hector Berlioz." Ph.D. diss., Yale University.

Rogin, Michael. 1996. *Blackface, White Noise: Jewish Immigrants in the Hollywood Melting Pot*. Berkeley: University of California Press.

Rorem, Ned. 1999. *Evidence of Things Not Seen: Thirty-Six Songs for Four Solo Voices and Piano*. CD. New World Records 80575-2.

———. 2000. *Lies: A Diary, 1986–1999*. Cambridge, MA: Da Capo Press.

Rosand, Ellen. 1971. "Aria in the Early Operas of Cavalli." Ph.D. diss., New York University.

———. 1991. *Opera in Seventeenth-Century Venice: The Creation of a Genre*. Berkeley: University of California Press.

Rosen, Alan. 2002. "'Teach Me Gold': Pedagogy and Memory in *The Pawnbroker*." *Prooftexts* 22(1–2): 77–117.

Ross, Alex. 2004. "Björk's Saga." *New Yorker*, August 23, 49–59.

Ross, Bill. 1956. "Glenn Gould Writhes, Soars." *Ottawa Citizen*, April 17: n.p. Document 1979-20, 41, 11, 3, Glenn Gould Papers, Music Section, Library and Archives Canada, Ottawa.

Roth, Martin, and Jerome Kroll. 1986. *The Reality of Mental Illness*. Cambridge: Cambridge University Press.

Rothenberg, Albert. 1990. *Creativity and Madness: New Findings and Old Stereotypes*. Baltimore: Johns Hopkins University.

Rubinstein, Renate. 1985. *Take It and Leave It: Aspects of Being Ill*. London: Marion Boyars.

Rushton, Julian. 2000. "Genius in Berlioz." In *The Cambridge Companion to Berlioz*, Ed. Peter Bloom, 41–52. Cambridge: Cambridge University Press.

———. 2001. *The Music of Berlioz*. Oxford: Oxford University Press.

Russ, Michael. 2000. "Ravel and the Orchestra." In *The Cambridge Companion to Ravel*, Ed. Deborah Mawer, 118–39. Cambridge: Cambridge University Press.

Sacks, Oliver. 1995. *An Anthropologist on Mars: Seven Paradoxical Tales*. New York: Knopf.

———. 1998. "Foreword," *Glenn Gould: The Ecstasy and Tragedy of Genius*, by Peter Ostwald New York: W.W. Norton.

Samson, Jim. 2003. *Virtuosity and the Musical Work: the Transcendental Studies of Liszt*. Cambridge: Cambridge University Press.

Sanjek, Russell. 1983. *From Print to Plastic: Publishing and Promoting America's Popular Music (1900–1980)*. New York: Institute for Studies in American Music.

———. 1996. *Pennies from Heaven: The American Popular Music Business in the Twentieth Century*. New York: Da Capo Press.

Scarry, Elaine. 1985. *The Body in Pain: The Making and Unmaking of the World*. Oxford: Oxford University Press.

Schatz, Thomas. 1981. *Hollywood Genres*. New York: Random House.

Schenker, Heinrich. 1935. *Der Frei Satz*. Vienna: Universal Edition. Trans. 1979 by Ernst Oster as *Free Composition*. New York: Longman.

Scherzinger, Martin. 1997. "Anton Webern and the Concept of Symmetrical Inversion: A Reconsideration on the Terrain of Gender." *repercussions* 6(2): 63–147.

Schilling, Britta. 1986. *Virtuose Klaviermusik des 19. Jahrhunderts am Beispiel von Charles Valentin Alkan (1813–1888)*. Regensburg: Gustav Bosse.

Schlaug, G., Jäncke, L., Huang, Y., Stagier, J. and Steinmetz, H. 1995. "Increased corpus collusum size in musicians." *Neuropsychologia* 33 (8): 1047–55.

Schlesinger, J. 2002. "Issues in Creativity and Madness: Part One, Ancient Questions and Modern Answers." *Ethical Human Sciences and Services: An International Journal of Critical Inquiry* 4: 73–6, 139–42.

Schoenberg, Arnold. 1941/1984a. "Composition with Twelve Tones." In *Style and Idea: Selected Writings of Arnold Schoenberg*, new exp. ed., Ed. Leonard Stein, trans. Leo Black, 214–44. Berkeley: University of California Press.

———. 1946/1984b. "New Music, Outmoded Music, Style and Idea." In *Style and Idea: Selected Writings of Arnold Schoenberg*, new exp. ed., Ed. Leonard Stein, trans. Leo Black, 113–23. Berkeley: University of California Press.

———. 1967. *Fundamentals of Musical Composition*. Ed. Gerald Strang and Leonard Stein. London: Faber & Faber.

Schorske, Carl. 1981. *Fin-de-Siècle Vienna: Politics and Culture*. New York: Random House.

Schuchardt, Sarah. n.d. "Music and the Autism Culture." http://www.autismforum.net.

Schumann, Robert. 1971. "A Symphony by Berlioz." Trans. Edward T. Cone. In Cone, 1971, 230–48.

Schwarz, David. 1997. *Listening Subjects: Music, Psychoanalysis, Culture*. Durham, NC: Duke University Press.

Seelman, Kate. 2004. "Trends in Rehabilitation and Disability: Transition from a Medical Model to an Integrative Model." *Disability World* 22 (January–March). http://www.disability-world.org/01-03_04/access/rehabtrends1.shtml.

Seletzky, Robert. 2004. "The Performance Practice of Maria Callas: Interpretation and Instinct." *Opera Quarterly* 20(4): 587–602.

Shakespeare, Tom. 1999. "Arts and Lies? Representations of Disability on Film." In *Disability Discourse*, Ed. Mairian Corker and Sally French, 164–72. Buckingham: Open University Press.

Sheinberg, Esti. 2000. *Irony, Satire, Parody and the Grotesque in the Music of Shostakovich: A Theory of Musical Incongruities*. Aldershot: Ashgate.

Shenner, Gladys. 1956. "The Genius Who Doesn't Want to Play." *MacLean's Magazine*, April 28, 69(9): 20, 98–103.

Shoham, S[hlomo] Giora. 2003. *Art, Crime and Madness*. Brighton: Sussex Academic Press.

Shore, Steve. 2001. *Beyond the Wall: Personal Experiences with Autism and Asperger Syndrome*. Shawnee Mission, KS: Autism Asperger Publishing Company.

———. n.d. "Music for the Child on the Autism Spectrum," http://www.autismtoday.com/articles/Music_for_the_Child.htm

Silverman, Kaja. 1988. *The Acoustic Mirror: The Female Voice in Psychoanalysis Cinema*. Bloomington: Indiana University Press.

Sinclair, Jim. 1993. "Don't Mourn for Us." *Our Voice* Newsletter of Autism Network International 1(3). Available at http://web.syr.edu/~jisincla/dontmourn.htm.

———. 2005. "Autism Network International: The Development of a Community and its Culture." http://web.syr.edu/~jisincla/History_of_ANI.html.

Skal, David J. 2001. *The Monster Show: A Cultural History of Horror*. New York: Faber & Faber.

Slater, Eliot, and Adolf Mayer. 1959. "Contributions to a Pathography of the Musicians: Robert Schumann." *Confinia Psychiatrica* 2: 65–94.

———. 1960. "Contributions to a Pathography of the Musicians: II: Organic and Psychotic Disorders." *Confinia Psychiatrica* 3: 129–45.

Slide, Anthony. 1994. *The Encyclopedia of Vaudeville*. Westport, CT: Greenwood Press.

Slonimsky, Nicolas. 1984. *Lexicon of Musical Invective*. 2d ed. Seattle: University of Washington Press.

Smith, Phil. 2004. "Whiteness, Normal Theory, and Disability Studies." *Disability Studies Quarterly* 24(2). Available at http://www.dsq-sds.org.

Smith, Ronald. 1976. *Alkan, Volume One: The Enigma*. London: Kahn & Averill.

———. 1987. *Alkan, Volume Two: The Music*. London: Kahn & Averill.

Snyder, Bob. 2000. *Music and Memory*. Cambridge, MA: MIT Press.

Solie, Ruth. 1993. "On 'Difference.'" Introduction to *Music and Difference: Gender and Sexuality in Music Scholarship*, Ed. Ruth Solie, 1–22. Berkeley: University of California Press.

Sontag, Susan. 1977. *Illness as Metaphor*. New York: Farrar, Straus & Giroux.

———. 1988. *Illness as Metaphor and AIDS and Its Metaphors.* New York: Farrar, Straus & Giroux.

———. 1989. *AIDS and Its Metaphors.* New York: Farrar, Straus & Giroux.

Southall, Geneva H. 1979. *Blind Tom, The Post-Civil War Enslavement of a Black Musical Genius, Book I.* Minneapolis: Challenge Books.

———. 1983. *The Continuing Enslavement of Blind Tom, the Black Pianist-Composer (1865–1887), Book II.* Minneapolis: Challenge Books.

———. 1999. *Blind Tom, the Black Pianist-Composer (1849–1908): Continually Enslaved.* Oxford: Scarecrow Press.

Springsteen, Bruce. 1993. "Streets of Philadelphia." *Philadelphia: Music from the Motion Picture.* CD. Epic Soundtrax EK 57624.

Staum, Myra J. n.d. "Music Therapy and Language for the Autistic Child." http://www.autism.org/music.html.

Steiner, Max. 1970. "Max Steiner." In *The Real Tinsel,* Ed. Bernard Rosenberg and Harry Silverstein, 387–98. New York: Macmillan.

Stevenson, Jack. 2002. *Lars von Trier.* London: British Film Institute.

Stiker, Henri-Jacques. 2000. *A History of Disability.* Trans. William Sayers. Ann Arbor: University of Michigan Press.

Stine, Gerald. 2000. *AIDS Update 2000.* Upper Saddle River, NJ: Prentice Hall.

Stoecker, Philip. 2003. "Studies in Post-tonal Symmetry: A Transformational Approach." Ph.D. diss., City University of New York.

Stok, Danusia, Ed. 1993. *Kieślowski on Kieślowski.* London: Faber & Faber.

Storr, Anthony. 1972. *The Dynamics of Creation.* London: Secker & Warburg.

———. 1988. *Churchill's Black Dog, Kafka's Mice, and Other Phenomena of the Human Mind.* New York: Grove Press.

Straus, Joseph. 2000. *Introduction to Post-Tonal Theory.* 2d ed. Upper Saddle River, NJ: Prentice Hall.

———. 2006. "Normalizing the Abnormal: Disability in Music and Music Theory." *Journal of the American Musicological Society* 59(1): 113–84.

Studlar, Gaylyn. 1996. *This Mad Masquerade: Stardom and Masculinity in the Jazz Age.* New York: Columbia University Press.

Subotnik, Rose Rosengard. 1991. "Adorno's Diagnosis of Beethoven's Late Style: Early Symptom of a Fatal Condition." In *Developing Variations: Style and Ideology in Western Music,* 15–41. Minneapolis: University of Minnesota Press.

Szatmari, Peter, Rebecca Bremner, and Joan Nagy. 1989. "Asperger's Syndrome: A Review of Clinical Features." *Canadian Journal of Psychiatry* 34(6): 554–60.

Szegedy-Maszak, Marianne. 2001. "A Lesson before Dying." *U.S. News and World Report,* June 25, 48.

Takeuchi, Annie H., and Stewart H. Hulse. 1993. "Absolute Pitch." *Psychological Bulletin* 113(2): 345–61.

Tantam, Digby. 1991. "Asperger Syndrome in Adulthood." In *Autism and Asperger's Syndrome,* Ed. Uta Frith, 147–83. Cambridge: Cambridge University Press.

Taves, Brian. 1987a. "Universal's Horror Tradition." *American Cinematographer* 68(4): 36–48.

———. 1987b. "Whose Hand? Correcting a Buñuel Myth." *Sight & Sound* 56(3): 210–11.

Taylor, Harvey. 1956. "Gould Great, Antics Upsetting." *Detroit Times,* March 16: 18.

Taylor, Timothy D. 2001. *Strange Sounds: Music, Technology, and Culture.* New York: Routledge.

Terry, Jennifer, and Jacqueline Urla. 1995. *Deviant Bodies: Critical Perspectives on Difference in Science and Popular Culture.* Bloomington: Indiana University Press.

Thaut, Michael. 1984. "A Music Therapy Treatment Model for Autistic Children." *Music Therapy Perspectives* 1(4): 7–13.

———. 1988. "Measuring Musical Responsiveness in Autistic Children: A Comparative Analysis of Improvised Musical Tone Sequences of Autistic, Normal, and Mentally Retarded Individuals." *Journal of Autism and Developmental Disorders* 18(4): 561–71.

The ICD-10 Classification of Mental and Behavioural Disorders: Diagnostic Criteria for Research. 1993. Geneva: World Health Organization.

Thomas, Adrian. 1997. *Górecki.* Oxford: Clarendon Press.

Thomas, Carol. 1999. *Female Forms: Experiencing and Understanding Disability.* Buckingham: Open University Press.

Thomas, Tony. 1996. "The Max Steiner Factor (1888–1971)." Liner notes. *The Lost Patrol / The Beast with Five Fingers / Virginia City.* Marco Polo Film Music Classics, 8.223870.

Tovell, Vincent, and Eric Till, producers. 1985. *Glenn Gould—A Portrait*. Film. Unpublished transcript of Herbert Gould interview, Glenn Gould Papers, Music Section, Library and Archives Canada, Ottawa, n.d.

Treffert, Darold. 2000. *Extraordinary People*. 2d ed. Omaha: BackinPrint.com.

Treichler, Paula. 1999. *How to Have Theory in an Epidemic: Cultural Chronicles of AIDS*. Durham, NC: Duke University Press.

Trethowan, W. H. 1977. "Music and Mental Disorder." In *Music and the Brain*, Ed. Macdonald Critchley and R. A. Henson, 398–442. London: Heineman.

Trippett, Frank. 1977. "Sweet Singer for All Seasons." *Time*, October 24, 106.

TrKelly. n.d. "TrKelly Autistic-Artist." http://www.raventones.com/autism.html.

Tsou, Judy. 1997. "Gendering Race: Stereotypes of Chinese Americans in Popular Sheet Music." *Repercussions* 6(2): 25–62.

Tumpane, Frank. [c. Fall 1955.] "Sincerely Yours." *Toronto Telegram*, n.d., n.p. Document 1979-20, 41, 9, 10, Glenn Gould Papers, Music Section, Library and Archives Canada, Ottawa.

Uprety, Sanjeev Kumor. 1997. "Disability and Postcoloniality in Salman Rushdie's *Midnight's Children* and Third-World Novels." In Davis, 1997, 366–81.

Vanhoutte, Jacqueline. 2002. "Cancer and the Common Woman in Margaret Edson's *W;t*." *Comparartive Drama* 36(3–4): 391–410.

Vitouch, Oliver. 2003. "Absolutist Models of Absolute Pitch Are Absolutely Misleading." *Music Perception* 21(1): 111–17.

Vogel, Frederick G. 1995. *World War I Songs: A History and Dictionary of Popular American Patriotic Tunes, with over 300 Complete Lyrics*. Jefferson, NC: McFarland.

Volkmar, Fred R. 1998. *Autism and Pervasive Developmental Disorders*. New York: Cambridge University Press.

von der Linn, Michael. 2001. "'Durch und durch entartete': Musical Modernism and the German Critics (1900-1936)." *Current Musicology* 65: 7–34.

von Trier, Lars. 2000. *Dancer in the Dark*. Film. Hvidovre, Denmark: Zentropa Entertainment and Fine Line Features.

Vrticka, Karel. 2000. "Stottern auf der Opernbühne." In *Sprache und Musik*, Ed. Johannes Pahn and others, 173–8. Stuttgart: Franz Steiner Verlag.

Walrod, Stephen T. 2005. "Review of *Crying at the Movies*, by Madelon Sprengnether." *American Imago* 62(1): 137–42.

Walter, Lynne. 2000. "Aspects of Glenn Gould: Glenn Gould and the Doctors." *Glenn Gould* 6(2): 88–9.

Ward, Keith. 1999. "Musical Responses to HIV and AIDS." In *Perspectives on American Music since 1950*, Ed. James Heintze, 323–52. New York: Garland Press.

Waters, Ethel. 1992. *His Eye Is on the Sparrow*. New York: Da Capo Press.

Watkins, Glenn. 1988. *Soundings: Music in the Twentieth Century*. New York: Schirmer Books.

———. 2003. *Proof through the Night: Music and the Great War*. Berkeley: University of California Press.

Welch, Graham. 1988. "Observations on the Incidence of Absolute Pitch (AP) in the Early Blind." *Psychology of Music* 16(1): 77–80.

Welten, Ruud. 1996. "'I'm not Ill, I'm Nervous'—Madness in the Music of Sir Peter Maxwell Davies." *Tempo* 196: 21–4.

Whalen, Robert Weldon. 1984. *Bitter Wounds: German Victims of the Great War, 1914-1939*. Ithaca: Cornell University Press.

Wiggins, Thomas ("Blind Tom"). 1862. *Wellenklange (Voice of the Waves)*. Score. New York: J.G. Bethune.

———. 1866. *The Battle of Manassas*. Score. Cleveland: S. Brainard's Sons.

———. 1888. Variations on "When This Cruel War Is Over." Score. Boston: Oliver Ditson.

Williams, Alan E. 2000. "Madness in the Music Theater Works of Peter Maxwell Davies." *Perspectives of New Music* 38(1): 77–100.

Williams, Donna. 1992. *Nobody Nowhere*. London: Transworld Publishers.

———. 1994. *Somebody, Somewhere*. New York: Three Rivers Press.

———. 1995. "In the Real World." *Facilitated Communication Digest* 3(2): 5–9.

———. 2000. "Nobody Nowhere." CD. Label: Donna Williams.

Wills, David. 1995. *Prosthesis*. Stanford: Stanford University Press.

Wilson, Elizabeth. 1994. *Shostakovich: A Life Remembered*. Princeton: Princeton University Press.

Wilson, Emma. 2000. *Memory and Survival: The French Cinema of Krzysztof Kieślowski.* European Humanities Research Centre, Oxford: University of Oxford.

———. 2003. *Cinema's Missing Children.* London: Wallflower Press.

Wing, Lorna. 1991. "The Relationship between Asperger's Syndrome and Kanner's Autism." In *Autism and Asperger's Syndrome*, Ed. Uta Frith, 93–121. Cambridge: Cambridge University Press.

Wingate, Marcel E. 2002. *Foundations of Stuttering.* San Diego: Academic Press.

Winnicott, Donald W. 1971. *Playing and Reality.* London: Tavistock/Routledge.

Wolf, Matt. 2000. "At the Movies: *Dancer in the Dark.*" Associated Press, September 19. http://web.lexis-nexis.com/universe, BC Cycle edition, Entertainment News. Available at http://olive.stage.advance.net/printer/printer.ssf?/movies/criticrev/00/10/ap_dancer001011.frame.

Wood, Robin. 1979. "An Introduction to the American Horror Film." In *American Nightmare: Essays on the Horror Film*, Ed. Andrew Britton, Richard Lippe, Tony Williams, and Robin Wood, 7–28. Toronto: Festival of Festivals.

Woolf, Virginia. 1925. "On Being Ill." In *Collected Essays*, vol. 4, 193–203. London: Hogarth Press.

World Health Organization (WHO). 1993. *The ICD-10 Classification of Mental and Behavioural Disorders: Diagnostic Criteria for Research.* Geneva: World Health Organization.

———. 2002. *Towards a Common Language for Functioning, Disability and Health: The International Classification of Functioning, Disability and Health.* Geneva: World Health Organization.

Yungkans, Jonathan. 2004. Review of "Marc-Andre Hamelin Live at Wigmore Hall." *The Flying Inkpot* 121. http://inkpot.com/classical/hyphamwigmore.html.

Zacharek, Stephanie. 2000. "Dancer in the Dark." *Salon.com*, September 22. Available at http://archive.salon.com/ent/movies/review/2000/09/22/trier_dancer/index.html

Žižek, Slavoj. 2001. *The Fright of Real Tears: Krzysztof Kieślowski between Theory and Post-theory.* London: BFI Publishing.

Index